Best to Mary!

Thanks for a great
"Girls Night Out!"

Peter Baker

A FUNNY THING HAPPENED ON THE WAY TO THE 21st CENTURY

*A FACTUAL AND IRREVERENT SURVEY OF AMERICAN HISTORY
FROM THE BEGINNING THROUGH THE MODERN ERA*

Peter Bales, Ph.D.

Maple Hill Press

First printing 2012

Printed in the United States of America

ISBN 978-0930545-33-8

ACKNOWLEDGMENTS

I owe special thanks to Professor Jay Mullin, whose eagle eye improved my manuscript immeasurably.

I'd also like to thank friends and colleagues for their suggestions and encouragement along the way: Joe Culkin, Pedro Meza, Mark Van Ells, Alan Rauchway, Bobbi Brauer, Toni Denis, Beth Smucker Amaro, and my editor at Maple Hill Press, Christopher Fleck.

Thank you to my many students over the years, who have had to put up with lots of bad jokes and, if I do say so myself, plenty of good ones.

Mariette "Peaches" Rodriguez and my son Dylan have consistently shown love and understanding.

DEDICATION

For my mother and in memory of my father
who taught me at a very young age to love "old time"

TABLE OF CONTENTS

PART I:
HOW COME THEY ALWAYS HAD THE BATTLES IN NATIONAL PARKS?

PART II:
"WHO CARES...THEY ARE ALL DEAD ANYWAY"

A nation which does not know what it was yesterday,
does not know what it is today, nor what it is trying to do.

— *Woodrow Wilson*

Past is prologue.

— *William Shakespeare*

God, this stuff is boring.

— *Peter Bales (in seventh grade History class)*

PART I

HOW COME THEY ALWAYS HAD THE BATTLES IN NATIONAL PARKS?

PREFACE TO PART I

One afternoon I was strolling with a small gaggle of friendly strangers up a hill known as Little Round Top, listening to a venerable tour guide pontificate on the nearly 150-year-old Battle of Gettysburg. When we paused and were asked if we had any questions, one earnest young woman raised her hand, stopped chewing her gum and queried, "How come they always had the battles in national parks?" I laughed, but covered it with a cough when I realized she was serious and the rest of the group was actually waiting for an answer.

Our tour guide — a gray-haired man with a handlebar mustache and thick glasses, a thirty-two-year veteran of the National Parks Service who knew everything there was to know about the Civil War and then some — stared wide-eyed and opened his mouth. But he could not bring himself to speak, and the only sound that escaped was a low moan. He placed both hands around his stomach, bent over slightly and appeared to be suffering some sort of gastric distress to which, I thought to myself, he was quite entitled. I stepped forward to defuse the awkward moment. "It was an incredible coincidence," I announced, "...all those battles in the national parks were just a coincidence and very convenient." Everyone nodded and seemed satisfied. I turned, placed my arm around our guide and nudged him forward. He blinked a few times, glanced around to get his bearings and in a few seconds all was back to normal.

We must ask ourselves, how can so many Americans be so confused about U.S. History? Why is it so difficult for many of us to distinguish between George Washington the president and George Washington the bridge? Why is the name Britney Spears more readily recognized than Franklin Roosevelt? Where did we go wrong?

When it came to the study of American History, we took ourselves too darn seriously, that's what happened. Too many of our grade school teachers made us memorize state capitals and the dates of wars and turned us all off. In truth, History is about people, about how they used to live and why we live the way we do today. And because people are always both good and bad, sensible and silly, so is History.

There have been lots of laughs in History. Sometimes we have to laugh because — to paraphrase Abraham Lincoln — it hurts too much to cry. This book is a tongue-in-cheek (but true) survey of historical events that begins to raise the boring black veil off our heritage. As we navigate the new millennium, it is more important than ever to understand where the heck we come from. Why not have a good time doing it? The following pages will not explain in excruciating detail the intricate ebb and flow of our nation's past. But they will make you smile and say, *hmmm*. And reading this may even make you curious enough to delve deeper into all those battles that took place "in national parks."

P. B.

CHAPTER 1

A NEW WORLD AND A NEW LIFE

or

Hi, We're Your New Neighbors...Now Get Out!

The discovery of America came about as a result of events in the Old World: the Crusades, the Renaissance, and the rise of national states ruled by absolute monarchs with money to burn. By the late 1400s, Western Europe was primed to pull a Star Trek and boldly go where no one had gone before. Great Britain founded ten colonies along the northern Atlantic seaboard and carved three more from territory purloined from the Dutch. These English colonists soon found out that life in the wilderness presented new and different challenges...such as teatime interrupted by a charging moose.

THE AGE OF EXPLORATION

or *I Thought You Knew Where We Were Going*

With all due respect to the Flintstones, tens of thousands of years ago during the **Ice Age,** primitive hunters and gatherers crossed a land bridge from Asia into what is today Alaska. Supposedly they were chasing woolly mammoth, though it was more likely the woolly mammoth were chasing them. Some of these **Native Americans** got sore feet and decided to settle in North America in small scattered tribes. Others trekked south and developed complex societies such as the **Incas** in Peru, the **Mayas** in Central America and the **Aztecs** in Mexico. In those places they built large stone cities, developed advanced agricultural techniques, engaged in commerce, studied mathematics and made some darn sophisticated astronomical observations. The Aztecs practiced human sacrifice so gruesome that even Freddy Krueger would be grossed out. The Incas built suspension bridges which centuries later influenced the designers of the Brooklyn Bridge. They even had toll collectors. They probably also had con men who tried to sell those bridges to the less intelligent Incas.

By some weird coincidence, both the ancient Aztecs in Mexico and the Egyptians in North Africa shared such things as pyramids and sun worship. Some people believe the lost continent of Atlantis sank into the ocean but sent out ships at the last moment. Others think flying saucers visited both places and spread ideas around. Then again, some people see Elvis at their local Burger King.

The first Europeans to "discover" America were the **Vikings**. Around 1000 C.E., **Leif Eriksson** spent a miserable winter in what is today called Newfoundland. His fellow barbarians called him "Leif the Lucky" but his stay in the New World was anything but. Unfriendly Indians constantly attacked, giving the Norse bullies a dose of their own medicine, so finally Leif and company said the hell with it and returned to Greenland (the Vikings called the natives *skrelings* which loosely translated meant buttheads). This ignominious and brief experience with the indigenous population frequently results in the Vikings' heroic achievement being overlooked. The Vikings also rarely get credit for wearing animal skins, leather helmets topped with bullhorns and pointed breastplates over a thousand years before Madonna made her first music video.

The Middle Ages is frequently divided between the Dark Ages (after the fall of Rome, from 476 C.E. to 1000 C.E.) and the High or Late Middle Ages (to about 1400 C.E.). Conditions supposedly began to improve in the High Middle Ages, but this is all relative. If you consider that during this time, one-quarter of the European population succumbed to the Black Death, and add to that a Hundred Years War between France and England, the earlier Dark Ages must have really been the pits. Anyway, in 1295 an Italian adventurer named **Marco Polo** returned from a remarkable overland trip to China with a cargo of silks, spices, perfumes and takeout food (just kidding.) By the way, in modern times "Marco Polo" is commonly remembered as the name of a game children play in swimming pools, a connection which is incomprehensible. In an age before refrigeration and zip-lock bags, spices made it a little easier to gag down food that was invariably rancid. And medieval nobility needed the perfumes desperately because, quite frankly, they all smelled: back then, refusing to bathe was considered a sign of wealth and leisure. Many an aristocrat bragged of never having taken a bath in their lives, and when wives contrived to walk ten paces behind their husbands it was mainly to keep them upwind. Soon Europeans were paying through the nose for the treasures of the Far East, and Italian trading cities such as Venice, Genoa and Milan grew rich functioning as middlemen and jacking up the prices. Their customers — the northern Europeans — soon longed for a cheaper route to the treasures of the Far East.

Europe in the 1300s began to enjoy a **Renaissance** that started in Italy — hard to believe if you've ever seen Tony Danza in a serious role. Renaissance means "rebirth" and it's how we all feel for the first three minutes when we try to get back into jogging. It was a time when many people realized how incredibly stupid they were, so they rediscovered the virtues of classical Greco-Roman civilization, began to emphasize reason and nonreligious aspects of life, and generally acted like they were really cool. By the 1400s most educated Europeans had finally figured out that — duh — the earth was round.

One person pretty sure that the earth was round was **Christopher Columbus**, and in 1492 he decided to sail the ocean blue to prove it. But he needed money first. Columbus was an Italian by birth, but since the country of Italy did not even exist yet, he asked Spain's King Ferdinand and Queen Isabella to pick up his tab. They were about to send him packing when he mentioned there might be loads of gold on the other side of the ocean. Suddenly, the King and Queen became like the doorman in *The Wizard of Oz* who shouted, "That's a horse of a different color!"

After seventy days at sea, Columbus' men were plotting to throw him to the sharks when just in the nick of time, a lookout named Rodrigo became the first person to cry "Land ho!" and actually mean it. Others had probably called "Land ho!" as a joke, which would have been funny at first but increasingly annoying as weeks turned into months. Rodrigo was especially psyched because Columbus had promised a reward for the first person to spot land. Unfortunately, Captain Chris claimed he himself had spotted land the night before and kept the reward for himself. Nice guy.

Columbus never stopped believing he had reached the island outposts of China, when in reality he had landed on San Salvador and then explored the Bahamas, Cuba, and Santo Domingo. He called the natives **Indians** (still thinking he had reached the Indies or Indonesian Islands) causing the problem we still have today when people tell you they are Indian. They might be from the country of India or Native Americans, but you never know for sure. Luckily, Columbus did not call the natives Chinese because then we would have Chinese American Indians and, while the cuisine sounds intriguing, it's all way too confusing.

Keep in mind Columbus and his men enslaved the natives and began the period in history in which the indigenous population of the Americas was decimated. In the one hundred years after Columbus' arrival, about ninety percent of the Native American population perished, mostly from European diseases. So next Columbus Day, don't celebrate Christopher Columbus, commemorate him and remember *everything* that happened. Above all, keep your mouth shut about all this so some overly zealous government bureaucrat doesn't try to take away our day off from work.

So how come we live in the United States of America and not the United States of Columbus? The word America is believed to be in honor of the Italian explorer **Amerigo Vespucci.** Vespucci supposedly reached the "New World" in 1497, five years after Columbus. The difference was Vespucci knew he had reached a "New World" while Columbus still thought he was in Asia. And Vespucci quickly published an account of his exploits, proving that even five hundred years ago it paid to have a good press agent.

Most of his contemporaries thought he was nuts, but in 1519, **Ferdinand Magellan** set out with several ships from Spain to attempt the first circumnavigation of the world. Magellan's expedition succeeded and will always be remembered, though Magellan himself probably had mixed feelings as natives in the Philippine Islands were killing him. Nevertheless, the journeys of Columbus and Magellan created quite a stir, causing the leading west European countries to send explorers to the New World for a variety of reasons: to (1) seek a **"northwest passage"** through North America to the Far East and GET RICH, (2) establish claims to new lands and GET RICH, (3) create settlements and trading posts and GET RICH, (4) convert the natives to Christianity and GET RICH, (5) satisfy curiosity, seek adventure and GET RICH, and (6) just plain GET RICH. Money motivated just about all the explorers. Most of Europe back then subscribed to **primogeniture**, the right of the eldest son to inherit the fortune and title of the father to the exclusion of all other children. Lots of young noblemen knew they were cut out of the will and said in effect, "Screw you Pops, I'm going to America to make my own fortune my way."

Spain really got the jump on exploring and colonizing the New World, but then Portugal got in on the act by pure luck. A Portuguese sea captain named **Pedro Alvares Cabral** was heading to Africa when winds blew him to the other side of the ocean; he landed in what was to become Brazil, and figured he might as well claim it. That's why it is really dumb to ask someone from Brazil if they speak Spanish or even worse, Brazilian. Remember, Spain settled most of Latin America, but in 1494, the Pope issued the **Treaty of Tordesillas** granting Brazil to Portugal, which was important at the time, even though today "tordesillas" sounds like a menu item at Taco Bell. This divided the New World between Spain and Portugal and ensured that Brazilians would forever speak Portuguese and generally act snobbishly toward their neighbors.

For Spain, **Vasco Núñez de Balboa** (no relation to Rocky) crossed the **Isthmus** (a narrow strip of land connecting two larger bodies, and a difficult word to pronounce quickly without spitting) **of Panama** to its western edge and waded into the Pacific Ocean. He was not particularly impressed and misnamed it the South Sea because in Panama the Pacific Ocean appears to be facing south. **Ponce de Leon** discovered Florida and wandered around drinking water from every stream and puddle (and peeing behind every bush) hoping to find the **Fountain of Youth.** All he ended up with was a lot of gray hair and a severe case of dysentery. Ironically, today many old people still trek to Florida, if not to find their youth, at least a little sun and maybe some shuffleboard.

The Spanish called their explorers **conquistadors** (which means conquerors) and that alone ought to give you an idea of the attitude they had toward the indigenous population. **Hernando Cortes** looted and destroyed the Aztec empire in 1519-1521 and **Francisco Pizarro** did the same to the mighty Incas in Peru about a decade later. Obsidian swords and spears and really gorgeous *quetzal*-feather-fan head dresses proved no match for iron muskets and cannons. The Aztecs had never seen horses before, so when they saw a Spaniard sitting on one they thought it was an entirely new and weird type of creature. They also thought if they gave Cortes and his men lots of gold and precious stones they would be satisfied and go away. This was roughly analogous to giving hungry fat people a wagonload of twinkies. Of course, the conquistadors were soon hungry for more. The Aztecs were confused about a lot of things; before he conquered them, they allowed Cortes into their midst because they thought he was a god. They changed their minds when they spied on him and noticed the great Cortes squatted to go to the bathroom just like everybody else. But by then it was too late.

One of the cruelest conquistadors was **Hernando de Soto,** who from 1539 to 1542 marched from Florida westward and discovered the Mississippi River. Hugely disappointed because he did not find any of the gold he was looking for, he expressed his frustrations by attacking every Indian village he came upon, even those that tried to be nice. **Francisco Coronado** heard rumors of Seven Cities of Gold, but after tramping through the American southwest for a few years found only the Seven Cities of Squat.

Particularly horrible for the Native Americans was the **encomienda system**, which was instituted by the Spanish colonial government from the 1500s through the 1700s. Spanish colonists were given the right to force labor out of any Indians living on their land, resulting in conditions that were far worse than any Kathie Lee Gifford sweatshop. It wasn't long before Spanish treatment of the Indians had given birth to what has always been known as the **Black Legend**. This legend states that all the Spaniards did was torture and murder the Indians, steal their riches, infect them with European diseases and basically screw things up wherever they went. Uh...that's all true, but there's a *but* here. The Spanish intermarried with the Indians and gave birth to **mestizos** — people of mixed European and Indian ancestry. They also bequeathed their language, culture, and Roman Catholic religion, a conglomeration which is to this day unique to the independent nations of Latin America. And there were many Spanish missionaries who, while laboring to convert the Indians to Christianity, also labored tirelessly to promote their welfare. True, the natives were generally forced to convert, but many of them were willing, since their own pantheon of Gods had let them down and allowed their world to be turned upside down. Centuries later, Jose Feliciano would record and make a fortune with a song entitled *Feliz Navidad*...it's all connected.

When the King of France heard that the Pope's Treaty of Tordesillas had divided up the New World between the Spanish and the Portuguese, he demanded to see "the clause in Adam's will" that excluded his country. Lots of people probably had no idea what he was talking about but were too intimidated to say anything; in any event, it soon became clear that France was going to get in on the action. In 1524 another courageous Italian seafarer hired himself out, this time to France; **Giovanni de Verrazzano** explored the Atlantic coast of North America and sailed into New York Harbor. It wasn't named New York then and Verrazano didn't hang around, but he did reportedly remark to one of his men "Hey, this looks like a great place for a bridge." In 1535 **Jacques Cartier** discovered and sailed up the St. Lawrence River. Seventy years later, **Samuel de Champlain** hoped to establish a "New France" in North America and founded Quebec. About seventy years after that, **Sieur de La Salle** descended the entire length of the Mississippi and named the territory Louisiana after King Louis XIV, who really loved being memorialized. Despite these facts, when the Canadian national anthem is sung in French at hockey games, many American fans don't have a clue what is going on.

The extensive French colonial holdings in North America never became extensively populated like other colonial empires. The main reason for this is that the French men who crossed the ocean were looking for beaver. Most French colonists had little interest in farming and permanently settling in the wilds of America; their scheme was to trap or trade with the Indians for lots of furs, get rich and then return home to France. It seems the New World wasn't good enough for the French even back then, and that goes a long way towards explaining the snobby Parisian waiters American tourists encounter today.

HERE COME THE BRITISH

or *Come On Everybody, Just Speak English*

In 1609, **Henry Hudson**, an Englishman in the employ of the Dutch, sailed into the harbor of New York and noticed a wide river running north. Hudson was the captain, so when he shouted, "Hey, there's the Hudson River!" nobody dared challenge him. The Dutch were also interested in the fur trade, so in 1621 the **Dutch East India Company** founded the colony of **New Netherland**. It is true the Indians sold Manhattan Island for about twenty-four dollars worth of beads and other stupid stuff to Dutch settlers led by **Peter Minuit**. The proliferation in recent years of tribal-owned gambling casinos is, in this light, truly poetic justice.

In the 1600s England and Holland became colonial and commercial rivals, and in 1664 an English naval force appeared in the harbor of **New Amsterdam** (present day New York City) and ordered the Dutch governor, **Peter Stuyvesant**, to surrender. Stuyvesant went ballistic and cursed a lot (which must have sounded really funny in Dutch), but since he was low on munitions he was forced to comply. The British took over and renamed the city New York, but the Dutch left behind lots of place names and cool customs (such as Easter eggs and Santa Claus and games like bowling and golf) which have unfortunately always been overshadowed by their ridiculous wooden shoes.

In the 1500s, England had no colonies of her own in the New World, so in an extreme expression of sour grapes, English sea captains frequently attacked Spanish treasure ships. Wanting to put the Protestant English in their place, Catholic Spain's King Philip II in 1588 sent what he called his "Invincible" **Armada** into the English Channel in preparation for an invasion of the British Isles. "Invincible" proved to be a relative term, and in short order one hundred and thirty heavily armed ships were sunk and otherwise disabled by English "sea dogs" in their smaller but faster and more maneuverable ships. The Brits deliberately set some of their ships on fire and sent them crashing into the Armada, which is something that would impress even Indiana Jones. Spain went downhill for the next three hundred years and Great Britain rose to become the world's predominant (and most pompous) sea power. By the way, you can insult a Brit by calling him a "limey." That's because English sailors used to suffer from scurvy (a deficiency in vitamin C), until some genius figured out that sucking on limes would take care of the problem. Adding a piece of lime, lemon or a pearl oyster to a cocktail came much later in history and has absolutely nothing to do with this.

Great Britain would eventually get around to colonizing the Atlantic seaboard of North America, and in 1587, they took their first shot at it on the island of **Roanoke** off the coast of present-day North Carolina. Three years later a resupply ship found the place completely empty. Starvation probably killed off most of them, and the rest were either adopted by the Indians (if you're an optimist) or killed. The only clue left behind was the word CROATOAN carved into a tree, undoubtedly by a crazed colonist muttering under his breath, "Ha, let the bastards try and figure this one out."

The first permanent North American settlement for England was **Jamestown**, Virginia, which was established in 1607. The survival of this colony is notable because of how completely clueless these early settlers really were; many were gold-hungry "gentlemen" who flatly refused to perform the hard labor necessary for survival in the harsh wilderness. Locating their settlement in the midst of a mosquito-infested swamp was another bonehead maneuver. Fortunately, **John Smith** took charge and declared (doubtless with musket in hand): "He that will not work shall not eat." After John Smith returned to England, the winter of 1609-10 became known as the starving time and Jamestown became a truly charming place to live — if you were a maggot. When the food gave out, the hapless colonists ate horses, rats, dogs, snakes and lizards. One hungry man killed, salted and devoured his wife, for which he was duly burned to death and eaten (just kidding, it is probably safe to assume they buried the guy). Take note: there is no solid evidence that Pocahontas ever stepped forward and begged for John Smith's life. Let's face it, the entire Disney film "Pocahontas" is more fiction than fact. The talking tree is definitely a stretch.

As early as 1619, the citizens of Jamestown elected representatives to a colonial legislature called the **House of Burgesses**. The first meeting ended inauspiciously on kind of a sour note — an outbreak of malaria — but this was the first appearance of representative government in America. Ironically, today many would argue that a malarial outbreak in Congress would not necessarily be a bad thing.

Meanwhile, back on the other side of the Atlantic, the **Puritans** wanted to purify the Church of England of practices that reminded them of Roman Catholicism. Most

English people looked upon these Puritans the way we look upon those extremely early risers who ring our doorbells on Saturdays to give us religious pamphlets. The Puritans were divided into different sects (groups) themselves, one of which was the **Pilgrims**. Fed up with their treatment in England, the Pilgrims moved to Holland, where they still continued to catch "attitude" from the neighbors. Finally, in September of 1620 they decided to sail to the New World on a ship called the **Mayflower**. They were supposedly headed for Virginia, but sixty-five days later the wind (yeah right) had blown them to the rocky coast of New England at Plymouth Harbor. In truth, the Pilgrims initially landed on Cape Cod before they ventured around to more hospitable moorings. Perhaps they could sense the future traffic nightmares the summer months on the Cape would bring. Plymouth Rock, the place where legend states they stepped ashore first, is probably a fabrication by some guy who just wanted to sell tee shirts.

Even before setting foot on land, the Pilgrims wrote the **Mayflower Compact**: the first written constitution in North America. The idea was to create a set of laws for the good of the colony as a whole. Today, you can call an 800 number and order a Mayflower Compact along with some lipstick and eyeliner...now that's progress for you. **William Bradford**, the Pilgrims' first governor, was elected every year for thirty consecutive years. Obviously, Bradford himself was the only one who counted the votes but historians never seem to mention this.

That first winter only 44 out of 102 of the Pilgrims survived, but nobody gave up. The next year brought good harvests, lots of beaver and fish, and the famous first Thanksgiving. Friendly Indians came to the feast and there were all kinds of good things to eat including roasted wild turkeys — but there was no football and no drunken relatives falling asleep on the couch in front of the television set. **Squanto,** a Pawtucket Indian, brought food to the hungry Pilgrims, showed them the best places to hunt and fish, and demonstrated how to plant strange crops like corn, beans, squash and pumpkins. Conveniently, Squanto spoke English. It's like on *Star Trek* when every time they go to another planet there are beings there speaking English. You just have to go with it.

Most important in the settlement of New England were the Puritans, those religious zealots who believed everyone in Great Britain was having too much fun. These pious sticks-in-the-mud, organized as the **Massachusetts Bay Company**, came to America and proceeded to wear black and walk around with long faces all the time. The Puritans worked hard and prospered — the "Protestant work ethic" served them well — and Governor **John Winthrop** declared, "We shall be as a city upon a hill," a holy city for all of humanity to emulate. These stirring words really inspired the Puritans, so much so that they all frowned and continued about their business. No one remarked on it at the time, but if the Puritans were such an uptight, dour bunch that didn't believe in enjoying themselves, how come they had such an incredibly high birthrate?

A courageous woman named **Anne Hutchinson** got kicked out of Massachusetts for arguing that people could get into heaven whether or not they had led virtuous lives. She's my hero. **Roger Williams**, minister of the church in Salem, advanced the shocking idea that it was wrong to seize land from the Indians without paying for it. He also denied the right of the Massachusetts government to interfere in religious matters. Despite their own experience with religious intolerance in England, the hypocritical Puritans expelled Williams, whereupon he and his followers founded the colony of Rhode Island. The Puritan clergy back in Boston referred to Rhode Island as "that sewer," "a sink" in which the "Lord's debris" had collected and rotted. Williams and his friends sneered back "Whatever you say bounces off me and sticks to you like glue" (or words to that effect) and they were even.

AMERICAN SOCIETY GROWS MORE SOPHISTICATED
or *Would You Please Put A Shirt On For Dinner*

The chief of the Wampanoag was called **King Phillip** by the New Englanders because of his adoption of European dress and customs. In 1675, when he got fed up with English encroachment on Indian land, he initiated the bloodiest war (if you take population into account) in American history. The colonists thought King Phillip violent and uncivilized so — to teach him a lesson — when he was captured he was shot, beheaded, drawn and quartered and had his head displayed on a pole for several years. Native Americans introduced the Europeans to corn, beans, tomatoes and the potato. The Europeans gave the Native Americans smallpox, yellow fever and malaria. That pretty well sums up the relationship.

In 1692, the Puritan town of **Salem** played host to a hysterical witch-hunt. Nineteen people were convicted of practicing witchcraft and hanged; one man was "pressed" to death under heavy stones. Even some dogs were executed, reportedly when they were ratted out by some of the local cats. Puritan passions run amok? Mass hysteria? Proof of what can go wrong when church and state merge into one? But wait — *The New York Times* in 1976 reported the scientific theory that the witches of Salem had eaten bread contaminated with a fungus similar to LSD. There, see? Everything has a logical explanation. Not.

In the **New England Colonies** (Massachusetts, New Hampshire, Connecticut, and Rhode Island), **freemen** (men who owned property and belonged to the local church) conducted town affairs and enacted local ordinances in **town meetings**. This **direct democracy,** in which citizens show up and personally participate (as opposed to **representative democracy** in which citizens elect legislators), provided the colonists with self-government and a real taste of freedom. Notably, most New England towns set aside land for public schools. The town meeting generally worked well; the only downside occurred when some loudmouth had to be shouted down or, in extreme cases, tarred and feathered and chased through the town square. Wooden "stocks" served as an alternative punishment in which malcontents had their arms, legs and heads shackled for days in public. In colonial times this type of bondage was considered a deterrent to anti-social behavior and not kinky fun on the weekends among consenting adults.

Life in the **Southern Colonies** (Maryland, Virginia, North Carolina, South Carolina and Georgia) came replete with hardships; the warm climate spawned malaria, dysentery and typhoid, and life spans were short. Men outnumbered women and it was extremely difficult to find a mate, which was especially frustrating in an age before *Playboy* and *Penthouse*. Most people in the colonial south were dirt poor and without a pot to piss in — literally. Toilets and plumbing of any kind were unknown, chamber pots a luxury, and most impoverished farm families had to do their "business" squatting in the woods while birds and chipmunks snickered at them. But for a lucky few in the southern colonies, fertile soil resulted in a plantation economy that raised tobacco, indigo (plants that yield a blue dye) and rice (plants that go really well with Moo Goo Gai Pan). The plantation owners grew richer and richer and evolved into an aristocracy that — while seeking to emulate the well-born in England — usually ended up looking like the Beverly Hillbillies at a formal dinner party.

In 1676, a demagogic Virginian named **Nathaniel Bacon** organized a group of about 400 malcontents who were frustrated over their inability to obtain farmland and women — they were both poor and horny, a volatile combination. When Governor Sam Berkeley refused to retaliate for Indian attacks on some frontier settlements because he did not want to jeopardize the fur trade in which he had a stake, Bacon and his rabble took matters into their own hands. They attacked a bunch of peaceful Indians, (hey, the warlike ones could be dangerous) and then marched to Jamestown and burned it to the ground. Bacon died of dysentery before English forces called in from New York could track him down, but about a dozen of his followers were hanged and the rest chased into the woods. During the colonial period there were actually about three hundred episodes similar to **Bacon's Rebellion,** which goes to prove that (1) the poor have always resented the rich in America, (2) Hollywood's portrayal of colonial times as totally genteel and homespun is really a crock, and (3) then, as now, it was always a good idea to lock the door at night. On the positive side, admission to colonial Williamsburg was free back then.

The **Middle Colonies** (New York, New Jersey, Pennsylvania and Delaware) lacked a distinctive institution such as slavery or the town meeting, so they've always gotten a lot less press than the South or New England. Also known as the **bread colonies**, family-sized farms produced surplus grain that was exported to other colonies and Europe. Many opportunities existed for artisans and merchants, who tended to congregate in the growing large cities: by 1750 Philadelphia had passed Boston as the most populous city in English America, although it was New York City, as always, that was known as the best place to party and meet colonial chicks.

One Swedish observer in 1744 noted the multiethnic nature of the Middle Colonies, reporting numerous Scots, English, Dutch, Germans, French, Irish and — hold on to your hats — one Jew. Most of the time, greater religious toleration prevailed in the region than anywhere else. In 1681, **William Penn**, the founder of Pennsylvania, declared his colony a "Holy Experiment," and by 1775, devout pacifist **Quakers**, inspired by Penn, numbered about 40,000, mostly in New Jersey, Pennsylvania, and Delaware.

When they were hassled about their beliefs or those silly hats they all wore, the Quakers proved more than willing to kick some serious colonial butt...peacefully of course.

During much of the 1600s, many of Britain's poor contracted with southern planters to work as field hands for 4-7 years in exchange for the cost of the transatlantic passage. (Others sold, or "indentured," themselves to artisans in the North.) By the beginning of the 1700s, the South's chronic need for labor caused planters to switch from these white **indentured servants** to more readily available black slaves. Slavery spread slowly throughout the colonies, but spread it did; in 1670 there were only a few thousand slaves, but by 1750 there were 400,000. Regulations sprang up to deny blacks their civil rights and forever put them in their place. Commonly, slaves were denied freedom of movement, freedom of assembly, and the right to earn money or even to learn to read. Black men could be killed or castrated for having sex with white women, even though the vast majority of interbreeding took place because white men used their power as masters to have sex with female slaves. This "race lightening" has been a constant component of American history. This has nothing to do with the late Michael Jackson's bleaching of his face, something that was just plain weird.

The British government promoted policies that modern economists have dubbed **mercantilism,** meaning that the British viewed their colonies as potential sources of raw materials that should benefit the mother country and *only* the mother country. Towards that end, they passed a series of **Navigation Acts** that were supposed to keep the colonies trading with England and not with those dirtbags in France, Spain or Holland. The colonists took these laws just about as seriously as we take a fifty-five mile per hour speed limit, and they quickly adopted prosperous trade routes that history teachers have always described as **triangular trade**. In fact, these trade routes were more of a pentagon in shape, and one sea captain with an inner ear infection was rumored to have taken his crew on a voyage that resembled an octagon. Anyway, one example would be New Englanders shipping rum to Africa in exchange for black slaves. The slaves were then sold in the West Indies for sugar and molasses, which in turn were carried back to New England and distilled into rum. The colonists loved triangular trade because they usually ended up with both a profit and a mixed drink.

Appointed by the King, colonial governors were usually content to lay low, collect their ample salaries and live in their nice mansions. The colonists happily governed themselves through elected assemblies. Even if he had really wanted to, Governor Edward Cornbury of New York (1702-08) had little chance of asserting royal authority after being spotted on the streets wearing a dress. Some have suggested that his purse did not match his shoes, a *faux pas* that caused even greater outrage.

In the early 1730s, New York's Governor William Cosby (no relation to the famous comedian) was vilified in **John Peter Zenger's** *Weekly Journal*. Infuriated, Cosby brought Zenger to court on charges of seditious libel. The judges were biased toward the governor from the start, but Zenger's attorney persuaded the jury to acquit his client because the articles he printed were true. This court decision laid the foundation for America's tradition of a free press. Little did they know that in the future, certain sleazy journalists would blatantly lie and then seek legal cover behind "freedom of the press," but hey, at the time Zenger and his friends felt pretty good about themselves.

In the 1740s, a wave of religious fervor swept through the colonies. **Jonathan Edwards** and **George Whitefield** worked up a sweat preaching fire and brimstone and declaring everyone to be "Sinners in the Hands of an Angry God." This **Great Awakening** ran its course in a few years, but it caused religious divisions and gave people the idea that it was okay to challenge authority and, in this case, create their own churches. It's always called the first truly American national event, and it fostered religious tolerance in the colonies — but let's face it, a lot of people shrieked, trembled, lost their lunch and generally behaved like the audience on *The Jerry Springer Show*.

The great achievements of the Scientific Revolution all took place far from America; Copernicus, Galileo, Newton and company all were Europeans. But the colonies did produce one man who could hang out with those guys, one of the most remarkable people of the American colonial era: **Benjamin Franklin**. Franklin was a writer, printer, philosopher, politician, diplomat and scientist all rolled into one. From 1732 to 1758 he edited *Poor Richard's Almanac,* which was packed with all sorts of witty expressions, most of which make little or no sense today. "What maintains one vice would bring up two children." Huh? But "Honesty is the best policy" is always relevant, and so is "Fish and visitors stink in three days" for anyone who has ever had in-laws visit. As a scientist, Franklin invented the Franklin Stove and bifocals, and by flying a kite in a thunderstorm (luckily not getting his colonial posterior toasted), he proved that lightning and electricity were the same substance. Crossing the Atlantic, he noted ocean currents and temperatures, and correctly theorized about the existence of the Gulf Stream. (Most of us on a cruise today just try to sleep it off in the deck chairs.) Due to his reputation with the ladies (and rumors about illegitimate children), he was credited both with inventing the lightning rod and having one.

By the mid-1700s, the colonists had shed many of their European customs and traditions. Their New World with its limitless and sometimes dangerous frontier demanded a different point of view. A new person evolved: individualistic, self-reliant and fiercely proud...an American...with an attitude. No one expected it or planned it, but the seeds of self-government were being sown as Americans placed more and more faith in the idea of a free people making their own laws. Then suddenly the British government started to act as if the king exercised final authority in the colonies. Uh oh...stay tuned...don't touch that dial!!!

This Really Happened!

When Daniel Boone turns 12 years old, his father gives him a brand new rifle, and he spends long days in the Pennsylvania woods learning how to shoot and trap. By the time he reaches Kentucky, the great frontiersman and Indian fighter has a way of turning a solitary stroll into a year-long adventure. After one such disappearance he returns to Boonesborough and announces generally where he's been — up river to its source, south maybe a hundred miles or so, west again, through a fine valley with many deer and splendid stands of oak and pine, and then back. But someone persists in asking, "In all that time, didn't you ever get lost?" In Kentucky, the legend of Dan'l Boone's answer still survives: "Nope, warn't lost none, though I was a mite confused there for a few months."

And the rest is History...

Quiz yourself on Chapter 1

Multiple Choice (circle the correct answer).

1. Europeans were able to dominate the New World because they possessed technological superiority in
    a. agricultural equipment
    b. weapons
    c. architecture
    d. evening wear
    e. none of the above

2. The colonists in Virginia did not find gold or silver but they did find they could make a lot of money growing
    a. pot
    b. corn
    c. wheat
    d. tobacco
    e. none of the above

3. Jamestown survived in part because _____ recognized the importance of building houses and raising food.
    a. Mel Gibson
    b. John Peter Zenger
    c. John Smith
    d. Bob
    e. Darrell, Darrell and Darrell

4. Spain could not block English penetration of the New World after the defeat of its _____ in the English Channel.
    a. bullfighters
    b. armada
    c. synchronized swimmers
    d. mariachi band
    e. none of the above

5. The Dutch were the first to claim and settle the area that is now New York City. They called it
    a. New Amsterdam
    b. New Netherland
    c. The Big Apple
    d. Gotham City
    e. none of the above

6. The Middle Colonies produced surplus grain and soon became known as the
   a. Cracker Colonies
   b. Seafood Coloniesb
   c. Bread Colonies
   d. Drunken Colonies
   e. a and b

7. The _____ was a British revenue ship that ran aground and was burned by angry Rhode Islanders.
   a. Minnow
   b. Niña
   c. Pinta
   d. Gaspee
   e. answer is in chapter two

8. The movement to instill evangelical zeal in the colonies has become known as the
   a. Enlightenment
   b. Renaissance
   c. Great Awakening
   d. Sweeps Period
   e. b and d

9. The British promoted mercantilism, the idea that
   a. colonists were too stupid to run their own affairs
   b. the colonies should exist for the benefit of the mother country
   c. the colonies should do what is best for themselves
   d. colonial goods should be sold as "Buy one, get one free"
   e. all of the above

10. Benjamin Franklin was not only a statesman but also a
    a. dentist
    b. slave owner
    c. scientist
    d. crossdresser
    e. b and d

CHAPTER 2

REVOLUTION AND A NEW GOVERNMENT

or

Trust Me, This Will Never Work

The British colonies prospered and the French were kicked out of North America. But when the British started to give the colonists attitude, the colonists gave attitude right back and before anyone knew it...REVOLUTION! The American War for Independence was bloody and bitter on both sides and extremely inconvenient for anyone trying to run a small farm or business. Against all odds, the colonists won and suddenly realized they weren't colonists anymore. They were Americans! They had a country to create and it was not going to be easy. After a few years, a number of people were fed up enough to wonder if somehow King George III could be persuaded to let bygones be bygones and take us back.

THE ROAD TO REVOLUTION
or *Let's Get Ready To Rumble!*

Starting in the late 1600s, Great Britain and France engaged in a series of wars. At stake was mastery of Europe, colonial superiority throughout the world, though it was also unclear which side made the best cheesecake. The first three of these wars were indecisive but in the fourth, called the **Seven Years' War** in Europe, the British really kicked butt.

The American counterpart of the Seven Years' War was called the **French and Indian War.** This was not the French against the Indians; the colonists and the British called it the French and Indian War because they were fighting against the French and their Indian allies for control of the Ohio Valley, fertile lands to the west of the Appalachian mountains. The war began in 1754, and for the first few years the French really had the upper hand. The British gave command of their forces to General **Edward Braddock,** who really should have been in a different line of work. When the French ambushed him, Braddock had five horses shot from under him before he was mortally wounded, probably by a French soldier who figured it might be more effective to aim higher. Braddock's aide-de-camp during this debacle was twenty-one-year-old **George Washington,** who gained valuable military experience (a polite way of saying he screwed up a lot) that would come in handy in the future.

In 1757, **William Pitt** became Prime Minister of England and declared "I am sure I can save this country and nobody else can!" which was really unnecessary because he already had the job. Pitt did send lots of money, supplies and reinforcements into North America and finally called on some generals — **Jeffrey Amherst** and **James Wolfe** — who actually knew their business. Wolfe and his men got past a French sentry simply by speaking French, proving that the French army did not require IQ tests for its recruits. Wolfe lost his own, life but the British captured Quebec, and forces led by Amherst secured Montreal. The fighting dragged on for a couple more years, but finally, in 1763, the **Treaty of Paris** was signed, really sticking it to the defeated French. They were forced to give the Louisiana territory to Spain (who had been their ally) and all they could say was *au revoir* as Britain gained the rest of its North American holdings. France did manage to hold on to Haiti, Martinique, St. Lucia and Guadeloupe in the Caribbean, nice places where they serve drinks with umbrellas in them, but pretty insignificant in the overall picture of North America. *C'est la vie.*

As the French were being defeated, American colonists poured into the Ohio Valley. They proceeded to get the Indians drunk and steal their best lands, business as usual as far as the white settlers were concerned. But Ottawa chief **Pontiac** was fed up and determined not to take it anymore. Along with assistant chiefs Buick and Camaro (just kidding), Pontiac formed an alliance among eighteen tribes including the Delaware, Shawnee, and Seneca. With great gusto, they massacred and pillaged western outposts until, by June 1763, only three forts remained. The British quickly struck back, and an ugly war ensued which included biological warfare (the British deliberately gave the Indians blankets infected with smallpox) and massacres of peaceful Indians who simply happened to be in the wrong place at the wrong time.

Demanding more protection from Pontiac's raiders, a mob of outraged pioneers known as the **Paxton Boys** threatened to attack Philadelphia. Fearing his own country-men more than the Indians, Ben Franklin talked them out of it by assuring them the Pennsylvania legislature would begin paying bounties for Indian scalps. To prevent fur-ther bloodshed between the colonists and the Indians (and preserve the fur trade for British companies), **King George III** announced the **Proclamation of 1763** prohibiting the colonists from settling west of the Appalachian mountains. As soon as the more clever colonists realized this proclamation was just a line drawn on a map in London, and not a real barrier they would trip over in the woods, they completely ignored it.

After the French and Indian War the British realized that they were nearly bank-rupt, despite having won. In 1763, **Parliament** (England's legislature) decided to termi-nate the decades-old policy that British statesman **Edmund Burke** famously described as **salutary neglect** — the belief that the American colonies benefited from the lack of interest in their affairs. After evading British mercantilist laws and exercising virtual self-government for as long as anyone could remember, the colonists basically replied, "What, are you kidding me?" Prime Minister **George Grenville** was not kidding, and determined to make the colonies bear their share of maintaining the British Empire, he sent over lots of customs collectors (the kinds of people who used to be hall monitors in high school) and naval patrols to stop the smuggling. He also authorized British officials to issue **writs of assistance**, general search warrants for colonial buildings and ships.

Any contemporary American who hid fireworks under the bed as a teenager can sympathize with how horrified the colonists must have been by these revolting develop-ments. Bostonian **James Otis** appeared before a Boston court and eloquently denounced the writs of assistance for violating the long-held English common law principle that "a man's home is his castle." He lost the case and later in life went insane, but at the time, virtually all the colonists believed he was right. They were also enormously gratified to find a lawyer who would work for free...even if he was a little nuts.

New taxes included the **Sugar Act** (1764) which infuriated fat colonists, and the **Stamp Act** (1765) requiring the purchase of stamps to be inked on all printed materials such as mortgages, almanacs, pamphlets, newspapers and even wills...which infuriated dead colonists. Britain's Chancellor of the Exchequer (a fancy name for chief accoun-tant) **Charles Townshend** came up with a plan for new duties on paint, glass, paper and tea. In an era before coffee was commonly drunk (and there was no such thing as a Starbucks or Dunkin Donuts), the **Townshend Acts** (1765) really freaked out colonial caffeine junkies. Anyone caught trying to avoid paying these taxes was denied a jury trial and judged in British military courts, where the fix was obviously in.

Another new law that really ticked off the colonists was the **Quartering Act of 1765,** requiring them to provide food and living quarters for British soldiers. Suppos-edly, the soldiers were in the colonies to defend against Indian attacks, but in practice most of these redcoats took up residence in cities like Boston, New York and Philadelphia. A lot of these soldiers snored, which was particularly galling to colonial homeowners tossing and turning on the couch.

Naturally, the headstrong colonists did all they could to violate the new British regulations. When an English naval patrol vessel named the **Gaspee** ran onto a sandbar off Rhode Island in June 1772, colonists, not exactly in a helpful mood, boarded the ship and set it on fire. British authorities were determined to bring the perpetrators to justice but could not find any Rhode Islanders who would testify against their neighbors. Some potential witnesses may have suggested the Captain's careless smoking in bed started the fire...which was really rubbing it in.

The Stamp Act angered the colonists so much that they called a big meeting, and delegates from nine colonies showed up in New York City for the **Stamp Act Congress** (1765). They urged a boycott of English goods, and declared that the colonies could be taxed only by their own elected legislatures, not a far away Parliament in which they had no voice. Unfortunately, none of the visitors had a chance to visit the Statue of Liberty or the Empire State Building because they didn't exist yet.

An organization of colonial patriots with a really cool name — the **Sons of Liberty** — helped to enforce the boycotts of British goods. They also set up **Committees of Correspondence** in each of the thirteen colonies. These committees sent messages up and down the eastern seaboard to keep each other informed of the latest resistance against the British. The colonists had to rely on riders on horseback because no formal Post Office existed yet. In other words, people who lost their tempers and got violent were "going postal" — they just didn't know it yet.

Boston in the early 1770s became a particularly tense place. British soldiers went to certain taverns while the colonists favored others, and there were often drunken brawls in the streets at closing time. In 1770, a colonial mob started throwing snowballs (with rocks in them) at a squad of British sentries manning a guard post. Under intense provocation, the soldiers panicked and fired blindly into the crowd, killing five men. It should be remembered that one of the first to fall was a black man, **Crispus Attucks**, although getting shot to death is a lousy way to achieve immortality. This incident was called the **Boston Massacre** by the colonists...talk about a snowball fight getting out of hand!

Parliament had backed off on all the new taxes by 1770 except for the tax on tea. Then they passed the **Tea Act** (1773) which exempted the British **East India Company** from paying taxes in England on tea shipped to America. This actually gave the colonists access to the cheapest tea ever, but colonial merchants were angry that their smuggled tea from Holland couldn't compete any more. Besides, it was the principle of the thing. The Townshend tax on tea remained in effect, and this was still **"taxation without representation!"** Angry mobs on the shorelines in New York and Philadelphia turned away the tea ships, but in Boston the ships anchored in the harbor. After nightfall, colonists dressed up as Indians boarded the ships and dumped the tea in the harbor. The Indian garb was a creative way to disguise the lawbreakers — nobody actually believed they were real Indians and, besides, real Indians would never refer to each

20

other as Nigel and Jeremy. This wanton destruction of British property (and rollicking good time for the colonial scofflaws) became known as the **Boston Tea Party.**

Appalled that the colonists had deposited the tea in the water unaccompanied by cucumber sandwiches, and determined to punish Massachusetts and assert British authority, Parliament passed a series of harsh measures. The official name for these acts was the **Coercive Acts** but the colonists found them so odious they called them the **Intolerable Acts,** with the term usually preceded by an expletive. They certainly didn't call them the "Awesome Acts!" In any event, the port of Boston was closed until the colonists paid for the destroyed tea, and no town meetings were allowed without the Royal Governor's permission. The **Quebec Act** was instituted at the same time and was also considered "Intolerable," but losing claims to lands west of the Ohio River was the least of the colonists' problems.

To present a united front against the Intolerable Acts, twelve colonies (where the heck was Georgia?) sent representatives to a "Continental Congress" in Philadelphia. This meeting is now known as the **First Continental Congress** because they would later have another one. Of course, they didn't call it the First Continental Congress at the time. In the same vein, Alexander the Great was just called Alexander when he was an infant. And when he was born, William the Conqueror's mother did not know "William the Bastard" was going to successfully invade England in 1066. Anyway...

The First Continental Congress demanded an end to the Intolerable Acts and voted in favor of another boycott of British goods. By now, emotions were running so high that patriots began training militias and storing supplies. Most colonists at this point still hoped some sort of accommodation could be reached with England, but a few radical hotheads were more than ready to call for independence. Speaking before the Virginia legislature, **Patrick Henry** declared, "Give me liberty or give me death!" In this age before microphones, some people in the back of the room may have thought he said, "Give me Lillian or give me Beth." But Henry was deadly serious and lots of people were beginning to listen.

THE AMERICAN REVOLUTION
or *Oh My God, How Do You Stop This Thing?*

In Boston, the British General **Thomas Gage** ordered his troops to march out to **Lexington**, capture patriot leaders **Sam Adams** and **John Hancock**, and then move on to Concord to confiscate military supplies. The British plan to surprise the colonists failed when, in the early morning, Sons of Liberty on horseback rode around shouting, "The British are coming! The British are coming!" Certainly at that hour it would have been more considerate to shout "Rise and shine, the British are arriving!" but this was no time to worry about good manners. **Paul Revere** is always remembered for being one of the riders because his name rhymes neatly in a famous poem, "The Midnight Ride of Paul Revere" by Henry Wadsworth Longfellow. Actually, **William Dawes** and **Samuel**

Prescott accomplished as much if not more than Revere that early morning, but since there were no such things as public relations firms back in those days, few people have ever heard of them.

At Lexington, patriot **Minutemen** were waiting on the village green. Today, it is an insult when a woman calls a guy a minuteman, but back then, the term referred to local militia, pledged to be ready at a minute's notice. Suddenly, a shot rang out. Nobody knows who fired first, the British or the Americans. It would have been really ironic if some kid behind the barn had lit off a firecracker. Anyway, a volley of shots commenced and the Minutemen were driven off with eight dead and ten wounded. The British soldiers next marched on to **Concord** and burned only a small amount of supplies because the Americans had carried most of them off. There was another skirmish, and the Brits turned back for the safety of Boston. That's when the real action started. Three or four thousand American militiamen showed up and fired at the soldiers from behind trees and rocks and anything else they could use for cover. The red coats of the "**Redcoats**" made them perfect targets, and they had never experienced **guerrilla warfare** before. By the time they got back to Boston the British had lost 73 killed and 174 wounded, compared to 49 killed and 39 wounded for the Americans. The battles of Lexington and Concord started the American Revolution, and the you-know-what hit the fan.

Three weeks later, Connecticut sent a group of frontiersmen led by **Ethan Allen** to capture a supply of weapons at **Fort Ticonderoga** on Lake Champlain, near the Canadian border. Allen and his volunteers, the **Green Mountain Boys,** attacked so early in the morning on May 10, 1775 the British were caught snoozing. On the very same day, delegates gathered in Philadelphia for the **Second Continental Congress**. Obviously something had to be done, because the colonists were definitely at war with the British, but there was no organization or central planning. They created a **Continental Army** and realized they needed someone to be in charge. **John Adams** proposed George Washington as Commander in Chief, because he was a moderate acceptable to all the delegates and he had military experience from the French and Indian War. Everyone took the hint that George wanted the job when he showed up wearing a new bright blue uniform he had specially designed for the occasion.

Meanwhile, up in Boston, more fierce fighting took place when the British attempted to seize a strategic position overlooking the city. The colonists were dug in up there, but the Redcoats repeatedly charged up the hill. Rebel Colonel William Prescott yelled, "Don't shoot until you can see the whites of their eyes!," causing considerable confusion until someone else shouted, "He means let them get close and save your ammunition!" Even so, after resisting the third charge the Americans' supplies ran out and they were forced to retreat. Nevertheless, the Patriots celebrated because their losses were much lighter than the enemy's, and they only lost because they had depleted their ammunition. This battle took place on Breed's Hill and is remembered in history as the **Battle of Bunker Hill**. Sorry, but it is too late to fix this dumb mistake now.

At this time it was still unclear to most Americans whether they were fighting for their rights as Englishmen or for complete independence. In July, 1775, the delegates at the Second Continental Congress sent the **Olive Branch Petition** to King George III, still hoping a compromise could be worked out. In November, the Americans found out the King had refused to even read their petition, and no one believed his dog had eaten it. The fighting went on: defeat at Quebec but victory when the British were forced to evacuate Boston and sail for Halifax, in Canada.

By the summer of 1776, many Patriots were giving up the idea of ever settling this conflict peacefully. Particularly galling was the British use of German **mercenaries** (hired soldiers) called **Hessians.** An English accent was irritating enough, but it was unacceptable to be shot at by foreigners using words like *dumkopf* and *bratwurst*. A lot of Americans were influenced in the direction of independence by a pamphlet written by **Thomas Paine** entitled **Common Sense**. Paine had studied the new ideas of the **Enlightenment,** an intellectual movement in Western Europe that grew out of the Renaissance, when reason replaced religion as a guide to politics, philosophy, and government. Paine argued persuasively that "there is something very absurd in supposing a continent to be perpetually governed by an island." Paine even called King George a "royal brute," a remark that outraged the British but which many Americans thought to be an understatement. If there had been a *New York Times* bestseller list back then, *Common Sense* would have been on it; even parsimonious Americans borrowed a friend's copy.

On July 4, 1776, the Second Continental Congress formally adopted the **Declaration of Independence**. With an official declaration, the Americans hoped they might secure some respect from foreign nations, especially France, which always seemed to be nursing a grudge against England. Now, hopefully, captured American soldiers would be entitled to status as prisoners of war (and imprisoned) rather than traitors to the crown (and executed). As news of the Declaration spread up and down the thirteen newly-independent states, many Americans cheered and celebrated. In New York City, the Sons of Liberty destroyed a large statue of King George III, failing to realize that, centuries later, antique collectors would have been willing to pay a fortune for it.

Thomas Jefferson of Virginia wrote most of the Declaration of Independence, basing his ideas on those of the English philosopher **John Locke**, but since Locke had died nearly a century earlier, he was not around to try to claim any credit. Benjamin Franklin and John Adams also made contributions, and it was rumored that there was particularly intense discussion over whether the correct term was unalienable rights or inalienable rights. There is no denying that the Declaration of Independence is a beautiful and eloquent document: "all men are created equal" and "endowed by their Creator with certain unalienable Rights" especially "Life, Liberty, and the pursuit of Happiness." When a government becomes "destructive of these ends," it is "the Right of the People to alter or abolish it" and establish a new government that won't be so obnoxious. Today, we know the framers of the Declaration of Independence did not intend the term "People" to refer to everybody, but because our founding fathers were all wealthy white men, they were satisfied that at least they had themselves covered.

Most historians agree that, during the war, only about one-third of the colonists were actually Patriots. Another one-third, called **Tories** or **Loyalists** (conservative rich types with business ties to England), stayed faithful to the Crown. The last one-third were opportunists, ready to jump on any winning bandwagon (like a lot of so-called Yankee fans today). Unfortunately for the real Patriots, just around the time the Declaration was issued, the Continental Army started to lose some major battles.

The **Battle of Long Island** (which took place mostly in Brooklyn) was a disaster, and in September, Washington and his men were forced to abandon New York City. Over the next couple of months, the British pushed Washington out of New York and across New Jersey into Pennsylvania. Fortunately, winter set in and the Redcoats decided to back off and seek shelter in the comfortable city of Philadelphia. Back in those days, warring armies often took the winter off because fighting in the wind and snow was such a bummer. But Washington knew his army was cold, hungry and depressed (and lots of his men were deserting), so he decided to try something really bold. On Christmas night, he and his men crossed the ice-clogged Delaware River back into New Jersey. At **Trenton,** the Continental Army surprised and ruined the drunken holiday celebration of a garrison of Hessians. A week later, after fierce fighting, Washington forced the British to withdraw from **Princeton**. The Trenton and Princeton victories exhausted the Continental army, but at least now they had the morale to fight on and create many other tourist attractions in the area.

In February, 1777, the British government approved a plan to isolate New England, split the colonies, and end this inconvenient war once and for all. Three British armies were supposed to converge on Albany in upstate New York. The plan could have worked, but only one of the armies showed up and was soundly defeated at **Saratoga**. The Americans were superior wilderness fighters, and this proved to be crucial along with the incompetence and pomposity of British General "Gentleman Johnny" **Burgoyne,** who found it difficult to march an army through thick woods laden with fifty-two cannon, his enormous wardrobe and wine cellar, and a female entourage. If Burgoyne were alive today, he would probably go camping and stay at a Hilton Hotel.

Saratoga should be remembered as the turning point of the Revolutionary War. When the French heard about it they thought: *Alors, these Americans actually have a good chance to win...especially if we help them.* In February, 1778, France signed a treaty of alliance with the United States and started sending Washington lots of men, muskets, military supplies and croissants. England now had another enemy to worry about (they were also concerned about Holland and Spain) so they had to keep a lot of their "first string" soldiers on alert back home and only send the scrubs across the Atlantic.

To the south, things were not going as well for the Americans. They had lost Philadelphia and been forced to withdraw twenty miles away to **Valley Forge** to spend the winter. Washington himself had a small house to live in, but his men had to make do in hastily constructed wooden huts. Needless to say they were freezing, starving and just plain miserable. Maybe it was patriotism, loyalty to their commander, or fanatical commitment to weekly bingo tournaments, but Washington miraculously managed to hold his army together. When the British evacuated Philadelphia in the spring, Washington followed and gave them a sound thrashing at **Monmouth Court House** (June 28, 1778) in New Jersey. Perched up in the hills around New York City, warmer now and with a few good meals in them, George and the boys waited for French reinforcements to arrive.

In the Northwest Territory, **George Rogers Clark** and his fellow frontiersman won a series of victories and firmly established American claims to the area north of the Ohio River, west of Pennsylvania, and east of the Mississippi. But most of the action in the war from now on was going to be in the South. British forces captured Savannah and Charleston but were unable to crush the Americans in the rural areas. Led by the hit and run guerrilla tactics of General **Nathanial Green**, the patriots drove the Redcoats to distraction. British soldiers hated fighting in the swamps because it was hot, sweaty and the Patriots rudely wouldn't reveal where the quicksand was. In early 1781, fed up with his heavy losses, British General **Charles Cornwallis** withdrew northward to **Yorktown**, Virginia.

Yorktown was on the Chesapeake peninsula, so with his back to the sea and the British fleet in nearby New York harbor, Cornwallis felt secure. But a French army reinforced Washington's Continental Army and together they moved south. When a French fleet under **Admiral Francois Joseph de Grasse** arrived in Chesapeake Bay, Cornwallis realized somewhat belatedly that he was completely boxed in. His forces held on for three weeks, but they were outnumbered on land (9000 Americans and 7800 French versus 8000 British and Hessians), and the British fleet sailing south from New York was diverted by de Grasse. On October 19, 1781, Cornwallis surrendered. Cornwallis himself was a spoilsport and sent his second-in-command to surrender his sword to General Washington. The British band played *The World Turned Upside Down* which at that moment it certainly was. The Americans sang "**Yankee Doodle** went to town riding on a pony, stuck a feather in his hat and called it macaroni." This line makes no sense unless you realize that back in those days they used the word "macaroni" like today we use the word "cool." Give them a break. After defeating the world's most powerful nation against all odds and winning their freedom, they were cool.

Yorktown did not cripple the British militarily but British public opinion turned sharply against continuing the fight. (Hey, right now take a break and look up the Tet Offensive during the Vietnam War. History really does repeat itself in strange ways.) The rich aristocrats would have loved to press on, but the masses of poor and middle class sympathized with the upstart Americans, who seemed to be fighting for rights any man justly deserved. Without French help, America never would have won the Revolution, so the next time you go to France and get treated snobbily by a taxi driver, try to chill out.

Individual French volunteers were invaluable, including **Marquis de Lafayette**, who joined Washington's staff and became his best pal, and **Baron de Kalb**, a soldier of fortune who had served in the French army. (When they are on our side we call them "soldiers of fortune" rather than "mercenaries.") Prussia's **Baron von Steuben** became drillmaster of the Continental Army, which really helped, because before he showed up there were lots of embarrassing collisions and pileups during parades. Two Polish guys,

25

Count Casimir Pulaski, a cavalry officer, and **Thaddeus Kosciusko**, a military engineer, offered vital assistance that ought to make you feel really guilty for all those Polish jokes you've laughed at. **Haym Salomon**, a Jewish refugee from Russian rule in Poland, gave his entire fortune to the American cause. Get the message? Lots of different sorts pulled together.

Over in Europe in 1783, the new United States and Great Britain finally got around to signing an official peace accord called the **Treaty of Paris**. It was called the Treaty of Paris because it was signed in London. Just kidding, it was signed in Paris and was a different Treaty of Paris than the Treaty of Paris ending the French and Indian War. It seems our founding fathers did not take into consideration future generations of History students who would have to keep this stuff straight for the final exam! Most importantly, the British government recognized the thirteen American states as independent with boundaries that stretched to the Mississippi River, though poor old King George stubbornly referred to the United States as "the colonies" until his death in 1820.

THE CRITICAL PERIOD (1781-1789)
or *We've Won, Now What?*

By 1781, the Continental Congress had created the first government of the United States, called the **Articles of Confederation**. The major point here is that it turned out to be a lousy arrangement. The central government was extremely weak and the thirteen states each went their own way. The country was plagued by hard economic times because wartime demand for goods waned. Farmers suffered, and american merchants also felt the pinch because the British, sore losers, excluded them from all British markets — especially the West Indies. To top it off, each state printed its own money, which only added to the confusion. There was no chief executive, only a Congress, and no central courts. Congress had no power to tax, and could only request funds from the individual states. (Who ever thought that would work?) Congress had no power to regulate **interstate commerce** and no power to regulate foreign commerce. Let's face it, Congress was lucky to have heat in the winter. Historians call this America's **Critical Period** because they are too polite to call it crappy.

But before we totally trash the Articles of Confederation, we have to give Congress credit for enacting at least two really terrific pieces of legislation: the **Land Ordinance of 1785** and the **Northwest Ordinance** (of 1787). After the Revolution, the states grudgingly ceded to the federal government their claims in the newly acquired Northwest Territory. In the Land Ordinance of 1785, Congress planned for the orderly sale and settlement of this area. With great foresight, they decreed that the income from one section of every township be used to support public education. Two years later, the Northwest Ordinance set the rules for how a territory could become a state: 60,000 inhabitants meant a territory could apply for statehood "on an equal footing with the original states in all respects whatever." This was exactly the opposite of how England had treated the original thirteen colonies, and evidence that our leaders had learned a good lesson. Eventually, five states were formed from the Northwest Territory: Ohio, Indiana, Wisconsin, Illinois, and Michigan. Slavery was abolished in the region, public education encouraged, and the new states did not have to feel second-class to the original thirteen. Not only did they not feel inferior, even back then people in Northwest Territory could not resist making fun of New Jersey.

The root of most of the problems under the Articles of Confederation was the economy. Merchants and artisans complained about a slowing of trade and falling prices. Farmers, as usual in American history, suffered the most. Oversupplied markets led to low prices for crops, and a lot of farmers found they could not pay their debts. Back in those days a person could be imprisoned for debt, which is difficult to imagine considering how we use our credit cards today. In Massachusetts, courts were foreclosing on mortgages and many farmers were losing their land. In January 1787, a poor, hot-tempered farmer and war veteran named **Daniel Shays** and about a thousand followers marched on the Confederation arsenal at Springfield to steal a cache of arms. Their plan made sense in the short term: keep judges from getting to court so they could not foreclose mortgages or send debtors to prison.

What was so shocking about **Shays' Rebellion** was that the federal government was powerless to do anything about it — under the Articles of Confederation, the central government did not have the authority to directly raise troops. Eventually the Massachusetts state militia crushed the rebellion, but not before Americans had received a rude awakening. A stronger central government was definitely needed to maintain law and order and solve the economic problems that had so ticked off Shays and his mob. At the time, Thomas Jefferson was over in France serving as our minister to that country. When he heard about Shays' Rebellion he proclaimed, "A little rebellion now and then is a good thing...The tree of liberty must be refreshed from time to time with the blood of patriots and tyrants." Lots of Americans inevitably thought to themselves, *PUH-LEEEZE... that's easy for you to say, you're three thousand miles away in Paris!*

A NEW CONSTITUTION
or *You Scratch My Back, I'll Scratch Yours*

Even before Shays' Rebellion, many Americans had been concerned about all the problems the country was having under the Articles of Confederation. In 1786, there was a convention at Annapolis, Maryland to discuss the confused commercial arrangements among the states. Delegates from only five of the states showed up at the **Annapolis Convention** (apparently Annapolis back then lacked appeal as a place for conventioneers to party, meet women, and wear funny hats), but they did petition Congress to call another conference for the express purpose of removing the weaknesses of the Articles. Congress gave in and called for a convention to be held the following year in Philadelphia, which would no doubt be better attended because in Philly the hotels were better, there were a lot more hot babes, and Shays' Rebellion had scared the heck out of everyone.

Fifty-five delegates (from all the states except Rhode Island — is it possible that state was so tiny it was overlooked when the invitations went out?) met at the **Constitutional Convention** in Philadelphia in the summer of 1787. These delegates were not exactly representative of America's general population, which at the time was mostly made up of small farmers, city workers and frontiersmen (and women). Let's not sugarcoat it: the delegates who set about to write our new constitution were all rich white men — mostly lawyers, large landowners, merchants, and bankers. They were educated devotees of the Enlightenment (don't feel bad if you've forgotten what the Enlightenment was, just check page 26) and especially familiar with the steps England had taken towards democracy. Collectively, they may have been the most brilliant gathering of statesmen in the history of the world, the galaxy and even the universe!

George Washington was unanimously chosen to be the president of the convention because everybody still loved him. **Alexander Hamilton** of New York attended and advocated strenuously for the wealthier classes. Benjamin Franklin was there, even though by this time he was eighty-one years old. If he nodded off once in a while, everyone was understanding, because when he woke up he was the same old genius, if a little groggy. **James Madison** of Virginia did so much of the work that he is often referred to as the "father of the Constitution." He also took detailed notes, which are virtually the only source of information about the proceedings because the meetings were held in secret, under conditions of what today we call a press blackout. Nobody blabbed; this would have driven the modern news media crazy, but back then, the secrecy created a dignified atmosphere in which to work out some extremely complicated issues.

John Adams was not present because he was in London serving as our ambassador, and Thomas Jefferson was not present, because he was in Paris serving as our ambassador and chasing married women. Revolutionary hotheads Sam Adams and Patrick Henry were also not in attendance, which was probably a good thing, since they both pathologically distrusted any kind of serious central government. You need people like Adams and Henry to get a revolution going because they have spirit and guts. But after the revolution, when it comes time to calmly sit down and conscientiously hammer out a workable plan of government, hotheads like them are a pain in the butt.

When the meeting convened, it immediately became clear that everyone was in agreement on one major point: the Articles of Confederation were too screwed up to be fixed; what was needed was an entirely new constitution. The delegates also agreed that this time they had to create a federal (central) government with some teeth, incorporating the power to tax, raise and support an armed forces, regulate commerce and foreign relations, enforce laws and, when necessary, buy furniture. But this government could not be so strong that it could become a tyranny and deprive citizens of individual liberties. In short, it had to be subject to the will of the people. It had to be strong, yet weak at the same time. Sensitive yet forceful. Invincible yet vulnerable. Unlimited yet controlled. Inclusive yet concise. Fierce yet cuddly. Sorry, I got carried away.

When it came to creating a national legislature, the delegates ran headlong into controversy. The more populous states wanted representation to be based upon population, and called for the acceptance of the **Virginia Plan**. The less populous states wanted each state to have equal representation and advocated for the **New Jersey Plan**. It was hot and humid that summer in Philadelphia, and the delegates themselves got pretty steamed over this issue (Luckily, they had no idea that air conditioning would be invented one day.) The delegates from the small states threatened to bolt the convention, but they subsequently loosened up over drinks at the local taverns. In what has come to be called both the **Great Compromise** and the **Connecticut Compromise**, the legislature (called the **Congress**) was to consist of two houses: a lower house (the **House of Representatives**) with representation based on population, and an upper house (the **Senate**) where each state would have equal representation. This two-house setup gives the United States what is called a **bicameral** legislature. Remember, the word is bicameral, not bisexual, although John Hancock reportedly looked really hot in his velvet knee breeches.

Next, the southern states as a group got into the act. They wanted their huge population of slaves to count for representation in the House, but not to count for purposes of direct taxation. Slavery was dying out in the north, so the northerners naturally took the opposite position. Tempers flared again but cooler heads prevailed, and the **Three-Fifths Compromise** settled the issue: slaves were to be counted as three-fifths of a person. In another unseemly compromise on slavery, Congress was forbidden for another twenty years to interfere with the slave trade. To our modern sensibilities these measures in regard to African Americans are nothing less than stomach turning, but they did keep the convention from falling apart. The brutal truth is that virtually none of our founding fathers cared one bit about the dignity or welfare of the slaves.

In another compromise, Congress was given the power to levy tariffs on imports but not exports. A **tariff** is a tax, and if placed on a product coming from abroad, raises the price of that product, thereby making it easier for domestic companies to offer competitive prices on their goods. A **protective tariff** was popular in the North because that's where American industry was rapidly developing. The South hated protective tariffs because they raised the prices of their imported consumer goods, and foreign countries retaliated with tariffs of their own against southern exports of indigo, rice, tobacco and, later, cotton. Arguments over the pros and cons of tariffs went on for a long time and, in fact, bald men with nerdy glasses are still arguing about it on cable news shows.

When it came to creating an executive officer for the country, there were a lot of different opinions. Some wanted the term of office to be three years, some wanted it to be for life. Some wanted the President to be elected directly by the people, some wanted him to be elected by the Congress. Some slow learners even suggested that America select a king and begin a hereditary monarchy just like they had in England. Once again, the delegates compromised and created the office of the presidency, in which one person serves a term of four years after being elected by the people...sort of.

Our founding fathers well knew that Roman mobs used to select popular generals to be emperors just because they passed out free food, drink and engravings of a naked

Cleopatra. Could this happen in the United States? To safeguard the country from the excesses of true democracy, the founders created an obnoxiously complex system for electing the President through an **electoral college.** Here's how it works: each state receives as many electors as the total number of its Representatives (based on population) and Senators (two) in Congress. (Today, under this formula, California has the most electors and a state like Wyoming, with lots of tumbleweed but relatively few people, has the least.) America's elections run on a winner-take-all principle, so if a candidate gets the most votes in a state, he (or she) receives all the electors (hence those red and blue states on the TV news maps.) The electoral college now consists of 538 electors and a candidate needs a majority of 270 to win.

Way back in the late 1700s when they were making up these rules, it was presumed the electors would be educated aristocrats who could exercise their own judgment in case the people (who were not completely trusted yet) elected some lunatic to the presidency. As we will discuss, the evolution of political parties, and the naming of electors who are pledged in advance to vote for the party's Presidential candidate, has made the electoral college results representative of the people's wishes — most of the time. There can still be convoluted screwups — just ask Al Gore, when he gets finished mowing his own lawn.

The founding fathers decided that each state would hold a convention on ratifying (approving) the Constitution, and if nine of the thirteen states approved it, it would go into effect. Those in favor of the Constitution were called **Federalists,** but ratification was not a slam-dunk because a lot of folks had doubts. These doubting Thomases (they had other names as well) were called **Anti-Federalists**. (If it is too difficult for you to keep the Federalists and the Anti-Federalists straight then stop reading this book immediately and head for the nearest tractor-pulling contest.)

The Federalists tended to be men with property and business interests who favored a strong central government that could maintain the law and order necessary to keep commerce flowing smoothly. Anti-Federalists consisted mainly of city workers and farmers who feared a strong national government would restrict both the rights of the states and an individual's civil liberties. The Federalists presumably bathed more often and dressed better.

The Federalists were much better organized and, being rich, may have greased a few palms in the states where the vote was close. Besides, back in those days most states still had property qualifications for voting, and many Anti-Federalists were too poor to make the cut. Alexander Hamilton, **John Jay** and James Madison wrote a series of articles for the New York newspapers explaining exactly what they thought the Constitution was all about, and why it should definitely be ratified. Published together in May, 1788, these essays became known as *The Federalist,* and even today serves as a useful reference when we are confronted with constitutional questions. When President Clinton was impeached, lots of people ran to the nearest copy of *The Federalist* and were disappointed that there was no reference to nookie in the oval office with an intern.

The most telling argument the Anti-Federalists had against the proposed Constitution was that it failed to include a bill of rights. The Federalists, believing the Constitution already offered sufficient protection of individual liberties, nevertheless promised that upon ratification, the first order of business would be insertion of a formal bill of rights. Most everyone believed them — lying by politicians back then was not automatically taken for granted — and one by one the states started to ratify. The small states approved quickly because they had more than their share of power in the new government and didn't want any of the large states to have second thoughts. (Delaware was actually the first state to ratify in December 1787; nothing much has happened there since, so it still says "THE FIRST STATE" on Delaware license plates. New Hampshire was the ninth state, and its license plates say "LIVE FREE OR DIE," which must be particularly galling to the convicts in the platemaking shop.)

Everyone knew the big states had to come on board or the new government would really be in jeopardy. Pennsylvania ratified on December 12, 1787, though opposition had been fierce; just to get a **quorum** (enough members present) for a vote on calling a ratifying convention, the Federalists had two Pennsylvania state legislators forcibly detained and their coats wrinkled against their will. It was also close in Massachusetts (a "large" state in those days because of its population), but a couple of months later it ratified. Patrick Henry led the opposition in Virginia, but Washington and Madison conspired together to convince everyone Henry was nothing but a radical crybaby.

In New York, Alexander Hamilton had his hands full with the Anti-Federalists, and even went so far as to throw a temper tantrum and threaten to break New York City away from New York State if he didn't get his way. Word of ratification by New Hampshire, the ninth state, and then Virginia in late June 1788 convinced just enough New York legislators to back a winning horse. The "EMPIRE STATE" ratified by three votes. North Carolina got around to ratifying the Constitution in November 1789, and stubborn little Rhode Island waited until the spring of 1790. It had been a difficult labor, but a new government was born...with a kind of caesarean section.

No one knew if this new government would actually work. Benjamin Franklin summed it up best when a woman approached him as he was departing the last session of the Constitutional Convention at Philadelphia in September 1787:

"What kind of government have you given us, Dr. Franklin?" she asked.

"A Republic, Madam," he answered, "if you can keep it."

Afterwards, given Franklin's amorous predilections, he probably hit on the woman. But precisely what happened next has been lost to History.

The constitutional foundations of the United States had been built. Not much else had been built yet so washed-out roads delayed for two months the formal beginning of the new government. Details remained to be worked out. Who was really going to do all the work? Who was going to get the credit? Would foreign nations respect us in the morning? Uncharted territory lay ahead (literally and figuratively) and the first officers of the new government realized it was in their hands to either build a great nation or screw it up and end up getting conquered again by some pompous European king. Uh oh...stay tuned...don't touch that dial!!!

This Really Happened!

A number of American presidents have actually grown marijuana. As a source of fiber, marijuana was a major crop in colonial America. George Washington imported seeds and planted them in his vineyard at Mount Vernon and Thomas Jefferson planted an acre of marijuana at Monticello because he wanted to research hemp. Later, Theodore Roosevelt grew fields of it and other medicinal drugs so he would not have to import them into America. There is absolutely no evidence that any of these presidents ever realized marijuana could be used for recreational purposes ... but in the case of George Washington ... why would he cross the Delaware River in the middle of winter in a small boat standing up?!

And the rest is History...

Quiz yourself on Chapter 2

Multiple Choice (circle the correct answer).

1. The British decisively defeated the French and Indians in
   a. the War of the Roses
   b. the French and Indian War
   c. the Hundred Years War
   d. Scrabble
   e. all of the above

2. Under the terms of the Treaty of Paris signed in 1763, France
   a. gained a tremendous amount of land in North America
   b. lost a tremendous amount of land in North America
   c. agreed to stop acting so pompous and stuckup
   d. admitted that they talked funny
   e. d and c

3. Most English leaders regarded the colonists as
   a. good dancers
   b. their loving cousins
   c. brilliant philosophers
   d. uncouth and inferior
   e. none of the above

4. In order to keep the colonists from coming into conflict with the Indians, a new British policy (The Proclamation of 1763)
   a. prohibited settlement across beyond the Appalachian divide
   b. announced that Indians should always be called Native Americans
   c. granted a prize for the nicest Indian costume
   d. closed some of the best gambling casinos in North America
   e. none of the above

5. The colonists considered tariffs to
   a. be taxation without representation
   b. really suck
   c. both a and b
   d. maybe a but not b and definitely not c
   e. e

6. Parliament repealed the Townshend Act but retained a tax on tea
   a. because they forgot
   b. because they wanted to drive Starbucks out of business
   c. because Townshend was found in bed with a goat
   d. because they wanted to preserve the principle that England had a right to tax the colonies
   e. all of the above

7. Samuel Adams and Thomas Paine were noted
   a. Tories
   b. lovers
   c. Siamese twins
   d. Patriots
   e. all of the above

8. General Washington's continual pressing problem during the Revolution was
   a. finding privacy when he wanted to go to the bathroom
   b. remembering where he had left his teeth
   c. obtaining sufficient supplies for his troops
   d. explaining to his wife why Betsy Ross was dressed only in an American flag
   e. b and d

9. The Articles of Confederation were
   a. memorized by all true Americans
   b. too weak
   c. too strong
   d. recommended by four out of five dentists
   e. none of the above

10. The United States Congress decided to create a new Constitution because
    a. some stupid secretary lost the old one
    b. they wanted a chance to go to Philadelphia and party
    c. the federal government could not exert authority over the states
    d. the Articles of Confederation failed to guarantee the rights of all Americans to do whatever the heck they wanted to
    e. a and b

CHAPTER 3

A YOUNG NATION
TACKLES ITS MANY PROBLEMS

or

Don't Call Me Your Majesty

After the adoption of the Constitution, the United States was one big happy family — for about ten minutes. The new government took off running and new questions arose. What kind of a country should America be? Whose side should we be on in the European conflicts? Who should really run things, the few rich or the many poor? Above all, who has more power, the national government or the individual states? About the only thing anyone agreed on was the color to paint the President's House (White).

THE CONSTITUTION SPRINGS TO LIFE
or *Did Anybody Proofread This Thing?*

The Constitution set up a system of government called **federalism,** whereby powers are divided between the state governments and the **federal** (or **central** or **national**) government. People from New Jersey don't have to be totally depressed because they are also citizens of the country of the United States. Powers specifically delegated to the federal government by the Constitution are called **enumerated** powers, but to this day Americans still argue about the proper roles of the federal and state government. One thing is certain: thanks to the **supremacy clause** in the Constitution, when a state law and a federal law conflict, the federal law takes precedence.

The powers of the federal government are divided among three independent branches, and this is called **separation of powers**. The **executive branch**, headed by the President, carries out, and enforces, the laws. The **legislative branch**, consisting of the Congress, makes the laws. The **judicial branch**, made up of the Supreme Court and the lower federal courts, interprets the laws, which means it steps in and settles arguments regarding exactly what the laws mean. Today, even constitutional scholars disagree over which branch is the most powerful, and that is just the sort of confusion the Founding Fathers intended. They didn't want any one person or group to definitively have the most power. Which branch is the coolest is another matter. Think about it. It's got to be the executive branch, because there are 100 Senators and 435 Representatives who are jealous and think they should be President.

The Founding Fathers ingeniously incorporated a system of **checks and balances** into the Constitution, whereby each branch can counteract the powers of the other two branches. For example, the President can **veto** (cancel) laws passed by Congress. It really ticks off the President, but Congress can **override** the President's veto with a two-thirds vote in both Houses (the Senate and the House of Representatives). The President makes treaties with foreign nations, but the Senate must approve them. The President nominates **Supreme Court** justices and the Senate approves (or sometimes disapproves) the appointments, but once in office, the justices serve a life term in order to *supposedly* stay aloof from politics. Supreme Court Justice is such a cushy job that some justices serve for decades until they croak in office, which after a few weeks has got to be noticed by the cleaning crew.

Probably the best thing about the Constitution (and the reason it still works so well today) is that it is flexible; it can be changed as the times require. An **amendment** (change) to the Constitution requires a two-thirds vote in each house of Congress and then approval by three-fourths of the state legislatures. The procedure is deliberately lengthy and difficult to make it impossible to accomplish on the spur of the moment. Clearly, a silly amendment to make everyone wear bell-bottoms would never pass, because long before the end of the process, Americans would come to their senses and demand the right to wear straight pants.

The Federalists lived up to their word and swiftly proposed amendments to the Constitution, collectively known as the **Bill of Rights**. These ten amendments were ratified by the state legislatures by the end of 1791. The **First Amendment** is the biggie because it addresses **civil liberties**, the rights of all persons that cannot be denied by governmental power. Freedom of speech, press and religion are all specifically mentioned, as are the rights to peaceably assemble and petition the government. This sounds fairly basic, but Americans love to test limits, and that's why the Supreme Court has frequently had to step in and decide what types of behavior the First Amendment covers. Some constitutional questions facing Americans today: Is topless dancing covered under freedom of expression? How about burning the American flag? Is the sacrificing of animals covered under freedom of religion? Is there any way to prevent Britney Spears from coming out with any more music videos?

The **Second Amendment** states "the right of the people to bear arms shall not be infringed." This made sense to our Founding Fathers and still makes sense today, if only the gun-toting fanatics in the National Rifle Association would be a tiny bit less dogmatic. They didn't have drive-by shootings back in 1789 because wagons were slow and muskets only fired one shot and then took forever to reload. They definitely didn't have automatic weapons. Today, sensible regulation and registration of handguns would reduce violent crime, and would not seriously threaten hunters, sport shooters, and the time-honored right of every red-blooded American to blow somebody away if they really want to.

The **Fourth Amendment** forbids the unreasonable search and seizure of persons and property, and it also disallows the use of general warrants for search or arrest. This means that the authorities must show a judge **probable cause,** and obtain a search warrant describing the particular object being sought. Courts have ruled there is a "plain sight exception" to all this, which basically means that anyone stupid enough to leave stolen goods or drugs in public view deserves to be arrested. By the way, cops frequently ignore the Fourth Amendment in traffic stops of young people and minorities.

The **Fifth Amendment** states that a person accused of a crime may not be tried twice (**double jeopardy**) for the same offense. O.J. Simpson can now stand up and say, "Ha, I did it!" and there is nothing anybody can do except throw up. People also may not be compelled to be a witness against themselves (give **self-incriminating** evidence). This means you can "**plead the fifth**" when they have you nailed dead to rights and try to ask you about it. It sure looks bad to the jury when you refuse to answer a question, but it does force the police to come up with evidence to prove their charges. By the way, the government cannot suspend the **writ of habeas corpus** except in extreme emergencies such as rebellion or invasion, or they think they can get away with it. This means that once a person is arrested, he/she must be quickly produced before a judge, along with a statement of charges. If a person is being held illegally, the judge is supposed to set the prisoner free and give the prosecutor a dirty look. If the prisoner is being held legally, he/she may be released on bail or returned to prison pending a speedy trial, which in America today could mean years, especially for illegal aliens of Middle Eastern descent.

GEORGE WASHINGTON TAKES THE REINS
or *There's a First Time for Everything*

George Washington was sworn in as the first President in the spring of 1789. There was no popular election, but he was the unanimous choice of every elector. As he rode north from his home at **Mount Vernon** in Virginia to the nation's first capital in New York City, he was met by cheering crowds and celebrations. Lots of folks wanted to party and put off worrying about the huge debts left behind by the Confederation Congress. No mechanism existed as yet for collecting taxes, and with no money coming in, the army had shrunk to 672 soldiers and the navy consisted of three dinghies that leaked.

Everything presidential that Washington did, he did for the first time. What should a president wear? Where should he sit at ceremonies? What should we call him? Should we laugh when he slips on the ice? Fortunately for the country, George Washington was a man of great dignity and moderation. He insisted on being called "Mr. President" not "Your Majesty," "Your Highness," or "Yo Dude." (Presumably only his wife, Martha, was allowed to call him Georgie late at night.) He demanded and received well-appointed accommodations, servants, and an expensive coach, but he purposely rejected the wasteful ostentation common to European monarchs. In short, he had good taste, and set a standard for all future presidents to aspire to.

The Constitution does not specifically mention the President's **cabinet**. It does mention "executive departments," so Washington created some agencies and appointed men to head them, men who collectively became his close advisors or cabinet. Every President since then has had a cabinet; Washington's consisted of four members, but currently that number has grown to twenty-two. There are reports that nowadays cabinet meetings are so crowded, the Secretary of Housing and Urban Development has to sit in the hall.

Washington named Thomas Jefferson Secretary of State, Alexander Hamilton Secretary of the Treasury, **Henry Knox** Secretary of War, and **Edmund Randolph** Attorney General. Hamilton had his hands full trying to get the country's finances back on track. Towards that end, he advocated full payment of the foreign and domestic debt, assumption of state debts, and organized money management through the creation of a **National Bank** or **Bank of the United States**. He also prevailed upon Washington to urge Congress to pass an **excise tax** (a fee imposed on products produced and consumed in the United States) on whiskey.

The **Whiskey Tax** was approved by Congress and became law, but the farmers in western Pennsylvania refused to pay it. They shot at federal "revenuers" trying to collect the tax, thereby brewing up some trouble that has become known as the **Whiskey Rebellion**. This first major challenge to the new government under the new Constitution infuriated Hamilton, and he convinced Washington not to take it lying down. In October, 1794, the two of them donned their old Revolutionary War uniforms and marched fifteen thousand militiamen to Pennsylvania to meet the threat. Their uniforms were way too tight and they inevitably must have burped a lot, but the rebellion was crushed. There was no real fighting because most of the farmers just stayed home and got drunk. But the federal government flexed its biceps, biceps that had not yet been developed a few years earlier when Daniel Shays had gotten out of line. Times had changed, and the Pennsylvania moonshiners took the punch.

States in the South balked at the proposal for the federal government to pay off state debts. It didn't seem fair, since most of the Southern states had already paid off their debts. Hamilton secured Southern support by **logrolling** — trading votes for one proposal in exchange for another. Southern congressmen supported Hamilton's financial plan in exchange for establishment of the nation's permanent capital in the South, on the banks of the Potomac River between Virginia and Maryland. President Washington picked out the exact location of the new capital, coordinated the design, and was especially pleased when it was named **Washington, D.C.** (D.C. stands for **District of Columbia**.) Hamilton undoubtedly would have preferred the name Hamilton, D.C., but he was smart enough not to be too pushy.

Jefferson and Hamilton soon realized they were the two main competitors for the ear of President Washington, so they handled the situation in a mature adult manner — they stopped talking to each other. Jefferson particularly hated Hamilton's plan for the creation of a National Bank, because the Constitution had not specifically granted Congress the power to do any such thing. Hamilton pointed to the section of the Constitution which states that Congress has the right "to make all laws necessary and proper" for carrying into effect the powers it has been granted. This **necessary and proper clause** (Article I, Section 8, Clause 18) is the basis for what is known as a **loose interpretation** of the Constitution — the idea that some governmental powers are implied and not specifically spelled out. Jefferson and his followers, fearful that the federal government would love to get carried away and give itself powers it was never meant to have, insisted on a **strict interpretation** of the Constitution. President Washington listened to arguments from both sides, and then decided in favor of Hamilton's position. Some of Jefferson's supporters swore they overheard Washington whispering "eeny, meeny, mincy, moe," but serious historians have generally discounted this as sour grapes.

The bitter struggle over financial policy resulted in the formation of the nation's first two political parties. Washington thought it was a bad idea, but pretty soon Jefferson and Madison were heading up the **Democratic-Republicans**. (To make this a little easier, from now on the Democratic-Republicans will be referred to simply as the Republicans.) Alexander Hamilton and Vice President John Adams in turn led a faction called the **Federalists**. The Federalists are distant ancestors of the modern day Republican Party, while the Republicans are related to the contemporary Democratic Party. Of course this is very complicated, but the study of history is not supposed to be a cakewalk.

At least what the two parties stood for is fairly easy to understand. The Federalists favored the wealthier people while the Republicans appealed to the common people. The Federalist Party was strongest in the North, especially New England, while the Republicans dominated in the South and West. The Federalists feared too much democracy and believed in government by and for rich aristocrats. The Republicans also believed that the educated wellborn should govern, but paternally, in the interests of the common people. Hamilton's side favored a strong central government and a loose interpretation of the Constitution. Jefferson's side favored states' rights and a strict interpretation of the Constitution. Hamilton's Federalists favored the National Bank just as much as Jefferson's Republicans hated it. Really the only thing they agreed upon was that it was inappropriate to serve red wine with fish.

The two parties couldn't even agree on foreign affairs. The Republicans favored France because the **French Revolution** of 1789 seemed to be a struggle for liberty and equality that closely paralleled our own. The Federalists, fearing that the French masses were chopping off way too many aristocratic heads, favored the British, whose government was controlled by the upper classes. When the French King, **Louis XVI**, had his head rudely severed from the rest of his body in 1793, other European monarchs, fearing for their own necks, formed an alliance (consisting of Prussia, Austria, Great Britain, the Netherlands and Spain) and declared war on France.

Federalists urged President Washington to aid England, and the Republicans called for an alliance with France. President Washington, with more wisdom than Jefferson and Hamilton put together, concluded that it would be rash and possibly self-destructive for the young nation to become involved in a European war. In 1793, the President issued a **Proclamation of Neutrality**. He really ticked off most Americans, who had taken sides, and France and England were also mad, but good old George was a very wise man, interested only in doing what was best for the United States. Federalists and Republicans alike hurled vicious criticism at him in their respective newspapers, but the President publicly stayed above the fray. Privately, he was reported to have had temper tantrums, which may have been due to the bitter politics or the fact that his false teeth — at one point made out of hippopotamus ivory — never seemed to fit right.

The French Ambassador to the United States, **"Citizen" Edmond Genêt**, really infuriated President Washington. Completely ignoring America's Proclamation of Neutrality, Genêt precipitated what is known as the **"Citizen Genêt Affair"** by traveling up the eastern seaboard commissioning **privateers** to raid British commerce. The difference between **pirates** and **privateers** is somewhat nebulous: pirates attack every ship they can get their hands (or hooks) on, while privateers supposedly have a letter from the government of one country giving them permission to capture the ships of enemy countries and keep the profits for themselves. Both pirates and privateers were total dirtbags; a lot of them had eye patches, peglegs, parrots on their shoulders, sang "yo ho ho and a bottle of rum" and danced on a "dead man's chest" which, if you think about it, is really gross.

Washington finally blew his top and ordered France to recall Genêt. That is a polite way of saying that Genêt was kicked out of the country. But as Genêt was preparing to leave, he received word that the political chaos in France had accelerated to the point where he might be executed if he returned. Washington resisted the urge to say "naaa naaa na naaa naaa" and allowed Genêt (stripped of his power) to remain in the United

States. Genêt found himself a nice rich woman, got married and lived out the rest of his days happily eating pastries in New York.

The war in Europe was made to order for the United States. The **belligerents** (warring nations) were desperate for supplies, and American merchants were more than happy to sell them to anyone who could pay. But Britain got really mad about our sending supplies to France, so the British navy started seizing American merchant ships heading for French ports. This violated the time-honored principle of **freedom of the seas**, the right of a neutral nation to trade with all sides in time of war. The British also **impressed** (kidnapped and forced) American sailors into the British navy. America was helpless against this bullying behavior because we had no navy of our own to fight back with, and the British knew we still wanted to trade with them. The most Americans could do was curse the British behind their backs and smile sweetly if they turned around.

To add insult to injury, the British still held forts in the Northwest Territory they were supposed to have evacuated after the Revolution. To top it off, they were encouraging the Indians to raid American frontier settlements. The British justified their conduct by pointing out that the United States had utterly failed to settle financial claims resulting from the war. Folks in the United States took a different view, calling the British nothing but a bunch of wig-wearing lime-sucking sore losers.

President Washington sent John Jay to England to try to negotiate some sort of a deal that would keep America out of war with England. Jay was in a tough position because he had little bargaining power, and Hamilton, favoring England, revealed Jay's weak poker hand to the British minister in America. Great Britain made few concessions, and with little choice, Jay returned home with what even he admitted was a really crappy treaty.

In **Jay's Treaty,** Britain did agree to withdraw its troops from the Northwest Territory and submit financial claims to an arbitration commission, but there was *no* mention of freedom of the seas and no agreement to halt the seizure of ships or the impressment of American sailors. Americans soon heard about the terms of the treaty and used terms a lot stronger than crappy. When John Jay looked out his window and saw a crowd hanging and burning a straw-stuffed dummy with the name Jay written on the shirt, he concluded it would be best if he stayed indoors for a while.

When Washington first saw the treaty in March 1795, he knew it was a piece of garbage, but he agreed with Hamilton that it was in the best interests of the United States to swallow hard and accept the damn thing. The two of them prevailed upon the Senate to ratify the treaty. Jay's Treaty was an insult to American pride but it did keep the country from going to war with England, a war that probably would have cost the United States its newly won independence. But most red-blooded Americans would not forget the slight, and they longed for a chance in the future to really sock it to those insufferable English "gentlemen" who kept their handkerchiefs tucked into their sleeves.

As the British were bullying the United States, Americans gleefully realized the United States could bully Spain. Spain was worried that England and the United States would form an alliance to seize Spanish territories in North America. No such plan ever existed — at this point in history, the Americans were not about to cooperate with those British jerks on anything — but the Spanish did not know that. American envoy to Spain **Thomas Pinckney** held all the cards, so the **Pinckney Treaty** with Spain achieved everything America wanted: free navigation of the Mississippi River, permission for American traders to deposit goods for shipment at the mouth of the river (in Spanish New Orleans), acknowledgment of the American southern boundary at the thirty-first parallel and the western boundary at the Mississippi, and an agreement by each nation to prevent Indians within its territory from raiding into the territory of the other. Crowds in America hailed Thomas Pinckney as a hero, which really must have bummed out John Jay, as he was still hiding in his attic.

Lots of people hoped George Washington would accept a third four-year term as President. It became clear this would not happen in 1796, when he issued his **Farewell Address**. His main point was that Americans should stay out of foreign entanglements and concentrate on building the country. Just about everyone thought that sounded like a good idea. Washington also warned against the dangers of political parties and excessive partisanship. But the Federalists and the Republicans were too busy yelling at each other to listen.

Washington retired to his beloved Mount Vernon plantation in Virginia, where he died in 1799 at the age of sixty-six. Modern doctors believe he probably died from a streptococcal infection of the throat, which is something people routinely recover from today with a dose of antibiotics. Washington's doctor, following the custom of the time, believed bleeding his patient would eliminate the disease. Washington was essentially bled to death by his own doctor which can still happen today if a person is covered by an especially lousy HMO.

A FEDERALIST PRESIDENT
or *We're Rich, So We Know Best*

Federalist John Adams beat Republican Thomas Jefferson for the Presidency in 1796 by the close electoral vote of 71 to 68. Jefferson had the second most electoral votes, so according to the rules of the time he became Vice President. Being from the other party and real cranky at having lost, Jefferson returned home and basically had nothing to do with the new administration. At first, Adams would turn around and look for Washington when someone addressed him as "Mr. President." Indeed, Washington had left some big shoes to fill, but luckily the short and chubby Adams had brought his own shoes and presumably an entire wardrobe. Eventually he became used to being the head honcho just in time to deal with a crisis involving France.

The French were enraged by Jay's Treaty and suspected it was a first step towards an American alliance with Great Britain. French warships commenced seizing unarmed American merchant ships, and they refused to even talk to our officially appointed envoy. Americans, acutely aware of their young country's short time upon the world stage, were hypersensitive about any insults from the old established French. President Adams bit his lip and decided to send a second diplomatic mission to France. French Foreign Minister Talleyrand sent three "secret" agents to intercept the Americans and demand a bribe of $250,000 before he would even consent to meet with them. Insulted, but no doubt impressed by the set of balls on Talleyrand, the American diplomats replied, "How about $225,000?" Just kidding. Reportedly, they cried, "No, no, not a sixpence!" Obviously, that was not the counter offer the French agents had been looking for.

Messages back to the United States identified Talleyrand's agents only as Mr. X, Mr. Y, and Mr. Z, and congressional and public outrage forever christened this episode the **"XYZ Affair."** Hotheads called for war against France with the slogan, **"Millions for defense, but not one cent for tribute."** Even though tribute would have been a heck of a lot cheaper, a patriotic Congress authorized increased military expenditures, the country prepared for war, and suddenly croissants did not taste so good.

Adams, to his great credit, kept his bald head on straight. Many in his own Federalist party called for open warfare — the so-called "High Federalists" led by Alexander Hamilton. They were not literally "high," but with their mindless belligerence they certainly appeared to be smoking something wacky. For two years an undeclared naval war bobbed across the waves. But neither country really wanted war — trade relations were too important for both sides — and in September 1798 France appeared to back down. With great forbearance, President Adams sent a third mission to France, and this time they did not even have time to pick up a magazine in the waiting room. Both countries agreed to the principle of freedom of the seas and war was avoided.

The crisis with France played right into the hands of many Federalists, who attempted to use the anti-French hysteria as fodder against the Republicans. The Federalists, who dominated Congress, pushed through a series of laws known as the **Alien and Sedition Acts**. The **Naturalization Act** increased the amount of time it took immigrants to become citizens from five years to fourteen. Immigrants had become associated with French sympathizers, but of greater concern to the Federalists was that these low-income newcomers invariably gravitated to the egalitarian Republicans rather than the aristocratic Federalists.

Other odious provisions of the Alien and Sedition Acts allowed the president great leeway to kick out of the country any aliens suspected of treason. The Sedition Act was deliberately designed to muzzle the Republicans — any person speaking out against the government could be subject to fines, imprisonment, and not being invited to dinner parties. Republican newspaper editors, printers and others numbering twenty-five were prosecuted for simply speaking their minds. Unconstitutional? A violation of freedom of speech and of the press? You bet. But the Federalist judges on the Supreme Court couldn't have cared less, providing early proof that even that august institution is partisan at heart. Many Europeans who had planned to come to America stayed on their side of the ocean out of fear of the Alien and Sedition Acts, depriving the Republican party of potential support, and ironically making it much more difficult for wealthy Federalist families in New England to find good help.

Thomas Jefferson and his friend James Madison gagged over the Alien and Sedition Acts, seeing them not only as an attack on the Republican party (of which they were the leaders) and the Constitution, but also the first step towards a Federalist tyranny. After lining birdcages with, and throwing darts at, copies of these acts, they decided to do something more substantive, so they folded up the Alien and Sedition Acts and used them to make funny paper hats. Then they approached the state legislatures of Virginia and the new state of Kentucky for support. Accordingly, the two state legislatures passed the **Virginia and Kentucky Resolutions** (1798-9) stating that **nullification** (cancellation) by the states was the proper response to unconstitutional actions by the federal government. No other states followed suit, and eventually the Alien and Sedition Acts expired on their own terms. But the big question had been asked, and one of the ugliest words in the American lexicon had been written — *Nullification*. The Philadelphia Convention had not clearly defined which level of government held the final authority, the federal government or the states. Today, we know the idea of states nullifying acts of the central government has been cut out of the body politic by the bayonets of the Civil War. Back then the cancer was just starting to grow.

Adams and Hamilton constantly squabbled over strategy towards the French, and the Federalists bickered and backstabbed as the election of 1800 approached. Consequently, Jefferson won the rematch against Adams, while his Republican colleagues gained control of both houses of Congress. Never again would the Federalist Party control the presidency or the national legislature. If there'd been a Las Vegas back then, a lot of folks would have lost bets. The Federalists would sputter on for a few more years — and be a pain in the butt during Jefferson's years in office — but basically they were done. Cooked. Stick a fork in 'em.

In March, 1801, Jefferson was inaugurated as America's third president. Power was peacefully transferred from one party to another for the first time and there were no shots fired, no riots in the streets. Adams was steamed at Jefferson for attacks on him during the campaign, and he did not attend the inauguration, but he did return home uneventfully to Massachusetts. That's quite an accomplishment that today we take for granted. Turn on the news, right now; in other places around the world the losers don't always go home peacefully. We were lucky.

America was also lucky to be led briefly in its infancy by the Federalists, men like Adams and Hamilton who did a good job getting the diapers on just in time. The Federalists held the country together during a difficult period and got the new government off to a solid start. Hamilton almost single-handedly put the country's finances in order after the Revolution, all the while successfully advocating for a federal government with some muscle. Adams put patriotism ahead of party and kept the nation out of a potentially catastrophic war with France. But the Federalists were a party of wealthy elites, and by 1800 American democracy was clearly heading in a different direction, away from fancy dinner parties and fine clothes, away from the idea that a person is automatically born into their position in life, and definitely away from stuckup rich guys who automatically assumed they knew what was best for everyone just because that's the way things had always been. Billionaires like Donald Trump and Ross Perot would have made great Federalists, but today they need to stay the heck out of politics.

In an interesting footnote to the election of 1800, Republican Vice-Presidential candidate **Aaron Burr** tried to steal the presidency. The original Constitution stipulated that each elector was to cast two ballots. The candidate with the most votes became President while the second place finisher settled for the Vice Presidency. The Republicans were so unified that their candidates, Thomas Jefferson and Aaron Burr, ended up in a tie. Everyone knew that Burr had intended to run for Vice President, but Aaron-the-all-American-sleazeball seized his chance to take home all the marbles. (Look up the word "opportunist" in the dictionary and see Burr's portrait.) With the tie, the election was thrown into the House of Representatives, not the newly elected Republican House but the **lame duck** (officials who have not been reelected and are serving out the remainder of their terms) Federalist bunch that had been elected in 1798. Many Federalists hated Jefferson, so Burr had a chance, and the House deadlocked for 35 ballots. At this point Alexander Hamilton stepped in. He disagreed with both Jefferson and Burr on virtually all the issues, but he considered Jefferson an honorable man and Burr a dangerous egomaniac and an all-around slimeball. On the 36th ballot, at Hamilton's urging, a number of Federalists who had been backing Burr abstained and Jefferson became president.

Soon after this debacle, the **Twelfth Amendment** was added to the Constitution requiring separate ballots for President and Vice President. As for Aaron Burr, he became Vice President, but because of his antics it was understandable that his relationship with President Jefferson was somewhat frosty.

PRESIDENT THOMAS JEFFERSON
or *Oh My God, He's Wearing a Bathrobe!*

Thomas Jefferson described his election to the highest office in the land as the **"Revolution of 1800,"** but most historians today feel he was just getting carried away. What had actually occurred was the peaceful transfer of power on the basis of election results both sides accepted. There were plenty of dirty looks but no physical fighting; the American democratic experiment appeared to be working! Most Americans were so pleased they didn't seem to mind Jefferson's bragging.

Thomas Jefferson always cut a striking figure. He was over six feet two inches tall (gigantic for that day and age) with reddish hair and large hands and feet that probably caused lots of women to jump to conclusions. His inauguration speech was brilliant, though few people were able to hear it due to the new President's chronically weak speaking voice. But when they read copies of the speech, most were impressed. Jefferson tried to calm the Federalists by insisting, "the minority possess their equal rights, which equal law must protect...We are all Federalists, we are all Republicans." At first only schizophrenics understood what he was saying, but soon it became clear to everyone that President Jefferson respected political opponents who held divergent views, and he did not consider those who disagreed with the actions of the government to be unpatriotic. It is frightening how many Americans today are clueless on this vitally important point.

Jefferson as President frequently reminded people he was no European king; on more than one occasion he greeted official visitors in slippers and nightclothes. He also turned out to be flexible and pragmatic, and he did not automatically overturn all the Federalists' policies. He hated the excise tax (he was a farmer and farmers really hated that tax) so he persuaded the Congress to get rid of it, but he left most of Hamilton's economic policies (notably including the National Bank) alone because it was clear by 1801 that *they were working*! He allowed the horrid Alien and Sedition Acts to expire on their own and the Republican-dominated Congress repealed the Naturalization Act. Once again, after five years, an immigrant could be lucky enough to become a U.S. citizen and be discriminated against by native-born Americans.

President Jefferson pathologically hated the judiciary, particularly the federal circuit courts the Federalists had set up with Federalist judges appointed for life terms (This had occurred in the **Judiciary Act of 1789**). Legend has it that when Jefferson showed up for his first day on the job, he found that outgoing President Adams had stayed up until twelve the night before, signing commissions for Federalist judges who soon became known as the **"midnight justices."** (Actually, he only stayed up until about nine-thirty, but why spoil a good story?)

When President Jefferson noticed that several of the commissions had not yet been delivered, he ordered Secretary of State Madison not to deliver them. **William Marbury** sued to force the delivery of his commission, creating the famous case of *Marbury versus Madison.* Chief Justice John Marshall and the rest of the Court were in a quandary. They knew Jefferson would probably refuse any writ (order) to deliver the commission, thereby provoking the nation's first serious constitutional crisis. But wily fox Marshall outsmarted everybody. He ruled that the section of the Judiciary Act under which Marbury had sued was unconstitutional and therefore void. Marbury lost his case, and he remains nothing but an historical afterthought, showing up once in a while on multiple-choice tests.

Marshall had asserted for the first time the power of the Supreme Court to overturn a federal law — thus establishing the principle of **judicial review**, the power of the Supreme Court to void acts of Congress that are found to violate the Constitution. Most Americans today accept this idea without qualms, but back then resolving that situation was pretty hairy. Jefferson hated the courts even more after this decision, and he urged the Republicans in Congress to the repeal the Judiciary Act, which they did in March, 1802, but John Marshall, the Supreme Court and judicial review lived on.

President Jefferson and his Secretary of the Treasury **Albert Gallatin** immediately set out to balance the federal budget and pay off the nation's debts. Accordingly, they slashed the army and navy, forcing a lot of military men to grudgingly pack their uniforms in mothballs. Jefferson truly believed the two great oceans on either side of the continent could keep America apart from foreign quarrels, but he was painfully naive.

For more than twenty years, the United States had been paying bribes to the leaders of the **Barbary States** of North Africa: Morocco, Algiers, Tunis, and Tripoli. Basically this was protection money to keep Barbary pirates from capturing our merchant ships. England, France, and Holland also paid the tribute, and it was considered business as usual. But in May of 1801, the Pasha of Tripoli (acting like a Mafia Godfather way before there ever was such a thing) demanded more money. This ticked off a sanctimonious (and penny pinching) President Jefferson, and he sent a naval squadron over there to kick some Barbary butt.

Butt was kicked, but unfortunately the U.S.S. *Philadelphia* ran aground on the shores of Tripoli while chasing some pirates. (That's where we get the "shores of Tripoli" for the Marine Corps hymn.) The crew was held for a $3 million dollar ransom, and they were not treated courteously when they asked for a room upgrade. A young lieutenant named **Stephen Decatur** became a hero by leading a raiding party that burned the *Philadelphia* before it could fall into enemy hands. That was good, kind of like cutting (or in this case burning) your losses. The crew was kept in custody for two more years until an aggressive U.S. naval blockade forced Tripoli to release the prisoners, for the blue light special price of $60,000. Americans felt pretty good that they had flexed their muscles and forced a bunch of cutthroats to back down. But as soon as Jefferson recalled the naval force the pirates resumed their skullduggery.

Remember that France had ceded the Louisiana Territory to Spain as a result of its defeat in the French and Indian War. In 1800, the new "emperor" of France, **Napoleon Bonaparte**, bullied Spain into giving it back. First he wanted to conquer Europe, then march on to North America...perhaps forgetting that a long boat ride would be required first. President Jefferson fretted about the pompous pipsqueak's intentions. (Nappy's lilliputian stature easily qualified him for membership in the Lollipop Guild.) Control of New Orleans at the mouth of the Mississippi River was essential to farmers west of the Appalachians, who would float their goods down the river and then ship them out through the Gulf of Mexico to the rest of the world.

Jefferson decided to try and buy New Orleans. James Monroe, former governor of Virginia, joined Robert Livingston, ambassador to France, and together they were authorized to offer the little dictator $10 million. To their enormous surprise, the two American envoys were informed that Napoleon was willing to sell not only New Orleans but also the entire Louisiana Territory for $15 million. Monroe and Livingston excused themselves, and as soon as they were out of earshot, presumably started giggling and slapping five. True, they had only been authorized to spend $10 million for New Orleans. But this was way too incredible a deal to pass up, so they jumped on it.

Napoleon did have his reasons. Black slaves led by one of their own, **Toussaint L'Ouverture**, revolted against their white masters and successfully took over the French owned island of Haiti in the Caribbean. Napoleon sent a fleet and thousands of troops to take it back, but they failed, due to a combination of L'Ouverture's military genius and mosquitoes carrying yellow fever. Napoleon reasoned that, with Haiti such a headache, and the British fleet bobbing around out there making anything he might try to do in the New World problematic, he might as well get his hands on some badly needed cash for his wars in Europe. Since Napoleon was an erratic and ruthless despot, prone to exterminating those who challenged his authority, no one dared to advise him to at least sleep on it. Fifteen million dollars purchased 828,000 square miles of fertile farmland and abundant natural resources, at approximately three cents an acre with no brokers' fee. Way to go, boys!

President Jefferson was thrilled with the **Louisiana Purchase** until some wise guy suggested he look up the word hypocrite in the dictionary. All of his political life, Jefferson had argued for a strict interpretation of the Constitution. He well knew that at no point in that still-relatively-fresh document was the president given the authority to purchase territory for the country. But Jefferson had been pragmatic in allowing Hamilton's successful financial policies to continue, and he decided again to take the same course. He gathered his friends and advisors and told them a good deal was a good deal, and it would be best to keep quiet about any constitutional questions. Doubtless, Alexander Hamilton smiled contentedly and slept well that night.

Nobody really knew what was out there, so Jefferson arranged for explorations. In 1804, **Meriwether** (a ridiculous name) **Lewis** and **William Clark** started out from St. Louis and journeyed up the Missouri River to the Snake and Columbia Rivers, and eventually all the way to the Pacific Ocean. Luckily, they found a skillful Native American woman named **Sacajawea** to guide them. (Sacajawea, at least in the Hollywood movie, was really hot.) Meanwhile, **Zebulon** (an even more ridiculous name than Meriwether) **Pike** explored much of the Rockies and discovered a mountain now named **Pike's Peak** in present-day Colorado. He did not climb Pike's Peak; he just pointed to it in the distance, so he was not as much of a hotshot as you might think.

The **Lewis and Clark Expedition**, given up for dead after more than two years, arrived back in St. Louis with extensive journals detailing the bountiful land they had just beheld. They journeyed to the capital and presented President Jefferson with many mementos, including two live bear cubs. The president acted appreciative — after all, little bear cubs are cute — but eventually the darn things grew up and had to be kept in a large pit on the White House grounds. Fortunately, America's third president was not a sleepwalker.

Vice President Aaron Burr continued to be a nightmare. The Republicans would have nothing to do with him after what he tried to pull during the election, so in 1804, he switched to the Federalists and ran for the governorship of New York. He also got involved in an outrageous plot to separate New York and New England from the rest of the country in order to create an independent (and presumably Federalist) Northern confederacy. Alexander Hamilton blew the whistle on the scheme, and Burr subsequently lost the New York election. Furious, Burr challenged Hamilton to a duel and honorably (but stupidly), Hamilton accepted. On July 11, 1804, on the palisades overlooking the Hudson River, Burr and Hamilton stood back to back, marched forward several paces, turned and fired.

Tragically, Burr's pistol ball extinguished the most brilliant star the Federalists ever had. But the story does not end here. Burr next found himself arrested for treason in another scheme to detach parts of the Southwest from the United States and create a new nation. Though found not guilty in his first trial, he fled to Europe for four years to avoid more charges, then returned to live a scandalous life in New York City. In his seventies he fathered two illegitimate children, and was sued for divorce on the grounds of adultery at the age of *eighty*! Ah, poetic justice...representing Mrs. Burr at the divorce proceedings was the son of the man he had killed: **Alexander Hamilton, Junior.**

All things considered, President Jefferson's first term went pretty well, and in 1804, he won a second term in a landslide over the Federalist candidate, **Charles C. Pinckney.** The electoral vote was 162 to 14, so the Federalists probably shouldn't have bothered. But Jefferson's second four years proved much more challenging than the first term, mainly due to the almost continuous warfare between England and France and the inability of the President to keep the United States out of it. Napoleon's army held supremacy on land, but England's navy ruled the sea, resulting in a stalemate often referred to as **"the tiger against the shark."** Naturally, merchants in the United States wanted to take advantage of the wartime demand in Europe to make lots of money. And just as naturally, neither England nor France wanted their enemy to benefit from trade with the United States. They took steps to prevent it: Britain issued the **Orders in Council** and Napoleon issued the **Berlin and Milan Decrees**. American shippers tried to ignore these threats and simply shouted, "Show me the money!" to anyone who would listen.

Great Britain's navy hassled the United States the most, capturing our ships and impressing our sailors. In 1807, the humiliating **Chesapeake-Leopard Affair** occurred in which an American ship (the *Chesapeake*) was roughed up and boarded by the crew of a British ship (the *Leopard*). If Rodney Dangerfield had been around back then, he would have said Americans "never get no respect." Outraged, the American public demanded that the President do something. Jefferson smiled and nodded but undoubtedly thought to himself, *What can I do? I cut the navy's budget and now most of the little ships we have leak when they go out past the lifeguards' ropes.* Too parsimonious (a nice way of saying cheap) to build up a navy that could stand up to the Brits, but also too proud to ignore all the indignities on the high seas, President Jefferson was really at his wit's end. With apologies to Dr. Seuss...

Then he got an idea!
An awful idea!
the grinch
GOT A WONDERFUL, AWFUL IDEA!

Grinch Jefferson requested that Congress pass the **Embargo Act,** which made it illegal for American ships to sail to any foreign ports. The President believed he could really stick it to the French and English and force them both to stop hassling our ships and beg for our cotton and foodstuffs. The whole idea proved a complete failure, the perfect example of cutting off your nose to spite your face. New England merchants and shippers were virtually wiped out. Farmers in the South and West lost foreign markets for their products. Smuggling became commonplace, France and England found alternate sources for the products they needed, and President Jefferson spent his last couple of years in office stomping around in a fog of massive crankiness. Basically, he just gave up. In 1809, Congress modified the Embargo Act a bit, making only trade with England and France illegal. This new law didn't work either, and was given the depressing name the **Non-Intercourse Act,** which reminds this author of several bad years he had after college.

By the end of his second term, Jefferson's policies had brought national scorn. But the anger for most did not seem to be at Jefferson personally. True, the embargo experiment had failed miserably, but Jefferson still retained enough popularity and power to secure the 1808 Republican nomination for his friend and protégé, James Madison. Again, the Federalists continued to fizzle. Even with the embargo fresh in everyone's minds, Madison clobbered his opponent Charles Pinckney (running again) 122 to 47 in the electoral college.

Jefferson was in great spirits at Madison's inaugural ball, mainly because he was relieved to be leaving the pressures of the presidency and heading home to his beloved farm at Monticello. Ironically, President Madison's beautiful wife, **Dolley**, received nearly as much attention as he did. He was short, skinny and bald, so it was easy for eyes to stray to the new First Lady, whom historians have graciously described as "portly," "buxom," "corpulent." "rotund," "plump" and "stout." Get the picture? Dolley Madison must have had great cakes! She would enliven the social scene in the nation's capital (Jefferson had been a widower) and, though frozen desserts were first enjoyed in America in the 1700s, Dolley would make ice cream immensely more popular by making it the official dessert at White House parties.

Back home at Monticello in Virginia, Thomas Jefferson would live for another seventeen years. His life demonstrates that no one...*no one*...is perfect. Perhaps the most brilliant man ever to occupy the presidency, Jefferson nevertheless possessed serious character flaws. He never learned how to manage his money and ended his life with his hands out to friends. He never understood that the judiciary needed to be respected as an equal branch of the government, in spite of the Federalist reprobates temporarily wearing the robes. He voiced misgivings about slavery, but owned slaves throughout his life. There is no doubt that he had a longtime affair with one of his slaves, **Sally Hemmings**, and fathered several children by her. It seems he truly loved Ms. Hemmings (and she him) but she had been his *slave*. That makes Jefferson flawed just like everyone else — including our immortal founding fathers. Look closely at History and try to find the perfect godlike man or woman. If you do find someone, then you have completely missed the point here.

Contrary to what many folks feared, the transition from a Federalist to a Republican government in 1801 produced only a small amount of acid indigestion. The country prospered during Jefferson's first term, and the Louisiana Purchase more than doubled its size. Burp! But war between Britain and France once again threatened to suck the United States into the maelstrom (Maelstrom, by the way, is a really cool word that derives from a dangerous whirlpool off the northwest coast of Norway). Lots of Americans demanded freedom of the seas and an end to the British pushing us around once and for all. Would this mean war for our fourth President, James Madison? Uh oh…Stay tuned…don't touch that dial!!!

This Really Happened!

The story goes that in 1799 an American privateer, the *Nancy*, is being chased around the Caribbean by a British warship. Just before he is captured, the Yankee captain, Thomas Briggs, throws proof of his American citizenship overboard and replaces it with forged Dutch papers. He is taken to Jamaica and put on trial for running a British blockade during wartime. They are about to set him free because no one can prove he is an American, when another British ship appears in port and produces the incriminationing evidence. The sailors had caught a shark off the coast of Haiti, cut it open and inside found the proof of Captain Briggs' American citizenship. Now you know why the U.S. Department of State always recommends that travelers keep their passports in a safe place at all times!

And the rest is History…

Quiz yourself on Chapter 3

Multiple Choice (circle the correct answer).

1. The main reason the Constitution still works so well today is that it is
   a. ignored most of the time
   b. flexible
   c. translated into Spanish
   d. posted on the Web
   e. all of the above

2. The federal government's response to the Whiskey Rebellion proved that
   a. alcoholism was rampant in early America
   b. drinking and horseback riding don't mix
   c. Alexander Hamilton had a serious drinking problem
   d. under the Constitution federal laws would be forcefully upheld
   e. all of the above

3. Alexander Hamilton favored
   a. a loose interpretation of the Constitution
   b. a strict interpretation of the Constitution
   c. Communism
   d. Brunettes
   e. d and c

4. President Washington's Proclamation of Neutrality
   a. meant war with France
   b. meant war with Great Britain
   c. meant war with New Jersey
   d. aimed to keep the United States out of European conflicts
   e. c and a

5. Jay's Treaty was
   a. an insult to the British
   b. an attempt to keep the United States out of war with France
   c. a chance for Britain to play hardball with its former colonies
   d. followed by the Kay Treaty
   e. none of the above

6. Marbury vs. Madison
    a. was a boxing match between Marbury and Madison
    b. is a new reality show on NBC
    c. ended with Madison running away
    d. established the principle of judicial review
    e. all of the above

7. The XYZ Affair was
    a. a *menage a trois* between Robert Livingston and two French midget wrestlers
    b. a novel by the American suspense writer Thomas Paine
    c. a triumph for those who wanted to add three new letters to the alphabet
    d. a scandal in which French secret agents demanded a bribe from American emissaries
    e. b and a

8. The Virginia and Kentucky Resolutions stated that
    a. nullification by the states was the proper response to unconstitutional actions by the federal government
    b. the states were subordinate to the federal government
    c. country music should be respected in the North
    d. the South was superior to the North
    e. none of the above

9. When he purchased the Louisiana Territory, President Jefferson
    a. compromised his usual strict view of the Constitution
    b. put the whole amount on his credit card
    c. had to borrow a few bucks from Hamilton
    d. demanded that Napoleon give him a receipt
    e. all of the above

10. The Nonintercourse Act was
    a. named by somebody totally clueless
    b. depressing to many Americans for a variety of reasons
    c. a misguided attempt to keep American ships from coming into conflict with France and Britain
    d. none of the above
    e. all of the above

CHAPTER 4

THE WAR OF 1812
FOSTERS AMERICAN PRIDE

or

Does Anyone Remember Why We're Fighting?

President James Madison had as little success as his predecessor in utilizing diplomacy to protect American rights on the high seas. When he trusted Napoleon's false promises and restored trade with France, the President further enlarged the chasm between the United States and Britain. James Madison's friends called him "Jemmy" not "Jimmy." Napoleon Bonaparte called him Sucker ("Le Sucker" in French).

THE WAR FOR FREEDOM OF THE SEAS
or *So What If I Can't Swim*

In 1810, Western and Southern voters elected a fresh bunch of Republican Congress-men who demanded war with Britain as soon as possible. They talked a lot about honor and freedom of the seas, even though many of the westerners had never even seen the ocean. The truth was that these guys viewed the war as an opportunity to steal Canada from Britain and rip off Florida from Spain, Britain's ally. Led by dashing and debonair **Henry Clay** of Kentucky and intelligent but way too intense **John C. Calhoun** of South Carolina, these young legislative bucks became known as **War Hawks.** They would have been really cool, except they had no idea what they were getting themselves — and the country — into.

Meanwhile, blood flowed out in the western wilderness. The Indians were resisting white encroachment on their ancestral homelands, and this time the tribes threatened to do something they had never really done before — cooperate in a unified Native American confederacy. Two Shawnee twin brothers, **Tecumseh** and the **Prophet**, recruited the tribes east of the Mississippi in a last ditch attempt to stop the onrushing white tide. This was the American settlers' worst nightmare, except of course for throw-ing up in public, or is that just me? Anyway, General **William Henry Harrison**, gover-nor of the Indiana Territory, advanced on an indian settlement called Prophetstown (quite an ego, the Prophet) and, unfortunately for the Indians, the more astute Tecumseh was away on a recruiting mission.

The Prophet actually believed he could control the movements of the stars and foretell the future — alive today he would doubtless have a really popular website — but he was no military strategist, and when he precipitously ordered an attack that failed, the Indians' spirit was broken. Harrison's men burned Prophetstown, and after that, the continuing battles between the pioneers and the Indians were disorganized and bloody, just as they had always been. Americans on the frontier convinced them-selves that the British in Canada were aiding and encouraging the Indians — true in the 1790s but probably not the case in 1812 — and this false conviction inspired even more reckless calls for war with England.

In June, 1812, President Madison, sick of ice cream and, more significantly, out of ideas, asked Congress for a declaration of war against Britain. He got one, but only by bare majorities in both Houses. The Northeast, the region most directly affected by the maritime insults (and where the Federalists still had influence) gen-erally opposed the war, so obviously this ruckus was mainly about land stealing. Ironically, a few days earlier the British government had repealed the Orders in Council, thus signaling an intention to finally leave our ships alone. If telephones had existed at the time, we could have avoided a dumb, unnecessary war. The coun-try was ill-prepared and disunited, and heading for a confrontation with the mighti-est nation in the world. Deja vu all over again.

By this time, some of the officers of the regular army dressed impressively, but were so old they thought they were back fighting the original Revolution, and most of the men in the poorly trained militia could not even spell Revolution. Several American invasions of Canada failed miserably. Major General **Henry Dearborn** (so fat he could hardly walk) headed north from Plattsburg, New York, and stood dumbfounded when his army of militiamen refused to cross the border into Canada. Since his mission was to capture the critically important Canadian city of Montreal, Dearborn was understandably upset. Yelling and stamping his feet did not help the situation, so he decided to sit down and have a bite to eat. By 1813, it was clear the Americans were far from taking Canada, and British troops were readying themselves to march south.

Fortunately, the British counter-invasion was stymied by American naval victories led by Captain **Oliver Perry** on Lake Erie and Captain **Thomas Macdonough** on Lake Champlain. Captain Macdonough reported his victory with the stirring words, "We have met the enemy and they are ours." He probably hoped his quote would put him in history books for centuries to come, and in this case it did.

On the oceans, American naval ships and privateers initially gave the limeys splitting headaches. The **U.S.S. Constitution** earned the nickname **"Old Ironsides"** because cannonballs seemed to harmlessly bounce off her hull. But after a few months, somebody in the British Admiralty probably said, "Hey — we've got over eight hundred fighting ships and they've got sixteen. What's the problem here?" Accordingly, the Brits assumed their customary supremacy on the seas and instituted a choking blockade on America's coast. The Constitution escaped destruction and remains today a commissioned ship in the United States Navy. She sits in Boston Harbor, and you can take a tour. You'll be amazed how small she is compared to modern warships, and below decks even short guys can hit their head on the ceiling. Ah...but she's a proud old lady, a living part of our history.

In 1815, Napoleon Bonaparte "met his Waterloo." He should have known to stay away from any town with that name. Anyway, the British now felt free to concentrate their best efforts on the pesky Americans on the other side of the Atlantic. Four thousand redcoats landed in the Chesapeake Bay area, drew their bayonets and advanced on Washington. Six thousand American militiamen peed in their pants and fled. The crimson interlopers cheerfully entered the city and burned most of the public buildings, including the White House and the Capitol. Dolley Madison was knocked to the ground in the public panic, but she courageously commandeered a wagon and managed to save some important papers and a priceless portrait of George Washington. Before torching the White House, the British officers generally behaved like the fraternity guys in the movie "Animal House." It is doubtful they lit their farts on fire, but they ate the food they found and made obscene toasts to "Jemmy's health." President Madison and other officials galloped out of town just ahead of the British, but they were easily able to turn around and see the smoke billowing up from a city in flames.

Next, the redcoats marched north towards Baltimore, but here American bladders held firm. The British fleet tried mightily to pound **Fort McHenry** into submission, and for one long night the outcome was in doubt. **Francis Scott Key**, an American lawyer who had boarded a British warship to arrange a prisoner exchange, spent hours watching "the rockets red glare, bombs bursting in air." When by the light of first dawn he realized "that our flag was still there," he got the idea to jot some of his observations down. At first a poem and then later set to music, **"The Star Spangled Banner"** remained popular through the years, and was officially designated our national anthem in 1931. Basically, we all agree the tune stinks — we've all heard even professional opera singers botch it up before ballgames — but the words are stirring and, well, we're stuck with it.

In early January, 1815, a British fleet sailed north from Jamaica and invaded the American Southwest by attacking the city of New Orleans. American defenses were under the leadership of General **Andrew Jackson,** who commanded a motley crew of regular army soldiers, Tennessee, Kentucky and Louisiana militia, free blacks, sailors, pirates, Frenchmen and a partridge in a pear tree. Jackson's men set up barricades, and bravely, but unwisely, the redcoats marched in rows straight for them. The Americans, most of them crack shots, mowed them down like little metal ducks in a shooting gallery. Any American who might have thought of turning tail did not dare do so because they were much more frightened of their commander than the British. Jackson had a violent temper and had literally executed those under his command who dared to defy him. He got involved in so many brawls and duels all his life — and had so many bullets permanently lodged in his body — he was lucky to have lived in an age before airport metal detectors. Doubtless, he had a touch of madness in his eyes that fateful day in New Orleans...precisely what his forces needed to spur them on to victory.

Peace negotiators for the United States and Britain had already started meeting in the Belgian city of Ghent. With Napoleon defeated, both sides suddenly came to a collective epiphany: there was no longer any reason to be fighting. Britain would be happy to resume trade and leave our ships alone. And with American invasions of Canada stymied, and British invasions of the United States likewise stalled, the whole hullabaloo suddenly seemed like one giant waste of time. So they signed a peace treaty (the **Treaty of Ghent**) on Christmas Eve. The United States and Britain basically agreed to stop fighting and go home: there was no mention of freedom of the seas in the treaty, and prewar boundaries were left as they had been. Ironically, at the time the **Battle of New Orleans** was fought, the War of 1812 had already been officially over for two weeks. Details, details. Proud Americans considered it a grand victory and bestowed upon General Jackson the title of the "Hero of New Orleans." Still, it was not wise to mention the inadvertent mistiming of the battle in front of Andrew Jackson, because no one ever knew when he would flip out and go nuts.

Nationalism means pride in your country, and Americans were pretty darn proud of themselves in the years immediately following the War of 1812. History teachers in the U.S. frequently refer to the war as a victory, while history teachers in England often prefer to skip it all together. With no territory changing hands, and Napoleon's defeat making the issue of freedom of the seas irrelevant, the war realistically should be judged a tie. But for America it was a good tie, and if you are a soccer or hockey fan you know what that means. It was a tie that helped us, a tie that encouraged the growth of new American industries because, cut off from European imports, we were forced to start building our own factories. Westward migration got a real boost as bankrupt merchants and shipbuilders headed toward the setting sun for a fresh start. Isolationist sentiments hardened as Americans turned away from European squabbles and focused on domestic affairs. Basically, the country survived and continued on to the playoffs.

The Federalists pulled one last bonehead maneuver in the waning days of the war and managed to put a cap on their decline into oblivion. Meeting at the **Hartford Convention** in 1814, diehard New England Federalists condemned the war and advocated a states' rights doctrine of nullification. (Again, there's that ugly idea that a state can cancel a federal law.) They demanded a Constitutional amendment which would require a two-thirds vote of Congress to declare war or admit new states and, sounding eerily similar to the Republicans' Virginia and Kentucky Resolutions of about fifteen years earlier, they bandied about the idea of secession from the Union. When news of the Treaty of Ghent and Jackson's big victory in New Orleans hit the press, the Federalists really had egg on their faces. They were accused of treason (which was accurate) and placed in "time out." Just kidding. The Federalists had so disgraced themselves, they basically went out of existence, like that early nineties group that got caught lip-synching, Milli Vanilli.

THE ERA OF GOOD FEELING
or *All This Smiling Makes Me Nervous*

After the war of 1812, the Republicans running the federal government tended to view problems from a national perspective. For a short time at least, they acted as Americans rather than residents of the Northeast, South or West. Speaker of the House Henry Clay (a man who loved whiskey, gambling, and married women, and who nevertheless labored tirelessly for his country) advocated for legislation he collectively called the **American System**: a strong banking system, protective tariffs to promote manufacturing, and extensive internal improvements at federal expense. The charter of the first National Bank had expired in 1811 and — surprise, surprise — financial havoc ensued, as lots of local bankers conducted business as if they were executives at Enron. In 1816, the Republicans (tossing their previous constitutional concerns aside and behaving like Federalists) chartered the second Bank of the United States to serve as a stabilizing influence.

That same year, they passed the **Tariff of 1816,** a high tax on imports intended to protect nascent American industries. Most of these new businesses were in the Northeast, but all sections supported the tariff in the interest of national unity, even though consumers everywhere would have to pay more for manufactured goods. Congressman John C. Calhoun sponsored the **Bonus Bill,** which called for the federal government to fund a countrywide network of roads and canals. He argued that the entire nation would benefit by being more closely bound together, and he made perfect sense. But President

Madison vetoed the bill on dubious constitutional grounds and Congress never appropriated sufficient funds, proving that when it came to spending federal money, nationalism only went so far. The **Cumberland Road** (from Cumberland, Maryland west across the Appalachian mountains to Wheeling on the Ohio River) got built, but most other road and canal building was done by states, cities and even private individuals who licked their chops at the prospect of charging tolls. Travelers paid their fee and then turned a wooden barrier or pike, hence the term *turnpike*. Going was slow because there was no electronic EZ Pass back then.

Governor **DeWitt Clinton** managed to get the state of New York to fund the construction of the **Erie Canal,** which would connect the Hudson River to Lake Erie. Laborers started digging in 1818, and for eight years detractors called the project **"Clinton's Big Ditch."** The mule population especially hated the canal because, lacking effective influence in the state legislature, they were forced to tow barges loaded with goods on towpaths alongside the canal. Horses mostly got off scot free and probably snickered at the poor overworked mules, but the Erie Canal soon became a sensational triumph. New York City established itself as the nation's leading commercial center, causing the rest of the country to respond with an orgy of canal building. No, not real orgies — just lots of canal building, some of which succeeded, and some of which turned out to be just a bunch of guys sitting around wondering why they were there.

The **Industrial Revolution** refers to the great shift in manufacturing from hands to machines, and from in-the-home to in-the-factory. It began in Great Britain around the middle of the eighteenth century and should not be confused with the Renaissance that originated in Italy about four hundred years earlier. You had to have a Renaissance in order to have an Industrial Revolution; with all that questioning and experimenting going on, it figured eventually there would be some really cool technological advances.

In the 1780s, **James Watt** of Scotland put down his bagpipe, took off his kilt, put on some men's clothing and perfected the steam engine. Factories in England began to use waterpower and steam engines to run spinning machines, and the mill owners were so thrilled with their profits, they schemed to keep their methods secret from the rest of the world. Metal detectors had not been invented yet, so workers were searched by hand when they left for the day. Carry-on luggage was strongly discouraged. But **Samuel Slater** memorized the plans of a British textile mill and traveled to Rhode Island, where he helped build one just like it. Slater had a genuinely photographic memory; others who tried the same thing quickly realized that their own supposedly photographic memories lacked film.

In 1807, an American inventor named **Robert Fulton** built the first steamboat, nicknamed **"Fulton's Folly"** by his doubting countrymen. Fulton must have felt a lot of satisfaction when his *Clermont* and other steamboats quickly proved they could successfully transport goods both downstream and (for the first time) upstream, and he was way too polite to flip his neighbors the bird even though they deserved it.

In 1813, **Francis Cabot Lowell** built the first New England factory that could turn raw cotton into thread and then into cloth. These early spinning factories turned to adolescent girls as workers, because they would presumably take orders better and work for less than men. Young women, the male factory bosses theorized, would be thrilled to leave their family farms for a few years so they could earn money that would make them better marriage material. They would live in strictly supervised boarding houses intended to foster Protestant morality and profits.

It worked for a few years, but by the 1830s the "**Lowell Girls**" were getting decidedly bitchy. They went on strike to protest wage cuts and oppressive regulations in their dormitories. This was not the beginning of the women's rights movement, but it was a harbinger of things to come. Factory owners increasingly turned to immigrants for their labor because these recent arrivals, new in town and desperate simply to survive, would work for even lower wages and could be more easily bullied. Nobody ever said the Industrial Revolution had a heart.

As the Northeast turned to industry, the South and West remained tied to agriculture. By the 1830s the western states could utilize **Cyrus McCormick's** mechanical reaper and **John Deere's** steel plow to produce vast amounts of wheat and corn to complement huge herds of livestock. The southern states grew tobacco, rice, sugarcane, hemp (relax, they used it to make rope), and, increasingly, cotton. Back in 1793 **Eli Whitney** had invented the **cotton gin,** which could remove the infuriating little seeds from raw cotton fifty times faster than by hand...and with much less cursing. From then on, thanks to the cotton gin ("gin" was short for engine), the more cotton plantation owners could grow, the more money they could make. Slavery — which by the late eighteenth century was slowly being replaced by wage labor in many parts of the South — experienced a rebirth and grew to unprecedented levels. As is so often necessary for understanding historical events, follow the money trail. More slaves meant more cotton, which in turn meant bigger profits. Pure greed — a perfect illustration of human nature's ugly side.

During this period, the Supreme Court contributed to Americans' increasing sense of nationalism. President Adams appointed a Federalist, John Marshall, to be Chief Justice in 1801, and he would serve for the next thirty-four years — a long tenure back in those days. Fortunately, Marshall exuded wisdom and patriotism, and in case after case, he convinced his fellow justices to rule in favor of federal power at the expense of the states.

We've already observed how, back in 1803, the case of *Marbury versus Madison* established the Supreme Court's authority to declare a law passed by Congress unconstitutional. In **Dartmouth College versus Woodward** (1819), the New Hampshire state legislature had messed with the college's original charter and placed the college under state control. The Marshall court said, "hold your horses," Dartmouth's charter was a contract and the sanctity of contracts was protected under the Constitution. Thus, Dartmouth remained a private school and the perfect place for rich kids to attend after Harvard, Yale, and Princeton had rejected them.

In **McCulloch versus Maryland** (1819), Maryland's state legislators, favoring state banks and hating the second Bank of the United States (BUS), levied a heavy state tax on the federal bank. McCulloch, an officer of the BUS, refused to pay it. Reports that he also mooned the state tax collectors are, at best, sketchy. When the Supreme Court finally decided the case, Marshall wrote that **"the power to tax implies the power to destroy"** and the state of Maryland had no right to threaten the existence of a federal agency. This decision also supported loose interpretation of the Constitution because the BUS, not mentioned specifically in the Constitution by our founding fathers, nevertheless was constitutional under the doctrine of implied powers.

In *Gibbons versus Ogden* (1824), two guys ran competing ferries across the Hudson River from New York to New Jersey. Ogden had a New York State grant of monopoly while Gibbons held a federal license. Rather then settle it like real men, with fisticuffs, or like gentlemen, and secretly agree to fix prices, the whole mess landed in the lap of the judiciary. Marshall's Supreme Court ruled Ogden's deal with New York State to be unconstitutional because it violated the Constitution's delegation of the regulation of interstate commerce to the federal government. That's why to this day the federal government regulates transportation, communication and every single business that crosses state lines...even something as stupid as professional wrestling.

James Monroe lived a long and fortunate life; he fought in the Revolution (and was wounded), served as minister to France, helped negotiate the purchase of Louisiana, and was appointed Secretary of State by President Madison. He ascended to the presidency in 1817 by crushing his Federalist challenger, Rufus King, 183 electoral votes to 34. Monroe was the last of his "revolutionary generation" to hold the reins of power. He dressed in the old-fashioned cocked hat, knee breeches, silk stockings, and buckled shoes, kind of like a guy today who still wears leisure suits and bell bottoms.

When Monroe toured New England as newly elected President, even the folks in this former Federalist stronghold greeted him warmly (That means only a few eggs were thrown and they all missed.). A Boston newspaper was moved to declare that an **"Era of Good Feelings"** had descended upon America. Even though there was a severe economic downturn in 1819 (**The Panic of 1819**), Monroe was reelected without opposition the following year. The Era of Good Feelings lasted for only eight years (1817-1824) and if you blink when you study American History, you miss it. The "Era of Hurt Feelings" is impossible to miss; it's all the rest of the time.

It is true there was an absence of open political strife during Monroe's two administrations, but just beneath the smooth stones, politicians continued to scamper about. **Sectionalism** refers to divisions between the North, South and West, based upon their differing geography and economic concerns, and during this brief interlude the fungus of sectionalism silently ate away at national unity. Louisiana had been admitted to the Union in 1812 and in the next four years Indiana, Illinois, Alabama and Mississippi joined.

In 1819 Missouri applied for statehood. No big deal, right? Wrong. Congressman James Tallmadge of New York offered an amendment to abolish slavery in Missouri. This **Tallmadge Amendment** passed the northern dominated House but failed to pass in the evenly divided Senate. It rates a mention in the history books because it stirred up such a hornet's nest; a bitter debate between northerners and southerners over whether Congress had the right to outlaw slavery in a territory or state. At this time, Thomas Jefferson wrote, "This momentous question, like a fire-bell in the night, awakened and filled me with terror." Whether it was the slavery question or an enlarged prostate that woke up the former President, it was clear to many that slavery had the potential to rip apart the country.

Fortunately for the United States, Speaker of the House Henry Clay was waiting in the wings, hoping for a chance to earn the nickname, "The Great Compromiser." Gossipers had been calling him "Homewrecker" and he wanted to get past that. With the balance in the Senate standing at eleven free states and eleven slave states, Clay worked out the **Missouri Compromise** (1820) wherein Maine was separated from Massachusetts and admitted to the Union as a free state. Missouri then came in as a slave state, with the delicate balance in the Senate maintained. Added to the compromise was the stipulation that the territory in the Louisiana Purchase north of the 36° 30" parallel would be forever closed to slavery. Southerners swallowed hard (especially those who chewed tobacco) and realized that they would always be a minority region of the country. Northerners went their merry way, but astute southerners noted that the compromise left much more territory closed to slavery than open to it. They also worried that in the future, the North would try to tell the South what do in their own home states — like abolish slavery or stop talking with such a funny accent.

Compared to most Presidents, Monroe had to spend a relatively small amount of his time dealing with domestic feuds (the Missouri debate notwithstanding), and was able to further the cause of nationalism by conducting a real kick-ass foreign policy. The man who did most of the work was Secretary of State **John Quincy Adams**, the son of our second president. Adams had been a Senator, foreign minister to four different countries, and served at Ghent as a negotiator in the talks that officially ended the War of 1812. He was also, reportedly, a hall monitor in grade school. Like his father, John Quincy was an uptight, stuffy New Englander and a great patriot; the apple fell directly under the tree.

In 1817, Acting Secretary of State Richard Rush worked out a treaty with Britain's ambassador to the United States, Charles Bagot. Rush was pleased that Adams had not arrived in town yet, so the treaty could be called the **Rush-Bagot Treaty** rather than the Adams-Bagot Treaty. Both nations agreed to naval disarmament on the Great Lakes, and for the first time Britain treated the United States as a legitimate country that was going to be around for a while. Today, this unfortified border extends 3000 miles to the Pacific. Until very recently, this friendly relationship between America and Canada had proven practical for both. Lately, however, unsavory Muslim fanatics have taken advantage and waltzed into our country, though it is important to keep in mind that only a tiny percentage of dancing foreigners are terrorists.

In the **Convention of 1818**, the United States and Britain addressed some of the confusion that had arisen from the Treaty of Ghent. The two nations agreed to share fishing rights in the waters off Newfoundland and Labrador, which back then teemed with fish that did not glow in the dark due to mercury poisoning. They also fixed the boundary line between the United States and Canada at the 49th parallel of latitude, from Lake of the Woods (in northern Minnesota) to the summit of the Rocky Mountains. Then there was the question of the Oregon Territory. Great Britain, the United States, Spain, Russia and a drunken frontiersman named Eddie all claimed the area. The United States and Britain blew off all claims but their own and agreed to jointly occupy the area. Joint occupation was a dumb idea from the start, but both sides knew they otherwise had a pretty good treaty on their hands so future generations were left to deal with the problem of Oregon.

Then there was Spanish Florida — alone, unprotected and a nesting ground for pirates, runaway slaves, smugglers, hostile Seminole Indians, and — rumor has it — North America's first personal injury lawyer. Native Americans in particular were raiding Georgia, and then slipping back into Florida for the legal protection of Spanish territory. Furious that the Spaniards could not control the Indians within their jurisdiction, President Monroe ordered General Andrew Jackson into Florida to subdue the Seminoles. Historians have traditionally pointed out that at this time the zealous Hero of New Orleans "exceeded his instructions." That is a polite way of saying that "Old Hickory" went postal. Not only did his force crush the Seminoles, they also captured two Spanish forts and executed two British subjects who had been inciting the Indians.

Members of Monroe's cabinet back in Washington demanded that the President disavow Jackson, discipline him and order him back to Tennessee where hopefully he would stay out of trouble — and politics. But crafty Adams saw an opportunity. The Secretary of State knew that the Spanish government understood they could very well lose Florida by force in the near future. He suggested to them that they might as well negotiate and get something out of it. The result was the **Adams-Onis Treaty** (1819), in which the United States grabbed Florida for $5 million (paid not to Spain but to Americans pressing lawsuits due to border raids) and the 42nd parallel was agreed upon as the boundary between Mexico and the Oregon Territory. The Adams-Onis agreement also renounced U.S. claims to Texas — fine print that future red-blooded Americans would claim they never heard of.

In the early decades of the 1800s, Spain had become embroiled in the Napoleonic Wars. Spanish New World colonists, sick and tired of being treated like second-class citizens by the *peninsulares* (Spaniards born in Spain), revolted and gained their independence. (Brazilians did the same to the Portuguese.) Virtually all Americans cheered these new republics because they had thrown off the monarchical yoke of Europe just as we had done in our Revolution. And now, with the Spanish mercantilist restrictions banished from the scene, American merchants and shippers envisioned friendly commerce with their little cousins to the south. The Latin Americans had no idea what they were in for, so they welcomed Anglo-American commerce with open arms. *Here come the Gringos! Watch when they drink the water!*

In Europe, a **Quadruple Alliance** of France (where the monarchy had been restored), Austria, Prussia, and Russia all agreed this revolutionary genie needed to be stuffed back in the bottle. After all, their royal necks could be next on the guillotine. Rumors abounded regarding a European military expedition on the horizon, intent upon getting Spain her colonies back. It turned out this was virtually all hot air, but Monroe and Adams grew concerned. Weak southern neighbors were greatly preferable to one giant European pain in the butt. The British were apprehensive as well because their merchants had also gotten in on the act in Latin America. Talk about a changing world! The United States and Britain were actually on the same side in this one. They both wanted Latin American profits to keep flowing in their directions, so Spain and the Quadruple Alliance better darn well keep themselves far away on their side of the Atlantic. *Klemens, Pedro, Ivan, Hans, Andre...you guys want coffee? Then buy it from us. Good to the last drop.*

British Foreign Minister **George Canning** suggested the United States and Great Britain issue a joint declaration warning the Europeans to stop threatening Latin American independence. Secretary of State Adams said no thanks — the United States will issue its own declaration. Still a young nation, we wanted to prove we could walk on our own without banging our head on the coffee table. The British, who preferred tea, made a mental note to remember the slight the next time the Americans needed a favor.

President Monroe knew Adams was on a roll so he wisely accepted his Secretary of State's counsel. In his annual message to Congress in 1823, the President flatly told the Europeans that any attempt to recolonize the western hemisphere would be regarded as "dangerous to our peace and safety." *Europe keep out*, the President essentially said. *You stay out of our affairs, we'll stay out of yours.* Boldly, he seemed to be announcing to the gang of Europeans that Latin America was the United States' turf. Statesman across the Atlantic guffawed at the gall of the militarily weak Americans, but straightened up when they realized the British navy would in reality back up the American **Monroe Doctrine**.

There was no way Britain would allow **reactionary** (turn the clock back) European forces to mess with their profitable Latin American trade. In making a declaration, then having another country do all the work, Adams and Monroe really pulled a rabbit (or a British lion) out of a hat. If only all diplomacy could work like magic! The Monroe Doctrine survived and continued to be a cornerstone of U.S. foreign policy (with both good and bad results) well into the twentieth century. Today, if you were to ask members of Congress about the Monroe Doctrine, most would give you a blank stare and head for a fundraiser. But you might find one or two who will solemnly state it is still in effect.

FACTIONS EMERGE AGAIN

or *Hug Me One More Time and I'll Punch Your Lights Out*

By the end of Monroe's second term, the nationalism of the post-war years had definitely run its course. Especially in the South and West, most folks favored states' rights over the federal government because individual states could be trusted not to threaten their precious institution of slavery. The presidential election of 1824 thus featured four candidates, each a sectional favorite who professed to be a Republican: **William H. Crawford** of Georgia (a states' righter), Henry Clay of Kentucky (a nationalist still pushing his "American System"), John Quincy Adams of Massachusetts (also a nationalist), and Andrew Jackson of Tennessee (vague on the issues but a really popular Indian fighter and war hero who impressed everyone by wearing buckskin, even though he changed into a velvet smoking jacket in the evenings). John C. Calhoun of South Carolina observed a crowded field that included Crawford from neighboring Georgia, so he decided to run for vice president and wait his turn for a chance at the presidency.

When Election Day rolled around, the big surprise was the strength of the support for Andy Jackson; he captured first place in both the popular vote and the electoral vote. But he still did not have a majority in the electoral college, so (as stipulated in the twelfth amendment to the Constitution) it fell to the House of Representatives to decide from among the top three finishers, Jackson, Adams and Crawford. Clay finished fourth and was eliminated, but he had an ace up his sleeve.

Henry Clay was the **Speaker of the House** (the highest ranking member of the majority party in the House of Representatives) and he wielded a lot of influence. He hated Jackson and Jackson hated him; they were rivals for western support, and Clay had vociferously condemned the General's 1818 foray into Florida. Crawford suffered a paralytic stroke, eliminating him, though the idea of a politician who could no longer speak seemed appealing. That left Adams, and even though Clay preferred parties and Adams preferred prayers, the two did share a belief in strong central government.

Clay threw his weight behind Adams, and obedient House Republicans responded by choosing him by a bare majority on the first ballot. "President John Quincy Adams" — Jackson and his supporters cringed at the sound of it. But their sullen silence changed to a roar of outrage when a mere three days later, Adams announced that his new Secretary of State would be none other than Henry Clay. Amid the curses, shouts echoed of **"corrupt bargain"** and the cries did not die down because they were, well, true. There has never been any "smoking gun" — the two men never signed anything and that subterranean crawler Linda Tripp was not around to blab everything — but the circumstances sure looked bad. Adams and Clay didn't break any laws, but they misjudged the outrage among the public in general and Jackson and his supporters in particular. In a real sense, the presidential election campaign of 1828 began at the precise moment in early 1825 when Adams and Clay clinked their glasses and drank.

John Quincy Adams was the country's first minority President, meaning that his paltry 32% of the popular vote fell far short of a majority. So many people were angry about the circumstances of his election that it would have been difficult for anyone to get much accomplished, but Adams was the worst man for the job. He was an uptight intellectual with a stuffy personality that made even his cold fish father look like the life of the party. (It has been reported that President Adams regularly enjoyed swimming completely nude in the chilly Potomac River, which is particularly difficult to envision because Adams looked shriveled even with his clothes on.)

Adams' character void had not mattered much when he was Secretary of State, so in that role he excelled, but to be President you have to care about politics and be able to schmooze and slap backs. Worse, Adams remained a devoted nationalist at a time when most of the country was turning to sectionalism and states' rights. When he proposed creation of a national university and astronomical observatory, establishment of a department of the interior, and federal funding for science, literature and the arts, most Americans thought he was nuts. All that stuff would cost money, and the protective tariff that would surely need to be raised to pay for it all was controversial enough already. Adams' proposals — and presidency — went nowhere. But John Quincy Adams was not nuts. His ideas were visionary and his countrymen and women were simply not ready for them.

Meanwhile, Andrew Jackson and his supporters strode towards the election of 1828 with a vengeance, and now they were calling themselves **Democrats**. Jackson and Adams did not personally condescend to name-calling and rumor-mongering, but their supporters and friendly newspaper publishers had no such inhibitions. Adams had used his own money to purchase for the White House a chess set and a billiard table. Rabid Jacksonites conjured them up to be "gambling devices" that were a disgrace to the highest office in the land. They also accused Adams, when he had been minister to Russia, of procuring a woman for the Russian czar. It did not matter that it was inconceivable that the puritanical Adams could ever have been a pimp — he did not own any purple leather jackets and he had never even heard of rap music — but the mud-slinging thrived on nonsensical nastiness.

Adamsites constantly called attention to Jackson's duels and even went so far as to call his mother a prostitute. Jackson's wife even became a target of charges of bigamy. Unfortunately in the case of his wife, the charges were technically true. Way back in 1791 Andrew and Rachel had mistakenly believed that she had been granted a divorce from her first husband. They got married, but discovered two years later that her original marriage was still in effect. They swiftly took all the legal steps to correct the snafu but rumors simmered for decades, only to be fanned in 1828 by conscienceless politicos. Rachel Jackson, a very pious woman, was devastated by the accusations, and though she lived to see her husband win the election, she died before he could be inaugurated. Jackson blamed his political enemies for destroying her health and carried the bitterness for the rest of his days. Out of spite, some claim he never returned the wedding gifts from his first reception.

On Election Day, Jackson creamed Adams in both the popular vote and the electoral college. Jackson generally carried the South and West while Adams maintained the support of the propertied interests in New England, along with virtually all cranky bald men with whom he felt a kind of kinship. But the small farmer and the laborer with calloused hands — most of the poor men everywhere — voted for "Old Hickory." They saw in him a man who respected them even though their clothes were dirty. And they now believed that even a regular guy could take part in American democracy and make it even more real. The Common Man had arrived.

It is hard to imagine today, but after Jackson was sworn in, the general public was invited to an "open house" at the White House. After all, President Jackson was reputed to have faith in the Common Man and they had elected him. Well, the common men showed up (without having bathed) and the party soon got out of hand. Basically, the White House got trashed. Luckily, someone got the bright idea to put tubs of spiked punch out on the lawn, and when the rabble sprinted for the booze, the doors were locked behind them. This "Inaugural Brawl" forced President Jackson to spend his first night in office at Gatsby's Hotel. What is going on here? Is the regular Joe really ready to participate in the national government? Uh oh...Stay tuned...don't touch that dial!!!

This Really Happened!

Before the invention of the refrigerator, preserved food tastes terrible: smoked, dried, salted ... *yuk!* Spices from the Far East sure come in handy to hide the taste of rotten meat. But in the early 1800s, twenty-one year old Frederick Tudor of Boston has a better idea — chop ice from the local ponds during the freezing winter months and then ship it around the world. Tudor builds ice houses insulated with wood shavings and straw, and now Australian gold miners can toast their new wealth with drinks cooled by New England ice. Persian hospitals pack the Boston ice around patients to lower fevers and save lives. Pretty soon local natives in the tropics are enjoying ice cream, iced drinks, chilled fruits and all the other "luxuries" of a cold Massachusetts winter... and perhaps even a "brain freeze!"

And the rest is History...

Quiz yourself on Chapter 4

Multiple Choice (circle the correct answer).

1. Young men who were elected to Congress in 1810 became known as War Hawks because
   a. they partied hard
   b. they wanted war with England
   c. they wanted war with France
   d. record company executives thought it was a good name
   e. all of the above

2. Captain Thomas Macdonough reported his victory on Lake Champlain with the stirring words
   a. "We have met the enemy and they are ours."
   b. "We have met the enemy and they seem like regular guys."
   c. "We have met the enemy and it was all a big misunderstanding."
   d. "Shout outs to my thugs in the hood!"
   e. a and d

3. The Battle of New Orleans
   a. barely interrupted Mardi Gras
   b. made a hero out of Aaron Burr
   c. occurred after the War of 1812 was already over
   d. popularized Cajun cooking
   e. all of the above

4. The idea that a state can cancel a federal law is known as
   a. intercourse
   b. nationalism
   c. eroticism
   d. nullification
   e. none of the above

5. Henry Clay's American System called for a strong banking system, protective tariffs to promote manufacturing and
   a. extensive internal improvements at federal expense
   b. prostitutes for the Speaker of the House at federal expense
   c. legalized marijuana
   d. a relaxed dress code on Capitol Hill
   e. a and c

6. For the most part the South and the West wanted cheap land; the people in the North tended to regard the national domain as
   a. an asset that should be converted into as much cash as possible
   b. wasteland in between New York and Los Angeles
   c. rightfully theirs
   d. the perfect place to build condominiums
   e. all of the above

7. Supreme Court Chief Justice John Marshall
   a. was an idiot
   b. was arrested for punching James Madison
   c. favored states' rights
   d. generally convinced his fellow justices to rule in favor of federal power at the expense of the states
   e. none of the above

8. The "Era of Good Feelings" was so called because
   a. everybody drank heavily during the Panic of 1819
   b. there was more sexual freedom after the War of 1812
   c. there was an absence of open political strife during the presidency of James Monroe
   d. Congress frequently stopped work to engage in a group hug
   e. all of the above

9. The crisis created when Missouri applied for entrance to the Union as a slave state resulted in
   a. the Missouri Compromise
   b. the Tallmadge Amendment
   c. Henry Clay's first divorce
   d. "Peace in our time"
   e. all of the above

10. The Corrupt Bargain was
    a. a drug deal gone bad
    b. Monroe's claim that he rather than Adams had written the Monroe Doctrine
    c. Henry Clay's promise to call the next day
    d. John Quincy Adams' appointment of Henry Clay as Secretary of State in return for Clay's support of Adams for the presidency
    e. a and c

CHAPTER 5

JACKSONIAN DEMOCRACY BRINGS REFORM

or

The Common Man Steps Forward — And Trips

By the third decade of the 1800s, many mainstream folks felt a new sense of dignity. Don't feel sorry for the rich guys, they were still plenty snobby, it's just that now they had to share the government and figure out new devious ways to dominate the country. The election of Andrew Jackson was only the first breeze of a tornado of reform that would swirl across the land. Anyone who got in the way of this American twister was best off hiding in the cellar or they risked getting blown away.

THE DEMOCRATIC SPIRIT OF THE TIMES
or *Hey, This Is Our Country Too*

Many aspects of American politics were definitely loosening up by the 1820s. One by one, states removed property qualifications for voting and holding office, many appointed government jobs were made subject to election, and terms of office were shortened. All this gave the people a greater check upon officials, who at least now had to stop bragging about all the public money and stationery supplies they were stealing at work.

By 1832, the Presidential candidate of each party was named by party delegates at a **nominating convention** rather than by a few political leaders over drinks and cigars. Wheeling and dealing still went on, it's just that now more party members were in on the action. By this time, almost all the states had transferred the selection of presidential electors away from state legislatures and awarded it directly to the voters. Only South Carolina was still doing it the old way, so don't be surprised when we see that this state becomes one continual pain in the American butt for the next several decades.

Andrew Jackson frequently stated that the President should be the direct servant of the people. Even though he always did precisely what he personally wanted to, he always tried to make it appear he was furthering the interests of "the people." Jackson became the most powerful President relative to Congress thus far in American history, and he used the "veto" more often than all his predecessors put together. His enemies called him *King Andrew* or *King Veto*, but not to his face.

Jackson was the first President to formalize the use of the **spoils system** on the federal level. The spoils system refers to the awarding of jobs to friends and political supporters. Jackson believed any semi-intelligent individual could handle a government job and these jobs should be rotated in order to involve more people. Jackson replaced only about 20 percent of officeholders under his control, but in succeeding administrations the spoils system got totally out of hand. Countless qualified government employees who were doing a good job found themselves replaced by the brother-in-law of a friend of a friend of a cousin of a winning candidate. The next time someone smiles and says to you, "To the victor belong the spoils," brace yourself because you are about to get screwed.

Speaking of getting screwed, that's precisely what President Jackson did to the Indians still living on their native lands east of the Mississippi. The tribes stood in the path of white settlement, so the President endorsed a plan to move them west and out of the way. Jackson and the vast majority of Americans convinced themselves that this would actually be best for the Indians, since they were increasingly unhappy living among whites and their tribal culture was at risk of destruction. But in reality this Indian removal policy was cruel and barbarous. Most of the tribes were coerced into moving, some by military force. In 1834, Congress set aside special Indian areas in the Arkansas territory. (Most of these Indian **reservations** were situated on inferior lands that would eventually be incorporated into the new state of Oklahoma and, much later, an overly sappy Broadway musical.) With little concern or planning on the part of the government, some of the tribes were forced to march west in the dead of winter. Many Indians, particularly children and the elderly, died.

A few tribes, notably the **Sauk** and **Fox** tribes in the Illinois and Wisconsin regions, decided to fight. Led by **Chief Black Hawk**, nearly all these out-gunned and outnumbered Native Americans were decimated in what became known as the **Black Hawk War**. In Florida, the **Seminoles** led by **Chief Osceola** hid in the swamps and put up fierce resistance that would last for seven years. The **Cherokees** in Georgia actually won a Supreme Court decision stating that the state of Georgia had no jurisdiction over lands that had been legally obtained for a Cherokee nation. President Jackson, clearly misplacing his copy of the Constitution, simply refused to enforce the order. In 1838, the Cherokees were forced to trek west. Conditions were horrific, the conduct of the U.S. Army inhumane in the extreme, and 4000 of 15,000 Cherokees died along this **"Trail of Tears."** Except for a few humanitarian reformers up north, nobody in America cared or lost any sleep.

Even an astute politician like Andrew Jackson could not avoid infuriating some of the people some of the time. Settlers out west wanted the opportunity to purchase cheap federal land, while eastern industrialists wanted the land to be expensive, to discourage their low-paid factory workers from heading west. President Jackson remained true to his western roots and called for cheap land, thereby infuriating the Northeast. On the question of internal improvements at federal expense, which by this time was opposed generally in the South and Northeast but greatly desired in the transportation-starved West, Jackson let his frontier brethren down. He remained true to his states' rights principles and issued the **Maysville Veto,** which effectively killed a Congressional plan to provide federal funds for a sixty-mile road project from Maysville on the Ohio River to Lexington, Kentucky. Henry Clay still believed in his American System and especially supported the Maysville Road because much of it would lie in his home state of Kentucky. When Jackson spiked the project, no doubt remembering Clay's "Corrupt Bargain" as he did so, Henry must have certainly realized that payback is a bitch.

THE NULLIFICATION CRISIS
or *Those South Carolinians Sure Are Full of Themselves*

In 1828, Congress passed an extremely high protective tariff. Northerners and Westerners wanted the protection from foreign competition, but Southerners complained that their costs for imported goods would shoot up and foreign countries would cut back on their purchases of Southern cotton. Officially called the **Tariff of 1828**, Southerners sneeringly dubbed it the **Tariff of Abominations** and tended to hyperventilate when discussing it. Hotheads in South Carolina, secretly inspired by Vice President John C. Calhoun, issued a document entitled the **South Carolina Exposition and Protest**. This document declared that states should have the right to declare laws passed by Congress unconstitutional. States should then have the option of declaring that law (in this case the Tariff of Abominations) null and void. If differences could not be reconciled between the Union and the State, according to Calhoun and his cohorts, a State should then have the right to secede from the Union...kind of like what little kids do when they stamp their feet, take their ball and go home. If you are thinking, *Wow, this is just like the Virginia and Kentucky Resolutions of 1798*, you have made an astute historical connection that you should brag about to anyone who will listen.

In 1830, there was a big debate about all this on the floor of the Senate. Senator Daniel Webster of Massachusetts and Senator **Robert Y. Hayne** of South Carolina, both eloquent orators, really went at it in what has always been appropriately remembered as the **Webster-Hayne Debate**. By this time everyone knew Hayne was speaking also for Calhoun, who as Vice President watched the spectacle as presiding officer of the Senate. Hayne vigorously defended the doctrine of nullification and pointedly reminded New Englanders that they had toyed with the idea themselves during the war of 1812. Webster spoke about "the people's Constitution, the people's government" and declared that the Union was not supposed to be voluntary, butmandatory and perpetual, and any attempt to quit now would be treason and lead to civil war. When he concluded with the words, "Liberty and Union, now and forever, one and inseparable," some listeners were reported to have tears in their eyes, either because they were touched by the emotion of the moment, or because scalpers had charged a hundred bucks for the supposedly free seats in the visitors' gallery.

Soon after all this, there was a formal banquet celebrating the birthday of Thomas Jefferson, who couldn't be there because he was dead. But, as always, it was the thought that counts. All the big Washington politicos were there, including the President. Twenty-four toasts were drunk, so it would seem a good number of these guys must have been thoroughly hammered. When it came time for President Jackson to make a toast, he raised his glass and said, "Our federal Union. It must be preserved." Calhoun had been tipped off this was coming, so he offered a counter toast that began "There once was a man from Calcutta ... " Just kidding. Calhoun returned Jackson's stare and said, "The Union: next to our liberty, most dear." This was a tense, dramatic moment, and everyone probably whispered, "Whoa, can you believe that?" to the person next to them. Jackson's friendship with Calhoun was clearly on the rocks.

An almost unbelievable incident involving Cabinet wives hammered another wedge between the two men. Secretary of War Eaton married an attractive woman named Peggy O'Neill, the daughter of a Washington boardinghouse keeper. Rumors abounded that Peggy had engaged in "yakahoola" with some of the boarding house guests ("Yakahoola" sounds like a board game similar to Parcheesi or Yahtzee, but in this case it refers to sex). True or not, this woman had a reputation for having fun and was probably good at it. Today, lots of us like that kind of a person but Mrs. Calhoun, an uptight social snob if there ever was one, arranged to have all the Cabinet wives snub Mrs. Eaton.

Jackson thought all this was a bunch of garbage, and you can be sure he remembered all the meanspiritedness his late wife had dealt with. He made it conspicuously clear he admired Peggy, ensuring Calhoun and the others got an earful from their wives. One member of the Administration who refused to snub Peggy was Secretary of State Martin Van Buren, who saw this soap opera episode as a chance to further ingratiate himself with Jackson. It worked. In 1831, Calhoun's allies were forced out of the Cabinet, and the following year, Calhoun resigned the Vice Presidency to become Senator from South Carolina. The President, who had been informed that back in 1818, Calhoun had advocated severe censure for Jackson's headstrong invasion of Florida, was happy to be rid of the scoundrel. Van Buren jumped in the air, clicked his heels and asked Jackson if he could fetch his slippers.

A new tariff law passed in 1832 did not reduce the Tariff of Abominations enough to satisfy the South. The South Carolina legislature thereupon declared the tariff null and void within South Carolina. They announced they would secede from the Union if the federal government tried to enforce tariff collection. President Jackson went ballistic, and threatened to hang Calhoun and the "nullies" from the highest tree. He asked for the authority to use military force if necessary against South Carolina, and Congress obliged by passing the **Force Bill**. Other Southern states sympathized with South Carolina, but they were not prepared in 1832 to take the drastic step of leaving the Union and provoking a Civil War.

Jackson glared and the "nullies" blinked. Henry Clay dressed in tights and a cape and cried, "This is a job for the Great Compromiser!" (I'm kidding, he didn't wear a cape.) Congress passed the **Compromise Tariff of 1833** that gradually reduced rates over a ten-year period to the level of the Tariff of 1816. The South Carolinians grumbled and skulked around, but "Old Hickory" had backed them down. Just like Thomas Jefferson, Andrew Jackson had advocated states' rights all his political life. But it seems there's a unique and solitary view from the office of the Presidency of the United States that changes minds. (If you are remembering President Jefferson's purchase of Louisiana even though such action was not provided for in the Constitution, again, pat yourself on the back.)

KILLING THE NATIONAL BANK

or *Because I Feel Like It, That's Why*

The Bank of the United States (BUS) effectively regulated the economy and maintained a sound currency, but Jacksonians hated it anyway. They argued that the BUS restricted state banks from issuing large quantities of bank notes, which would cause inflation of farm prices and help farmers pay off their debts. Lots of folks hated paper money altogether, and hoped the Bank's demise would convert the country exclusively to the use of gold and silver (**hard money**). They despised the way the "Monster" monopolized the nation's credit and currency. Most of the Bank's big investors were rich eastern industrialists and foreigners, and hardly anyone had any sympathy for those types. Besides, the Bank's director, **Nicholas Biddle**, was a pompous and arrogant blowhard who highhandedly made loans to friends and supporters while being notoriously tightfisted with poor folks who really needed the money. If this reminds you of your own bank today, switch banks and make sure you get free checking.

Jackson really wanted to deliver the BUS a knockout punch. Henry Clay noted the President's hatred of the Bank, and determined to make it the main issue in the election of 1832. He and Webster contrived to have Biddle apply four years early for the Bank's recharter. When the Congress passed the recharter and Jackson scornfully vetoed it, Clay, standing as the candidate of the National-Republicans, took off sprinting. But he quickly ran out of breath. Poor people (who generally hated the Bank) greatly outnumbered rich people (who generally supported it), and in this era of Jacksonian Democracy, poor men voted in large numbers. In November, 1832, Jackson blew Clay away, 219 electoral votes to 49. The popular vote was closer: 687,502 to 530,189, but Jackson never really broke a sweat.

Jackson thereupon set out to destroy the Bank. He withdrew government funds and opened up new federal accounts in state banks that became known as his "pet banks." (Unfortunately, toasters had not been invented yet or Jackson would have cleaned up.) Biddle and the BUS went down for the count. As events soon proved, Andrew Jackson had basically a fifth-grade understanding of the nation's financial system. Reforms of the BUS had been needed, but Jackson obliterated it completely. Biddle's expensive suit needed rumpling, but the President stripped him naked — not literally, but you get the idea.

State banks, now unbridled, made loans to anyone who could sign their names and smile. Teeth were not required. These **"Wildcat Banks"** printed so much paper money that Jackson had to issue the **Specie Circular** requiring that federal land agents accept payment only in gold or silver. Just as Jackson was wrapping up his second term and heading home to Tennessee, overspeculation along with other crack-brained Jacksonian financial policies caused the economy to nosedive. The big financial mess would be the next President's problem. Instead of pet banks, it would have been much better for the country if Jackson had kept goldfish.

Martin Van Buren's long-term commitment to butt-kissing paid off when Jackson secured the Democratic presidential nomination for him in 1836. In that same year, opponents of Jackson started calling themselves the **Whig Party,** which sounds dumb today but at thr time hearkened back to British opposition to royal authority in the 1700s. The Whigs came from many walks of American life, and just about the only thing they agreed on was that they hated Jackson and his toady, Van Buren. Clay wanted to be the Whig candidate, but other Whigs forcefully informed him that he was already a two-time loser who should sit this one out on the bench. The Whigs ran four favorite sons (regional favorites) in the '36 election, hoping to deadlock the electoral vote and leave the outcome up to the House of Representatives. The strategy failed and Martin Van Buren became President. That Henry Clay walked around whispering, "I could have won... " made the Whigs even more frustrated.

Clay was lucky he didn't run. The **Panic of 1837** devastated both the country and Van Buren's presidency. Even though Jackson's financial policies had brought about the financial collapse, everybody called it "Van Buren's depression." Van Buren did not believe it was the position of the federal government to regulate the economy or provide direct relief to suffering citizens, so the depression was still going strong in 1840. The Democrats didn't have the guts to deny a sitting president (the **incumbent**) the chance to run for a second term, so the unpopular Van Buren ran again.

The Whigs were overjoyed at this turn of events and, determined to make sure they didn't blow this one, Henry Clay was again told thanks but no thanks. The Whigs offered their nomination to William Henry Harrison, the old general who in his younger days had defeated the Indians at Tippecanoe. The Whigs figured Harrison was a good choice because he didn't have enemies, due to the fact that he seemingly didn't have any opinions about anything. Even when discussing the weather, Harrison would say, "It looks like rain...or not." In short, he was the perfect candidate.

Harrison was a refined gentleman who had been raised in comfortable circumstances, but Whig campaigners, learning from Jackson's appeal to the common people, fabricated that he had been born in a log cabin and loved hard cider, the odoriferous beverage of frontier folk. When they balanced the ticket with a Democratic Virginia legislator named **John Tyler**, the Whigs found an alluring slogan: **"Tippecanoe and Tyler too."** Voters jumped at the lure hook, line and sinker, and the Whigs reeled them in. Van Buren was swept from office and the Whigs took control of the Presidency and both houses of Congress. Henry Clay was pleased because, even though he had been denied the high office, he had every expectation that he (and other big Whigs like Daniel Webster) would be telling the compliant Harrison what to do.

President Harrison delivered an overly long inaugural address outdoors in lousy weather and died of pneumonia a month later. The doctors had no clue back then how to treat infections, although they were skilled at submitting their bills. Harrison was the first President to die in office; it was a shock to everyone, and the Whigs soon realized they should have planned better. Vice President Tyler became President Tyler, and to the surprise of everyone he refused to take orders from the Whig elders. Clay and Webster et al had placed Tyler on the Whig ticket to pick up support in the South; after the victory, it was expected that as a good Vice President, he would return home to Virginia and keep his mouth shut. Harrison dropping dead ruined everything. As President Tyler vetoed bill after bill passed by the Whig-controlled Congress, Whig leaders went increasingly bananas. The President thus found that he was a man without a party — Democrats and Whigs alike hated him. The game of solitaire was invented for people like John Tyler. He was a man of principle, and his fellow politicians looked at him like he was speaking Greek.

MANIFEST DESTINY
or *There's a Nice Mountain — Let's Live There*

Manifest Destiny refers to Americans' belief that they had a God-given right to spread their white Christian civilization across the North American continent from sea to shining sea. By the 1840s, Manifest Destiny seemed to make perfect sense. Abundant fertile land prevailed west of the Mississippi with just a few Indians in the way who could always be shoved aside. Eastern shipping companies had begun trading with Asia and they needed ports on the Pacific coast. The pesky British still could not be trusted to keep their grasping colonizing hands to themselves, so Americans figured they better get there first. Back then, a person could go bankrupt, make enemies, screw up their lives altogether and simply start over by heading west. The frontier seemed mighty appealing, especially when an angry father with a shotgun wanted you to get married to his suddenly expanding daughter.

Due to the arrival of lots of immigrants from Europe, some of the big cities in the Northeast were getting downright crowded. Ireland in the 1840s experienced widespread starvation when a blight afflicted its staple crop, the potato. The more affluent English declined to provide aid while continuing to deny Irish requests for home rule. One million died and another one million emigrated to the United States due to the **Potato Famine**. Reports that around this same time there was a Potato Knish Famine in Israel proved unfounded. Lots of Germans fleeing political unrest also journeyed to America in the 1840s. These were mostly liberal democratic-minded Germans, not the conservative authoritarian types that would come to dominate the country of Germany as it formed over the next several decades.

Established white Anglo-Saxon Americans discriminated against the newcomers, who tended to live in their own ethnic enclaves in cities like New York, Boston, and Philadelphia. Sometimes the only employment the Irish could get would be domestic help for the women and the police and fire departments for the men. Why do you think so many of the cops in the old black and white movies had names like O'Hara, O'Reilly and Flynn? Many of the German immigrants had enough money to push on out to the Midwest. Why do you think Budweiser is a German-sounding word and Anheiser Busch is headquartered in St. Louis? See, all this stuff eventually comes together in a way everyone can relate to.

There were so few people in Mexico's northern province of Texas in 1821 that Mexican authorities (newly independent of Spain) actually encouraged Americans to move there. **Stephen Austin** led the first group of settlers, and by the 1830s over 20,000 Americans had followed. These newcomers brought slaves, refused to forsake Protestantism for the Catholic faith, demanded self-government, and generally refused to transform themselves into good Mexicans. Their boisterous Fourth of July celebrations proved a particular bone of contention. Belatedly, the Mexicans realized they had invited a red, white and blue monster into their midst.

Friction increased, and in 1836 the Texans rose in rebellion. They claimed inspiration from the American Revolution against Britain, which actually made good sense. The Mexicans sent an army of about 6000 under the command of General **Santa Anna** to crush the uprising. Santa Anna was a bombastic egomaniac if there ever was one, and would have referred to himself as "Lord and Savior" had the name not already been taken. At San Antonio, a small Texas force of under 200 refused to retreat and took refuge in the **Alamo** mission. (A mission is a building that serves as both a church and a fort.) They held out for thirteen days before the Mexican army blew apart the walls, stormed inside and massacred all the Texans left alive.

Courageous heroes such as Colonel **William Travis**, **Jim Bowie**, and **Davy Crockett** died fighting, probably bummed out that no help arrived in time. (Jim Bowie invented a wickedly large hunting knife still called the Bowie knife; David Bowie is an aging rock star, and it's embarrassing when you confuse the names...believe me, I've done it. Davy Crockett was a frontier hero who also happened to be a former Congressman. Crockett lived in a later century than Daniel Boone, but is often confused with him because they both wore coonskin caps. The Walt Disney Corporation added to this confusion when they cast the same actor, Fess Parker, to play Daniel Boone in a TV series and Davy Crockett in the movies. An entire generation of Americans in the sixties and seventies saw the same guy in the same hat and are still mixed up to this day.)

Two weeks after the Alamo massacre, the Mexicans surrounded 400 Texans at **Goliad** and forced them to surrender. As soon as the Texans threw down their arms, the Mexicans entered the town and slaughtered them — not the surrender terms the Texans thought they had arranged.

The main bulk of the Texan army waited to the north under the command of **Sam Houston**, a former Tennessee governor, protégé of Andrew Jackson and notorious alcoholic. But don't blame Houston for the Alamo and Goliad. The headstrong Texans caught at those two places had disobeyed his orders to stay with the group. This was not a field trip — it was war, and Houston, drunk or sober, knew what he was doing. He retreated east for thirty-seven days while Santa Anna's army followed him. Despite the fact that many called him a coward, Houston waited for precisely the right moment to attack. At **San Jacinto,** the Texans took full advantage of the Mexicans' siesta hour to surprise and decisively defeat them. (It is stupefying that the Mexicans could not forgo their afternoon nap considering that they were in the middle of a war. One wonders if some of the officers shouted, "Hey, it's nap time!" before being slashed to death by a bright-eyed and bushy-tailed Texas cavalryman.)

Shouting, "**Remember the Alamo! Remember Goliad!**" and "Where are my pants?" (don't forget, Houston was a boozer), the Texans delivered the Mexicans a dose of their own medicine. Tragically, for several hours the Texan officers lost control of their troops. Most of the Mexican soldiers tried to surrender but were struck down by vengeful out-of-control Texans. Victims even included little twelve-year-old drummer boys. If you consider that the Texans were Americans by extension — they had come from America and still wanted to be part of America — then this barbarism at San Jacinto can be considered the lowest and sorriest point in the history of the United States Armed Forces. Santa Anna was captured while hiding in tall grass in his underwear — presumably boxers rather than briefs since he was overweight.

Victorious Texans immediately declared themselves an independent nation: The **Lone Star Republic**. (That five-pointed star on the helmet of the Dallas Cowboys now should make some sense. The Dallas Cowboys Cheerleaders also wear the star, but nobody notices.) They drafted a constitution similar to that of the United States, elected Sam Houston president — and immediately requested annexation by the United States!

To the surprise of many, President Andrew Jackson did not jump at the chance to welcome Texas into the Union. The question of whether or not the Texas territory would allow slavery was a hot potato on which the President did not want to burn his mouth, especially since annexation would almost certainly provoke war with the Mexicans and their chili sauce. On his last day in office in 1837, Jackson extended diplomatic recognition to Texas as an independent country, but the Texans felt like they had been left hanging. Like a high school kid ditched by his friends, the Lone Star Republic hung out alone outside the American Union for about eight years. When President Houston, out of desperation for new friends, started pounding down drinks with British diplomats, the Texas question became a big issue in the presidential election of 1844.

The Democrats passed over Martin Van Buren and nominated **James K. Polk**, Speaker of the House and a former Tennessee governor. Polk and his supporters were completely under the spell of "Manifest Destiny," and they unambiguously called upon the country to take possession of Texas and any other land that might be out there to be grabbed. President Tyler had so angered the Whigs that his own party refused to even consider his renomination. Unanimously, the Whigs decided to give Henry Clay another shot at the presidency, and characteristically, Henry blew it. He failed to comprehend the extent to which "Manifest Destiny" had shaped most Americans' outlooks. While trying to appeal to both the North and the South, he was wishy-washy and confusing on the pivotal issue of Texas' annexation.

Clay ended up eroding much of his support in both regions, the one time his instincts for compromise may have been in error. Insults flew fast and furious from both sides and the Democrats actually made a big deal out of labeling Clay a slave owner. Since their own candidate, Polk, was a slave owner himself, this is yet another example of the level of inanity to which an American presidential election can descend. Polk won decisively in the electoral college but the popular vote was extremely close. Ironically, Clay could have won the electoral college, and thus the election, had he not lost New York State by a mere 5000 votes. A small anti-slavery third party, the Liberty Party, polled about 16,000 votes, most of which otherwise would have gone to Clay. This ensured the election of Polk, whose policies, much more so than Clay's, favored the annexation of Texas and the extension of slavery. Ralph Nader and his Green Party would have done well to study this little piece of History before they handed the 2000 presidential election to George W. Bush.

Lame duck (an officeholder serving out his term and not running again) President Tyler viewed the election as a mandate to annex Texas. He knew he could never get two-thirds approval for a treaty through the Senate due to Northern opposition, so in February 1845 he arranged for annexation through joint resolution, a simple majority vote in both the House and the Senate. Slavery was permitted in the new territory, and two months later Texas jumped happily into the American pool. Meanwhile, the Mexicans fumed in the desert heat.

No doubt about it, Americans had a prodigious appetite for land. Even though baseball had not been formally invented yet, back in 1842 President Tyler had played hardball during a dispute with Britain over the boundary between Maine and Canada. Both sides possessed conflicting maps even more confusing then those lousy maps we get today over the Internet from Map Quest. Secretary of State Webster worked out a favorable treaty (the **Webster-Ashburton Treaty**) and the Brits even threw in some rugged land out in what is now Minnesota. It was unintentional, but we really pulled a fast one on the Brits...this Mesabi mountain range later turned out to contain extensive deposits of iron ore.

Since 1818 the United States and Britain had jointly occupied the Oregon territory, but by 1845 about 5000 Americans had succumbed to the "Oregon fever" and migrated there. **Marcus Whitman** and other missionaries inspired by him energetically trashed Native-American religions and hawked Christianity. Polk had promised during his campaign to annex all of Oregon, endorsing such slogans as "**Fifty-four forty** or **fight!**" and the lesser known "Come on, we can get away with it." He even brought up the Monroe Doctrine, which most folks had forgotten about. Lots of hotheads on both sides of the Atlantic clamored for war. But cooler heads in Parliament and Congress concluded war was not worth it, so they negotiated a compromise agreement dividing the Oregon territory, and extending the boundary between the U.S. and Canada straight across to the Pacific at the 49th parallel. Canada's Vancouver Island dips below the 49th parallel, but it's no big deal; it's a beautiful place to visit and we'll get our hands on it eventually.

THE MEXICAN WAR
or *Come On, You Want a Piece of Me?*

In the fall of 1845 President Polk sent an envoy, **John Slidell** of Louisiana, to hopefully calm the Mexicans down. He was ordered to negotiate for a southern boundary of Texas at the Rio Grande River (not the more northern Nueces River the Mexicans wanted) and offer cold hard cash for the New Mexico and California territories. If the President thought Slidell's mission would mollify the Mexicans, he was badly mistaken. He would have done better offering Valium had it been available. The Mexican authorities were in such a snit they refused to even meet with Slidell, and he did not dare ask if they would validate parking. Polk was furious, but he cheered up when American troops, looking for trouble in the disputed area above the Rio Grande, ran into a small Mexican force and engaged in a minor skirmish. Accusing Mexico of invading U.S. territory and "shedding American blood on American soil" was definitely a stretch, but the President sufficiently whipped up Congress to elicit a declaration of war. Many Northeasterners knew this was a case of the United States bullying a weaker neighbor in order to gain territory and extend slavery, but hawkish Westerners and Southerners shouted them down.

The Mexicans also approached the war enthusiastically, embracing the dream that they could teach their domineering northern neighbor a lesson. As events would prove, they should have renamed their country Fantasyland or *Tierra de la Fantasia*. The Mexican Army was equipped with outdated weapons, and led by generals who looked good in gold braid and epaulets but knew precious little about tactics. The United States Army was no great shakes either, but it was better supplied with arms and leadership in the person of General **Winfield Scott**. Scott was a young officer during the War of 1812, and had subsequently dedicated his military career to professionalizing the American armed forces. Give the guy a lot of credit for the accomplished manner in which the U.S. army whipped their Mexican counterparts.

General **Zachary Taylor** won lots of victories in northern Mexico. His nickname, "Old Rough and Ready," suited him perfectly on the battlefield, though that same attitude probably caused strains in his domestic life. General Scott captured Vera Cruz and Mexico City, the capital, despite encountering fierce resistance. This feat by Scott and his men was all the more impressive because Pepto-Bismol had not been invented yet. Colonel **Stephen Kearny** defeated the Mexicans in New Mexico and pushed on to California, probably thinking to himself, "What the heck else do I have to do to make General?" Captain **John C. Frémont** encouraged American settlers in California to drive out Mexican authorities and establish a temporary California, or **"Bear Flag" Republic.** Temporary is the operative word here; if California had actually stayed independent, Ronald Reagan would have been ineligible to become President of the United States.

Mexico was completely pinned to the mat. Utilizing a chokehold, the U.S. virtually dictated surrender terms in the **Treaty of Guadalupe Hidalgo**. Mexico (1) accepted the

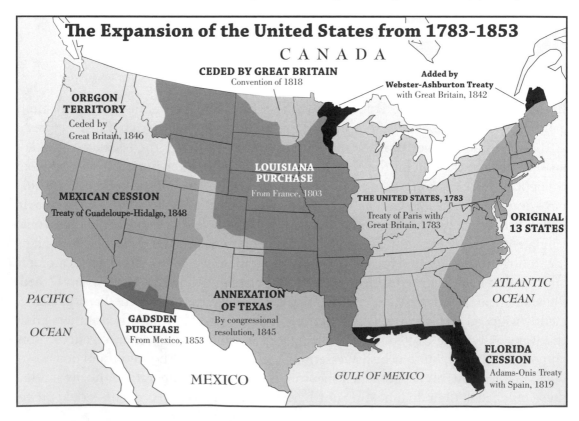

The Expansion of the United States from 1783-1853

CANADA

CEDED BY GREAT BRITAIN
Convention of 1818

Added by Webster-Ashburton Treaty with Great Britain, 1842

OREGON TERRITORY
Ceded by Great Britain, 1846

LOUISIANA PURCHASE
From France, 1803

THE UNITED STATES, 1783
Treaty of Paris with Great Britain, 1783

MEXICAN CESSION
Treaty of Guadeloupe-Hidalgo, 1848

ORIGINAL 13 STATES

PACIFIC

ANNEXATION OF TEXAS
By congressional resolution, 1845

ATLANTIC OCEAN

OCEAN

GADSDEN PURCHASE
From Mexico, 1853

MEXICO

GULF OF MEXICO

FLORIDA CESSION
Adams-Onis Treaty with Spain, 1819

Rio Grande as the southern boundary of Texas, (2) surrendered the California and New Mexico territories (collectively known as the **Mexican Cession**) and (3) was forced to drop its pants and say "U.S.A. grande, Mexico pequeno." Ironically, as some of us look back from a different perspective, it was the other way around. The U.S. agreed to pay Mexico $15 million and assume the claims of American citizens against the Mexican government. Unemployed American negotiator John Slidell doubtless said, "You *estupidos*, that's about what I offered you before the war." But all the Mexicans could do was turn away, take a shot of Tequila, and begin nursing a grudge that still exists to this day. They might have felt better had they known that in succeeding years, the issue of slavery in these newly-seized territories would lead America directly into civil war. Now you know why there are so many Spanish names out west as far north as San Francisco. You've also got to agree it's outrageous so many Americans have no sense of the irony when they complain about "all these damn Mexicans sneaking into our country."

Five years later, the United States, needing an extreme southern route for a railroad, bullied Mexico into accepting $10 million for a small strip of land that could be added to southern New Mexico and Arizona. Except for Alaska, the United States' acquisition of territory in North America was complete. Some historians have labeled this Gadsden Purchase as "conscience money." We may never know the truth because a lot of Americans when questioned at the time felt way too guilty about the Mexican War to even discuss it.

REFORMING SOCIETY
or *Would You Please Get This Busybody Off My Back*

In the decades after the election of President Andrew Jackson, some people wanted to reform not only politics but society as well, and believe it or not, most of these folks were actually sincere and trying to do what was right for the poor and disadvantaged.

The mentally challenged in America had always been treated like something distasteful that needed to be locked away out of sight. **Dorothea Dix** spent many years enlightening the public in regard to mental illness and advocating for the establishment of mental hospitals. She certainly had no idea that in the future, criminals would attempt to claim insanity in order to avoid responsibility for their crimes, but that's another story.

Education had always been important in America. During the colonial period, the Puritans had stressed the teaching of reading as necessary for getting closer to God through the Bible. Thomas Jefferson described the need for an educated citizenry that could participate in the new Democracy. In the 1820s, social reformers came up with additional reasons to focus on education: it offered a path away from poverty and crime. **Horace Mann** of Massachusetts championed tax-supported public education, and by the 1850s most communities offered free elementary schools (open to all ages), with some states even adding compulsory attendance laws. It thus became possible to cut school and go fishing (or "play hooky") and kids have continued to come up with creative reasons for missing school ever since. I personally know students who have attended their grandmother's funeral six or seven times.

Opportunities for men in higher education were limited during the first half of the 1800s, but the number of private, state and church-affiliated colleges steadily grew and broadened their curriculums. Women were generally excluded from colleges, but in the 1830s Mount Holyoke in Massachusetts became the first all women's college, and Oberlin College in Ohio became the nation's first coeducational college. Not surprisingly, this was about the time reports first surfaced of male students attempting to sneak into the girls' dormitories.

In 1848 in upstate New York, a remarkable event took place: the **Seneca Falls Convention**. This was the first women's rights convention in the nation. Women had always been accorded inferior status in America but attendees at this meeting declared, "all men *and* women are created equal." Some really exceptional women such as **Angelina Grimké**, **Lucretia Mott**, **Elizabeth Cady Stanton**, and **Susan B. Anthony** advocated forcefully for women's rights, particularly the right to vote, which earned them the name **suffragettes**. As we will discuss, women have made steady gains in America, but nobody should pat themselves on the back until all women get the same pay as men for the same job and we elect a female President. Also, guys should be forced to wear high heels just for one day so they can sympathize when women say their feet hurt.

These early women activists had their hearts in the right place and they naturally gravitated toward other causes as well, like **temperance**. The temperance movement refers to the drive to outlaw intoxicating liquors and ruin all the really fun parties that were going on. America had always been a hard-drinking place. Men did most of the imbibing since taverns and saloons were almost exclusively a male domain. You can bet that once in a while some women would sneak a snort, but it was mostly their fathers, sons, and brothers who ruined their lives with drink. Wives coming home from their temperance meetings to find their husbands drunk only aggravated the situation.

Of course, organized religion got in on the act. Remember the first Great Awakening during the colonial period? Well, in the early part of the 1800s along comes the **Second Great Awakening**. In the late 1700s, church attendance had been low as Americans embraced the reason and attendant **secularism** (the belief that religion should play no role in public institutions) of the Enlightenment. Then, in the early decades of the 1800s, the country (particularly among the poor and uneducated in rural areas) experienced an intense religious revival that denigrated reason and focused on free will, personal salvation, and emotion. In this Second Great Awakening, huge crowds of up to 25,000 would gather at **camp meetings** to gyrate and convulse and get "saved." Traveling preachers like **Charles Grandison Finney** and **Peter Cartwright** huffed and puffed and whipped their audiences into a frenzy by offering folks hope and security during rapidly changing times. New Christian denominations emerged, and your neighbors would really give you a dirty look if you didn't go to church on Sunday. Being drunk the night before was not considered a good excuse. America is to this day a nation of great religious diversity. We were then and are now a nation of God. That's great, but cross to the other side of the street when the religious extremists out there try to tell you they know what God wants and you don't.

Some Americans tried to set up experimental communities, called **Utopias**, in which idealists were supposed to live in tranquility and share all work and possessions. But places like New Harmony in Indiana, Brook Farm in Massachusetts and Oneida Colony in New York met with only limited success. Organizers found that communistic sharing of everything goes against human nature (or at least American nature) and suspicion and jealousy are difficult feelings for people to suppress. It was particularly awkward when a young child would call "Daddy!" and all the men within earshot would answer. In a similar vein, transcendentalists believed that reality is essentially mental or spiritual in nature and that true knowledge can only be attained by the cultivation of the mind. Some great writers in the Northeast adopted **transcendentalism** (such as Ralph Waldo Emerson, Henry David Thoreau, and Walt Whitman), and believe it or not, these guys actually came up with their ideas without smoking pot.

In 1830, a man named **Joseph Smith** claimed to be a prophet. He swore that while sober, an angel had bestowed upon him a revelation that turned out to be a third book of the Bible. He started a new religion called **Mormon** or the Church of Latter Day Saints. These Mormons were different, particularly in their practice of **polygamy** which allowed men to have as many wives as they wanted at the same time. Women were not given the same option, so draw your own conclusions. Anyway, everywhere the Mormons went, they encountered violent hostility from neighbors who were still having difficulty comprehending the idea of religious tolerance.

After Joseph Smith was murdered in 1846 by a raging mob in Illinois, **Brigham Young** stepped forward and led the Mormons way out west to the Utah territory. They founded Salt Lake City, and through sheer hard work and perseverance succeeded in building a flourishing community. In 1848, their crops were about to be devoured by a swarm of crickets, when suddenly a flock of seagulls appeared a thousand miles away from the ocean and ate the crickets. That's the story that has always been told, and if — *if* — it is true, wow! The Mormons wanted to be left alone but they also claimed they wanted to be Americans, perhaps figuring that eventually they would have no choice. Polygamy proved a sticking point, but after the Mormon Church renounced the practice, Utah became a state in 1896. But polygamy still goes on out in Utah — at least according to *60 Minutes*. And now you know there is much more to the Mormons than Donnie and Marie Osmond.

When many women looked at African American servitude, they realized were in the same boat. Women formed the backbone of the early American abolition movement in the 1830s and 1840s. It was not a popular position to take during that time, even in the North, but these ladies were on a roll. Lots of guys ducked into an alley when they saw them coming, but that would only work for a while. Soon many men joined the cause. Most Northerners, although not active abolitionists, eventually became convinced that the institution of slavery had to go. White Southerners collectively replied, "Screw you. And your mother is a #$%@$&*#." How are they going to settle all this? What about slavery in the new territories? Can the country survive all this jive? Uh oh...stay tuned...don't touch that dial!!!

This Really Happened!

Early railroads are torture chambers on wheels and no place for weaklings or cowards. Live cinders from wood burning locomotives cause fires and even burn holes in passengers' clothing. The brakes are so bad the engineer often misses the station many times both coming in and backing up. With steep hills and sharp curves there always seem to be accidents. But the Pullman sleeping car is introduced in 1859 and from now on many people find railway travel much more, uh, enjoyable.

And the rest is History...

Quiz yourself on Chapter 5

Multiple Choice (circle the correct answer).

1. Americans' belief that it is their God-given right to spread their Anglo-Saxon Christian culture from sea to shining sea is known as
   a. Conservatism
   b. Sectionalism
   c. mental illness
   d. Manifest Destiny
   e. all of the above

2. President Monroe's two terms in office became known as
   a. the Era of Good Feeling
   b. the Time of Trouble
   c. the Reign of Terror
   d. Party Time
   e. none of the above

3. Southerners hated the Tariff of 1828 so much they called it
   a. not very nice
   b. just plain mean
   c. the Tariff of Abolition
   d. the Tariff of Abominations
   e. none of the above

4. John C. Calhoun favored the South and
   a. federal supremacy
   b. the power of Congress
   c. nullification
   d. long romantic walks with Peggy O'Neill
   e. all of the above

5. The Webster-Hayne debate focused on
   a. the nature of the federal Union
   b. Bud Lite – great taste or less filling
   c. the rights of women
   d. the rights of slaves
   e. none of the above

6. President Jackson's handpicked successor was:
   a. John Quincy Adams
   b. Daniel Webster
   c. Martin Van Buren
   d. Dan Quayle
   e. Jimmy Kimmel

7. After the Texas Revolution in 1836, Texas became an independent republic. But they requested annexation by
   a. Great Britain
   b. France
   c. the United States
   d. OZ
   e. none of the above

8. _____ received the most popular votes in the Election of 1824.
   a. John Quincy Adams
   b. Andrew Jackson
   c. Henry Clay
   d. Ralph Nader
   e. Steven Colbert

9. "Sam" Houston became the chief leader and hero of
   a. the Texas rebels
   b. the Redcoats
   c. the U.S. Army
   d. Alcoholics Anonymous
   e. all of the above

10. The Mexican War was fought between the United States and
    a. Mexico
    b. Spain
    c. this question is an insult to my intelligence
    d. a and c
    e. c and a

CHAPTER 6

STUMBLING INTO WAR

or

We're Running Out Of Compromises

Ever since the Constitutional Convention, America had always found ways to compromise on the issue of slavery and keep the Union together. But the 1850s brought new leaders to center stage. Unfortunately, most of them turned out to be bad actors, and the American people soon found out it was too late to get their money back. This "Blundering Generation" hesitated and bumbled, and in the ensuing brouhaha raised the curtain on Civil War.

NORTHERN LIFE AT MID-CENTURY
or *Hey, I've Never Seen That Before!*

Alexis de Tocqueville, a French historian and political philosopher, journeyed across the Atlantic in the early 1830s and was quite impressed. He produced a remarkably insightful book entitled ***Democracy in America,*** in which he described the United States as a nation of great opportunity and equality. He was also amazed at how restless and constantly in motion Americans seemed to be compared to staid Europeans. De Tocqueville was particularly annoyed during his trip when he would go to visit someone only to find they had moved.

At mid-century, Americans were on the move all right, but nobody seemed to be sure where they were going and how they were going to get there. Back in 1830, **Peter Cooper** had built a steam locomotive (nicknamed *Tom Thumb*) and challenged a horse to a race. There was an uncomfortable few moments when the horse did not respond, but then his owner accepted. The *Tom Thumb* broke down and the horse won, but everyone realized the railroad bugs would be quickly worked out. By 1860 railroad tracks wove across the land like spider webs. Industry flourished as raw materials sped east to factories and finished products returned rapidly west to eager customers. Keep in mind these early railroads were quite dangerous. Derailments were common, deadly accidents the norm and flying sparks sometimes set passengers' clothing on fire...circumstances eerily similar to travel today on Amtrak.

Beginning in the mid-1840s, American shipbuilders produced sexy fast moving sailing vessels called **clipper ships**. Northern merchants made their move and began trading profitably as far away as Asia. But the clippers' star shone very briefly. Within ten years the Brits were building faster and more spacious ironclad steamships that, though homely, soon monopolized Neptune's dance floor.

By 1854, the United States boasted warships powered by steam, and Commodore **Matthew Perry** (no relation to the guy on the TV show *Friends*) commanded nine of them on a visit to the Japanese islands, where the inhabitants lived in a manner similar to medieval feudalism, completely isolated from the western world. The Japanese wore what looked like bathrobes, carried samurai swords and bowed a lot, which the Americans at first found difficult to do without bumping their heads. They were intimidated enough by the steam-powered show of force to sign the **Treaty of Kanagawa,** establishing diplomatic relations and opening some ports to U.S. trade. A few years later the Japanese decided to industrialize (and create a modern army and navy) so they wouldn't fall into the clutches of western imperialist nations. They would be so successful that about eighty years later they'll have the rice balls to launch a sneak attack against Pearl Harbor, Hawaii. But we are getting ahead of ourselves.

Samuel B. Morse discovered how to send electrical impulses over wires so people miles away from each other could communicate instantaneously. In 1844, he strung wires from Washington to Baltimore, and using **Morse Code** (how convenient!) sent the immortal message: "What hath God wrought?" Clearly Morse took himself very seriously, but everyone had to admit the **telegraph** was groundbreaking. Soon, telegraph poles and wires snaked about the country alongside the railroad tracks; it became possible to send good and bad news via telegram, and for an extra fee a messenger would deliver a "singing telegram." A "stripogram" is a late twentieth-century innovation that Samuel B. Morse and his contemporaries never would have imagined.

Up in the North, improvements in transportation and communication fueled industrial growth, and vice versa. Existing cities expanded and new cities sprang up as many Americans deserted the drudgery of farm life and hopped a train for the new factories. Unfortunately, they soon found that conditions in the factories actually made shoveling out a pigsty seem appealing. As early as the 1820s, workers formed labor unions and attempted strikes, demanding better working conditions and higher pay, but to no avail. These early unions were both illegal and unsuccessful, and due to the hostile actions of factory owners and police, hazardous to the members' health. Besides, more and more immigrants were pouring in every day — Irish fleeing famine and Germans fleeing political unrest and the increasing popularity of the accordion — so there was always a ready supply of able-bodied men, women and children willing to work for starvation wages.

The 1830s and 40s were decades of considerable mob violence, as native-born Americans and immigrant groups formed neighborhood gangs and clashed in city streets. This led to the formation of the first professional police forces in this country, and thus the first arrest for DHWI (driving a horse while intoxicated). In the 1840s, **nativists** (native-born Protestant Americans contemptuous of immigration in general and Catholics in particular) formed the American party, which everybody called the **"Know-Nothing"** party. Ironically, the name is appropriate given the stupidity of the party's credo, but in reality it derived from a member's required pledge to say "I know nothing" when questioned about their activities. Parades and banners blew the whole secrecy thing anyway, and to America's lasting shame the Know-Nothing party gained considerable support in both the North and South; by 1855 the party controlled several state legislatures, and in Congress had elected five senators and forty-three representatives. Forget that melting pot your fifth grade teacher told you about — America was really one big boiling cauldron.

LIFE IN THE SOUTH AND SLAVERY

or It Is Not "Peculiar," It Is Immoral

While the Industrial Revolution percolated in the North, the South remained tied to agriculture, producing tobacco, sugar cane, rice, and to a lesser extent wheat, rye and oats. But cotton was king. Thanks to Eli Whitney's invention of the cotton gin to easily remove those pesky little seeds, and the ravenous appetites of cotton mills in the North and England, a few large plantation owners got even richer than they had been before, lived in columned mansions and owned hundreds of slaves. This wealthy one percent dominated state politics and local society, and generally expected to get exactly what they wanted exactly when they wanted it...kind of like my ex-wife. It is important to note that about eighty percent of white southerners did not own a single slave, and nineteen percent owned five or less, but poorer whites fiercely defended the institution of slavery. Why? You could ask your psychology teacher for more info (or your therapist if you are older), but it seems lower class whites liked having another group worse off to look down upon. And there was always the long shot that someone might strike it rich and graduate up to the drinking-mint-juleps-on-the-veranda class.

Treatment of African-American slaves varied depending upon circumstances, particularly the personalities of the slave owner and his **overseer**, a white (or sometimes black) man in charge of making sure the slaves continually worked hard. Physical brutality and murders did occur, but they were definitely not the norm, as slaves were valuable property and an investment. Field hands fared the worst, followed by slave artisans (like bricklayers or carpenters) and household servants who might even be entrusted with child care and treated affectionately like a family pet. If your name was Kunta Kinte you were really screwed, even though your television miniseries "Roots" in the 1970s would open many eyes. To be sure, black slaves were not treated as humans, though, looking back, it was really the slave owners who debased their humanity.

Of course, African-American slaves hated their chains. They engaged in work slow-downs, sabotage, and did not produce nearly as efficiently as a free wage earner would. Even though the whites had all the power, weapons and organization, there were violent slave revolts. In 1822, **Denmark Vesey** organized a slave uprising in Charleston, South Carolina that failed when one of his co-conspirators squealed. In 1831, **Nat Turner** led a band of escaped slaves through the Virginia countryside that killed 57 whites. State troops responded and exacted a bloody revenge. Southerners became so terrified of the possibility of slave revolts they enacted **slave codes** to control African-Americans' behavior. Both slaves and free blacks could not vote, move freely from state to state, or congregate in groups larger than three. Days off to honor the likes of Vesey and Turner were definitely out of the question.

Believe it or not, white southerners actually tried to defend the institution of slavery — what they called their **"peculiar institution"** — with logic. They pointed out that ancient Greece and Rome embraced slavery, neglecting to mention that slavery in those places had not been based upon race but upon prisoner of war status. They announced that life on the plantation was better for blacks than life in Africa or a northern factory town. What they refused to admit, of course, is that life in bondage is never better than a free life no matter what the circumstances. Southern "Christians" claimed the Bible condoned slavery while being continually vague on page numbers. "Physicians" declared blacks were mentally and physically inferior, claims that have been put to rest once and for all in our modern age by the decoding of DNA and the career of Denzel Washington.

Naturally, all the proslavery arguments were a bunch of garbage. This was an age before washers and dryers and irons and refrigerators and all the mechanized gadgets we now take for granted. With one group of people determined to live the pampered good life, another group of people was forced to do the dirty work. All forms of slavery are cruel and barbarous, but the American model based upon race is probably the worst of all. At slave auctions, children were pulled from their parents' arms and husbands and wives separated. Sickening...and in some Northern stomachs at least, bile began to rise.

Up until the mid-1800s, most Northerners felt that slavery, as unpleasant as it might be, was the South's business. Free blacks up North encountered lots of race prejudice, particularly from arriving immigrants with whom they competed for low-wage jobs. In 1817 the **American Colonization Society** proposed shipping blacks "back where they came from," and the country of Liberia (with its capital of Monrovia named after the President) was established for this purpose on the west coast of Africa. This was a dumb idea from the start because logistically, the ships did not exist that could provide transportation for such massive numbers, and more importantly, most African-Americans by this time were generations removed from Africa and had no desire to relocate to a foreign land. They were Americans — discriminated against and enslaved — who nevertheless desired to stay home. Lots of bright people who should have known better (like Abraham Lincoln) advocated for colonization for decades, proving that even smart people can believe in stupid things. This partially explains the popularity of streaking on college campuses in the 1970s...it seemed like a good idea at the time.

Abolitionists (men and women actively opposed to slavery) risked life and limb if they spoke out publicly. In 1831, **William Lloyd Garrison** began publishing a radical anti-slavery newspaper called *The Liberator*. Garrison pulled no punches about the evils of slavery, went so far as to advocate that the North secede from the Union to get away from the wicked South, and most galling of all, failed to include a sports section. His presses were frequently trashed and he was beaten time and time again. The **American Anti-Slavery Society** was founded in 1833 but failed to put forth any practical plan for the abolishment of slavery. Boycotting slave-produced cotton and sugar cane was a nice gesture, but wealthy southerners barely noticed. Great Britain abolished slavery in its New World colonies that same year by paying compensation to the slaveowners — expensive and distasteful, but at least they were done with it.

In the United States, great African-American voices cried out against slavery. **Frederick Douglass**, an escaped slave, was a gifted writer and lecturer who continually endured beatings and threats. **Sojourner Truth** moved audiences to tears as she focused on religion and the "sin" of slavery. **Harriet Tubman** started the **Underground Railroad.** No, it was not actually a railroad running underground — then they would have called it the Underground Subway — but it certainly functioned like a railroad. Originating in the South, traveling mostly at night, escaped slaves were spirited from one "safe house" to another until they reached the North or sometimes all the way up to Canada. Harriet Tubman was one of many "conductors" who risked their lives on the Underground Railroad, on which passengers considered themselves fortunate to be able to ride for many hours under a pile of hay.

By the 1850s, the antislavery agitation in the North had clearly made a huge dent in public opinion. Diminutive **Harriet Beecher Stowe** hefted a sledgehammer when she published a novel entitled *Uncle Tom's Cabin*, the first major work of American fiction to dramatically portray slave characters as sympathetic human beings. Without ever being an Oprah Winfrey Book Club selection, *Uncle Tom's Cabin* became a best seller in the North. Millions of people read the book or saw the stage adaptation and came to hate slavery. There is no more important book in American history, even though in the South copies were banned and burned.

THE POLITICS OF SLAVERY
or *We're Running Out Of Compromises*

During the Mexican War, a Congressman from Pennsylvania named David Wilmot introduced a resolution forbidding slavery in any territory the United States might win from Mexico. The **Wilmot Proviso** passed in the Northern dominated House of Representatives but went down to defeat in the evenly divided Senate. When America defeated Mexico and gained Texas and the Mexican Cession, few were surprised when the status of slavery in the new territories reignited sectional passions. President Polk worked himself so hard that he developed chronic diarrhea and was forced to limit himself to one four-year term and increase his fiber intake.

In 1848 the Democrats held their convention in Baltimore and nominated an aging veteran of the War of 1812, General and now Senator from Michigan **Lewis Cass**. Seeking support from both the North and the South, the Democratic **platform** (a formal statement of the party's views) completely ignored the divisive issue of slavery. Cass himself had come up with an idea he christened **popular sovereignty**, the view that people of a territory should vote and determine for themselves the status of slavery. Unfortunately for Cass, his opponents would have a field day with a name that rhymed with both "Gas" and "Ass."

The Whigs met in Philadelphia and chose a hero from the just-completed Mexican War, General Zachary Taylor. Taylor was perfect because he was the "Hero of Buena Vista" and, more importantly, had never publicly committed himself on the issue of slavery extension and in fact never bothered to vote in his life. His supporters quickly changed the subject when someone mentioned that the general owned a huge sugar plantation with many slaves who called him *Massa*.

Lots of anti-slavery folks in the North didn't trust Cass or Taylor, so they created a new party the **Free Soil Party** and wheeled out the old former president, Martin Van Buren. Taylor won the general election in November, probably because American voters are continually infatuated with war heroes, but Cass came close, though the Free-Soil Party garnered enough votes from Cass in New York to swing that critical state and thus the entire election to Taylor. Whigs and Democrats alike worried how much longer they could continue to excuse themselves and run to the bathroom every time someone brought up the slavery question.

The issue of whether or not the federal government possessed the authority to ban slavery in the new territories came to a head after gold was discovered in 1848 out in California. The next year, thousands of **Forty-Niners** (a great name for a football team) raced out there to try their luck panning for nuggets (a great name for a basketball team). Few of these fledgling excavators actually struck it rich and when they did, crafty businessmen frequently swindled them out of their claims. A more reliable way to get rich during the gold rush was to set up a business catering to the miners and then rip them off. Smelly, thirsty, horny miners with a smidgen of gold dust in their pockets would pay almost any price for a bath, a bottle of whiskey and a woman, not necessarily in that order.

California applied to enter the Union as a "free" state in 1849. Since this eventuality would upset the balance of free and slave states, the you-know-what hit the fan just as it had done in 1820 (Remember the Missouri Compromise?). Henry Clay sprang into action once again. By this time he was seventy-three years old, and lacking access to Viagra, he had nothing better to do. Assisted by a young senator from Illinois named **Stephen A. Douglas**, Clay urged a series of concessions upon both the North and South. South Carolina's John C. Calhoun died during the debate, and that was probably just as well because he had been adamantly opposed to the South making any concessions. Supposedly his last words were "The South! The South! God knows what will become of her?" But always be suspicious when you hear about famous last words.

Sixty-eight-year-old Daniel Webster had one great speech left in him, in which he urged the North to make concessions to the South in the interest of preserving the Union. He declared that he was speaking "not as a northern man but as an American." Most southerners, completely missing Webster's point, thought to themselves, *Yeah, but you're an American from the North.* The debate in Congress seesawed back and forth and it looked for a while like there would be a deadlock. Then suddenly President Taylor died, reportedly of a severe intestinal disorder. Given what had befallen President Polk, it is surprising the White House chef was not brought up on charges, or at least told to stop serving chili. Anyway, Taylor had been opposed to compromise, but his Vice President — now President — **Millard Fillmore** threw his support behind it and the congressional logjam was broken.

Here's the deal that became known as the **Compromise of 1850**: (1) California was admitted to the Union as a free state; (2) the rest of the Mexican Cession was divided into the territories of Utah and New Mexico, and would follow the principle of popular sovereignty (the citizens themselves would vote to determine whether or not they would allow slavery); (3) Texas was paid $10 million to help with its debts in exchange for a strip of land that was given to New Mexico; (4) slave trading (but not slavery itself) was outlawed in the District of Columbia; and (5) a strict **Fugitive Slave Law** was put in place to assist southerners in recovering slaves who had escaped to the North. Nobody on either side danced a jig over any of this.

Most historians now believe the North gained the most in the Compromise of 1850. The admission of free California permanently wrecked the delicate balance in the Senate, and the desert lands of Utah and New Mexico were not particularly suited to a slave economy. The Fugitive Slave Law caused the most controversy. Federal commissioners were paid ten dollars if they ruled blacks to be escaped slaves and five dollars if they set them free — a bribe no matter how you slice it. Blacks captured in the North were not allowed a jury trial nor permitted to testify on their own behalf, and there were no African-American lawyers like Johnnie Cochran around back then to cry foul. But by this time most Northerners had come to detest slavery, so the vast majority of them refused to cooperate, and in numerous cases aided escaped slaves and harassed federal commissioners. This "Bloodhound Bill" and "Man-Stealing Law" appalled Northerners, and when they refused to be bound by it, Southerners were appalled in turn. Then South Carolina and company got a dose of their own nullification medicine when many northern states passed **Personal Liberty Laws** that contradicted the Fugitive Slave Law.

Even though most Americans from the North and South alike disagreed with parts of the Compromise of 1850, there was a general hope that the slavery controversy could finally be put to rest. In the presidential election of 1852, both the Whigs and the Democrats (as usual trying to appeal to all sections of the country) offered half-hearted support for the Compromise. The Democrats nominated a northern man with southern sympathies, **Franklin Pierce** of New Hampshire. The Whigs turned their backs on President Fillmore and chose yet another war hero, General Winfield Scott.

Nobody wanted to deal with the serious and difficult issues facing the country, so Americans endured another lowbrow campaign. Pierce, who did have a fondness for alcohol, was ridiculed for falling off his horse during the Mexican War. Scott, a talented military officer, was so pompous (his nickname was "Old Fuss and Feathers") that he alienated vast numbers of rank and file voters and even his horse, who resented his massive bulk. Though the popular vote was reasonably close, Pierce won a landslide in the Electoral College, mainly because southern Whigs didn't trust Scott to uphold the Fugitive Slave Law. This election hopelessly divided the Whigs and brought about their disintegration. But like the deceased Federalists of an earlier generation, the Whigs had contributed mightily to a still youthful United States. Their legacy was one of great leaders like Clay and Webster who labored tirelessly to preserve the Union.

President Pierce deeply believed in American expansion, and would have loved to annex Cuba and all of Central America, not to mention Hawaii and the whole planet if he could get away with it. Pierce's Secretary of State William L. Marcy conspired to release a State Department memorandum — the **Ostend Manifesto** — calling for the United States to purchase Cuba from Spain or, failing that, acquire it by force. European and Northern outrage forced President Pierce to repudiate the Ostend Manifesto, and Secretary of State Marcy (his face like the Sphinx) deftly blamed it on American Minister to Spain Pierre Soulé, who dutifully resigned.

Cuba, Central America, and Hawaii would presumably support slavery, so northern congressmen refused to allow "manifest destiny" to head overseas. In spite of the potential for incredible surfing vacations without having to leave the country, there was no way the United States could annex any foreign lands without reigniting the slavery controversy. For the time being, U.S. policy would only focus on keeping these strategic areas independent, weak, and free from foreign control.

In 1854, Senator Douglas declared that the Platte country, a largely uninhabited area to the west of Missouri and Iowa, should be granted territorial status. He claimed that he was patriotically dedicated to a "continuous line of settlement to the Pacific Ocean" but his investments in a railroad company no doubt colored his vision. He pushed through Congress a bill called the **Kansas-Nebraska Act.** It divided the remaining land of the Louisiana Purchase into the territories of Kansas and Nebraska, and allowed the inhabitants of those territories to decide for themselves the status of slavery according to the democratic principle of popular sovereignty. But because the Missouri Compromise of 1820 had outlawed slavery that far north, the Kansas-Nebraska Act also required the repeal of that hallowed legislation. Abolitionists in the North were furious, and Henry Clay rolled over in his grave only to realize he was sleeping alone for a change. Douglas hoped his measure would dampen flames in the North and South, but he actually added kerosene. In short, the stubby little schemer from Illinois screwed up big time.

When it came time for a vote in Kansas to set up a territorial legislature, both sides tried to stuff the ballot box. Groups like the New England Emigrant Aid Company had helped finance settlers who promised to be staunch abolitionists. Then on Election Day, "border ruffians" from proslavery Missouri poured into Kansas and made a mockery of the democratic principle of "one man one vote." The proslavery faction claimed victory in the fraudulent election, but the antislavery forces decided to elect their own governor and their own legislature, so for a while Kansas had two governments. Prominent Protestant preacher **Henry Ward Beecher** (brother of novelist Harriet Beecher Stowe) — in a convoluted interpretation of Scripture — proclaimed that guns would be more useful out in Kansas than Bibles, and northern abolitionists sent new breech-loading rifles nicknamed "Beecher's Bibles" to their allies. The proslavery forces were already armed and, not surprisingly, violence broke out, especially when someone made the mistake of saying the wrong thing in the wrong state capital.

Onto the Kansas stage stepped the schizophrenic personage of **John Brown**. Fiercely dedicated to the worthy cause of abolition but also a mentally unbalanced fanatic, Brown and his small band murdered and desecrated the bodies of five proslavers in retaliation for an attack on the free-soil town of Lawrence. Vengeance begat more vengeance, and soon a mini civil war ensued that newspaper headlines back east christened **"Bleeding Kansas."** President Pierce could have acted forcefully and brought down the curtain on the whole mess — another federally supervised election was clearly called for — but he was so afraid of offending both sides that he did nothing. Pierce was the sort of guy who would hide under the covers every time it thundered.

Around this time a remarkable event took place in the United States Senate that demonstrated how freaked out everyone was over the issue of slavery. Senator **Charles Sumner** of Massachusetts, a staunch but pompous abolitionist, gave an anti-slavery speech in which he made fun of South Carolina Senator Andrew Butler's tendency to drool. Two days later, Congressman **Preston Brooks**, Butler's nephew, strolled onto the floor of the Senate and pounded Sumner with his cane until the senator was unconscious and the cane shattered in pieces. Senator Sumner was so popular with his colleagues that no one moved a muscle to protect him. He was badly injured and needed over three years to recover, but his outraged constituents in Massachusetts defiantly reelected him anyway. Brooks resigned his seat in the House and returned to South Carolina, where the people showed their appreciation by reelecting him and sending him back to Washington with as many gold tipped canes as he could carry. It was not uncommon during this period for senators and congressmen to carry concealed pistols and knives under their jackets when they entered the Capitol Building. Tensions ran high and there was lots of showing off in the coatroom.

In 1854, fed up with their party's dithering on the slavery issue, a bunch of former Whigs and Democrats gathered in Wisconsin and Michigan and formed a party fiercely dedicated to stopping the spread of slavery to the territories and repealing the Kansas-Nebraska Act. They called themselves the Republicans, and this was the birth of the modern-day Republican Party. No matter what you think of what the party has become, with its general hostility towards government programs for the poor and antediluvian stances on social issues, it is undeniable that the GOP (Grand Old Party) sprang from noble beginnings. Within a couple of years the Republicans controlled most northern state governments, and had established credit accounts at many fashionable taverns.

In 1856, the Republicans hoped to capture the White House — no, not attack it with military force, this is America remember — so they nominated John C. Frémont, a Mexican War veteran and famed western "Pathfinder." Frémont had no political experience, no direct connection to the Kansas-Nebraska debacle, a pushy wife, and his name lent itself to a terrific slogan: "Free speech, free soil, free press, free men, Frémont and victory." When party leaders told him that he was an abolitionist he probably said, "Sure, but what is that?" (He had spent way too much time in the mountains). One prominent Republican who would never get the chance to run for the presidency was Senator **William Seward** of New York. During the Kansas debate, Seward had stated that a "higher law" should prevent the spread of slavery to the territories. Suggesting that the Bible supersedes the Constitution, however, doesn't fly in this country...ever.

The Democrats, still trying to soft-pedal the slavery issue and appeal to all sections of the country, nominated a northern man with southern sympathies, **James Buchanan** of Pennsylvania. Fortuitously, Buchanan had been having tea and crumpets (as minister to Great Britain) during the Kansas-Nebraska fracas. He was a bachelor with a longtime male roommate, so you can imagine the rumors that abounded at the time and still persist to this day. There is no record that Buchanan particularly enjoyed Broadway show tunes, and obviously his sexuality has nothing to do with his measure as a politician or a person. So let's show some class and just drop it.

The anti-foreign Know-Nothing party really galvanized itself for the election of 1856. They nominated ex-President Millard Fillmore and commenced throwing mud at both Buchanan and Frémont. Their favorite slogan — Americans Must Rule America — was about as anti-American as you can get. Fortunately, they got their butts kicked and began to disintegrate as a political force. A basic American credo seemed to assert itself: immigration and diversity brings our country strength and energy (and the low-wage workers we need to take the really lousy jobs established Americans don't want.)

Buchanan won. Frémont did not carry a single Southern state, but he came close in the Electoral College by carrying all but five of the free states in the North. President Buchanan began his term hoping everybody would just stay calm. But most Americans were really hyper, and unfortunately for the President, Ritalin was not available.

Next, the Supreme Court stumbled into the fray. A slave named **Dred Scott** had been taken by his master into the free territory of Minnesota. When they returned to Missouri (a slave state, remember), abolitionists created a test case in which Scott sued for his freedom on the grounds that his residence on free soil had made him a free man. The whole shebang ended up in the Supreme Court, whereupon America's distinguished "court of last resort" completely dropped the ball. Dominated by southerners, in 1857 it ruled in the **Dred Scott Decision** that Scott, being a black man, was not a citizen and therefore ineligible to bring suit. Confusingly, there were several northern states where blacks did have citizenship status, and about a quarter of a million free blacks in the South whose legal status was now completely muddled.

It was a horrible decision, but did the Court stop there? No. Chief Justice **Roger B. Taney** — an emaciated bag of bones whose appearance scared small children — convinced a majority of justices to rule that since slaves were property, and the Fifth Amendment to the Constitution specifically protected private property, Congress could not forbid slavery in the territories on the grounds that this would be depriving people of their property. The Missouri Compromise had been unconstitutional all along. Southerners were ecstatic, northerners outraged, and Taney earned a place in History as a committed racist who helped push the nation into civil war. There's a lesson to be learned here. Just because Supreme Court justices wear black robes and appear solemn doesn't guarantee they are always right. On occasion, they are biased and ignorant. Look at a photograph of the current Court. You definitely get the feeling that under those robes at least one of them is wearing just a thong.

When the proslavery faction out in Kansas demanded that Kansas be admitted to the Union as a slave state under the fraudulent **Lecompton Constitution**, President Buchanan, under the thumb of his southern advisors, compliantly assented. This assault on popular sovereignty outraged Senator Douglas, who in a meeting with the President basically told him to "stick the Lecompton Constitution where the moon don't shine." (Or words to that effect.) Douglas stood up to the leader of his own party and Congress temporarily blocked Kansas' bid to become a state.

In 1857, a severe economic depression hit the country. Many businessmen had speculated irrationally in land or railroads, and finally the bubble burst as bubbles always do (Ask anyone who bought internet stocks in the 1990s). At the same time, western wheat farmers were actually producing more than they could sell at home and abroad, causing prices (and their profits) to plummet. The South weathered the depression rather well because demand did not slacken for cotton, and as a result they got the mistaken idea that their southern cotton economy was stronger and more stable than northern industry. Boy, were they cruisin' for a bruisin'.

In 1858 (halfway through Buchanan's term) there was a midterm election for Senate that attracted nationwide attention. Democratic Senator Stephen Douglas ran for reelection against a relatively unknown Republican challenger, **Abraham Lincoln**. Lincoln had sprung from humble roots — a log cabin in Kentucky — to become a popular trial attorney in his adopted state of Illinois. All that legendary stuff you've heard about him is basically true. He probably did walk several miles through the snow to get to school, though it is not recorded how many times he was late. He probably did lie on his stomach in front of the fireplace to read, though it is not recorded how many times his hair caught on fire. He certainly excelled at "wrastlin" and rail splitting. Legend has it that when he worked as a store clerk, he accidentally shortchanged an old woman and walked hours to return her a penn,y though it is not recorded whether she handed him back the penny as a tip, making the whole exercise a waste of time. The point here is that lots of folks liked him and his nickname "Honest Abe" fit him well. He loved telling long stories, which were usually entertaining except when someone was in a hurry and all they wanted was a yes or no answer.

Lincoln had left the Whigs and, opposed to the spread of slavery to the territories, easily found a home in the new Republican Party. When he challenged Douglas to a series of debates and the senator accepted, the two men standing side by side on a platform presented a striking contrast. Douglas was short, stocky and impeccably dressed. Lincoln was six feet four inches tall, gangly, and perpetually wrinkled with his hair full of cowlicks. Douglas loved formal oratory, Lincoln would go for a joke, and they were both brilliant in their own way. Lincoln wore a tall stovepipe hat in which he would carry important papers and perhaps some fried chicken. It is not known whether or not anyone ever offered to lend Abe a briefcase.

At the **Lincoln-Douglas Debate** in Freeport, Illinois, Lincoln pressured Douglas to state his position on the spread of slavery to the territories. Douglas replied that it looked like it might rain. But finally he stopped stalling and announced that the Dred Scott decision made slavery technically legal in the territories, but the people living out there could keep slavery out by simply not keeping slaves. This half-assed answer (remembered as the **Freeport Doctrine**) was good enough to get Douglas reelected in Illinois in 1858, but two years later when he ran for the presidency, southerners didn't trust him. Lincoln, flat out opposed to the spread of slavery, received favorable newspaper coverage that made him popular among Republicans across the North.

With passions at a fever pitch, the last thing the country needed to deal with was another abolitionist outrage hatched in the mentally deranged mind of John Brown. This time his plan was to capture the federal arsenal at **Harper's Ferry**, Virginia, arm the local slaves and initiate a slave uprising. Brown and a few followers did manage to occupy the arsenal but then the plan, boneheaded from the outset, began to fall apart. Analogous to a scene in the woods when two campers look at each other and say "I thought you brought the food!" Brown and company realized no one had bothered to clue the local slaves in on the plot. A detachment of U.S. marines under the command of Lieutenant Colonel Robert E. Lee (oh, the irony) swiftly stifled the insurrection and captured Brown.

John Brown was obviously insane but the modern science of psychology did not exist yet in America, so Brown and his co-conspirators were tried for murder, treason, and conspiracy by the state of Virginia. Somehow, he managed to conduct himself with great dignity during the trial and solemnly spouted biblical passages right up to the moment in which he was hanged. Southerners considered John Brown an antichrist but Northerners made him into a martyr. Both sides sang songs about him, but the Southern songs weren't very nice.

Many people hoped the presidential election of 1860 would somehow goad the North and South into reaching a compromise, but the opposite occurred. The Democratic Party held several conventions and finally split apart — good for the hotel business, but disastrous for the party's chances of winning in November. The Northern Democrats nominated Stephen Douglas and proclaimed their support for popular sovereignty. The Southern Democrats nominated **John C. Breckinridge** of Kentucky and demanded the legal extension of slavery into all the territories. The Republicans were thrilled at this turn of events because, with the opposition now divided, they had a real chance of victory.

At their convention in Chicago, the Republicans passed over party leader Seward, whose big mouth (he had alarmingly called the slavery issue an "irrepressible conflict") made lots of folks nervous. They found a compromise candidate in the moderate personage of Abraham Lincoln. Abe and the Republicans pledged to oppose the extension of slavery to the territories but leave it alone in the states where it already existed. To make sure they would win in the North and West they promised a protective tariff, federal aid for internal improvements, a transcontinental railroad, free homestead farms and, on election day, free shots of bourbon. There were no bumper stickers back then because horses would have objected.

A fourth party, calling itself the **Constitutional Union Party**, announced support for the Union and the Constitution and nominated **John Bell** of Tennessee. Basically this was just a bunch of old Whigs, Know-Nothings, and fed up Democrats calling for all sides to calm down and remember the good old days. But it was too late for that and even Bell had to admit he had no new ideas.

Lincoln won basically by default. He carried the North and West solidly and crushed all the other candidates in the Electoral College. But he garnered only forty percent of the popular vote and did not carry a single Southern state. All this was legal, but Lincoln was clearly a sectional president taking office without much of a popular mandate, and the South freaked. They shouldn't have — the Democrats still held a majority on the Supreme Court and in the Senate — but it was hard to stop themselves in the middle of a temper tantrum. On December 20, 1860, South Carolina held a state convention and seceded. That troublesome state should have been placed in time out, but no one did anything. In the next several weeks six other states (Georgia, Florida,

Alabama, Mississippi, Louisiana, and Texas) followed suit. Lame duck Buchanan continued to dither, claiming that no state had the right to secede, but the President lacked constitutional authority to use federal force to prevent it. The spanking, apparently, would be left to Lincoln.

In early February 1861, the seceding states met in Montgomery, Alabama, and officially formed a new country called the **Confederate States of America**. They chose a red, white and blue flag of stars and crossed bars that would be perfect for future generations of redneck morons (unaware or not caring that the flag stands in large part for slavery) to place in the windows of their pickup trucks. They adopted a constitution very similar to the U.S. Constitution, with notable exceptions that slavery was guaranteed and ultimate authority rested in the hands of the states. Lots of folks on both sides still thought these **Confederates** were bluffing. In Washington, Senator Crittendon of Kentucky asked for yet another compromise, but none of his colleagues would even let him finish a sentence. The **Crittendon Plan** was too little too late.

Lincoln arrived at the Washington train station incognito out of fears that he might be assassinated. Rumors that he was in drag were unfounded and absurd, since Lincoln would have been about six feet eight in high heels. After he was sworn in, he gave an inauguration address in men's clothes that was both firm and conciliatory. Again, he promised not to touch slavery where it already existed, but he reminded the South that he had a taken a solemn oath to "preserve, protect and defend" the Union. "In your hands, my dissatisfied countrymen, and not in mine, is the momentous issue of civil war." In other words, the President was telling the South, *if you want to fight, you are going to have to start it.*

South Carolina had seceded, but forces loyal to the Union continued to occupy **Fort Sumter** in Charleston harbor, and soon they were running out of food and water. Lincoln did not want to wimp out and let them surrender, but he still wanted to avoid initiating a military clash, so he prudently ordered a halfway measure. He announced that he would send provisions to the garrison at Fort Sumter but no more men or ammunition. The South Carolinians bombarded the fort anyway and, running low on supplies, Major Robert Anderson lowered the stars and stripes and surrendered. He and his men were allowed to embark for New York on the relief ships, a nice gesture that could not hide the fact that a battle had been fought and blood spilled...even though relatively speaking it was just a paper cut. The Confederate states were in open rebellion, the fight had been joined, and finally the Civil War had begun. Lots of folks with scheduled vacations had to cancel.

Well, so much for compromise and peace. The South decided to sue for divorce and the North decided to fight it. As usual in war and marriage, both sides thought they were going to win quickly. But four years of frightful slaughter lay ahead. Which side is going to keep the furniture? Will America ever be able to live together again? Uh oh...stay tuned...don't touch that dial!!!

This Really Happened!

Abraham Lincoln, a Republican relatively unknown nationally, contests for the Senate seat from Illinois with the Democratic incumbent, the "Little Giant," Stephen A. Douglas. They engage in a series of seven remarkable debates on the subject of slavery in the territories, in which the well-groomed and polished Douglas, with stocky figure and bullish voice, offers a striking contrast to the six foot four Lincoln in his unshined shoes and baggy clothes. Well known for his often self-deprecating wit, Lincoln has a great comeback when Douglas calls him two-faced. "I leave it to my audience," honest Abe says. "If I had another face, do you think I would wear this one?"

And the rest is History...

Quiz yourself on Chapter 6

Multiple Choice (circle the correct answer).

1. Up in the North, improvements in transportation and communication fueled
   a. industrial growth
   b. greater respect between employer and employee
   c. a population shift back to rural areas
   d. more business trips by wayward husbands
   e. none of the above

2. The Know-Nothing Party
   a. was mainly composed of nativists
   b. was founded upon equal rights for all
   c. would have been perfect for George W. Bush
   d. both a and c
   e. not a or c

3. The institution of slavery
   a. sucked
   b. was a shameful part of our American History
   c. was actually defended by most Southerners
   d. all of the above
   e. none of the above, except d

4. The issue of whether or not the federal government had the right to ban slavery in the new territories came to a head after
   a. General Winfield Scott sat on his horse and killed it
   b. Henry Clay mistakenly opened his big mouth
   c. gold was discovered in California and Americans rushed out to the new territories
   d. the invention of the whoopee cushion
   e. d and a

5. The Fugitive Slave Law
   a. was generally ignored by Northerners
   b. was applauded by Southerners
   c. inflamed abolitionists in the North
   d. all of the above
   e. none of the above

6. The Whigs were
   a. bald
   b. a British musical group
   c. a political party in opposition to the Democrats
   d. the party of Jackson
   e. none of the above

7. Henry Ward Beecher was
   a. a Prostestant preacher
   b. full of himself
   c. brother of novelist Harriet Beecher Stowe
   d. all of the above
   e. none of the above

8. "Bleeding Kansas" refers to
   a. a guy named "Kansas" who kept falling down
   b. Royals fans after the Yankees purchase another superstar
   c. violent conflict between pro- and anti-slavery forces in that state
   d. none of the above
   e. all of the above

9. Senator Charles Sumner and Congressman Preston Brooks
   a. were lovers
   b. both loved grits
   c. fought together against slavery
   d. symbolized the violent nature of the slavery debate
   e. all of the above

10. The Dred Scott decision
    a. helped push America into the Civil War
    b. set Dred Scott free
    c. canceled one of the finest shows on Broadway
    d. demonstrated that the Supreme Court is always right
    e. none of the above

CHAPTER 7

THE CIVIL WAR

or

Blood, Sweat, and Lots of Tears

After the battle for Fort Sumter there were parties and parades, and lots of boys promised their best girl they would be married when the fighting was done. Guys making the same promise to several girls risked death both on the battlefield and at home. In any event, the War promised to be a grand adventure. No more talk about nullification and slavery...we would settle it with bullets and bayonets! Two civilizations clashed — the industrial North and the agricultural South, and because both sides were Americans, the Civil War proved to be the costliest of all our wars.

THE NORTH-SOUTH BALANCE SHEET
or *God Is On Our Side!*

It sure seems lame from the vantage point of History, but the South thought they were going to kick butt and be home eating grits in a matter of weeks or months at the most. Grits, by the way, is ground corn boiled into a mush which southerners still love to this day. Never order "one grit" down there — there is no such thing, and rednecks who flunked out of the fifth grade will try to beat you up in the parking lot.

The South only had to fight a defensive war; their supply and communications lines were shorter and they knew their own turf. The North had the more difficult task of conquering the Rebels and forcibly dragging them back into the Union. The boys from Dixie were more used to the outdoor life of riding and shooting hunting rifles...according to legend, babies down South were born gripping tiny muskets, which they refused to relinquish even when breast feeding. Lots of Union boys, by contrast, hailed from the big cities, where horses pulled cabs and a broken bottle sufficed for a street fight.

Most of the experienced military officers stayed loyal to their states in the South and joined the Confederacy — notably **Robert E. Lee** and **Thomas J. "Stonewall" Jackson.** Most of these officers were graduates of West Point or Virginia Military Institute, and many had fought in the Mexican War, but they were just too narrow in their outlooks to understand all the issues. It was true then and it is true now: we need our professional military forces to fight and protect us. They're good at it and we should honor them for their sacrifices, but most of these guys are behind the times when it comes to political or social issues, and just about all of them would really benefit from an appearance on *What Not To Wear*.

In reality, the North had the upper hand. It retained two-thirds of the states and boasted a population of 22 million, as opposed to the South's 9 million, of whom 3½ million were slaves and not exactly supportive. The South could not replace its losses while Northern recruiters could always grab another Irish kid getting off the boat in New York harbor. As casualties mounted, both sides resorted to **conscription,** (the **draft**).

Rich guys could legally buy their way out of serving by hiring a substitute, usually some poor schlep who desperately needed a few hundred bucks. In the South, slave overseers were exempt, and up North most wealthy businessmen opted for profits over patriotism. Many soldiers on both sides rightly derided the "rich man's war and the poor man's fight." Come to think of it, when in History has there ever been a "poor man's war and a rich man's fight?" Anyway, when the North offered a financial incentive for enlisting (a **bounty**), some ethically challenged young men got creative. They would enlist, get their money, desert, and rush to another place to enlist, get their money, desert and then start the process all over again. This **bounty jumping** was punishable by death, which was unfortunate because a lot of these guys might have made great politicians.

In 1863 the attempted enforcement of an unfair draft law in New York City sparked the worst riots ever in the United States — the **Civil War Draft Riots**. For four days, mobs took over the city — they even got hold of some cannons — and the police were afraid to go out after them even in groups of fifty. There were no precise statistics of the casualties of the fighting, only estimates kept by those who dragged the dead away to the East River or nameless graves in the city slums. Some African-Americans — hated because they competed for scarce jobs — were lynched in the melee. Conservative estimates put the number killed at over two thousand — roughly the number of American battle casualties in the War of 1812. The rioters were white, impoverished, and both Protestant and Catholic. This unsavory episode points out clearly that race or ethnicity does not predispose any one group of people to violent antisocial behavior. We must address poverty and stop the riots before they start. Liberals are right — nobody ever finishes a big meal, pats his stomach and yells, "Let's go riot." Now go outside and find a poor person and give them a big hug.

Virtually all the big banks and financial institutions were located in the North. The South printed mountains of paper currency without gold or silver to back it up, so lots of Confederate money ended up as wallpaper. The North successfully sold government bonds, raised the protective tariff, passed our nation's first federal income tax, and held one heck of an impressive bake sale in the hallway outside the White House cafeteria. The Union also retained control of the Navy and the merchant marine (The merchant marine consists of unarmed ships carrying cargo and manned by civilians who drink a lot while on duty). Lincoln ordered a naval blockade of the Confederacy that was pretty leaky at first (**blockade runners** took huge risks and made tidy profits), but within two years the Rebels were gagging over millions of tons of rotting cotton they couldn't export.

So desperate was the South to defeat the Union blockade, they raised a sunken Union gunboat named the **Merrimac** and covered its hull with iron plating. Cannon balls bounced off the Merrimac and the North's wooden warships bobbed about like sitting ducks. Luckily for the Northerners, their own version of an ironclad ship, the **Monitor**, showed up just in the nick of time. The two ships pounded each other for a whole day but neither was able to significantly damage the other. Both sides grew cranky and hot and finally decided to steam away. This was the first time ironclad warships had ever faced each other in warfare, and it demonstrated that wooden warships the world over were now obsolete. Eventually the Confederates had to destroy the *Merrimac* themselves to avoid her falling into enemy hands. Later, the South even tried building a primitive submarine but never successfully worked out the kinks. The sub sank a Union warship but blew itself up in the process. After that, it proved extremely difficult for the Confederates to recruit men to be submariners.

The North possessed ninety percent of the country's industry, more than twice the South's railroad mileage, and reportedly the world's first miniature golf course. Armament plants, iron mills and textile factories cranked out loads of war materiel for the Union, and food from western farms poured in continually. The South had to rely mostly on imports that quickly dried up due to the naval blockade. What were they supposed to do, throw cotton balls at the Yankees? Ever hear the expression *an army travels on its stomach?* It's true in any war: it doesn't matter how brave and well dressed you are, if you are hungry and out of ammunition you lose. That's precisely what happened to the Confederates.

Four wavering, slave-holding Border States — Delaware, Maryland, Kentucky and Missouri — stayed technically loyal to the Union. Lincoln swore this was a war to save the Union, not free the slaves, but when that wasn't enough the President proved more than willing to totally blow off the Constitution. At various times he declared martial law, suspended habeas corpus and sent in troops to make sure these critical states stayed faithful. Though Lincoln loved democracy and the rule of law, he wanted to win even more. State legislators in Maryland who favored secession were arrested on the road as they attempted to gather and vote. Virginia went south, but poor whites in the western mountains who resented the wealthy slaveholders would have none of it. In 1863 they entered the Union as the new state of **West Virginia**. Northerners were happy to welcome them and tactful enough not to mention their generally poor standards of dental hygiene.

The Confederacy expected both Great Britain and France to enter the war on its behalf, but it never happened. European aristocrats sympathized with their wealthy cousins in the South and fervently yearned for the creation of two competing nations out of one united (and frequently troublesome) nation. But the European masses hostile to slavery rooted for the North, causing government leaders in both London and Paris — fearing riots or at least nasty looks from the populace — to watch and wait. Unfortunately for the South, lots of folks in Western Europe depended upon Northern shipments of wheat, and English textile manufacturers found alternative sources of cotton in Egypt and India. In the battle of **King Cotton versus King Wheat**, King Cotton hit the canvas hard and stayed down for the count.

Despite this, England and France did cause problems for the North during the Civil War. In the **Trent Affair** (1861) a U.S. naval warship stopped the British steamship *Trent* and removed two Confederate commissioners, John Slidell and James Mason. Americans loved this turn of events, but British officials had a hissy fit and dropped their crumpets. They demanded an apology and the immediate release of the prisoners. Lincoln was practical and could bear insults for the good of the country, so to avoid a war with England which the North could ill afford, he ordered the release of the two men, who promptly continued on their merry way to London. After this, Great Britain continued to be a pain in the butt for the North. British shipbuilders provided the South with two warships, christened the *Florida* and the *Alabama*, that destroyed $15 million dollars worth of Northern shipping before the Union navy could capture them. Northerners wouldn't forget, even though those little yellow sticky notes had not been invented yet.

Then there were the French, who really had not been very nice since they helped us win the Revolution. Taking advantage of America's preoccupation with the Civil War, **Emperor Napoleon III** (nephew of the original Napoleon) decided to use French troops to install a puppet ruler in Mexico in the personage of his cousin Archduke Maximilian of Austria. The idea of a German-speaking Austrian ruling Hispanic Mexico at the behest of France sounds absurd, but that is precisely what Napoleon III tried to pull off. Secretary of State Seward reminded everyone who would listen that America resented this blatant violation of the Monroe Doctrine, but with the Civil War raging there was nothing else he could do. After the war, though, it was a different story. The United States sent thousands of soldiers to the Texas border with Mexico and threatened to invade. Napoleon III backed down in 1867 and pulled out his troops, but a delusional Maximilian convinced himself the Mexican people loved him and wanted him to stay. As soon as his French protectors left he was thrust before a firing squad under the command of Mexican nationalist **Benito Juarez**. The deposed ruler finally faced reality, and the **Maximilian Affair** came to an end with a bang.

The Russians, on the other hand, supported the North because they preferred a strong United States as a counterweight to British power. The Czar even sent the Russian fleet on friendly visits to San Francisco and New York City to not so subtly warn the British and French to mind their own beeswax and refrain from helping the South. Lots of hard drinking Americans who met the Russians were quite impressed when they tasted a clear beverage called vodka. After the war, Secretary of State Seward returned the favor by paying $7.2 million for territory everyone back then thought was nothing but frozen wasteland. Today we call it **Alaska**. Seward took a lot of heat — unfriendly newspaper editors called the purchase **"Seward's Folly"** and **"Seward's Icebox"** — but over time folks would change their minds. The discovery of vast amounts of gold and oil would have a lot to do with it.

The South faced one overriding problem it could do nothing about simply because of its very nature — it was founded to be a confederacy. A confederacy by definition consists of a weak national government and greater power to the states. In the midst of war, a nation is served best by a strong central authority that can command respect and, if necessary, force cooperation among the provinces (or in our case — states). President Lincoln had little problem with that. Confederate President **Jefferson Davis,** however, had to deal with state governors who thought they knew best, frequently refused his orders and called him names behind his back. For example, if soldiers from South Carolina needed boots and Georgia had extra pairs, Georgia would likely refuse to contribute outside its own borders — no way to fight a war.

In addition, Lincoln simply outclassed Davis. Jefferson Davis was sincere and hardworking, but frequently petty, meddlesome and a detriment to his subordinates, who were usually more capable than he was. Davis had been Secretary of War during the Pierce Administration, but he was a lousy military strategist who was completely clueless about how clueless he was. Lincoln was a man on a mission — to save the Union. He believed in God and the Constitution, handled cantankerous politicians and generals with infinite patience and good humor, and, unlike President Clinton, really did feel your pain. Abraham Lincoln is a great American hero, pure and simple, in a league with George Washington and Arnold Schwarzenegger.

THEATERS OF WAR

or *Down In Front — I'm Trying To Watch The Battle*

The North tended to name battles after the nearest body of water while the South preferred to name battles after the nearest town. I'm from the North and we won, so as far as I'm concerned the first big offensive of the war is called the battle of **Bull Run** and not **Manassas**. More and more people today refer to it as Manassas, which points to the possibility that the South is secretly plotting to rise again. I have no proof of this but it has been reported on the Fox News Channel, so draw your own conclusions. Anyway, in July of 1861 the Union army attempted to march across Virginia, capture Richmond and quickly put an end to the whole unfortunate misunderstanding.

Everyone knew about the plan and its precise timing because Confederate spies easily reconnoitered what was going on. Several women with southern sympathies took advantage of their Union officer lovers to garner precise details of the strategy. Apparently, in the midst of passionate lovemaking it was fairly easy to get these officers to yell, "Yes! Yes! Ohhh! Ohhh! We're leaving at seven in the morning on July 16th." So well known was the Union plan to march south, and the Confederates' counter plan to march north to meet them, that well dressed "high society" men and women packed picnic baskets and blankets and rode out in carriages to watch the fun.

At first it appeared the Union forces would prevail, as 30,000 soldiers under General Irvin McDowell pushed back the Confederates. But a Virginia brigade led by General Thomas J. Jackson held its ground and led a counterattack (Jackson, it was noted, stood like "a stone wall against the enemy," thus earning his immortal nickname "Stonewall" Jackson. Union commanders boasted monikers like "Rubber Legs" and "Rabbit Heart," but History thankfully tends to forget stuff like that). In the heat of battle the inexperienced northern men panicked and fled in chaos back to Washington, forcing a lot of confused picnickers to drop their chicken and champagne and run for their lives. But the Southerners were also inexperienced (and exhausted), so they failed to follow up their victory. Had they done so they might have captured Washington D.C. and ended the war then and there. But the North regrouped, dug into their defenses around Washington, and both sides suddenly realized that a long, bloody conflict lay ahead.

President Lincoln then appointed General **George B. McClellan** commander of the Union forces. McClellan, a popinjay in his thirties, skillfully drilled his **Army of the Potomac,** and soon these well-disciplined Union troops came to revere their youthful commander. Unfortunately, McClellan loved his army back and continually hesitated to place them in harm's way even when they were clearly ready to roll. Lincoln wrote McClellan a sarcastic letter stating "If you don't want to use the army I should like to borrow it for a while." But McClellan still dithered and Lincoln continued to fret.

Out west, Union General **Ulysses S. Grant** ordered attack after attack. His forces captured Fort Henry on the Tennessee River and Fort Donelson on the Cumberland River. When the Rebel commander at Fort Donelson asked Grant for his surrender terms, Grant replied that he had none, and demanded "unconditional surrender." He thus earned the immortal nickname "Unconditional Surrender Grant" while the Confederate commander's response, "Jeez, that's harsh!" has gone largely unreported.

General Grant was sloppy in appearance and frequently rip-roaring drunk, quite a contrast to the impeccable McClellan. When a Confederate attack surprised Grant at **Shiloh** in southern Tennessee, his Union army barely survived one of the bloodiest days of the war. Critics demanded Grant's removal but Lincoln, doubtless with McClellan's excess of caution in mind, replied, "I can't spare this man, he fights." In another famous exchange, the President responded to critics of Grant's drinking by proclaiming, "Find me the brand and I'll send a barrel to each of my other generals." One listener who shouted out "Jack Daniels" failed to grasp the sarcasm. But Grant's drinking really was a problem — perhaps he needed to dull the pain of sending so many young boys to their deaths — and finally officials in the War Department hit upon a remedy. They discreetly dispatched Mrs. Grant to her husband's various army camps. As soon as his wife approached, "Unconditional Surrender" immediately straightened up and switched to black coffee.

Back east, meanwhile, Union fortunes continued to sag. In March 1862, General McClellan finally decided to move his army by ship to the base of the Virginia peninsula below Richmond. He hoped to move up from there and capture the Confederate capital of Richmond, but he was overly cautious, and when the Rebels counterattacked his forces were beaten back. Reinforcements never arrived because Lincoln ordered them held back to protect Washington from the marauding troops of "Stonewall" Jackson in the Shenandoah Valley. The entire Peninsula Campaign was judged to be a disaster, and McClellan looked especially incompetent when it was revealed he had accepted bad advice and counted tree stumps the confederates had painted black as real guns. No mention was made at the time of straw dummies painted gray, though the Pinkerton "Intelligence" Agency may have covered up that bit of misinformation.

Though his army remained in fine fighting shape, McClellan was, perhaps unfairly, removed from his command and replaced by General **John Pope**. The overconfident Pope promptly screwed up and received a thrashing at the hands of General Lee at Manassas Junction, the same place where the first battle of Bull Run had occurred about a year before. This **Second Battle of Bull Run** went about as well as the first one and anyone within earshot of General Pope, who exclaimed "Oh wow, deja vu!," risked getting shot.

General Lee then decided to go on the offensive and strike north into Maryland. Lincoln restored McClellan to his command, and when the two sides met at Antietam Creek, Maryland, the Union forces repeatedly attacked even though the Confederate lines held firm. This was the bloodiest day of the war — over 18,000 wounded and nearly 5000 dead — and both armies battered and exhausted each other. The next day, Lee retreated back into Virginia and luckily for the Rebels, McClellan, demonstrating what today is referred to as a slow learning curve, hesitated and failed to follow up. This was probably the closest the South would ever get to victory. Had Maryland been wrenched from the North and Washington D.C. surrounded, the Union's ability to continue the war might have been fatally undermined.

The British would have been sorely tempted to jump on the soon-to-be-victorious Confederate bandwagon. But it was not to be. President Lincoln — in a masterstroke reminiscent of Napoleon Bonaparte after the Battle of the Nile over half a century before — publicly declared the battle of **Antietam** (militarily a draw) to be a magnificent Union victory. The Confederate veterans who had been there could do little more than mutter under their breath, "Bull#$%!, I was there." Then the President announced he was going to issue an executive order called the **Emancipation Proclamation.** Everyone ran to their dictionaries and realized emancipation means freedom. Finally, America's slaves would be freed — sort of.

The Emancipation Proclamation, announced in late September 1862 and formally issued on January 1,1863, did not in reality free one single slave. It applied only to slaves in those regions still under Confederate control, so of course Southern authorities in those areas ignored it. In the Border States and in territory conquered by the Union, the institution of slavery was left intact so as not to anger white slaveholders whose support Lincoln needed in the war effort. President Lincoln, remember, always aimed primarily to preserve the United States, so the Emancipation Proclamation was really a public relations maneuver and not the defining moment in American History that ended the institution of slavery. When one Southern plantation owner referred to the Emancipation Proclamation as a "fantasy like Santa Claus," other slaveholders still living in their dream world were forced to confront their belief in the Easter Bunny. After the war individual states were compelled to abolish slavery, and in 1865 the 13th Amendment to the Constitution accomplished the task on the federal level.

Lots of slaves deserted their plantations and headed north, and none of them received a parting gift. Almost 200,000 former slaves and free blacks from the North enlisted in the Union army. Most of the time they were assigned to labor battalions or as stewards for white officers, but when they did get the chance to fight, black troops excelled. Two Massachusetts regiments did so well and had so much pride that they would — as immortalized in the movie *Glory* — refuse to accept any pay unless it was equal to the amount white soldiers received. It is not true that actors Denzel Washington and Morgan Freeman tried to pull the same thing in regard to Matthew Broderick on the movie set.

Women on both sides also contributed mightily to the war effort. They proved essential in the collection and distribution of supplies, and many served as spies and scouts and nurses. **Clara Barton** is noteworthy as a battlefield nurse; a couple of decades later she would organize and head the **American Red Cross.** At home, women had to take the place of their men in the fields or behind the store counter. To be sure, the females in that sort of situation missed sex just as much as the males did, but due to the social conventions of the time, only men continually groused about it out loud.

After Antietam, Lincoln replaced McClellan with General **Ambrose E. Burnside,** who had thick bushy whiskers on his cheeks that reached down around his chin. This hairy affectation failed to distract from his bald head (a timeless tactic that never works) but it did become known as "burnsides" and then "sideburns." Burnside is remembered best for this contribution to the English language, but not his generalship, because he promptly led his army into a disastrous defeat at **Fredericksburg** outside Richmond.

Lincoln continued to play musical generals and replaced Burnside with General **"Fighting Joe" Hooker,** who at least sounded like he would be right for the job. But General Lee cleverly divided his smaller force and gave Hooker a sound thrashing at **Chancellorsville,** Virginia. "Stonewall" Jackson, however, was accidentally shot by his own troops in the gathering dusk, and Lee lost his ablest lieutenant and source of military advice (What do you say in such a situation? "Sorry about that?"). Though his arm was amputated, Jackson was expected to recover, but a few days later pneumonia set in and he became delirious. When he suddenly spoke the words, "Let us cross the river, and rest under the shade of the trees," those in attendance realized he was heading to some other place.

Lincoln promptly fired Hooker, though it is interesting to note that the "loose" women who followed his army came to be known as "hookers," a distinction the general was doubtless proud to share with his grandchildren. Buoyed by his victories, Lee decided to attack Northern territory once again. On July 1, 1863, totally by coincidence, Lee's Army of Northern Virginia met the Union general *du jour* **George G. Meade** and his Army of the Potomac outside a tiny town in southern Pennsylvania named Gettysburg. At places like Seminary Ridge and Little Round Top, men on both sides fought heroically, and after two bloody days the battle was basically a draw. On the third day, General Lee made one of his few military misjudgments, ordering a rash frontal attack up a slight incline against the fortified center of the Union lines. No one will ever know whether "Stonewall" Jackson — had he been alive — would have talked him out of it. **Pickett's Charge** failed as an avalanche of Yankee musket and cannon fire mowed down the courageous Confederates.

The next day, Lee was forced to withdraw southward but Meade did not pursue. Exasperated, Lincoln had to be reminded that it would be "unpresidential" to travel to the front solely to kick Meade in his hesitating rear end. However, this defeat in the **Battle of Gettysburg** was a turning point and the costliest defeat of all for General Lee and the Confederates. Never again would they go on the offensive. Never again would they have any real chance to win the war. Never again would they make serious long-range plans to open quaint tourist hotels in northern cities with names like "Southern Hospitality" or the "Jeff Davis Rebel Resort." But they would not surrender, and nearly two more years of horrific fighting lay ahead.

A few months later, President Lincoln journeyed to Gettysburg to participate in ceremonies dedicating the Soldiers' National Cemetery. Lots of dignitaries attended including the famous orator of the day, Edward Everett. Everett spoke for a full two hours, and after the singing of a hymn the President rose to offer the formal dedication. Lincoln spoke for about two minutes, and with stark, simple and passionate truths, blew Everett away. Lincoln believed with all his heart that the North should fight on to victory so "that this nation, under God, shall have a new birth of freedom — and that **government of the people, by the people, for the people**, shall not perish from the earth." Powerful and beautiful words, short and to the point, which was fortunate for those in attendance who by that time had to go to the bathroom. Legend has it that, while riding the train, Lincoln scribbled his **Gettysburg Address** on the back of an envelope. This sounds good but it is false. Lincoln had really put a lot of effort into that little (now immortal) speech and he tinkered with it right up to the moment of its delivery — all without a laptop.

Around the same time events were unfolding at Gettysburg, General Grant and his troops pressed relentlessly forward out west. In 1862, Admiral **David G. Farragut** had led a Union naval force into the mouth of the Mississippi and captured New Orleans. Lots of the people there still spoke French and had no idea what was going on, but Mardi Gras, as usual, was a blast. About a year later, General Grant remained determined to capture **Vicksburg**, one of the last remaining Confederate strongholds on the Mississippi River. Union troops surrounded the city and commenced a siege — an attempt to starve the inhabitants into submission. After six weeks of hiding in caves and reduced to eating rats, mules and horses (reportedly it all tasted like chicken), the men, women, and children of Vicksburg finally surrendered. Upon hearing the news of the fall of Vicksburg and another Confederate river position, **Port Hudson**, Lincoln remarked, "At last the Father of Waters flows unvexed to the sea." For a moment everyone thought the Commander in Chief was losing his marbles until one of his secretaries explained, "Don't worry, that's just how he talks. What he means is the Union now controls the Mississippi, supplies from the far West can no longer reach the South, and the Confederacy is effectively split in two."

Grant next concentrated on eastern Tennessee, where the Rebels had defeated a Union army near a stream called **Chickamauga**. Chickamauga was an Indian name meaning "river of death" and probably a good place to avoid at all times. Surrounded and trapped in the town of **Chattanooga**, now it was a Union army's turn to be under siege. It was not quite as bad for the North at Chattanooga as it had been for the Confederates at Vicksburg because (reportedly) when one soldier exclaimed, "Hey, this tastes just like chicken!" his officer replied (reportedly), "That's because it is chicken you idiot." Just in the nick of time, fresh from his victory at Vicksburg, General Grant showed up with a huge army and rescued his Union comrades at arms. To the east lay Atlanta, Georgia and the now vulnerable Confederate states of South and North Carolina.

At last President Lincoln realized he could stop playing musical generals. He called Grant east and appointed him supreme commander of all northern armies. Grant knew precisely what he needed to do and how to do it. He would drive his army forward, wear down the enemy's resources and break their will to fight. His plan — many historians call it an early example of **total war** — could hardly be called creative but it worked. Grant had more men and supplies than Lee and, unlike Lee, Grant could replace his losses. Horrible battles took place in the **Wilderness** of Virginia, at **Spotsylvania** and **Cold Harbor** (the perfect locale for a big Hollywood movie), and eventually Grant's Union army settled in for a siege of Petersburg and Richmond, the Confederate capital. Grant and his men could taste victory (and whiskey) while the Rebels, with their supplies dwindling and irreplaceable, barely had the chance to taste anything.

THE 1864 PRESIDENTIAL CAMPAIGN
or *An Election...Now?*

According to the Constitution, America is required to hold a presidential election every four years, even when current events make it inconvenient. So we always do, and if you think about it, it is a measure of strength, not weakness, when in the midst of war a country can afford a campaign to determine whether or not it should change horses. In 1864, Republican Lincoln desired to keep riding into a second term while unemployed General George McClellan, donning the armor of the Democrats, demanded to joust. Through most of that year, Lincoln believed he was going to lose and was reportedly spotted reading want ads in the newspaper. Union losses mounted daily, no end to the war lay in sight, and many northerners (dubbed **Copperheads**) demanded immediate peace with the Confederacy. But by the fall Union fortunes began to change.

Admiral Farragut's naval force captured Mobile, Alabama as he uttered his immortal words, "Damn the torpedoes, full speed ahead!" Luckily for Farragut, torpedoes had not been invented yet or he would have been toast. Actually, torpedoes back then referred to mines, so we should give Farragut his due. Union General **Philip H. Sheridan** galloped around Virginia's Shenandoah Valley, successfully destroying every last turnip and radish so the Confederates could no longer even scavenge for supplies. General **William Tecumseh Sherman** (Grant's replacement in the west) occupied Atlanta and then burned it, providing inspiration for 1930s Hollywood to make one of the classic movies of all time, *Son of Flubber*. Just kidding, it was **Gone With the Wind**, a powerful film you simply must see to have any clue what the American movie culture is all about.

President Lincoln's electoral fortunes rose with every Union victory. Lots of Northern troops — patriotic and sensing victory near — happily accepted furloughs so they could go home and vote (multiple times if they could get away with it) for their commander-in-chief. McClellan garnered 45% of the popular vote but Lincoln got the rest and creamed him in the electoral college 221 to 21. Now everyone in both the North and the South realized there would never be a negotiated settlement and the fight would be to the finish.

Next, General Sherman moved his army across Georgia, slashing a sixty-mile pathway of devastation to the Atlantic Ocean and then north through the Carolinas. His men raped (figuratively and literally) and pillaged as they advanced, and to make sure uprooted railroad tracks could not be repaired, they heated the iron rails and twisted them into "Sherman's neckties." Most importantly, they thoroughly accomplished their goal of denying the Confederates supplies and devastating the morale of the Rebel soldiers on the battle lines. Sherman's campaign almost certainly shortened the war and thus saved lives, but the idea that "you've got to kill people in order to save more people" still seems kind of sick. To this day the name Sherman is still an epithet in the South, and when you are down there it is definitely best not to mention this unsavory episode.

After nine months, Grant's army broke through Confederate lines and captured Petersburg and then Richmond. Lee realized that attempting to hold out any longer would be futile. At the town of **Appomattox Court House**, on April 9, 1865, General Grant and General Lee met to discuss the formal surrender of the Army of Northern Virginia. Lee dressed impeccably in a new dress uniform while Grant, rumpled and unshaven, was underdressed as usual and probably a little ripe. But the two men saluted and shook hands, and Grant, mindful of his instructions from Lincoln to be generous, wrote out surrender terms. Confederate officers were allowed to keep their swords and pistols. All soldiers were allowed to keep their horses, for there was still time for a desperately needed spring planting. "The Rebels are our countrymen again," Grant announced, and — red-eyed (lots of macho soldiers lied and said it was their allergies) — everyone headed for home. The United States was whole again but forgiveness — on both sides — would not be so easy to achieve.

"Other than that, Mrs. Lincoln, how did you enjoy the play?" That tasteless line is one of the sickest jokes of all time. But sometimes humor helps folks cope with events that are so tragic as to be virtually unfathomable. Five days after Lee's surrender at Appomattox, on April 14, 1865, Good Friday, the President and Mrs. Lincoln attended a play entitled *My American Cousin* at Ford's Theater near the White House. A fanatical Southern sympathizer and Lincoln hater, twenty-seven-year-old actor **John Wilkes Booth**, walked into the unguarded Presidential box and shot Abraham Lincoln in the head with a pistol at point blank range. He then jumped to the stage and before a horrified audience shouted "Sic semper tyrannis" — the motto of Virginia, and Latin for "Thus always to tyrants."

Having landed awkwardly and broken his leg, Booth limped off the stage, exited the theater, and galloped off on his horse. Incredibly, a few dimwits remained convinced all this was a part of the play. The unconscious President was carried across the street to a boardinghouse where, grotesquely, his feet dangled off the end of the bed. Lincoln never regained consciousness and died at 7:22 in the morning. Secretary of War Stanton was in attendance and commented, "Now he belongs to the ages." Folks who knew how Stanton had continually been a thorn in Lincoln's side probably could not help but think, *Nice comment Stanton but a little late. Now we're all going to realize how great Lincoln really was.*

There were no phones or radios back then, so Booth simply rode unmolested over the Georgetown Bridge and into the Virginia countryside, but twelve days later Union troops trapped him and an accomplice in a tobacco barn. He refused to surrender, so the barn was set on fire. Then a shot rang out and Booth was carried dead from the burning barn. Historians are still not sure whether Booth committed suicide or an enraged Union soldier managed to take a shot at him through a space in the slats of the barn. Rumors persist to this day that Booth had somehow managed to escape, but no hard evidence substantiates this. The CIA did not exist back then so don't blame them. Eight co-conspirators were eventually captured, tried and hanged three months later. These hasty executions illustrate one reason why capital punishment is a bad idea: further information is impossible to garner from a corpse. But maybe clandestine conspirators within the government wanted them dead as fast as possible. Hmmmm...sounds like a great idea for a cable documentary.

It has long been told that an army band assembled outside the White House shortly after the Confederates surrendered. Lincoln appeared and someone asked him what song he would like to hear in celebration. Solemnly, Lincoln chose "Free Bird" by Lynyrd Skynyrd. Just kidding. He actually chose "Dixie," the anthem of the South. Whether or not this story is actually true, it does accurately portray Lincoln's feelings towards his conquered southern brethren. He wanted to forgive them. He wanted to bring the South back into the Union as soon as possible and begin healing the nation's deep wounds. As it turned out, John Wilkes Booth hurt the southern cause when he murdered President Lincoln. He shot the only man who — with his prestige and greatness — might have been able to orchestrate a lenient **Reconstruction** of the South. Nice going, schmuck.

Now what? Can the North and South ever unite again? Will the wounds ever heal? Who should be in charge of Reconstruction — the President or the Congress? Can anyone step into Lincoln's shoes? Who has feet that huge? What will happen to the freed slaves? New President Andrew Johnson certainly has his hands full. Uh oh — the future of America is at stake, so stay tuned...don't touch that dial!!!

This Really Happened!

Boxing is popular in Rome during the Empire, and after the fall, it remains popular in England. By the end of the eighteenth century Americans have come to love the "sport" and there are bare-fisted prizefights for money. These matches are no holds barred — kicking, eye gouging and hair pulling are common, and when the referee is distracted, anything can happen. Sometimes one of the contestants is drugged. But eventually public opinion is aroused against this brutality, and in 1866, Britain's Marquess of Queensbury draws up a code of rules. Henceforth boxers wear padded gloves and wrestling is prohibited. Fights are divided into rounds and when a boxer is down he is allowed ten seconds in which to rise and continue the fight. Biting is definitely not allowed.

And the rest is History...

Quiz yourself on Chapter 7

Multiple Choice (circle the correct answer).

1. When the Civil War broke out, most of the experienced military officers stayed loyal to their states in the South – notably
   a. Robert E. Lee
   b. Thomas J. "Stonewall" Jackson
   c. James T. Kirk
   d. a and b
   e. f

2. Men who would enlist, collect their bonus, then desert and rush to another state to enlist again were called
   a. bounty jumpers
   b. break dancers
   c. New York City municipal employees
   d. Copperheads
   e. all of the above

3. The government of the following country favored the Union:
   a. Russia
   b. Great Britain
   c. France
   d. Iraq
   e. Iowa

4. "Seward's Folly" refers to Secretary of State Seward's
   a. affair with a chorus girl
   b. support for the Confederacy
   c. belief that he would one day be president
   d. his purchase for the United States of cold and snowy Alaska
   e. none of the above

5. When President Lincoln complained that General McClellan had "the slows" he meant that McClellan
   a. was constipated
   b. was too fat to run very fast
   c. was shy with women
   d. hesitated to use his army aggressively
   e. none of the above

6. Lincoln's Gettysburg Address
    a. dedicated a cemetery for the Union troops killed in the battle
    b. presented a short and poetic description of American democracy
    c. was kept a secret so he could sleep uninterrupted
    d. a and b
    e. none of the above

7. General William Tecumseh Sherman
    a. is to this day loved in the South
    b. surrendered to the Confederates while he was drunk
    c. moved his army across Georgia destroying everything in their path
    d. brought relief supplies to the wounded Southern soldiers
    e. all of the above

8. At the town of Appomattox Court House
    a. General Grant finally married his long time mistress
    b. General Lee was forced to pay off his parking tickets
    c. the judge told Lincoln to sit down and shut up
    d. General Lee formally surrendered his army
    e. all of the above

9. Actor John Wilkes Booth assassinated President Lincoln because
    a. he was not chosen to be on American Idol
    b. the President had cut funding for the arts
    c. he was a fanatical Southern sympathizer
    d. he wanted better treatment of the freed slaves
    e. Lincoln said "his brother, Edwin, was a better actor"

10. Many folks in the South today
    a. still resent the North
    b. talk funny
    c. believe the Confederate flag should fly over public buildings
    d. all of the above
    e. none of the above

PART II

"WHO CARES...THEY ARE ALL DEAD ANYWAY"

PREFACE TO PART II

One bright and early morning I faced an earnest group of college students on the first day of a new semester. My first order of business was to explain to them that History is an important subject...indeed vital for an understanding of the modern world. This American History class could be more than a letter grade and three credits required for graduation. In the back row a drowsy freshman yawned and reached toward his knapsack. "No Texting in class," I said, and pressed on.

Most of them admitted that they had hated "Social Studies" in high school...lots of boring facts, irritating memorization, and deadly dull teachers droning on and on. It doesn't have to be that way, I insisted. History is not about names and dates, it's about life and people and passion and understanding who we are by understanding where we came from. I turned to a high-haired girl down front and repeated, "I said no Texting."

I decided to lighten things up a bit. Many in the class acknowledged that they knew of their family's "roots," and calling on them individually revealed a veritable smorgasbord of ethnicities and cultures. My own ancestry, I proudly revealed, could be traced back on my mother's side to the first ship after the Mayflower. And an ancient family bible revealed that "one of my Great Great Great Great Grandfathers was the first person in this land that would one day become the United States of America...to be arrested for public drunkenness." This absolutely true personal tidbit drew chuckles from most of the class. I did not add that in my senior year of college a particularly wild party had enabled me to achieve a similar a destiny and link myself forever with my illustrious relative not only in blood but also in ignominy.

One gum-chewing girl did not seem amused. She raised her hand and I called on her.

"Is this going to be important?" she asked.

"Excuse me," I replied.

"I mean is this going to be on the test?"

Clearly this class was going to be another undergraduate challenge.

"I'm just trying to explain that history does not have to be boring; it can also be interesting and fun. To understand the present and predict the future we absolutely need to acknowledge those who have gone before."

"Who cares, they are all dead anyway," she said.

That took my breath away, but I recovered almost instantly, remembering my father's admonition to never let them see you sweat.

"I care," I said. And I'm going to try my level best over the next few months to show you all why you should care, too."

I really do care. And so must you if you are getting ready to read on. In the second part of this tongue-in-cheek but entirely factual American saga, enjoy the machinations of our predecessors as they faced challenge after challenge and shaped the world we live in today. As always, don't take things too seriously, and allow yourself to laugh. Most importantly — even though "they are all dead anyway" — never, ever forget.

P. B.

CHAPTER 8

RECONSTRUCTION AND THE GILDED AGE

or
Is Anyone Here An Honest Man?

The four-year Civil War hopefully will remain this country's costliest war. Think about it...both sides were Americans...360,000 Union soldiers and 258,000 Confederates dead plus countless wounded...an unspeakable tragedy. Defeated "Johnny Rebs" returned to devastated towns and ruined farms. Former slaves walked free but homeless and destitute. Folks on both sides were bitter and angry and unsure what to do next. President (by assassin's bullet) Andrew Johnson suddenly found himself thrust into Abraham Lincoln's large shoes. The new President tried to follow in "Honest Abe's" footsteps but, unfortunately for America, "Andy the drunken tailor" proved to be a man with really tiny feet.

COMPETING RECONSTRUCTION PLANS
or *My Way or the Highway*

Lincoln had probably never heard the Yiddish term *mensch*, but when it came to how he wanted to treat the conquered South, he certainly was one. He believed that since the South did not have the right to secede, it had never actually done so. He wanted to pardon any southerner who would swear a loyalty oath; in any Southern state, when ten percent of those who had voted in 1860 had sworn, they could set up a state government and be welcomed back into the Union with open arms and maybe a hug.

Many northern Republicans in Congress hated Lincoln's Ten Percent Plan and wanted to make the South pay dearly for their treason. In 1864, while the war was still raging, Congress had passed the **Wade-Davis Bill** calling for a majority to declare loyalty to the Union before a state could be readmitted. Lincoln refused to sign the bill and Congress adjourned, so it did not go into effect. When the president puts a bill that has been passed "in his pocket" and allows it to expire when Congress leaves town on vacation, it is known as a pocket veto. Lincoln almost certainly stuck the Wade-Davis Bill in his stovepipe hat, not his pocket — where it doubtless got smeared with fried chicken — but you get the point.

Andrew Johnson had been chosen as Lincoln's running mate in 1864 because he was a pro-Union Democrat from Tennessee who would underscore that the Republican Lincoln desired unity. (Andy was rip roaring drunk at his vice-presidential swearing in, claiming later that he had innocently been trying to cure a bad cold. Yeah, right.) But after Lincoln was killed, President Johnson generally refused to cooperate with Republican leaders. He agreed with Lincoln's Ten Percent Plan mainly because a quick reinstatement of Southern state governments seemed certain to bring large numbers of his fellow Democrats back into the Congress. Republican legislators, used to ruling the roost during the Civil War, were appalled when in December, 1865, smirking former Confederates (virtually all Democrats) showed up to reclaim their seats as if the war had never transpired. Congress, dominated by Northern Republicans, told them to take a hike. Presumably the wine and cheese "welcome back" reception was also canceled.

State governments down in Dixie did other obnoxious things that irritated northern Republicans. A few southern state legislatures refused to officially renounce secession. South Carolina and Mississippi would not repudiate their Confederate war debts. Mississippi failed to ratify the **Thirteenth Amendment** (1865) to the Constitution that outlawed slavery everywhere in the United States. Reportedly, there was lots of graffiti with phrases like "GRANT IS A DRUNK" and "GENERAL SHERMAN SUCKS" plastered all over the South. Worst of all, the new southern state legislatures passed laws that became known as **Black Codes**. These Black Codes aimed to keep newly-freed blacks subservient to whites. Blacks could not vote, bear arms, serve on juries, hold office and could even be arrested for "loitering" and assigned to "work crews." Slavery was gone in name but white southerners intended to keep it in practice.

Northerners fumed. Radical Republicans in Congress decided to take control of Reconstruction away from the President and run it their own (very intense) way. In early 1866 they provided for the **Freedmen's Bureau** — a federal agency set up to operate down South providing food, clothing, education, and job training for former slaves. Johnson, a southern bigot at heart, vetoed the bill, but Congress overrode his veto (remember how it's done?) with a two-thirds vote in both the House and the Senate. The Republican Congress then passed a civil rights bill outlawing discrimination based on race. The President vetoed this as well but was overridden again.

To make sure black citizens' rights would truly be permanent, Congress proposed the **Fourteenth Amendment** to the Constitution (ratified in 1868 when three-fourths of the states approved it) stating that the federal and state governments may not deprive any person of life, liberty, or property without due process of law; nor deny to any person within its jurisdiction the equal protection of the laws. Any former Confederate official, unless pardoned, was forbidden to hold federal or state office. And without doubt in the North, wearing the color gray at a social function was considered extremely bad taste.

Southern whites reacted to all this with such fury that horrible race riots broke out in several southern cities, notably Memphis and New Orleans, during which over eighty blacks were estimated to have been killed. President Johnson was undeterred, and as the November 1866 midterm elections approached, he embarked on a speaking tour to encourage the election of Democrats who supported his views (Midterm elections occur halfway through a President's term; the entire House of Representatives and one-third of the Senate stand for reelection, and the results are widely viewed as a referendum on how the President is doing).

Johnson's appearances hurt more than they helped. He was frequently heckled and decided to yell right back, turning red-faced and reportedly spitting all over the folks standing in front. A report that he turned around, dropped his pants and said, "Kiss this!" was probably exaggerated. Whether or not Johnson was actually intoxicated at any of these appearances has been wondered about ever since, but these emotional outbursts certainly reflected poorly on the dignity of the office of President. Turned-off voters sent huge Republican majorities (over two-thirds and thus veto proof) to both Houses of Congress. President Johnson could only console himself with a good stiff drink.

In March 1867, Congress passed the **Reconstruction Act** and the President couldn't do anything about it. Cursing and kicking the wall did not prevent his usual veto from being easily overridden, and presumably prodigious amounts of spackle had to be allocated to the White House maintenance crew. The South was split into five military districts, and Union troops dispatched to oversee the formation of new state governments composed of blacks and loyal whites. When Congress approved new state constitutions that ratified the fourteenth amendment and guaranteed suffrage for blacks, then and only then would a southern state be readmitted to the Union.

Former Confederates could bitch all they wanted, but there were "blue bellies" with bayonets and bad attitudes right outside their doors. This was probably the point when lots of white southerners — a couple of years after the fighting had ended — finally admitted to themselves, Wow, we really did lose the war. One by one the wayward southern states reentered the Union, defeated but still proud and defiant, and definitely unwilling to stop eating grits or be nice to visiting northerners.

THE IMPEACHMENT OF THE PRESIDENT
or *Just Do It...We'll Find a Reason!*

Thaddeus Stevens of Pennsylvania in the House, and Charles Sumner in the Senate (recovered physically from his beating but retaining a pathological fear of gold-tipped canes) led the Radical Republicans. Both of these guys were a passionate mixture of both political opportunism and a sincere desire to protect the rights of freed slaves. Both scowled a lot and looked scary, and neither was much fun to hang out with.

In 1867, obsessed with hatred for President Johnson and fearful that he would undermine the military Reconstruction going on, the Radicals went way too far. Basically, they tried to destroy not only Andrew Johnson but also the office of President. First, they restricted his power over the armed forces; then they passed (over a presidential veto) the infamous **Tenure of Office Act**. This law stated that the President could not fire any appointed officials approved by the Senate without getting the permission of the Senate first. Absurd — the idea that the President should not be allowed to determine the makeup of his own cabinet — but these congressional bullies thought they could get away with it. They probably also hoped the President would shine their shoes and dance a little jig for them.

President Johnson deliberately fired Secretary of War Stanton (a stooge for the Radicals who well deserved the boot) so the Tenure of Office Act (clearly unconstitutional) could be tested in the courts. Rumors that Johnson broke the news to Stanton with the words "So long dorkboy!" further exacerbated an already tense situation. Since the President had technically broken the law, the Radical Republicans smelled blood. The House of Representatives impeached Johnson: as stipulated in the Constitution, a majority of the Representatives (126 to 47) voted that the President had committed "high crimes and misdemeanors" and should be removed from office. With the Chief Justice of the Supreme Court presiding, a trial was held in the Senate, with a two-thirds vote necessary to remove the President.

President Johnson kept his job by one vote cast by courageous Republican Senator Edmund G. Ross, who bucked his party and (are you sitting down?) actually acted for the good of the country. Ross was not reelected to another term, but that sometimes happens when politicians rise above the public passions of the moment and decide to do the right thing. Unfortunately, American History's lengthening road is littered with far too many noble dreams abandoned by self-seeking politicians, so it's no wonder most folks today bestow the same amount of prestige on our elected officials as they do used car salesmen.

Andrew Johnson had delivered lots of intemperate speeches, and he really was a loudmouth without an ounce of tact, but what the Republicans truly couldn't stand was his opposition to their agenda — and that is not "high crimes and misdemeanors" or a good reason to kick the President out of office. The whole Tenure of Office Act imbroglio was simply an excuse to try get rid of a chief executive the Republicans hated and disagreed with, and had they succeeded, the presidency would have been greatly weakened — perhaps permanently — and our founding fathers' notion of three equal branches of government checking and balancing each other destroyed. Whew, close call! Another bunch of rabid GOP bloodsuckers tried to pull a similar stunt when they impeached President Clinton in 1998, but we'll get to that later on.

In the presidential election of 1868, neither party wanted anything to do with Johnson. The Republicans knew their haughty conduct had garnered them a lot of enemies, so they nominated the most popular and heroic figure they could think of — General Ulysses S. Grant — despite the fact that he had no political experience whatsoever. The Democrats' prospects were in even worse shape, since they were still looked upon (with considerable justification) as the party of secession. They talked a lot about improving the economy by allowing for inflation — rising crop prices would help strapped farmers struggling with fixed debt repayments — but their candidate, Governor **Horatio Seymour** of New York, remained uncommitted to his party's own cause and basically bored everyone to death.

The Republicans roused Americans by waving the **bloody shirt** — a phrase that initially served to remind the voters of the Republicans' loyalty and the Democrats' treachery during the Civil War (a Congressman on the floor of the House actually waved a real bloody shirt, at which point some observers were grossed out and exclaimed, "Jeez, wash that thing."). For the next half-century both parties would continually wave the bloody shirt, which eventually came to symbolize the promise of fat pension payments to the Civil War veterans who comprised a large part of the electorate. This kind of pandering or buying of votes when a party's agenda is not popular enough on its own merits has continually been a part of American politics. Currently, the Republicans trumpet huge tax cuts our country cannot afford, causing the budget deficit and debt to explode...but I digress.

Grant won an unimpressive victory, and immediately demonstrated he had no idea how to serve as a civilian Chief Executive. Personally trustworthy, he took lots of bad advice and allowed his friends and political appointees to run wild and loot the government. Two multi-millionaire speculators (pure scoundrels), **James Fisk, Jr.** and **Jay Gould**, bought the assistance of the President's brother-in-law and attempted to manipulate the gold market; failing to comprehend the situation, the President acted painfully slowly to stop it — too late to help many honest folks who were ruined (I can attest that idiot brother-in-laws are not uncommon, but when you are President you've got to keep a lid on them). In another sordid affair, the Union Pacific Railroad, which had been fleecing taxpayers for years, created a company called **Crèdit Mobilier** to bribe potentially nosey members of Congress with millions of dollars worth of stock. Even Grant's vice-president, **Schuyler Colfax**, couldn't resist a piece of that action.

Remarkably, the Republicans renominated Grant to run for a second term in 1872. Fed up "Liberal Republicans" broke away, and even more remarkably nominated New York Tribune editor **Horace Greeley**, even though he was essentially a hothead with no political experience. More remarkable still, the Democrats — desperate for a win any way they could get it — also nominated Greeley, even though he had long blasted that party as a bunch of unpatriotic scoundrels. Most remarkable of all, gullible Americans solidly reelected Grant. Poor Greeley had a particularly rough campaign during which he was attacked as a communist (which he wasn't) and a vegetarian (which he was, but what's wrong with veggies?). Then, in one month, he lost the election, his wife, his business, his sanity, and his life. Bummer...but he still might have been better than Ulysses S. Clueless.

Scandal followed scandal in Grant's second term. Officials in the war department granted contracts to the shipbuilding company offering the highest "under the table" payoff. Secretary of War William W. Belknap sold rights to set up trading posts on Indian lands and personally pocketed the cash. Whiskey distillers in Missouri — the Whiskey Ring — avoided paying excise taxes by bribing officials in the Treasury Department.

Grant cannot escape blame for allowing and ignoring all the malfeasance swirling in and around his Administration. A nonstop cigar smoker and serious boozer, there has been a longtime rumor that he had a hole cut in the wall of his office in the White House so he could conveniently discard his empty whiskey bottles, which would shatter and then fall directly into the trash in the cellar. Lesson here: a good general does not automatically make a good president. Grant may have been the worst of all.

RADICAL RECONSTRUCTION IN THE SOUTH
or *You Lost, So Shut Up and Do What We Tell You*

Black codes were removed in the South starting in 1867, but virtually all blacks remained desperately poor. Many African-Americans (and poor whites) became **sharecroppers** — a lousy arrangement in which a white landlord provided farmland, tools and seed, whereupon rent had to be paid in profits from the resulting crop. Usually what was left over was barely enough to eke out a living, and ironically, in terms of material comforts, many former slaves found themselves worse off than before. When sharecroppers inevitably needed to borrow money from landowners or banks, the interest rates charged were usurious, inhumane and just plain evil — kind of like what credit card companies charge today. Blacks were free, but it was a freedom embittered by unremitting poverty and debt.

Lots of northerners headed south, becoming known as carpetbaggers because they carried their belongings in small suitcases made out of samsonite...just kidding, carpet. Since airplanes had not been invented yet and none of these folks traveled on USAIR, most of these intrepid travelers arrived at their southern destinations without losing their luggage. Some of the carpetbaggers intended to make a fast buck by hook or crook, some came with honest motives such as business investment or to help blacks. Regardless, southern whites hated them all.

They hated **scalawags** even more — white southerners who had remained loyal to the Union and now supported Radical Reconstruction. Former confederates saw scalawags as traitors to the Rebel cause, so their loathing is somewhat understandable...go to the racetrack and bet a week's paycheck on the wrong horse and you'll see it's natural to want to throttle the winners. Don't literally do this, I'm just making a point.

Some of the Reconstruction governments in the South did positive things like building schools and hospitals and repairing damaged infrastructure. But a lot of carpetbaggers and scalawags were criminals who stole everything that wasn't nailed down. State legislators got rich by charging taxpayers for projects that never even existed; many an outhouse was paid for but never built. Historians sometimes point out that these Reconstruction governments were no more or less corrupt than local governments of the same period up North. Fair enough, but history shouldn't let these dirtbags off the hook.

Blacks in the South cast ballots in large numbers during Reconstruction. Almost unanimously voting Republican — the party that had sponsored emancipation and Radical Reconstruction — they were pivotal in the election of President Grant. Two African-Americans served in the Senate, fourteen in the House of Representatives, and many more in state and local positions, though there was never a black governor nor a black majority in a state legislature. Ironically, it's said that African-Americans newly allowed to dress as Santa Claus chafed the former Confederates the most...go figure. The Fifteenth Amendment to the Constitution passed in 1870, stating: "The right of citizens of the United States to vote shall not be denied or abridged by the United States or by any state on account of race, color, or previous condition of servitude." Dream on. Anyone who thought black suffrage would last in the South was wearing rose-colored glasses and oblivious of the bigots who were starting to dress in bed sheets.

In the late 1860s, secret societies such as the **Ku Klux Klan** and the **Knights of the White Kamelia** sprang up in the South dedicated to denying blacks their basic rights, particularly their right to vote. These morons disguised themselves in white sheets and hoods, and any Klansman who showed up wearing a floral pattern was heavily teased as a wussy boy who might, say, read a book or think independently. The Klan operated mostly at night and employed intimidation and violence; burning a cross in front of your house was a first warning, a lynching might come next.

In 1870 and 1871, the Grant Administration proposed and the Congress passed a series of **Force Acts** authorizing martial law, the suspension of habeas corpus and even military action to discourage anyone down South intent upon interfering with blacks' right to vote. But it was all talk with little action. Northerners were getting bored with Reconstruction and sick of bickering with obstinate white southern bigots. This description of the former Confederates might sound harsh, but it is true and, Who Cares, They Are All Dead Anyway. What are they going to do to me? Come back from the dead and haunt me? (Just in case, I use a nightlight.)

THE END OF RECONSTRUCTION
or *President Tilden...Not!*

In 1872 Congress passed the **Amnesty Act**, allowing all former Confederates, except for their top leaders, to hold office, and in short order southern whites regained control of state and local governments in the South. By 1875 only three states — South Carolina, Louisiana, and Florida — remained under Radical Reconstruction rule. The Freedman's Bureau had been disbanded in 1870 so dark clouds danced on the horizon, blowing fast toward the former slaves in the South. The last thing America needed was a fraudulent and divisive presidential election in 1876. But that's exactly what happened.

The Democrats knew they had a real shot at winning the presidency for the first time in about twenty years. They nominated Governor **Samuel J. Tilden** of New York who, although extremely bland, had a reputation as a reformer (it was rumored that one of Tilden's speeches actually put a corpse to sleep). Incredibly, Grant would have accepted a nomination to run for a third term had not Congress (urged on by a large majority of Americans including many in his own Republican party) passed a resolution informing him that, since he had completely messed up for eight years, it would be best if he honored the two term tradition and return home to die. Grant did soon die of cancer, personally of modest means and racing till the end to finish his memoirs so his family would have money to live on. Remember, it was the people he appointed who were corrupt. Grant himself was just clueless. The Republicans argued amongst themselves and finally settled on a compromise candidate — Governor **Rutherford B. Hayes** of Ohio. Hayes was a good choice because he had never been caught stealing anything and he hailed from a "swing state" — a state that normally split evenly between the Democrats and the Republicans and one in which the voters would be predisposed to vote for one of their own.

Florida, Louisiana, and South Carolina sent in two sets of electors, one for Democrat Tilden and one for Republican Hayes. Tilden had won the popular vote but the Republicans charged fraud. Congress appointed an "electoral commission" consisting of eight Republicans and seven Democrats to get to the bottom of all the confusion and — surprise,surprise — by a party line vote of 8-7 awarded all the disputed electors to the Republican Hayes. Democrats went ballistic, and in the South, lots of them went searching for their rifles. To calm the Democrats down, the Republicans offered to pull the Union troops out of the South and end Reconstruction if the Democrats would accept Hayes as President. The Democrats finally acquiesced two days before the inauguration, after the Republicans said "pretty please" and threw in promises to build some railroads in the South, and appoint a southerner to a cabinet post to be named later.

Hey, let's put it this way. Samuel Tilden won the election. But you say you've never heard of a President Tilden? That's because the man got the shaft. He was screwed royally, ripped off, robbed, purloined, pilfered...you get the picture. And you thought this kind of chicanery could only happen in a banana republic...no, not the store — a politically unstable country in Latin America.

BLACKS IN THE "NEW SOUTH"
or *Screwed For a Hundred Years*

The corrupt election of 1876 ended Reconstruction, and the removal of federal troops left southern blacks completely vulnerable. President Hayes (appropriately nicknamed "His Fraudulency") promised blacks that if they trusted southern whites, their civil rights would be respected, but he lied. Southern local and state governments immediately set about formalizing segregation, and they passed **Jim Crow** laws to enforce this separation of the races. These laws legislated totally separate facilities for whites and blacks: schools, prisons, hospitals, railroad cars and waiting areas in the stations, hotels, restaurants, theaters, bathrooms, drinking fountains, and even cemeteries.

In one of the worst Supreme Court decisions ever — **Plessy v. Ferguson** (1896) — the men in black sheets cited the Fourteenth Amendment (in a manner those who created it never intended) and ruled "**separate but equal**" could be constitutional as long as the facilities provided were truly equal. Of course, facilities were never equal, and America's so-called highest court effectively legalized segregation and second-class status for African-Americans. Ironically, some black-owned restaurants served collard greens and black-eyed peas (a terrific name for a musical group) — superior food that white southerners never got to experience. Their loss.

In the 1880s, southern blacks generally were allowed to vote, as various political factions offered false promises to gain their support, but in the nineties the ballot box slammed shut. Economic conditions worsened, and with blacks as competitors for jobs and power, whites commenced a campaign of **disfranchisement** (denial of voting rights) across the South. Blacks found that they had to pay a fee for voting, and since virtually all blacks were poor, this **poll tax** kept them home on Election Day (the poll tax was conveniently waived for poor whites). Then there was the **literacy test** — a reading exam voters had to pass in order to vote — and many former slaves had not yet learned to read or write. Illiterate whites received easier tests requiring them to read such difficult words as "A" and "I;" a black person who could read English would be handed a page of ancient Greek! Particularly insidious was the **grandfather clause** — a law stating basically that a person was ineligible to vote unless their grandfather had voted. This law made it impossible for most blacks to vote because their grandfathers had been slaves and certainly not able to vote.

White-dominated state legislatures also engaged in "**racial gerrymandering**." "Regular" **gerrymandering** has always been a part of American politics — the party in power creates legislative districts in which their supporters outnumber the opposition, in an attempt to guarantee that the candidate from your party wins every election. Gerrymandering got its name in 1812, when Massachusetts Governor **Elbridge Gerry** and Republican state legislators drew a district boundary in their favor that was so squiggly, some observers thought it looked like a salamander — thus "Gerry*mander*." Both parties often do this today; it stinks, but it is not illegal. Racial gerrymandering makes use of the same principle, except that southern legislatures drew district lines to ensure that whites always outnumbered blacks. The insidious result: a black man could never hope to run and have any chance to win an election. And to top it all off, very few African-Americans were able to vote in the South after 1890 because, if all else failed, Election Day brought out the genetically inbred Klansmen pathetically driven to make themselves feel superior to somebody.

An African-American named **Booker T. Washington** stood tall and spoke out. He was a former slave who obtained an education and founded **Tuskegee Institute** in Alabama. In 1895, he made a made a speech in which he declared that blacks should ignore white prejudices and concentrate on learning useful skills and improving themselves economically. This "**Atlanta Compromise**" delighted whites because it seemed to be so accommodating, but many blacks had mixed feelings. Washington was disparaged then (and still is today) for catering to whites and being too willing to accept discrimination. That criticism was (and is) unfair. Learning job skills, making money, gaining economic (and then political) power are certain avenues to equality, much more so than foot stomping and righteous indignation. Bigots are too ignorant to comprehend righteous indignation and they usually jump quickly out of the way when you try to kick them. But bigots are forced to treat African-Americans with respect when they find themselves in need of a black-owned service or product, or a job in a black-owned company. Go Booker T., Go!

William E. B. Du Bois — born in 1868, intellectually gifted, and the first African-American to earn a Ph.D. in history from Harvard — became a foot stomper. Understandably angry at the continued intransigence of white racism, in the early 1900s Du Bois ripped Booker T. Washington for his apparent willingness to accept inferior racial status. Du Bois and his **Niagara Movement** in 1905 loudly demanded the unrestricted right to vote, an end to segregation, and equal justice in the courts. Whites in America collectively yawned, as Washington had always known they would. But a few liberal whites got fired up and founded the **National Association for the Advancement of Colored People** (NAACP) of which Du Bois became an officer and the editor of its newspaper, The Crisis. (Little known fact: the NAASCP — The National Association for the Advancement of Swedish Colored People — folded almost immediately due to a lack of membership.) Washington died in 1915, and thanks to Du Bois and others, a new era of black pride and militancy was born. Sadly, most civil rights leaders of the time focused on their differences and never accepted how perfectly the two men complemented each other.

GILDED AGE POLITICS

or *Fill Your Pockets and Screw the Public*

America's greatest writer in the late nineteenth century was the one and only **Mark Twain** — we've all heard of him, particularly due to his authorship of books such as

Huckleberry Finn and *Tom Sawyer*. If you are a young person and you haven't yet encountered these books, check them out and shame on your English teachers. Even though there is no sex in these stories, and the action moves slower than you are used to in Star Wars, Harry Potter and the Lord of the Rings, etc., Twain is good, really good. He's funny, and offers insightful portraits of what our country used to be. It was Mark Twain who described politics after the Civil War as a **Gilded Age**: glitter on the outside, trash underneath.

Corruption pervaded every level of American government: local, state and federal. Most big cities were controlled by "bosses" who could turn out immigrant voters on Election Day and who, though never elected to public office, could handpick officeholders...naturally, men who would do what they were told. Mayors and governors across the country bowed to the Boss.

William Marcy "Boss" Tweed and his infamous Tweed Ring ran New York City from 1868-71. They bribed judges, bought votes, and tried to convince a whole generation of New Yorkers that the democratic process was a joke and the only sensible government was one in which you paid off the Boss. The rule of the day: "Addition, division, and silence." The "books" recorded a payment of $138,000 to a plasterer for two days of labor and a city hall estimated at $250,000 ultimately cost $8 million.

But Boss Tweed's luck finally ran out. The New York Times published damning evidence and gutsy young caricaturist **Thomas Nast** attacked him mercilessly in Harper's Weekly magazine. Tweed was arrested, escaped, rearrested after being recognized through a Nast cartoon, and put in prison, where he died alone, unforgiven, and probably the most despicable of the 19th century big city bosses. By the way, Thomas Nast's drawings popularized the tradition cartoonists still use today of representing the Democrats with a donkey and the Republicans with an elephant. Nast showed great restraint in this since he could just as easily have chosen rats, cockroaches, or any of the innumerable other species of vermin.

On the federal level, one undistinguished president followed another, all of them subservient to Congress and eminently forgettable (but don't totally overlook them in case someone brings them up or they turn up on an exam.) The Senate and the House of Representatives were no better, as both the Republicans and the Democrats focused on personal attacks against each other and enriching themselves. The issues of the day — the protective tariff (too high considering a treasury surplus?), currency reform (should there be inflation to help poorer folks who owed money?), and civil service reform (is the spoils system totally out of control?) — were all tough issues that were, well, tough, and most in this generation of indolent American politicians tried their best to ignore them. Unfortunately for lots of these guys, Alcoholics Anonymous had not been founded yet.

President Hayes came to office through a stolen election, so it is often forgotten that he had an otherwise well-deserved reputation for bravery as a Union officer in the Civil War, and integrity as a congressman and then governor of Ohio. He did actually try to curb the outlandish extremes of the spoils system, most notably the New York

Customs House, which collected about two-thirds of the nation's duties on imported goods and was essentially a den of thieves. One of the biggest crooks of them all, New York's Senator Roscoe Conkling, was particularly furious when his buddy and fellow criminal **Chester A. Arthur** was canned as head of the custom's house.

Hayes' brief flirtation with political reform caused the Republicans to argue amongst themselves and divide into two factions: the **Half-Breeds** and the **Stalwarts**. Conkling led the Stalwarts; they were unabashedly in favor of milking the spoils system for their own personal enrichment. Maine Congressman **James G. Blaine** led the Half-Breeds; this group also loved corruption but at least wanted to be at a little bit discreet about it. This pathetic state of affairs provides the perfect snapshot of the utterly unprincipled Gilded Age. First Lady Lucy Hayes — perhaps on some unconscious level trying to atone for sins swirling about the political landscape — earned the nickname "Lemonade Lucy" when she banned alcohol from the White House. But visitors devised ingenious ways to sneak intoxicating beverages onto the premises. One cabinet officer reportedly sneezed, cracking so many bottles tucked into his pants that he required hospitalization.

President Hayes had often proclaimed his intention to serve only one term, which was lucky for him since his streak of honesty had made his fellow Republicans utterly uninterested in renominating him. A Stalwart from the critical swing state of Ohio named **James Abrams Garfield** got the nod, but Conkling was able to get his Half-Breed partner in crime, Chester A. Arthur, nominated to run for Vice-President. Garfield had been a Union general in the Civil War, but the Democrats countered by nominating their own general, Winfield S. Hancock, who had been wounded at Gettysburg (reports that he had taken a musket ball in his butt scampering away from a Confederate infantry charge were Republican mudslinging and utterly false). Both sides barely addressed serious issues as they frantically waved the bloody shirt, tossed about insults and — on Election Day — cash and free drinks. Garfield barely won the popular vote but managed a solid majority in the Electoral College: 214-155.

Just about everyone who personally knew Garfield found him capable and a nice guy. And the new President did sincerely desire to follow up on his predecessor's efforts to at least begin to get the spoils system under control. But Garfield did not have the thick skin to turn people down when they asked him for favors — no wonder he had the reputation for being such a nice guy — so the usual mad scramble for jobs engulfed him as soon as he moved into the White House. For four months, President Garfield gasped for air in this swirling whirlpool of spoils when on July 2nd, 1881, disappointed (and deranged) office-seeker **Charles J. Guiteau** shot him in the back in a Washington railway station. Tragically, President Garfield lingered on in agony for about eleven weeks until he was almost certainly killed by his doctors, searching for the bullet in his body with all the subtlety of golfers trying to find an errant ball in the rough. Remember, back in those days (and for many decades still to come) a patient was more likely to be hurt by their physician than helped.

Thus the ultimate spoilsman Chester A. Arthur suddenly found himself elevated to the presidency. Job seekers licked their chops. But to most everyone's surprise, the shocking circumstances of President Garfield's death seemed to bring out a decent and digni-fied side of Arthur most people never knew existed. As President, he actually worked conscientiously and threw his support behind civil service reform.

The American public, outraged over the Garfield assassination, at last demanded decisive action. In 1883, Senators and Representatives, worried more about getting re-elected than anything else, did the right thing and passed the **Pendleton Act** — America's first real attempt to clean up the spoils system. The Pendleton Act set up a **Civil Service Commission** which was supposed to impartially guarantee that federal employees would be hired based on a merit system, rather than their political or familial connections. At first, the Act only covered about ten percent of federal employees, but today it has been expanded to cover just about all of them. And as long as we are on the subject of civil service reform, in 1939, Congress passed the **Hatch Act**, making it illegal to ask civil service (government) employees to make political contributions or actively engage in politics unless they choose to do so of their own free will. All this civil service reform was long overdue, and while it is good that we have these laws, let's not kid ourselves...if you are looking to get a government job, it still helps to know somebody!

In 1884, the Republicans once again had no interest in renominating a sitting Presi-dent who had turned out to be fundamentally honest. Chester A. Arthur was told to pack his integrity and hit the road, and being a hefty six foot two inches tall, he may well have replied, "Okay, which way to the nearest restaurant." Instead, Senator James G. Blaine of Maine, who had long craved the Republican nomination, finally got his wish. He was one slick operator, and a consummate Gilded Age politician. Now if you have been catching my drift these last several pages, that means he was also deeply corrupt — most blatantly in the favors he had thrown to railroad companies. Unfortunately for Blaine, solid proof of his malfeasance existed in the form of the **Mulligan letters**, one of which Blaine had closed with the admonition: "Burn this letter." It was pretty obvious to the American public that a politician was really up to no good when he asked a business-man he was corresponding with to torch their correspondence.

Even some Republicans couldn't stomach an obvious bribe-taker like Blaine, so they dramatically declared they were switching to the Democrats. Their former Repub-lican friends insultingly called them **Mugwumps**, an Indian name essentially describing a person who is totally full of themselves. Once again, here is an example of how history is not black or white, but gray; some of the mugwumps were honest reformers, but others probably were full of themselves and just looking for a better deal.

The Democrats nominated a former mayor of Buffalo and governor of New York named **Grover Cleveland**. Today, new parents rarely name a child Grover because of that annoying character on Sesame Street, but back then Grover was a perfectly good name. Cleveland had a terrific reputation as an honest reformer, but during the cam-paign it was revealed that he, like Blaine, had skeletons in his closet. One of them was a doozy; while living in Buffalo, the bachelor Cleveland had fathered an illegitimate child. Back then, this was unbelievably scandalous and the candidate was urged by his advi-sors to flat-out lie about it and deny everything. But Cleveland demanded that the truth be told; he had accepted responsibility for the child and provided financial support. Imagine the mudslinging in this campaign: the Mulligan letters versus the stigma of an illegitimate child. But the difference was Cleveland told the truth, while Blaine clung to his lies. Cleveland won in a squeaker, and we get an obvious lesson in American morality. You can screw up, but if you sincerely admit it and apologize, folks will generally forgive and give you another chance. Later on in our history, there will be plenty of examples of how the cover-up always damages a person's reputation much more than the initial mistake.

President Cleveland — the first Democratic President in twenty-eight years — proved to be just another post Civil War presidential stinker, though perhaps the best of a bad lot. He announced that he wanted to enforce the Pendleton Act, but ravenous office-seeking vultures still found themselves plenty of snacks. Republicans, with some justification, accused the President of virtuous words unmatched by deeds, and like the other presidents of his time, Cleveland willingly let Congress take the initiative on legislation.

Remarkably, in light of the federal deficits the United States regularly racks up in our modern era, the Cleveland Administration was embarrassed by a budget surplus that was due almost entirely to high protective tariffs that poured revenue into the national treasury. Remember, there were no income taxes in those days. To his credit, Cleveland essentially said, "Hey. This is crazy, let's lower these protective tariffs and give American consumers a break." His most famous quote was the more esoteric: "What's the use of being elected unless you stand for something."

Protectionist Republicans (and even some of his fellow Democrats) accused Cleveland of being hostile to American businesses. Politicians in both parties would have loved to see the surplus squandered on more perks for Civil War veterans, who by this time had waved their bloody shirts to shreds and received from the government as much as, or in many cases more than, they deserved. A couple of hardcore alcoholics in the House of Representatives reportedly suggested that a nationwide party with an "open bar" would be the best way to dispose of the troublesome surplus. But Cleveland held firm, demanded the tariffs be lowered, and in so doing angered lots of voters in both parties. This showed guts and fortitude — virtually unheard of among politicians of the Gilded Age — and President Cleveland's honorable stance cost him his chance to be reelected.

Super-psyched to knock off the unpopular Cleveland in the presidential election of 1888, the Republicans nominated just the man for the job: **Benjamin Harrison**. This senator from Indiana came from a famous family; his grandfather had been (briefly before he dropped dead in a month) the ninth president of the United States, and his great-grandfather had been a signer of the Declaration of Independence (there was an unsubstantiated rumor that his father — rarely mentioned by Benjamin — had been a female impersonator based out of New Orleans). Naturally, Harrison defeated the incumbent Cleveland by promising the sugary sweets most self-interested Americans craved: high tariffs and still more benefits for Civil War veterans. In an oddity, Cleveland received more popular votes than Harrison but lost out in the Electoral College. Since November 2000, Al Gore receives regular visits from Grover Cleveland in his nightly dreams, or rather nightmares.

President Harrison was one of America's worst presidents. He accomplished virtually nothing, and I hate to waste a paragraph on this guy. He turned his back on civil service reform, and squandered the surplus on the civil war veterans and **pork barrel** projects for influential Republican congressmen (pork barrel projects benefit an individual state or congressional district but are paid for out of federal revenue that is supposed to serve the entire nation). Senators and Representatives support each other's pork barrel projects (a form of vote trading political scientists refer to as **logrolling**) because it helps politicians who "bring home the bacon" get reelected. All this stuff still goes on today — some call it the lifeblood of American politics — but you'd be right if you said lots of this bacon really smells rancid and some parts of the country unfairly get more of it than others. I guess in some ways American democracy is like the state of New Jersey — most of it is something to be really proud of, but there are times on the turnpike when you absolutely have to hold your nose.

The Gilded Age was not America's finest hour...or minute or second for that matter. Reconstruction brought recalcitrant Confederate states back into the Union, and the federal government abandoned freed African-Americans to the purgatory of a segregated South. Corruption permeated politics and talk of reform was basically all hot air. As far as most of the Republicans and the Democrats of the time should be remembered, Shakespeare said it best: "A pox on both their houses." As the years passed, many Americans, disgusted with the stench of the dirty dealers, turned their noses to the sweet-smelling western frontier. Others stared wide-eyed at an expanding America that every day seemed to present new and greater opportunities to make a fortune. Who will get rich? Who will stay poor? And what the heck are those newfangled contraptions scaring the horses? Uh oh...stay tuned...don't touch that dial!!!

This Really Happened!

For centuries washing your clothes is so much trouble many people don't even bother. At sea, clothes are actually towed behind the ship for cleaning. Perfumes from the Far East become popular in Europe — not to entice or enchant, but to cover up body odor! Then around 1860 the idea of putting clothes, water and soap into a wooden box and tumbling them is beginning to catch on. In 1914 electric motors are introduced, but water often drips into them, giving paralyzing shocks to the operators. But soon the bugs are worked out, mass production makes the luxuries of the well-to-do the necessities of the middle class, and new standards of cleanliness sweep across America!!!

And the rest is History...

Quiz yourself on Chapter 8

Multiple Choice (circle the correct answer).

1. In the Compromise of 1877
   a. African-Americans ended up getting screwed
   b. Rutherford B. Hayes became President
   c. Democrats completely wussied out
   d. Samuel Tilden got screwed
   e. All of the above

2. During the Gilded Age politicians waved the bloody shirt
   a. because they hoped someone would volunteer to wash it
   b. they were too lazy to take it the congressional Lost & Found
   c. they wanted to appeal to veterans for their votes
   d. because they couldn't find the bloody pants
   e. none of the above

3. Ulysses S. Grant was
   a. a poor general but an excellent president
   b. an excellent general but a poor president
   c. a poor general and a poor president
   d. an excellent dancer and a fabulous lover
   e. a and d

4. Big city bosses such as "Boss" Tweed were
   a. basically "Robin Hoods" out to help the poor
   b. basically "Clara Bartons" out to help the injured
   c. basically Charlie Sheens completely out of their minds
   d. basically trying to enrich themselves
   e. none of the above

5. The assassination of President James Abrams Garfield
   a. made Mrs. Garfield's lover very happy
   b. dramatically demonstrated the need for reform of the military
   c. dramatically demonstrated the need for reform of the spoils system
   d. put an end to target practice in the White House hallways
   e. b and d

6. Radical Republicans
   a. insisted on a harsh Reconstruction
   b. took Control of Reconstruction away from President Johnson
   c. instituted a strict dress code for all congressional functions
   d. tried to impeach the President because they disagreed with him
   e. a, b, and d

7. Booker T. Washington's "Atlanta Compromise"
   a. delighted whites because it seemed so accommodating
   b. urged economic empowerment for blacks
   c. was contrary to W.E.B. Du Bois' calls for immediate equality
   d. allowed blacks and whites to attend Braves games together
   e. a, b, and c

8. During the Cleveland Administration
   a. stupid people thought the city of Cleveland was our nation's capital
   b. the federal budget had a surplus
   c. the federal budget had a deficit
   d. Cincinnati and Akron were jealous
   e. b and c

9. President Harrison
   a. survived in office a lot longer than his grandfather
   b. squandered federal money on more money for veterans
   c. squandered federal money of pork barrel projects for Congressmen
   d. should have been in a different line of work
   e. all of the above

10. During the Gilded Age
    a. government corruption was much worse than it is today
    b. the rich got richer and the poor got screwed
    c. millionaires had a blast
    d. Most politicians deserved to be put in jail
    e. all of the above

CHAPTER 9

INDUSTRIALIZATION, FADING FRONTIER, AND FURIOUS FARMERS

or

We're Mad As Hell and We're Not Going to Take It Anymore!

After the Civil War a vast western frontier beckoned, and lots of energetic, strong-willed Americans headed out toward the setting sun. Big cities, teeming with new immigrants, grew like crazy. Led by the railroad industry and plenty of really cool inventions, the late nineteenth century became an era in which a few crafty businessmen built huge companies and made fortunes beyond anyone's wildest dreams. But when regular folks — farmers and factory workers — started to demand fair treatment from the big bosses, not only were they told to get lost, but they also had to think fast and duck.

FREE LAND AND STRIKING IT RICH
or *Get Those Indians Out of My Way*

In 1862, Congress passed a remarkable piece of legislation called the **Homestead Act**. Basically, it meant free land — 160 acres out on the Prairie — for any citizen who wanted it. As usual, there were bumps aplenty in this supposed road to the American Dream. Back east, 160 acres was ample space for a successful family farm, but out on the prairie the uncertainty of rainfall made it tough. Besides droughts, "homesteaders" faced wickedly hot summers, bitterly cold winters, floods, dusty winds, swarms of hungry grasshoppers and, just when they thought life could not get any tougher, a sales person would arrive selling AMWAY products (I apologize; AMWAY did not exist back then and listing it alongside swarms of grasshoppers is insulting...to the grasshoppers).

Speculators (the types of guys who today are executives in the cable or oil business) and railroad companies got into the land-selling racket, so for many of the relatively poor settlers, their new land was far from free. But lots of hardy families — rich in guts and perseverance — made a successful go at it in houses built of baked sod. With steel-tipped plows, they dug deep and found soil moist enough (This is called "**dry farming**") to produce corn, oats and hardy new strains of wheat. In some places, windmills helped raise water up from depths of nearly 300 feet for drinking and irrigation. **Cyrus McCormick** (who earlier had invented the reaper) developed a giant "combine" that could actually cut, gather, thresh, and then bag wheat. Inventions tend to spawn related inventions, so demand for grain increased when **John S. Pillsbury** devised an improved flour-milling process. Yes, you are right to make the obvious connection. The Pillsbury Doughboy we know from television commercials is directly related to John S. Pillsbury — though not literally by blood, because the Pillsbury Doughboy is an animated figure and far too fluffy to be a real person.

In 1863, work on a transcontinental railroad finally began. A student of mine once wrote in an essay, "The transcontinental railroad ran from New York City to Albany in upstate New York." This was humorous because the word transcontinental obviously means "across the continent" from coast to coast. My former student is now an executive on Wall Street making millions of dollars: still clueless but now rich. There's no justice. Anyway, riding a train would sure beat those covered (often called Conestoga) wagons any day. The **Union Pacific Railroad** built westward from Omaha, Nebraska and the workers (mainly poor Irish guys) fought off blazing heat, blizzards and, sometimes, hostile Indians. The **Central Pacific Railroad** pushed eastward from Sacramento, California and those workers (mostly Chinese immigrants rudely referred to as **coolies**) dug, chiseled and dynamited through mountains. In 1869, the transcontinental railroad was completed when the tracks joined at **Promontory Point**, Utah. Posing for photographers and driving a ceremonial "**golden spike,** " one of the rich railroad executives, who probably had never wielded a heavy hammer in his life, swung and missed and broke his foot. Well, maybe sometimes there is justice.

The railroad industry grew like wildfire and became the most important driving force behind America's remarkable economic growth in the latter decades of the nineteenth century. The development of steel really boosted the railroads; steel was mass-produced from iron using the **Bessemer process**, invented in the 1850s by an American named **William Kelly**, who obviously got shafted since history books never refer to something called the Kelly process. Oh well, just understand that steel is stronger, lighter and more flexible than iron and thus a big technological advance. In addition, tracks were given a standardized gauge (meaning all railroad companies agreed to build their rails the same width apart) and the air brake, invented by **George Westinghouse**, made it possible to stop all cars at the same time with equal pressure. The Pullman sleeping car, invented by **George M. Pullman**, made longer hours on board easier to bear because now people could enjoy privacy to sleep or, uh, you know.

Building the railroads required iron, steel, wood, gravel, glass, etc., and all along the tracks sprang up train stations, restaurants, hotels, and finally, bustling towns. New workers were hired. Telegraph wires naturally got strung up alongside the tracks. People and products journeyed east to west and west to east faster than ever before, so fast that railroad companies needed to create America's "time zones" — Eastern, Central, Mountain, and Pacific. For example, it is seven in the morning in California when it is ten in the morning in New York. If you are now thinking: Gee, folks in New York get to sleep later than they do in California then it is time to stop reading this book so you can tune your radio to Rush Limbaugh. You get the idea — the railroads caused the entire economy to grow, and today economists refer to the railroads as the "multiplier" of America's nineteenth century economy.

Looking ahead, it's pretty obvious that the automobile would become the "multiplier" of the twentieth century. But what about the twenty-first century? Has the computer or internet become the multiplier of this new century we're living in? Maybe next big multiplier hasn't been invented yet. Maybe the next multiplier will be some sort of a teleportation device in which we need only think about where we want to go and, poof, we're there. Yes, I do watch way too much of the SciFi Channel.

From the 1860s well into the 1880s, cattle ranchers grazed huge herds across the open range — unclaimed lands owned by the government. Cowboys would herd the longhorns vast distances to cities such as Abilene, Kansas or Laramie, Wyoming, where the steers would be loaded onto "cattle cars" and shipped to slaughterhouses in the sprawling midwestern metropolis of Chicago, Illinois. Next, newly-invented refrigerator rail cars sped the beef to the hungry human carnivores back east. It was probably around this time that someone invented steak sauce. And, by the way, then as now, slaughterhouses are incredibly disgusting places. But as long as we get our burgers, who cares?

For a short while in the late nineteenth century, a "wild west" actually existed replete with saloons, gambling, and dance hall girls who definitely weren't respectable. And there really were duels in the center of town..."Draw"...and then the anguished cry "Somebody go find Doc and sober him up." Towns like Dodge City always seemed to need a new sheriff because the old one in the white hat was either shot dead or "run out of town" by bad guys who, as depicted in Hollywood movies, always wore black hats. Any sheriff who donned a hat in a muted pastel shade never had chance.

Occasionally, Americans moved west so fast that they found themselves in regions not yet organized as territories, lacking governments and laws. Out of necessity, "justice" had to be administered by vigilantes: self appointed police, prosecutors, judges, juries and executioners all rolled into one motley mob of drunken jerks with guns on their hips. Needless to say, many innocents were hanged along with the guilty...kind of like the situation that persists to this day in the state of Texas.

By the end of the 1880s the age of the true cowboy was virtually over. Farmers arrived out west and, utilizing newly-invented barbed wire, effectively began to fence off the open range. Sheep ranchers also showed up on the scene and became bitter competitors with the cattle ranchers. Apparently sheep and cattle don't get along, so for a couple of decades there were ugly range wars in which the cattle ranchers and sheep ranchers shot at and frequently killed each other. In any event, the era of the cowboy and his "long drive" to bring cattle to market ended quickly. But to this day we still fantasize about the romance and freedom of the cowboy life in the saddle and under the stars. We love cowboy movies and cowboy clothes and lots of folks out west think they're really cool in their cowboy hats. It's often forgotten that many of the real cowboys were black or Mexican (cowboy comes from the Spanish word *vaquero*) and life on the long drive was fraught with hardships. Sleeping under the stars was no great shakes when a thunderstorm rolled in. And in real life, that guy around the campfire with the harmonica playing Home On The Range got real annoying real fast.

Ever since 1849, gold and silver strikes had periodically sent hordes of prospectors out west to strike it rich. In the movies and on television, these prospectors are frequently really old bearded guys who seem to have a very weird relationship with their mule. In reality, Americans of all stripes joined the scramble for the glittery metals. The **Comstock Lode** (1859) in Nevada is probably America's most famous gold and silver strike of all time. The word lode can mean either "a deposit of precious metal" or "an abundant supply of something." Today there is still a common expression: "We've hit the mother lode!" I first used that expression as a teenager to my buddies upon our arrival at a dance at a Catholic all-girls high school. Anyway, wherever there was a gold strike, a town would spring up virtually overnight; Virginia City in the Nevada territory was a perfect example of one of these boomtowns. Then when the mine went bust everyone would skedaddle right away, leaving behind nothing but an eerie ghost town with buildings but no people...except for that strange old guy with his mule.

THE FATE OF THE PLAINS INDIANS
or *Never Mind the Treaty — Move!*

Let's not sugarcoat it, the Native Americans who had long lived out on the western lands really got treated abominably. By the 1850s, a steady stream of settlers poured into

Indian country and inevitably, arrows and bullets started to fly. The United States government facilitated the signing of treaties intended first to enforce tribal boundaries, and later create "reservations" that would keep the Indians contained and out of the way of the rising tide of white settlement. But Indians hunting buffalo and settlers seeking fertile farmland or the rumor of gold naturally paid scant attention to paper boundaries. Both sides broke treaty after treaty; the **Fort Laramie Treaty** (1851) and the **Medicine Lodge Treaty** (1868) are two of the better-known worthless pieces of scrap. United States government agents charged with distributing aid to the resettled tribes proved to be mostly crooked; by the time the conniving bureaucrats had pocketed their "take," the Indians often ended up receiving spoiled food and vermin-infested blankets. At a time when corruption pervaded virtually all levels of American government, the **Bureau of Indian Affairs** was the crème de la crème or, more accurately, the scum de la scum.

Fierce fighting ensued, with the Native American warriors proving time and again to be formidable adversaries. They won numerous battles against the U.S. Army, notably at the **Little Big Horn**, when the arrogant General **George Armstrong Custer** divided his forces and charged directly into an encampment of Sioux and Cheyenne, who were in no mood to be molested. This event has gone down in History as "**Custer's Last Stand**," so I'm sure you can tell how it turned out — General "Yellow Hair" and all 264 of his soldiers were massacred. The Indians were led by **Sitting Bull** and **Crazy Horse** who, of course, are famous. Another Indian chief named Herb has been completely forgotten.

Outnumbered and outgunned, eventually the Indians would be defeated. Led by the legendary **Geronimo**, the Apaches of the Southwest were finally forced to end their resistance in 1886. **Chief Joseph** of the **Nez Perce** surrendered by saying "I will fight no more forever," words that remain a sad and eloquent echo of this sorry episode in our History. Contributing to Native American destruction was decimation of the great herds of buffalo they depended upon for food, clothing and shelter. White hunters shot the docile beasts for meat, for their hides, and sometimes (this is really sick but true) through open windows while riding on the railroad for a hearty laugh as the defenseless creatures tumbled and died. Before the coming of "civilization" tens of millions of buffalo had roamed the Great Plains, but by 1875 only about one thousand remained alive as the species came within a few rifle rounds of total extinction. Personally, I've never understood the appeal of hunting for sport. I say give the animals guns and make it fair.

In 1889, the Sioux created a new religion called the "**Ghost Dance**": a mixture of traditional tribal faiths and Christianity that promised redemption for the vanquished Native Americans. Nearby white settlers did not understand it and thus felt threatened; at **Wounded Knee** in South Dakota the army put an end to it all by massacring nearly three hundred Sioux men, women, and children. **Helen Hunt Jackson** made some folks back then feel guilty when she forthrightly chronicled the treatment of the Native Americans in her book entitled *A Century of Dishonor*. It's an important book; somebody should call Oprah and suggest she put it on her famous reading list.

Unfortunately, even white reformers with good intentions supported legislation called the **Dawes Act** (1887) that stripped tribes of their legal status and attempted to "Americanize" the Indians. Individual Native Americans were given their 160 acres of free land so they could become peaceful little farmers and eventually earn their citizenship, which disgracefully took until 1924. Priceless tribal culture was lost forever, and in many cases conniving white speculators purchased much of the land at rock bottom prices from unsuspecting Indians, who traditionally had not recognized the concept of private ownership of land. Make that call to Oprah now.

THE RISE OF BIG BUSINESS
or *Here's the Deal — Take It or Leave It*

Thomas Edison labored tirelessly at his workshop in Menlo Park, New Jersey and produced many remarkable inventions, including the electric light bulb, the phonograph and the moving picture. It has long been told that Edison once arrived at work fully dressed except for his pants. That's because Edison truly was the ultimate "absent minded professor," a genius with way too much on his mind that day to remember his pants. I once forgot my pants, but it was after a fraternity party in college, and frankly, indefensible. Anyway, other cool inventions emerged in this era such as the sewing machine, the typewriter, the adding machine, the cash register, and the stock ticker. **Alexander Graham Bell** invented the telephone in 1876, enabling a girl to break up with her boyfriend without having to tell him face to face. Sorry, but I'm still bitter. What is most important here is that within about twenty years the telephone revolutionized communication in America.

After the Civil War, businesses continued to grow larger and larger. The great need of capital for their expansion caused the **corporation**, a type of company in which investors buy stock certificates and then share in the profits, to become dominant. Some companies organized themselves into **trusts**; shareholders of smaller companies would turn over their stock to a trust for management by its board of trustees, in exchange for a slice of the trust's profits. This arrangement gave birth to the **monopoly**, in which one company could virtually own and control an entire industry. And if one man maintained at least a fifty-one percent ownership of such a company, he could wield unprecedented economic power — including who gets the hot-looking secretary.

To be fair, monopolies did have a positive side; all aspects of production (including research and development) could be streamlined, allowing industries to operate more efficiently and expand faster. But there was a wicked downside; small independent companies were driven out of business and monopolies, lacking competition, could engage in price gouging, pay their workers starvation wages and, ultimately, screw the general public at will. Today, we get a taste of this kind of thing when a Wal-Mart or Home Depot comes to town. Of course, the classic board game "Monopoly" was originally inspired by these types of business practices, and is perfectly named because your goal is to make as much money as you can and drive the other players out of business. I'm pretty good at it and I usually choose to be the shoe.

The late nineteenth century was an era of **laissez faire** — an era in which government left businesses alone to function as they darn well pleased. Trusts and monopolies maximized their profits by stifling competition wherever possible. Railroads emerged as the first monster corporations when a man named **Cornelius Vanderbilt** played the real life game of Monopoly to perfection. **John D. Rockefeller** became the richest man in America when his **Standard Oil Company** achieved control of over ninety percent of the country's oil refining and transportation. **J.P. Morgan** became America's greatest investment banker, and an accomplished master at consolidating the many huge corporations that would come to control (some said strangle) the American economy. And **Andrew Carnegie** created the largest steel company in the world. At least Carnegie felt so guilty that he sold his company to Morgan and spent the rest of his life as a philanthropist, giving away most of his money to worthy causes (unlike a rich guy I heard about recently who died and was buried in his super-expensive Maserati, in kind of a sick attempt to circumvent the old adage that "you can't take it with you"). Carnegie got it right, so the next time you are at a concert at Carnegie Hall, give the guy a nod.

Eventually some of these trust titans felt the need to justify their enormous wealth — if not to the American people, than at least to themselves. They conjured up a conservative **Gospel of Wealth**, proclaiming that God had ordained them to be wealthy. There is of course no "Gospel of Wealth" in the Bible, but frequently, some people defend ungodly behavior simply by declaring that God is on their side. Other millionaires perverted the serious scientific work of Charles Darwin, who had articulated his theory of evolution in his book *Origin of the Species*, published in 1859. Darwin stated that humans (and all contemporary species of animals and plants) had slowly evolved from lower forms of life, basing his theories on what became commonly known as "survival of the fittest and natural selection." Rich guys said in effect: Okay, since only the strong survive, then I'm rich because I'm stronger than the poor who are weak.

By blaming the poor for their plight — in effect calling them unmotivated and lazy — the wealthy fabricated a philosophy called **Social Darwinism**, justifying both their ruthless business practices and their opposition to any government assistance for poor people, whom they believed were to blame for their own poverty in a world in which only the strong survive. Today nobody admits out loud to being a Social Darwinist — applying a biological theory to human society is really too stupid for anyone to try to defend in logical debate — but there sure are people out there who act like Social Darwinists. You figure out who they are; this book is an account of American History and not about my personal politics and beliefs. (Hint: it's the conservative Republicans who would cut every social program out there if they could.)

Obviously, the vast majority of Americans were lower- and middle-class and well aware that they stood no chance of ever joining the country club. These folks were not buying the Gospel of Wealth or Social Darwinism. In the 1880s, there emerged a clamor for government to step in and do something to curb the unrestrained power of big business. Thankfully, politicians required to periodically stand for re-election usually respond to the voice of the people, even though in many cases they wish they didn't have to hear it. In 1887, Congress passed the **Interstate Commerce Act** to begin regulating the railroads. Three years later, the **Sherman Antitrust Act** became law. Neither of these pieces of legislation had much effect at the time, though, because slimy lawyers immediately found loopholes and judges routinely ruled in favor of the big business owners, who also happened to be their good friends and golf partners. Nevertheless, these two Acts were the first crack in the aristocratic wall of laissez faire, the first time the federal government ever acknowledged its right (and perhaps its duty) to protect the American public from the abuses of big corporations, whose owners were commonly referred to as "malefactors of great wealth," "**robber barons**," and other names not to be repeated in a "family" book like this.

NEW IMMIGRANTS ARRIVE
or *Darn, We're Gonna Have To Move — Again*

In the 1870s, waves of "new" immigrants began to wash up on America's shores, joining the "old" immigrants — mainly the original English, plus the Irish and Germans who had arrived en masse starting in the 1830s. Now Italians, Greeks and other southern Europeans arrived, and from Eastern Europe came Jews, Russians, Poles, Hungarians and others — a cornucopia of additional ethnic groups. Some were fleeing poverty, some were escaping political or religious persecution, and all were chasing a dream — the American dream of a better life in a prosperous new land.

As always, the new immigrants were not welcomed by the citizens already here. The United States has always been a nation built and energized by immigrants (and don't forget the forced immigration experience of blacks from Africa), but nevertheless, every time a new ethnic group shows up, the families already settled here resent the newcomers and allow them only begrudgingly into the American neighborhood. It's a pattern we can't seem to shake. Currently Mexican-Americans and Muslim-Americans are having the same rough time. Maybe some day aliens from outer space — fleeing poverty, religious persecution or some scary guy like Darth Vader — will arrive in flying saucers hoping to join us. Let's hope we Americans show these aliens a lot more respect and acceptance than we've shown our fellow earthlings. Come on, it could happen.

Ever since 1849, lots of Chinese had been arriving out on the west coast. Times were tough in China, and most of these Chinese immigrants planned to make a few bucks (or find a few gold nuggets) and return back home. But over the next several decades, many Chinese stayed and became a vital part of the American labor force. Chinese who moved to eastern cities kept their native customs alive by clustering in a section of each city that came to be known as "Chinatown." Often, Chinatown was right next to "Little Italy," causing many arguments among the general population over which restaurant to go to.

In 1873, an economic depression hit the country that would last through the rest of the decade. With jobs scarce, many Americans started to resent the Chinese immigrants, despite the fact that their restaurants consistently prepared terrific takeout meals in under twenty minutes. Mainly out in California, there were numerous ugly episodes of anti-Chinese violence, and in 1882, Congress shamefully passed the **Chinese Exclusion Act** and other restrictions on immigration. For the first time, the United States started to turn away an entire ethnic group and, shockingly by modern sensibilities but back then hardly anyone cared, it became illegal to enter the country if you were a pauper (really poor), a criminal, a convict, a prostitute, a polygamist, insane, an alcoholic, a political extremist, an obvious carrier of infectious disease — or Chinese.

Ironically, Japanese began to enter the country, seeking the same opportunities the Chinese immigrants had sought. American bigots sprang into action once again, forming the **Japanese Exclusion League** in 1905. Generally, there was a lot of nativist (anti-foreign) feeling towards the end of the 19th century; in 1887 the **American Protective Association** started lobbying against Catholics and Jews from Southern and Eastern Europe.

The Statue of Liberty, a gift from France, opened to the public in 1886, standing tall in New York Harbor. Inscribed at the base of the statue were the words of the poet Emma Lazarus:

> *Give me your tired, your poor,*
> *Your huddled masses yearning to breathe free,*
> *The wretched refuse of your teeming shore.*

These are truly inspiring words, and America has accepted countless immigrants of all stripes. But to be fair, when you look at the Statue of Liberty closely through the binoculars of History, remember how poorly many were treated once they got here. Don't get me wrong, "Lady Liberty" will always be incredibly beautiful...but her slip is showing.

With immigrants pouring in and the folks already here having lots of babies, America's population almost doubled between 1870 and 1900, from about forty to nearly eighty million. From 1892 to 1924, **Ellis Island** in New York Harbor served as America's primary processing center for immigrants. Health officials performed a perfunctory examination and sent just about everyone (approximately 98%) on their way...kind of like what happens today in lots of hospital emergency rooms when patients admit they have no health insurance. Urban areas grew the most rapidly as many farmers sought out an easier and "faster" life in the city, where at least you could get simple directions out of someone in less than half an hour. Steel skeleton construction allowed for very tall buildings, the newly dubbed *skyscrapers*. Horse-drawn streetcars on tracks, and later electric trolleys, made it possible for city dwellers to live farther and farther away from their jobs in the inner city, and thus was born another new term: suburbs. Most middle and upper class city folk took up residence in suburbia. The poor newer immigrants, having no choice, remained behind in the "inner city" under increasingly squalid conditions.

As cities continued to expand with virtually no order or central planning, they soon began to resemble huge garbage dumps, with impoverished people living in them. There was no trash collection or clean water, and raw sewage collected in the streets. Greedy landlords erected substandard four- to six-story buildings called tenements, into which they crammed destitute immigrant families nearly out of money and completely out of options. There were no laws back then protecting "tenants," so unventilated windowless apartments were common, and some avaricious slumlords would even stick a family or two in the space under the staircase. The next time you call a plumber to come to your home to fix a leak in your sink and he charges you a fortune, don't forget that you at least have a sink with running water! And you also have a toilet. Back then poor city folks often had to go in a bucket and then empty it in the gutter and then...let's change the subject.

With so many people living in such close quarters, germs spread quickly and without mercy. The numbers of children who died before the age of five were staggering. Some good people noticed the poverty and tried to help through private charities. One notable example is **Jane Addams**, who founded America's first settlement house (named **Hull House**) in Chicago in 1889. Soon, settlement houses opened in big cities throughout America. They were essentially community centers, where Addams and her fellow settlement workers (mostly women, a few men, all of them with big hearts) could help the poor with classes teaching English, basic health care, and nutrition. Sometimes people down on their luck would drop by a settlement house for a cup of coffee and moral support in a huge metropolis that more often than not was cold and callous to the less fortunate. Obviously, there was no cover charge.

Some churches and synagogues pitched in to help; others were sadly indifferent or oblivious. The **Salvation Army** (founded in 1879 to redeem fallen Christians) commendably launched a full frontal assault on the beachhead of urban poverty. You better believe the hungry and homeless appreciated the free food and shelter — even if they had to recite a prayer and sing a couple of hymns to get it, accompanied by a Salvation Army band that was (let's be honest here) performing some of the worst music ever in the History of America, even worse than disco. But nobody should seriously knock the Salvation Army — they are selfless volunteers who (similar to Red Cross workers) do good works to this day.

In 1890, **Jacob Riis** published a book called **How the Other Half Lives** in which, through his words and photographs, he forthrightly chronicled the suffering of America's urban poor. The pain etched into the faces of so many families living in wretched conditions — and orphaned little children living on the street, always hungry and with no place to turn — were enough to make a lot of American men and women cry, though as usual the men would lie and claim they had something in their eyes. Now you might be wondering...where in dealing with this crisis was the government? The answer: the government was nowhere and uncaring. Local and state officials made inadequate, often just token, efforts to help the poor, and the federal government did absolutely nothing. Remember, this was a time when virtually no one — Democrat or Republican — believed it was the job of the federal government to directly aid the needy. But Riis and his book stirred the conscience of the nation, and within a few years the Salvation Army would receive some serious reinforcements.

LABORERS START TO ORGANIZE
or *Get Back To Work Or I'll Shoot!*

Thanks to the Industrial Revolution, by the second half of the nineteenth century most American workers no longer worked in their homes or small shops. They worked in factories run by large companies, and their livelihood depended directly upon the generosity of the company's owner. But in reality there was rarely any generosity. The big bosses viewed wage increases and investments to improve working conditions as money diverted away from their already-bulging profit margins. Workers frequently worked six days a week for ten hours a day, but lots of folks worked seven days for twelve hours or more. Workplaces commonly lacked adequate ventilation, heating, lighting, and accessible escape routes in the event of a fire.

Wages sucked — sorry for the crude language but I really want to make the point that many people could barely get by in terms of basic shelter and food. Raising a family was especially difficult. Women, blacks, and immigrants made less money than white men. And skilled laborers made more than unskilled laborers. This is just as true today as it was then, or in 1800, or 1700. There's a History lesson here — in America, <u>Skilled workers make a lot more money than unskilled workers</u> — so if you are reading this book and thinking about dropping out of high school or college, or that vocational training program you are currently enrolled in — don't do it. STAY IN SCHOOL. Of course, if you are lucky enough to have inherited a lot of money, congratulations, you can do what you want, just don't be rude and rub it in our noses like Paris Hilton. And don't ever drive drunk.

Most disgraceful and shocking to our modern sensibilities is the child labor that existed back then. Children toiled away for pennies a day performing menial tasks, while steam- or electric-powered machines did the heavy lifting. Not surprisingly, it was not uncommon for a ten-year-old working a twelve-hour shift to momentarily lose focus, move just a little bit too slowly, and get an arm or a leg crushed in some cold steel contraption that never daydreamed or slackened its pace. I bet I know what you're thinking right now, and I agree with you — it would be great if the movie *Back To the Future* was true; we could use a really cool time machine to go back and tell those factory owners to their faces how much future generations of Americans despise them for their unspeakably cruel exploitation of young children.

In the years after the Civil War, workers tried to elevate their standards of living by organizing unions, but it remained an uphill struggle or, more accurately, a steep mountain climb. During the depression of the mid-1870s, railroad company owners faced reduced revenues. In order to avoid having to cut back on their filet mignon consumption, they slashed their workers' wages. Stomachs churning, railroad workers across the nation cast down their bowls of rancid stew, declared a strike and paralyzed rail traffic. President Hayes was furious at the strikers and ordered the army to crush them, and in gun battles dozens died and the strikes collapsed. Then dessert was served at the White House.

In truth, many (probably most) Americans at the time supported the President. Many of the laborers were recent arrivals from Europe who had brought "dangerous" ideas with them. A few were communists who believed the government should protect exploited workers by taking ownership of all industries and safeguarding the economy. **Karl Marx** first postulated the theory of **communism** in *The Communist Manifesto of 1848* and ***Das Kapital***, published in 1867, and his radical views did sound intriguing in theory. But future world events would prove beyond a shadow of a doubt that communism is a fatally flawed system that, in practice, viciously oppresses the masses, exacerbates rather than alleviates poverty, and, worst of all, forces potentially hot women to dress in baggy peasant dresses and sensible shoes.

Socialists, less extreme than the communists, demanded that the government step in to forcefully regulate the unbridled American free enterprise system (capitalism) that so favored the rich over the poor. (Today, the American economy is a mixture of capitalism and socialism and is often referred to as regulated capitalism. Our continuing debate over precisely what the balance should be between the liberals/Democrats who lean toward government regulation and the conservatives/Republicans who prefer laissez faire capitalism sometimes gets nasty, but overall, it's healthy for our country.) **Anarchists** advocated the overthrow of the American government altogether — violently if necessary — then stammered idiotically when asked what alternative they had in mind to fill the void. Today, most anarchists can barely put a coherent English sentence together, and spend most of their time listening to old punk rock music from the seventies.

These new ideas confused and frightened lots of mainstream Americans who, as usual, had the potential to be quite bright, but chose the low road to ignorance. In the late 19th century, P.T. Barnum's circus and Buffalo Bill's traveling "Wild West Extravaganza" dazzled the easily beguiled; today we have NASCAR and Ultimate Fighting. Anyway, encouraged by the wealthy businessmen, some of whom owned the newspapers everybody read everyday, average Americans jumped to the emotional and incorrect conclusion that all workers who wanted to join unions were either communists, socialists, anarchists, or, worst of all, vegetarians. The truth was that the vast majority of workers in unions back then (and now and always in America) were extremely patriotic, loved a good thick steak, and all wanted a fair deal so they could support themselves and their families.

In the early 1880s, a union of skilled tradesmen called the **Knights of Labor** opened its ranks to women, blacks, immigrants, and unskilled workers. When the Knights pulled off a successful strike against railroad magnate Jay Gould, the union gained lots of prestige and membership soared to around 700,000. The Knights of Labor dreamed of creating a giant brotherhood of workers but, perhaps unavoidably, the union's various constituencies started arguing amongst themselves. Reportedly, skilled workers complained when unskilled workers misspelled words on banners, and male workers griped when women workers eschewed primary colors and produced banners in turquoise and lavender — but obviously the resentments ran much deeper. And, reeking of communism, the union attempted to own its own businesses (called "**workers cooperatives**") that naturally failed and further divided the membership.

As far as the Knights were concerned, in 1886 Murphy's Law really kicked in. Another strike against a Gould railroad collapsed. In Chicago, strikers at the McCormick Harvester Plant clashed with scabs (strikebreakers) and police. Four strikers were killed and several injured. The next day, May 4, 1886, in Chicago's Haymarket Square, someone — to this day unknown — threw a bomb at the police, igniting an all out battle that resulted in several dozen casualties, including seven dead policemen. Eight anarchists were rounded up virtually at random in a frenzied political climate in which officials and the public demanded that someone — anyone — pay. Four of the anarchists were hanged, three were given stiff prison sentences, and one committed suicide — perhaps in shock that the English departments at both Harvard and Yale had turned down his request for a teaching position. The Knights of Labor condemned the **Haymarket Square Bombing** but the public, wrongly, did not buy it, and soon the Knights found themselves unhorsed and irrelevant.

By July 1892, workers had been exploited for years at the Homestead Steelworks in Pennsylvania, owned by Andrew Carnegie. Living in a company town, they paid rent to live in company housing, shopped at the company store, worshipped at the company church, sent their kids to the company school, and, probably, cursed their bosses in the company outhouse. Then the company cut the workers' wages, but not their rent or the prices at the company store. Pushed to the breaking point, the unionized steelworkers went on strike. First, the company hired 300 armed Pinkerton guards (today we call these goons rent-a-cops) but the workers fought them off. Then, when Pennsylvania's Governor (with wide public support) ordered the state militia to crush the **Homestead Strike**, the steelworkers threw in the towel and received an even deeper pay cut as punishment.

Two years later, workers at the Pullman sleeping-car factory near Chicago received pay cuts of over 25 percent. The **American Railway Union**, led by **Eugene V. Debs**, declared a strike, whereupon union railroad workers refused to move any train that included a Pullman car. In support of a court order (an injunction) ordering an end to the **Pullman Strike**, President Cleveland actually sent in federal troops. Big business owners clinked their champagne glasses and toasted a nation in which the local, state, and even federal governments seemingly would go to any lengths to make sure oppressed and hungry workers stayed that way. Debs, who found himself locked up in jail, received a tin cup and dirty water.

In 1886, as the all-inclusive Knights of Labor skidded off a cliff, skilled workers representing many trade unions met at Columbus, Ohio to form the **American Federa-**

tion of Labor (AFL.) A Jewish immigrant named **Samuel Gompers**, a cigar maker and longtime advocate of organized labor, was elected president. Gompers and the AFL excluded unskilled workers and strongly discouraged the recruitment of blacks and women, reasoning coldly but correctly that skilled workers were much more difficult to replace than unskilled workers, and thus could throw a more lethal punch at management's protruding jaw during a strike. The AFL also stayed on message, demanding higher wages, shorter hours, and better working conditions, and they would have sounded like a broken record, except that records had not been invented yet. The AFL has fought countless rounds in support of the American laborer against management and its conservative supporters, and despite plenty of knockdowns for both sides, they're still in the ring today. When the twentieth century dawned, most Americans were still undecided about collective bargaining (the right of workers to join together in unions to bargain collectively) and whether or not unions had the right to — gasp — strike.

THE FARMERS' STRUGGLE GOES ON
or *Darn it Toto, We're Still In Kansas*

In good times the American farmer does well, but as we've seen, the economy periodically goes up and down, and in the down times farmers suffer first and worst. In good times, farmers borrow money to buy more land and equipment, and then when recessions or, worse, depressions hit, they miss payments and the bankers take away their farms. This pattern repeats itself throughout the entirety of American History. Today, Willie Nelson and others perform benefit concerts, a nice gesture, but not an answer to the fundamental problems that continually beset our farmers. By the way, I heard most real farmers hate the song "Old MacDonald Had A Farm," especially the part that goes with an oink oink here and an oink oink there.

Farmers in the late 19th century had a lot to be steamed about. Banks considered them to be bad risks (which they were) and charged them outrageously high interest rates. Railroad companies did what monopolies with no competition always do — they screwed the consumer — in this case charging farmers super high rates to ship their products to market. Meanwhile, manufactured goods the farmers needed to buy remained expensive because high protective tariffs kept low priced foreign goods out, allowing American manufacturing companies (many of them monopolies as well) to jack up their prices at will. Many poor and miserable farmers simply abandoned their farms and moved to the city, where they remained poor and miserable, but without that damn rooster crowing at dawn, at least they could sleep later.

Farmers who stuck it out began to pray for inflation, which is when prices go up. Usually everybody hates inflation; I recently paid eight bucks for a box of Special K cereal, so I'd personally like to take a shot at the greedy SOB who runs Kelloggs. Anyway, back then farmers continually demanded an increase in the money supply, which they reasoned would stimulate inflation and raise the price of their produce. During the Civil War, the United States government, desperate for fast cash, had printed about 400 million dollars worth of banknotes, called greenbacks, that were not backed by gold. In the years following the war, despite the protest of farmers, the government started to take the greenbacks out of circulation. In 1875, the **Specie Resumption Act** made greenbacks redeemable in gold, which would clearly reduce the money supply and stimulate *deflation* — lower prices, and the opposite of what the farmers wanted. Outraged, farmers formed the backbone (along with pro-union workers) of a new political party — the **Greenback-Labor party**. In 1878, the greenbackers polled a respectable million plus votes and elected fourteen members to Congress, but with only three percent of the vote, it was clear the Republicans and Democrats would always be the ones calling the monetary shots. The depression ran its course by 1878 and the Greenback-Labor party faded quickly, but its legacy reminds us that as early as the 1870s, lots of farmers and laborers were fed up with business as usual in Washington.

Farmers came together and formed an organization called the **Grange**, and by the mid 1870s — especially in the Midwest — there were local chapters with a combined membership of over 800,000. The Grange was a sort of "clubhouse" where local farmers and their families could meet to socialize and bitch about their lousy circumstances. On Saturday nights there was likely to be a dance, with plenty of foot stompin' music that would quickly result in a dance floor covered in horse manure. But what the heck...everyone had a good time. **Farmers Alliances** in the South and West were kind of the same thing and, as in the Grange, sometimes the farmers would form cooperatives to collectively own warehouses and feed-and-grain stores. Relax, the farmers were not communist — they were just trying to avoid getting ripped off by greedy businessmen.

The Grange and Farmers' Alliances provided moral support, but lots of farmers concluded that their salvation (inflation) could only be achieved through as much free coinage of silver as possible. For decades the U.S. had coined two metals — gold and silver — a monetary practice called **bimetallism**. Traditionally, sixteen ounces of silver equaled one ounce of gold. But to control inflation, conservative businessmen in the East successfully lobbied Congress to pass the **Coinage Act** of 1873, requiring the government to stop coining silver and just stick to gold — real gold, not those milk chocolate coins wrapped in shiny gold-colored paper. Farmers freaked — remember, they wanted inflation — and went straight to their local Grange, where they cursed a lot and denounced what they called the Crime of '73.

The government tried to shut the farmers up with the **Bland-Allison Act** of 1878 (which allowed for a modest amount of silver coinage) and the **Sherman Silver Purchase Act** of 1890 (which authorized the issuance of paper money backed by silver), but neither piece of legislation went far enough, so deflation and a money shortage persisted during this period. Then in the early 1890s the economy really took a hit. Silver miners hoisted so much silver out of the ground that its value started to decline, and folks rushed to trade in their silver (and paper money) for gold, which was considered to be the most secure and reliable of the monetary options available. The national treasury started to run dangerously low on gold as Americans rushed to dump their silver and stockpile their gold. Treasury agents who tried offering free coffee and a cheerful "come back next week" received some serious verbal abuse in return.

Farmers came to believe that eastern businessmen and bankers, in cahoots with both Republicans and Democrats in Congress, were sabotaging their interests. There was a lot of truth in this, since the easily bribed nineteenth-century politicians were much more influenced by gold than turnips and collard greens. In Omaha, Nebraska in the summer of 1892, farmers got together, scraped off their boots, and formed their own political party, the Populist Party, to advocate for their interests. The Populists naturally demanded much more free coinage of silver, a graduated income tax that would nail the rich much more than the poor, and government ownership of telegraph, telephone, and railroad companies to stop the greedy overcharging of the robber baron big business owners.

Eighteen-ninety-two was a presidential election year, and the Populists nominated Granger and Civil War veteran General **James B. Weaver**. The Republicans renominated President Benjamin Harrison, even though his four years in office had exposed him as nothing more than a petty party hack. The Democrats decided to give former President Cleveland another shot; Cleveland, remember, had already served one four year term and then been defeated by Harrison. On Election Day in November, Weaver did not come close to winning, but the Populists really stunned both the Republicans and the Democrats by polling over a million votes and sending over a dozen new members to Congress. Cleveland won because the poor city workers ignored the Populists and stuck with the Democrats, and thus Grover Cleveland became the first and only President thus far to be elected to two nonconsecutive terms. Unfortunately for the country, a few pounds heavier and a few IQ points lighter, Cleveland had become increasingly conservative.

In 1893, another wickedly bad depression struck. Cleveland blamed the whole economic mess on the Silver Purchase Act, so he cajoled Congress into repealing it, but still the treasury continued to bleed gold. In 1895, the nation's gold reserves grew so low that President Cleveland turned to a cadre of bankers led by J.P. Morgan, who (for a fat commission) agreed to lend the national Treasury sixty five million dollars in gold. This action did temporarily restore confidence in the nation's finances, but the spectacle of the President of the United States pleading with a private businessman for a financial bailout made lots of folks feel disgusted and actually ashamed for their country. Let's hope this never happens again, but given the way our government recklessly overspends tax dollars today, our current President might soon need to make nice with Bill Gates.

During the depression of the 1890s, the farmers were like canaries in a mine; they keeled over first, but quickly thereafter, industrial workers found themselves gasping as well. As thousands lost their jobs, Populist organizer "General" **James Coxey** led a march of hundreds of unemployed workers, nicknamed Coxey's Army, directly to Washington. Coxey demanded that the government print more paper money (to deliberately cause inflation) and use it to put unemployed workers back to work on public works projects.

158

Actually, Coxey was in some ways decades ahead of his time. We will soon see that, during the depression of the 1930s, the federal government entered into deficit spending to relieve unemployment by funding public works programs. But in the 1890s, Coxey was considered an extremist, and largely laughed at and ridiculed. Pathetically, when Coxey and a few of his followers were arrested for walking on the grass near the capitol building, his "army" basically disintegrated. Folks who, at the time, argued that the "freedom of assembly," provided by the first amendment to our Constitution, was more important than the trampling of a few petunias were basically told to shut up. And the depression raged on.

THE ELECTION OF 1896
or *I've Got More Money Than You Do, So I Win!*

In 1896, with the nation's economy still deep in the tank, many Democrats found themselves increasingly sympathetic to some of the ideas the Populists had been bandying about for years, particularly bimetallism and a lower protective tariff. They believed, with considerable justification, that President Cleveland had deserted them; Cleveland did not even bother attending the Democratic presidential nominating convention in Chicago because, let's be honest here, nobody likes to give a speech and be pelted with rotten tomatoes. Farmers and "silverites" gained the upper hand, and gleefully embraced a guy they thought would be perfect to lead them to victory: **William Jennings Bryan** of Nebraska. The Constitution states that a President must be at least thirty-five years old, and the youthful Bryan, thirty-six, reportedly needed to reassure folks that he did indeed need to shave every morning.

Bryan was a mesmerizing orator and a formidable presence on stage. At the convention, he gave one of the most famous speeches in American History: his pro-silver **"Cross of Gold" speech** in which he declared: "You shall not press down upon the brow of labor this crown of thorns, you shall not crucify mankind upon a cross of gold." As he held out his arms in imitation of Jesus Christ on the cross, lots of folks gasped and concluded that God must be on his (and now their) side. A few smart people — far too few — thought to themselves, Bryan, that sure is one cheap demagogic stunt and you should be ashamed of yourself.

Jesus Christ, of course, never mentioned the free coinage of silver or the protective tariff during his lifetime because those issues never came up back in ancient Palestine, but when politicians claimed to speak for him on contemporary issues, far too many Americans fell for it back then, and still do. (Today, it needs to be similarly noted that Jesus never mentioned issues such as abortion and gay civil rights, nor, for that matter, whether or not there should be a "designated hitter" in major league baseball.) But the die was cast back in 1896, and wide-eyed convention delegates nominated William Jennings Bryan to run as the Democratic candidate for president. Bryan immediately found himself nicknamed the "Silver Messiah," pleasing his campaign operatives, who knew full well that many unsophisticated Americans consistently failed to grasp a central foundation America was built upon — the separation of Church and State.

The Republicans nominated former Congressman **William McKinley** from the pivotal "swing" state of Ohio. Finally, here was an American presidential election in which the issues were clear-cut. McKinley stood for the gold standard, high tariffs, and the laissez-faire idea that government should leave big business alone; having served honorably in the Civil War, he could also point to many years of experience in the Congress (it's rumored that McKinley remarked during the campaign: "I have underwear older than my opponent."). So Bryan and McKinley disagreed on virtually all the big issues of the day — a clear and fair fight, right? Wrong. Suddenly, a force from the dark side came into play in American politics as never before. The man's name was not Darth Vader, it was Marc Hanna, and he had money...big money...to buy votes...and he was determined to play "kingmaker."

Hanna, a millionaire industrialist, had no use for Bryan's overall message that the government should assume a fair measure of responsibility for the economic well being of the American people, so obviously he threw his weight (and bank account) behind McKinley. (If you're thinking, gee, most millionaire businesspeople today still have that same attitude you're being pretty harsh — but you're right.) With Hanna padding his client's pockets with gold, McKinley spent about sixteen times more on his campaign than Bryan. (Sixteen times...get the irony?) But Bryan had a thousand times more energy than McKinley. He crisscrossed the nation, giving hundreds of speeches, and most of the time large crowds turned out and went bonkers. This is notable because, prior to this point in our History, presidential candidates did not actively "go on the stump" soliciting votes; it was considered "undignified." Nowadays we're used to presidential candidates jetting frantically to and fro, willing to say and do anything — literally begging — for votes. But back then, Bryan's baby kissing antics raised eyebrows.

McKinley stayed home, where, completely under Hanna's thumb, he occasionally gave tightly scripted speeches from his front porch before friendly Republican audiences, and paid for newspaper "reporters" to be brought in for the occasion. McKinley's invalid wife would sit behind him covered by a blanket, the sight of which, everyone had to admit, was a nice touch. (A rumor that McKinley's wife was faking her condition and was — out of sight of the public — an avid salsa dancer sounds like a cheap shot by the Democrats that fooled no one.) Meanwhile, to counter the manic Bryan, Hanna paid for mountains of campaign literature, and dispatched hundreds of professional mudslingers out across the country to paint Bryan as a dangerous fanatic. The Populist Party, realizing the Democrats had latched on to virtually all their ideas, endorsed Bryan, unfurled a "Gone Out of Business" sign, and promptly joined American History's lengthening list of short-lived third parties.

With Marc Hanna in his corner, McKinley in the Republican trunks knocked out Bryan in the Democratic trunks on Election Day. Bryan won the South and West but the much more populous industrial states of the North and East went for McKinley. Big money carried the day, and clear future trends emerged from the election of 1896. The

city beat the country. The factory beat the farm. The large American middle class —
doing okay and always hoping to move up — refused to join with the farmers, remained
suspicious of organized labor, and stuck with the Republicans and the status quo. The
independent farmers remained disappointed and angry. And when the victorious conservatives sat down to their sumptuous celebratory banquet, they still could not have
cared less about the well being of the men and women who produced the food.
EIEIO...whatever that means.

America began to lift itself out of depression in 1897 as new gold deposits were
discovered in Alaska, Australia and South Africa. Inflation returned and the farmers started doing better without their precious free coinage of silver that promptly
became a forgotten cause. McKinley and his fellow Republicans — merely in the
right place at the right time — gladly took credit for the economic upturn. As the
factories hummed louder than ever, American businessmen began to scout about
for new markets to sell their wares. Their eyes landed on foreign shores. What's
next? Will the United States abandon its obsessive isolation of the post-Civil War
decades? Is America going to get over its fear of commitment and get involved in
relationships overseas? And if we do are we going to behave ourselves or get in
trouble? Uh oh...stay tuned...don't touch that dial!!!

This Really Happened!

In the late nineteenth century, Emperor Menelek II of Ethiopia learns that newly
invented electric chairs are being used to execute criminals in the United States.
This sounds like a great idea to the king so he orders three of them. But when they
arrive, he realizes electricity has not yet been introduced into his country and
the electric chairs are useless. But just so they won't be a total loss, Menelek
decides to use one of the chairs for his royal throne, and the hot seat is actually
employed this way for many years.

And the rest is History...

Quiz yourself on Chapter 9

Multiple Choice (circle the correct answer).

1. In a monopoply
    a. one corporation controls a entire industry
    b. one corporation is capable of fixing prices
    c. cheaters hide their money under the board
    d. the shoe always wins
    e. a and b

2. The Homestead Act demonstrated that the U.S. was enormously rich in
    a. land
    b. steads
    c. gold
    d. fresh water
    e. a and b

3. The transcontinental railroad
    a. was always late
    b. ran from New York City to Albany
    c. ran across the continent from coast to coast
    d. gave free rides to Native Americans
    e. none of the above

4. The Comstock Lode (1859) in Nevada was
    a. a heavy metal band way ahead of its time
    b. located in New York's Greenwich Village
    c. a hit Broadway show
    d. America's most famous gold and silver strike of all time
    e. was just a rumor

5. At the Little Big Horn, Colonel George Armstrong Custer
    a. got married
    b. played his new trumpet
    c. proved the superiority of the U.S. cavalry
    d. got himself and his men wiped out by the Indians
    e. all of the above

6. Thomas Edison invented
   a. the moving picture
   b. the phonograph
   c. the light bulb
   d. the Snuggie
   e. a, b, and c

7. Social Darwinists
   a. blamed the poor for their plight
   b. believed the rich were superior
   c. perverted the theories of Charles Darwin
   d. were reminiscent of many wealthy conservatives today
   e. all of the above

8. The Sherman Anti-Trust Act and the Interstate Commerce Act were
   a. named after a guy whose last name was Act
   b. defeated in Congress
   c. the first crack in the wall of laissez faire
   d. the first crack in the wall of sheetrock
   e. very successful in vaudeville

9. Ellis Island
   a. was a great vacation spot for new immigrants
   b. had a beach famous for Shark attacks
   c. was located in the middle of Lake Michigan
   d. served as a primary processing center for new immigrants
   e. b and d

10. The Populist Party was formed by
    a. the Cowardly Lion
    b. George W. Populist
    c. angry farmers
    d. wealthy industrialists
    e. none of the above

CHAPTER 10

PROGRESSIVISM
AND OVERSEAS ENTANGLEMENTS

or

Check Out My New Muscles

Beginning in the 1890s, the United States is really going to start trying to boss around the weaker nations of the Western Hemisphere: Mexico, the Caribbean, Central America and South America...collectively referred to as Latin America. We'll even start sniffing around in Asia. Meanwhile, here at home an incredibly hyper group of reformers known as the Progressives will stick their noses into virtually all aspects of society, demanding that Americans start putting their own house in order. Let's face it, this is a time when lots of Americans are going to be really annoying both at home and abroad...determined to ignore the wise old adage: Mind your own @#%@#%$# business!

THE END OF THE FRONTIER
or *Now Where Do We Go?*

In 1890, the official U.S. census pronounced the frontier closed. That meant there was no more land left to be explored and claimed. Three years later a young historian named **Frederick Jackson Turner** published an essay entitled, "The Significance of the Frontier Upon History," in which he argued that the continually westward moving frontier had been the central force in the shaping of the nation's character. Turner argued in his now famous *Turner Frontier Thesis* that the wilderness with all its obstacles had transformed Americans into fiercely proud, inventive, individualistic, and tough SOBs. He had a good point, though he overstated it by — to use an expression students and teachers dealing with term papers both know — "shoveling with both hands." Certainly the richness of our natural resources, continual infusion of immigrants, and rapid industrialization shaped the American outlook as well. But folks were sad to see the frontier go, especially those who now had to turn around, face their neighbors and say hello for the first time in their lives.

A lot of people blamed the depression of the 1890s on the fact that lots of American factories were producing more goods than American consumers could buy. Incredibly, the robber barons found themselves too wealthy but still craving more, so these rich industrialists began to cast ravenous glances overseas both for potential customers and additional sources of raw materials. After all, the Europeans were getting rich exploiting Africa and Asia, so why shouldn't the United States get in on the action? This was a call for the country to embrace **imperialism**: the policy of seeking to extend the power and territory of a nation...music to the white Christian ears of Social Darwinists who longed to crank up the volume of "Manifest Destiny" so the "backward" people of the world could "enjoy" it. Many Republican and Democratic politicians in power also thought it was a catchy tune that could distract the American public from its ceaseless calls for reform, and they began to hope most people would dance to it.

But there was a problem. By the 1880s, the American navy had deteriorated to a point whereby it could conceivably be defeated in battle by any number of popular New England yacht clubs. So Congress took initial steps to upgrade the navy, and the imperialists (also called expansionists) found their bible — a book published in 1890 by naval **Captain Alfred Thayer Mahan** entitled *The Influence of Sea Power Upon History*. Mahan argued that naval power was indispensable for any nation aspiring to be "great." A *great* nation for Mahan presumably meant one that could take over foreign lands, make lots of money, and kick butt if anyone objected. It has been reported that a young politician named Theodore Roosevelt read this book in the bathtub while playing with his boats.

Historians often refer to our nation's "aggressive national mood" that began near the close of the nineteenth century, as several international incidents caused Americans to puff out their chests and bust some buttons. In 1889, the U.S. and German navies almost clashed over the Samoan Islands in the South Pacific until it was finally decided to share the islands and the Mai Tais. In 1891, Italy threatened war against the United States after eleven Italians were lynched in New Orleans (remember, Italians had started to arrive in America in large numbers in the 1870s and this is just another example of the ugly American pattern in which the old immigrants automatically hate the new immigrants). War was averted when the United States agreed to pay compensation and, reportedly, sprinkle prodigious amounts of garlic on the food served at the White House.

The following year another potential war loomed when two American sailors were killed in the Chilean port of Valpariso; luckily Chile showed restraint and paid damages, even though their navy at that time may have been a match for our own. In 1893, hotheads in both the United States and Canada called for war over the disgusting issue of seal hunting off the coast of Alaska (the Canadians had gained independent "dominion" status from Great Britain back in 1867 but, remaining as members of the British "commonwealth" family, they could still count on money and military support from their "parents" in London). Lots of Americans wanted to be pals with our northern neighbors, and fortuitously, this argument got settled through arbitration. All the testosterone in the international air caused the anti-imperialists in America to suggest that everyone take a chill pill and reflect on all this. But the imperialists were panting so loud they didn't even hear.

America's most alarming "near war" experience occurred in 1895 and is usually referred to as the **Venezuela Boundary Dispute**. Actually the original argument was between British Guiana (a colony, obviously, of Great Britain) and the independent "republic" of Venezuela over the precise location of the border. The area in question in northern South America was just a tangle of jungle and the dispute had been going on for years and nobody really cared...until gold was discovered in the region. Suddenly everybody cared. The British — feeling superior to the Venezuelans militarily and righteous in their snobby British way — rejected arbitration and essentially told the Venezuelans to kiss off...a message that confused the Venezuelans and then infuriated them when the Spanish translation was clarified.

President Cleveland, a big believer in the Monroe Doctrine, instructed Secretary of State **Richard Olney** to write the Brits a nasty letter reminding them that "the United States is practically sovereign on this continent" so they better stop bullying the Venezuelans and submit the dispute to arbitration. The British, insulted, took four months to answer, further irking the President. When they finally did reply, Great Britain denounced the Monroe Doctrine and essentially told the United States to stick it you know where. President Cleveland understood immediately what the British were saying and he was in his own words "mad clear through." Infuriated at the English insult and red-faced in anger (and from lots of vintage wine), he urged Congress to create a commission to decide where the stupid boundary would go and he let everybody know if the bloody limeys didn't like it the United States would be willing to fight.

Once again, transatlantic insults flew and hotheads on both sides called for war. As usual, the United States was ill prepared for a clash, considering the British navy boasted thirty-five battleships and the American navy had five. But, again as usual, the Brits were over extended. European rivals Russia and France posed a threat, and the newly unified (and psycho militaristic) nation of Germany was building a huge navy. And way down in South Africa, white Dutch-descended farmers called *Boers* had commenced armed resistance against Britain's Cape Colony.

When the Boers captured hundreds of British soldiers, the German Kaiser (King) publicly congratulated the Boers, and Britons shifted their anger towards both the Boers and the Germans. Kaiser Wilhelm II loved to strut about in his army helmet with the spike on top and in his annoying German way pronounced "W" like a "V". Thus the traditional English name William was pronounced in German as *Villhelm*; no wonder the British couldn't stand him. Anyway, fortunately for the U.S., the distracted Brits decided to let the whole argument over Venezuela slide. The boundary dispute was finally submitted to arbitration, America once again had successfully brandished the Monroe Doctrine, and in 1899 British Guiana officially received most of the disputed territory. Thank you, *Villhelm*.

THE UNITED STATES ANNEXES HAWAII
or *We've Got You Covered So Drop Your Pineapples*

Native Hawaiians descended from Polynesians who had paddled to the group of islands in the Central Pacific way back in the mists of time. Whether or not they paddled through any real mists we'll never know — the point is it was a long time ago. There is no such thing as paradise on earth, but the Hawaiian Islands were pretty close to it until white Christian "civilization" arrived. The perfect "truck stop" for merchant ships heading to Asia, Hawaii also enticed American businessmen, who established lucrative sugar plantations. In the 1820s, New England missionaries showed up. Smugly clutching their bibles and exuding disdain for any and all indigenous peoples, they immediately set about doing more harm than good.

The sugar money rolled in until 1890 when the McKinley Tariff leveled the field for all foreign nations wishing to export sugar to the United States. American importers immediately switched to Cuban-grown sugar, which was closer and cheaper, and the Hawaiian economy plummeted. American plantation owners together with rich Hawaiians pleaded with President Harrison to annex the islands so they could get a sweet deal that would make sugar exports to the United States profitable again. But in 1891, a strong willed native Hawaiian named **Queen Liliuokalani** assumed control of the government and promptly instituted a campaign to stamp out foreign interference. (It took me seven years of teaching before I actually pronounced Liliuokalani correctly on the first try in front of a class...I had botched it so many times I psyched myself out. Repeat after me: LIL-EEE-UUU-OOO-KAA-LAA-KNEE. By George, I think you've got it.)

Anyway, the wealthy planters orchestrated a revolution that soon forced Queen Liliokalaka (darn) Liliuokalani to abdicate her throne. Sympathetic U.S. Ambassador

John L. Stevens (power mad and completely out of line) obligingly ordered 600 marines ashore to help out. The "revolutionaries" immediately established a new "republic" and requested annexation by the United States. A treaty was drawn up, but before the Senate could approve it, President Cleveland replaced President Harrison. Cleveland was an anti-imperialist whose views were sincerely based upon his sense of ethics and morality — hard to believe, I know. The President pulled back the treaty because he believed honestly (and correctly) that most Hawaiians wanted to remain independent and the United States had acted disreputably by sending in an armed force.

For the next few years anti-imperialists battled imperialists as Hawaii remained independent, vulnerable and ripe for the picking. But by 1898, in tense international times, most Americans agreed that if we didn't grab the Hawaiian pear the British or the Germans might. So Congress authorized annexation and these beautiful people and their islands became a part of the United States. I've never been to Hawaii myself, but I plan to visit as soon as I win the lottery.

THE SPANISH-AMERICAN WAR
or *Come On, This Will Be Fun!*

The island of Cuba — a delectable morsel just 90 miles off the coast of Florida — remained a vestige of the once great New World empire of Spain. Cuban nationals had long hated their colonial masters who treated them *muy mal* by imposing heavy taxes and denying them political rights. A ten-year-long revolution was finally chopped up and swept off the table by Spanish authorities in 1878. By the early 1890s, most Cubans were still stuck working for a pittance on sugar and tobacco plantations, ironically unable to afford the famous Cuban cigars produced on their own island.

Then in 1894 the United States, reeling from a depression, imposed a high protective tariff on Cuban sugar imports, causing the Cuban economy to collapse. Cubans already in poverty got hit the hardest and, pushed to the breaking point, they dashed around madly, burning and pillaging plantations and businesses.

Spain sent troops commanded by **General Valeriano Weyler** to restore order. General Weyler's nickname was "Butcher," so the Cubans had to know he was not on his way to open talks or offer compromise (had he been nicknamed "Tickles" events might have unfolded differently). Unfortunately, Weyler immediately lived up to his reputation by rounding up thousands of rebellious Cubans (even children and old folks) and forcing them into "reconcentration camps." It is basically summer all year round in Cuba, but there were no Arts and Crafts or Swimming Lessons in these "camps;" conditions were atrocious, and 200,000 trapped *Cubanos* died from hunger and disease.

In an age before radio, television and the Internet, Americans avidly followed the events in Cuba by reading newspapers, sometimes several times a day. More newspapers sold resulted in higher advertising rates, so publishers competed fiercely. As always, "shocking" news proved most popular — crime, scandal, violence — and a new kind of newspaper reporting emerged called **yellow journalism** — really just a euphemism for exaggerating and outright lying to create outrageous stories that would sell more papers and make more money.

Newspaper titan **William Randolph Hearst** (hoping to scoop his rival **Joseph Pulitzer**) hired artist Frederick Remington to travel to Cuba and send back sketches of Spanish outrages. When Remington cabled back that he couldn't find much going on, Hearst replied, "You furnish the pictures, I'll furnish the war!" What Hearst really meant was: *Make it up if you have to you pinhead, I'm trying to sell papers here.* The bottom line: lots of the newspaper coverage from Cuba was fraudulent; conditions were bad but the yellow press sensationalized it, and in so doing whipped Americans into a frenzy of support for the rebellious Cubans.

Most Americans were naturally sympathetic to the Cuban revolutionaries; after all, they were just doing what our own Patriots had done to get rid of the British more than a century before. Besides, disorder in Cuba threatened U.S. investments and trade with the island, and if the Spanish couldn't keep a lid on the violence, maybe Uncle Sam needed to step in and keep the peace. But President Cleveland, a committed anti-expansionist, would have none of it. When Congress began to debate a declaration of war to "free" Cuba, Cleveland actually stated that if Congress declared war he would refuse to order the army into action.

Convinced of his own righteousness, Cleveland was threatening to override the Constitutional provision that Congress makes the laws (including the right to declare war) and the president enforces the laws. This is noteworthy because it is relatively rare that a president publicly threatens to blow off the Constitution; usually they try to do it secretly or through convoluted legal maneuvers only slick lawyers understand. Reportedly, when someone mentioned the Constitution to Cleveland, he placed his hands over his ears and started humming *The Battle Hymn of the Republic*.

Similarly, the next President, McKinley, was not especially psyched to lead a yelping United States into a war before all avenues for a peaceful settlement had been fully explored. But Spain refused his offer to mediate and as the situation worsened, it soon became clear he lacked the fortitude of his predecessor. Spain did recall Weyler and close down the reconcentration camps, but that caused riots by the other side in Cuba: Spanish "loyalists." Then Spanish ambassador to the United States, Dupuy de Lome, did something stupid: writing a letter to a friend in which he called President McKinley weak and incompetent. A Cuban spy stole the letter from the Havana post office and released it to Hearst's New York *Journal* (publication of the **De Lôme Letter** really sent circulation up big time for that edition.) Frothing at the mouth, Americans' calls for war got louder and louder. Reportedly, President McKinley put his hands to his ears and started humming *Happy Days Are Here Again*. Too bad he didn't have an iPod.

On February 15, 1898, the American battleship *Maine*, anchored in Havana harbor in case the violence escalated and Americans needed to be rescued, blew up. 260 officers and men died. Who could have perpetrated such an atrocity? Suspect #1: Spain — doubtful because it didn't want to provoke the United States while trying to finesse the

Cuban crisis by offering Cubans a form of self-rule that would satisfy both the revolutionaries and the Spanish people, who stubbornly wanted to retain "their" colony. Suspect #2: Cuban revolutionaries — doubtful, though it is intriguing to wonder if they might have concocted such a plot, confident that the explosion would be blamed on Spain and bring the U.S. into the war on their side. Of course, there has never been any evidence of this, and even lunatic conspiracy theorists aren't buying this one. Suspect #3: Vice-President Dick Cheney, Karl Rove, and "Scooter" Libby — these three guys weren't even born yet, but they deserve to be listed whenever sneaky schemes are discussed.

An initial American investigation blamed a Spanish mine — a cover-up in the grand tradition of the American navy (today experts agree that the explosion was an accident, caused by a spark in the powder compartment, and just plain stupid and tragic). Spain denied involvement, but without evidence or trial the yellow press convicted the *SPANISH MURDERERS* in banner headlines. Most folks had forgotten the Alamo but they were quite capable of shouting, "**Remember the Maine!**" A huge clamor for war erupted and President McKinley, a wimp for caring that he was being called a wimp, caved in to the pressure and asked Congress for a declaration of war. Congress, caught up in the hysteria, complied on April 20, 1898. But perhaps out of guilt, the anti-imperialist **Teller Amendment** was added to the resolution, promising to the world that the United States would keep its hands clean and free Cuba, not annex it. Western European imperialists, busy making mud pies in Africa, Asia and the Middle East, thought we were nuts.

With his boss out of town, Assistant Secretary of the Navy **Theodore Roosevelt** (more on this remarkable man later) cabled Commodore **George Dewey** in Hong Kong and basically told him to proceed to the Philippine Islands, Spain's colony in the South Pacific, and in the event of war, attack the Spanish Pacific Fleet anchored in Manila Bay. Well, that's precisely what happened, and when Dewey arrived, the overmatched Spanish vessels were demolished by America's more modern ships in a few bloody hours. Filipino "freedom fighters" had been fighting a guerrilla war to get Old World Spain off their islands and, led by **Emilio Aquinaldo**, they gladly accepted American help. When the U.S. army finally arrived in August, Spain promptly surrendered the Philippines to the United States. Back in Washington the Secretary of the Navy, observing the Assistant Secretary's toothy grin, swore never to take off for a long weekend again.

Back in the Caribbean, where the war was supposed to be in the first place, Spain's Admiral Pascual Cervera commanded a leaky flotilla of wooden ships totally overmatched by a U.S. steel fleet in fairly good shape. He didn't really want to fight but was ordered by his superiors to defend the honor of his country. In Cuba's Santiago Harbor, his fleet was demolished, with about five hundred Spanish sailors, and one American, killed. None of the Spanish politicians across the Atlantic in Madrid were injured in the battle.

The battle on land in Cuba featured "Dumb and Dumber." The American army was ill trained and ill equipped, and simply getting to the island proved to be a logistical nightmare. Utter chaos reigned at the embarkation port of Tampa, Florida. Theodore Roosevelt resigned his post in the Navy Department, and by pulling strings and spending money, organized a cavalry regiment — the famous **Rough Riders** — and got himself commissioned lieutenant colonel. The Rough Riders had to commandeer a boat to take them to Cuba, and when they arrived were disappointed to learn they didn't have their horses. In fact, most of the American soldiers in Cuba were real cranky, perhaps because they were wearing winter uniforms designed for fighting Indians in the Rocky Mountains. Their woolen mittens looked especially ridiculous on the beach.

The Spanish defenders proved even more inept and unable to muster sufficient troop strength to offer much serious opposition. But there was some fierce fighting, and the Rough Riders with Theodore in the lead — give them and him credit for guts — charged up and captured San Juan Hill. It has been rumored that up on top of the hill one of his men asked, "Colonel Roosevelt, now what do we do?" Smiling that toothy grin of his, Roosevelt supposedly replied, "Stand fast and allow yourself to go down in History." I doubt that exchange ever took place, but Roosevelt did become a huge hero who for the rest of his life frequently acted as if he had won the Spanish-American war all by himself.

Spain, honor satisfied, surrendered on August 12, 1898. The relatively quick military victory inspired Secretary of State **John Hay** to call the conflict a "splendid little war." Secretary Hay was not alone; lots of his fellow Americans were **jingoes** — smug, excessively patriotic flag-wavers who were convinced anyone who disagreed with them was a traitor. Reminiscent of most wars in History, lots of young men had marched off in anticipation of a grand adventure. And quite possibly some politicians in Washington made ignorant statements like "Bring it on!" But truthfully the **Spanish-American War** was far from "splendid." Even though only about 400 American soldiers died in the actual fighting, more than five thousand soon died from tropical diseases such as typhoid, malaria, and yellow fever. Some adventure.

AMERICA GAINS AN EMPIRE
or *We're Here, Now What Do We Do?*

Peace commissioners from the United States and Spain got together in Paris and enjoyed exquisite cuisine that contrasted sharply with the rancid food the soldiers in the field had to force down their throats. Eventually, over dessert they hammered out a peace accord. Clearly, the United States was holding the hammer: in the treaty signed Dec. 10, 1898, Spain granted Cuba its freedom and ceded Guam (in the Pacific), Puerto Rico (in the Caribbean), and the Philippines to the United States. The American diplomats could not conjure up any justification for capturing Spanish possessions half a world away from the Cuban conflict; saying *because we felt like it and you couldn't stop us, have some more wine* just wouldn't do. So the U.S. agreed to pay Spain $20 million for the Philippine Islands...a great deal for Spain, as events would soon prove. Suddenly and without much prior planning, the United States found itself in possession of an honest to goodness Empire.

In deciding the future of the Philippines, President McKinley did not really have any good choices. Anti-imperialists made good points when they argued that taking ownership of the Philippines violated the "consent of the governed" clause in the Declaration of Independence, and as that Democratic pain in the butt William Jennings Bryan kept repeating, "Despotism abroad might beget despotism at home." But the sugar trade was a huge economic incentive to stay, and granting the politically inexperienced Filipinos independence might lead to an anarchy that would allow a circling vulture such as Germany or Russia to swoop down on the sweet islands. All along, expansionists kept telling McKinley he would be a *girly man* if he decided to ever "haul down the flag." In the end, the President decided to be macho, and in the domestic shouting match that ensued between the chest thumping expansionists and the screw you too anti-expansionists, the Senate approved the peace treaty by one vote.

Ironically, William Jennings Bryan helped the President by calling for Democratic senators to support the treaty (no Republican senators would take his calls even though they had those really cool new telephones). Bryan passionately hated imperialism and hoped to be elected President in 1900, whereupon he would set the Philippines free, the sooner the better. Besides, if the occupation went badly, the President and the Republicans would get the blame. But Bryan's strategy didn't work. Democrats still loved him and renominated him in 1900, but Republicans and independents responded well to incumbent McKinley's reelection campaign, which focused on the nation's economic prosperity with the slogan that every American should be entitled to a "full dinner pail." (It was just a weird expression; most Americans back then ate off plates just like we do.)

The President stayed on his front porch next to his invalid wife, recreating the successful image that had been so effective in 1896. Bryan crisscrossed the nation and hyperventilated a lot, but the issue of free silver was dead, the economy solid, and Cuba and the Philippines seemed worlds away. McKinley beat Bryan by a larger margin than he had four years earlier. Ironically, during the campaign the hyper Bryan was out-hustled by McKinley's new and even more hyper vice-presidential running mate: Theodore Roosevelt. It is tempting to assume that Roosevelt must have been on steroids, but they had not been developed yet.

Still, by annexing the Philippines, America had stumbled into a hornets' nest. Native Filipinos, previously fighting the Spaniards and briefly grateful for American help, immediately realized they were still wearing a Western yoke, this one colored red, white, and blue. The United States spent millions to improve sanitation, infrastructure and education, but that did little to salve wounded Filipino pride; they had long craved freedom and no amount of humanitarian aid could satiate them. Emilio Aquinaldo and Filipino freedom fighters waged a vicious guerrilla uprising that lasted far longer and caused many more casualties than had resulted from the original war. Both sides committed horrible atrocities that were reported in the U.S. and sold lots of newspapers. (President Bush, uh, I mean McKinley, repeatedly complained that the press was focusing far too much on the bad news and ignoring the good news coming out of Iraq, uh, I mean the Philippines.) After three long years and about 4000 American and 20,000

Filipino deaths, Aquinaldo was captured and the uprising died. Ten thousand miles away, Americans were stung by the lack of appreciation for all the new schools and hospitals being built. American politicians in particular could not comprehend the Filipinos — a group of people who for some strange reason couldn't be bought off.

Cuba also became a problem child, even though, just as in the Philippines, the United States paternally built dams, hospitals, roads, and schools. Under the Teller Amendment, the United States could not annex Cuba, so after a few years American forces (loaded down with Cuban cigars) withdrew. But first we "supervised" the Cubans as they wrote a democratic constitution for themselves that turned out — big coincidence — to be remarkably similar to our own. But there was one big difference: the United States forced the Cubans to write the **Platt Amendment** into their own constitution, stating that America retained the right to intervene militarily if Cuba's independence was ever threatened or it became necessary to preserve "life, liberty and property." In other words, this provision provided legal cover for the U.S. Army to return at any time to slap the Cubans around if they ever got out of line...they had their "freedom" as long as they didn't look at Uncle Sam the wrong way.

Not surprisingly, over the next couple of decades, dictators and corruption flourished, the Cuban masses remained landless and poor, and the U.S. had to send in troops to restore order four times — not for the sake of the Cuban people (few Americans cared about them) but to protect the American investments which increasingly dominated the island. By the way, the U.S. Navy established a "temporary permanent" base on the island at Guantanamo Bay, where today suspected Muslim terrorists are being held "temporarily permanently."

GRABBING A PIECE OF THE ACTION IN CHINA
or *Don't Slam the Door, You'll Hurt My Foot*

By the 1890s, the Asian country of China — populous, rich in resources, but with a weak central government — had been carved up into **spheres of influence**: separate regions in which foreign nations held virtual sovereignty and control over commerce and trade. Great Britain, France, Russia, Germany, and Japan all clutched one of the wontons. In late 1899, at the behest of American businessmen who feared being cut out of the Chinese action, President McKinley and Secretary of State Hay addressed a series of letters to all the nations involved, insisting that China's sovereignty and trading rights for all nations be respected (what they really meant was that all countries, not just those with spheres of influence, should share equally in the exploitation of China). This audacious bit of diplomacy became known as the **Open Door Policy**.

Italy quickly endorsed it, buoying McKinley and Hay until someone reminded them that Italy did not control one of the spheres of influence and had probably been placed on the mailing list by mistake. China accepted (duh). Great Britain, France, Germany, and Japan grudgingly accepted, but only on condition of unanimity, and Russia — obviously plotting to steal China's northern province of Manchuria — declined. At this point, McKinley and Hay got even more audacious, declaring that all nations had accepted the Open Door Policy and it was now officially in effect. Reportedly, Hay tried to schmooze the Russian ambassador in Washington by saying, "Gee, there must be some problem with your translation."

In truth, the Europeans and Japan stubbornly clung to their spheres in China and only gave lip service to free trade. They never openly rejected the Open Door Policy, not because they were concerned about what the United States might do, but really because they were fearful of provoking war with each other. At best, the Open Door Policy helped American merchants snatch just a sliver of the China pie, so on a scale of one to ten give the McKinley/Hay Open Door Policy a four...five if you like *tofu*.

A nationalistic group of Chinese patriots called "Boxers" hated the way their country had been dismembered, and began a bloody uprising. Their cry of "Kill Foreign Devils" definitely hurt the Chinese tourist industry, particularly after a couple of hundred white people at a Club Med were murdered (actually, the dead were mostly missionaries and their families in the countryside). The **Boxer Rebellion** swarmed into the capital of Beijing and forced all foreigners to flee behind the walls of their embassies.

An international rescue force hastily gathered; Germany, France, Britain, Japan, and Russia had no problem cooperating when it came to teaching rebellious Chinese a lesson. The United States also contributed about 2500 troops, and in short order the trapped westerners were freed and China was forced to bow low, really low, and stay that way. The helpless Chinese government agreed to pay excessive damages of over $330 million. Recognizing the Chinese had been overcharged, the United States — you better sit down — returned most of its share. Lots of American capitalists fainted. But Chinese government officials, after throwing cold water in their faces, appreciated the gesture and inaugurated an era of Chinese-American friendship and cultural exchange that would last for decades.

THEODORE ROOSEVELT BECOMES PRESIDENT
or *Oh My God, What Have We Done?*

On September 6, 1901, the President hosted a reception at the Pan American Exposition in Buffalo, New York. Afterwards, a jovial McKinley was shaking hands when a deranged anarchist named Leon F. Czolgosz, holding a revolver in his hand covered by a handkerchief, walked right up to the President and shot him twice. One bullet ricocheted off McKinley's button, but the other pierced his stomach. The President was rushed to a hospital for surgery; he survived eight days before an infection, which his doctors were unable to treat, killed him. It has been reported that at Czolgosz' trial, his lawyer tried to sway the jury by chanting, "If the handkerchief don't fit you must acquit." But this particular jury was not entirely composed of morons, so Czolgosz was convicted of murder and fried in "Old Sparky" (electrocuted in the electric chair).

Vice-President Roosevelt rushed back from his vacation in the Adirondack Mountains and was sworn in as President the same day McKinley died (unfounded rumors persist to this day that the judge had to ask Roosevelt to remove the moose antlers he was wearing). Many bigwig politicians were shocked and dismayed that Theodore Roosevelt now occupied the White House. That was never part of the plan...

Theodore Roosevelt was born into a wealthy, influential New York family. He was a sickly, asthmatic child, and nearsighted (not that there's anything wrong with that). Luckily he had private tutors so he didn't have to deal with bullies during recess. "Teddy" became obsessed with conquering his bodily shortcomings, and he embraced exercise, sports, hunting, and physically intimidating anyone who disagreed with him. We've all seen people who try to compensate for their perceived shortcomings, most obviously the short guys at the gym whose shoulder width is greater than their height. If only back in early nineteenth century Napoleon Bonaparte could have showed off in a Gold's Gym, he might not have felt the need to take over the world.

After graduation from Harvard, Roosevelt served as a Republican Assemblyman in the New York State Legislature. Then, both his wife and his mother died in the same year. Devastated, Theodore left politics and literally became a cowboy, living out in the Dakota Territory for a few years. Upon returning to New York City, he served as a reform-minded Police Commissioner, Civil Service Commissioner under Presidents Harrison and Cleveland, and then (as we've seen) became Assistant Secretary of the Navy. After his Rough Rider adventure in the Spanish-American War, Roosevelt returned home, whereupon an adoring public elected him Governor of the Empire State.

As Governor, the personally honest Roosevelt energetically opposed corruption, and the Republican Party bosses in New York couldn't stand him. So they concocted a scheme in which Roosevelt would be nominated as McKinley's running mate in 1900 and "kicked upstairs" into the Vice-Presidency. Vice-President had long been a do-nothing job and nobody expected "that damned cowboy" to become President. But thanks to an assassin's bullet, "TR" did become President...the first one to overshadow Congress since Lincoln...and also the first President to box prizefighters on the White House grounds in his spare time. An alleged incident in which the nearsighted Roosevelt accidentally knocked out the Secretary of the Treasury has never been confirmed.

ROOSEVELT'S VERSION OF THE MONROE DOCTRINE
or *We're the Cops Around Here*

In 1902, Venezuela defaulted on debts owed to citizens of Germany, Great Britain, and Italy. Fuming at being stiffed, European warships chugged across the Atlantic. The Italians, in their first real attempt to meddle in Western Hemisphere affairs, supposedly had to be informed that getting to the Caribbean was much faster by the Atlantic route as opposed to the Pacific. The militaristic Germans, barbarians as usual, cheerfully bombarded a Venezuelan town. The Brits simply made tea, but they made it clear they wanted their cash with their crumpets. In 1904, the Dominican Republic similarly failed to make their interest payments on their European "credit cards."

President Roosevelt was worried the Europeans might use debt defaults as an excuse to go ashore and occupy the offending Latin American nations — a potential violation of the time honored Monroe Doctrine. So he flat out told the Europeans to butt out of Latin America; in the event of "chronic wrongdoing" by any nation in the Western Hemisphere, the United States would exercise "international police power." In regard to Venezuela, Roosevelt succeeded in getting all sides to submit the dispute to arbitration. The Dominicans agreed (yeah, like they had a choice) to let the United States seize their customhouses and pay off their debts to foreign creditors.

This was a real change to the Monroe Doctrine, which originally had been a fairly basic statement warning Western Europe to stay out of the Western Hemisphere. In what became known as the **Roosevelt Corollary** to the Monroe Doctrine, Roosevelt added the provision that "if there is any problem the United States will handle it." His favorite expression to explain his philosophy was, "Speak softly and carry a big stick." The science of psychiatry was still in its infancy back then, but today many professionals in the field think it is obvious this guy had "issues."

Thus the Caribbean truly became an American lake with Uncle Sam as the cop on patrol. Lots of Latin Americans shook their heads and wondered, *who gave the United States the badge?* But there was nothing they could do about it. The Europeans, satisfied they would get their debts repaid, backed off. It's been said the Italians were so intimidated by the aggressive Roosevelt that they grabbed themselves, muttered "*Fugghetaboudit*," and returned to Italy...the long way.

A CANAL ACROSS THE ISTHMUS OF PANAMA
or *Give It To Us or We'll Take It*

In an age before Jet Blue, getting from the east coast of North America to the west coast (and vice-versa) had always been incredibly expensive and difficult. Crossing the plains and mountains didn't cut it, and neither did traveling down to Central America and cutting across on foot. Navigating the stormy seas around the Cape of Good Hope, the most southerly part of South America, was dangerous and enormously time consuming— even if you made it in one piece. Everyone who looked at a map of the Western Hemisphere had been saying for decades: *Man, we really need a canal across that skinny area in between North and South America.* In 1869 the French completed construction of the Suez Canal, which connected the Mediterranean to the Red Sea, so they felt confident enough to tackle the tropical Isthmus of Panama. They failed utterly, for a number of reasons: (1) digging in Egypt's desert had proven much easier than digging in Panama's jungle with its incessant mudslides, (2) mosquitoes carrying yellow fever and malaria depleted the work force, and (3) corporate corruption underfunded the work effort, and (4) they were French.

President Roosevelt and many Americans still believed a canal was necessary and any obstacles could be surmounted. It was a national embarrassment that the U.S.S. *Oregon* left San Francisco to fight the Spanish in Cuba, but arrived late for the war because it had to round Cape Horn to get there — a sixty-four-day voyage (there is to this day still some suspicion that the crew of the *Oregon* stopped in Rio de Janeiro to party for a about a week). Teddy especially wanted to start construction because, with the election of 1904 fast approaching, "making the dirt fly" would really look good to the voters.

Panama back then was the northern province of Colombia, so Secretary of State Hay negotiated a treaty with Colombia under which the U.S. would pay $10 million and a $250,000 annual rent for a six-mile strip of land across the Isthmus. But the Colombian Senate rejected the treaty, hoping to squeeze the U.S. for more money. President Roosevelt had no respect for the Colombian Senate (he could barely stand the U.S. Senate) so he "discreetly" encouraged the Panamanians to revolt. The Panamanians had long resented Colombian rule and were happy to rise up — particularly after they were paid off by a representative of the failed French canal company, who stood to make a fortune if the U.S. paid the agreed-upon $40 million for the dilapidated French assets and began construction.

The Panamanian army (basically a bunch of guys from Panama's fire department) swiftly secured Panama's independence from Columbia in a "revolution" that succeeded virtually without bloodshed when the "discreet" U.S. Navy prevented the Colombian army from entering Panama to put down the insurrection. Roosevelt immediately extended diplomatic recognition to Panama, and the new nation — not wanting to get hit in the head with a "big stick" — agreed to improve upon the deal the Colombians had turned down. Thus the U.S. took possession in perpetuity of a *ten-mile* wide **Panama Canal Zone** and picked up where the French left off. When criticized for his utter audacity, President Roosevelt did not back down. In fact, he proudly boasted, "I took the canal and left the Congress to debate." His description of the Colombian senators is unprintable in a classy book like this.

A brilliant army medical officer named **William C. Gorgas** convinced stubborn skeptics that mosquitoes were the reason nearly everybody working on the canal was dropping dead. Improving sanitation (and draining standing water or spreading oil on it) depleted the mosquito population and made it possible for construction to move forward. Equally brainy army engineer **George W. Goethals** conquered all manner of technical obstacles and designed a system of locks to raise and lower ships. In 1914, the Panama Canal — truly an engineering marvel — finally opened and became an instant success. Eventually, in 1921, the United States paid Colombia $25 million to stop bitching.

The American public loved their vigorous young President, and he clobbered a forgettable Democratic challenger to win a term in his own right in 1904. That same year, war broke out between Japan and Russia, basically because both sides wanted to call the shots in China's northern province of Manchuria. To the astonishment of the white western world, the Japanese navy administered several crushing defeats to a Russian navy that bobbed about as if its crews were pounding down shots of vodka rather than manning their guns. But the obstinate Russians refused to back down, and when the Japanese asked Roosevelt to mediate, he characteristically replied, "Bully!" ("bully" was another of his favorite expressions, and it basically meant "Good" or what hip people today mean when they say "Word!")

The President brought peace envoys from both sides to Portsmouth, New Hampshire, whereupon the Japanese demanded a huge indemnity and possession of Sakhalin Island off the coast of China. The Russians replied, *No way, we're not paying anything, we want Sakhalin Island, now get us some vodka!* Reportedly, Roosevelt locked both sides in a room, yelled at them, disallowed bathroom breaks, and then broke the impasse by threatening to smother everybody's meals in maple syrup. Finally, the two sides agreed to a compromise peace settlement, and the Russians and Japanese each occupied half of Sakhalin Island. Both sides felt cheated — such is the nature of compromise — so ironically, by brokering peace, America made a couple of new enemies. For his efforts, Theodore Roosevelt ultimately won the Nobel Peace Price, an announcement greeted in much of Latin America with cries of *What...are you kidding me?*

Japanese-American relations took another hit in the wake of the horrific San Francisco earthquake of 1906. With many local schools transformed into piles of rubble, the San Francisco Board of Education decreed that to make room for American students, all Japanese immigrant students would be sent to a separate school. When news of this racial segregation reached Japan, the ethnocentric Japanese people were offended that there was actually another country as bigoted as they were. Hotheads on both sides of the Pacific called for war (especially in stupid newspapers) and Teddy, wanting to avoid war (note how his bellicose demeanor often belied his actions), called the California school authorities to the White House to diffuse the crisis. The maple syrup threat didn't work, but baring his teeth and pulling out his big stick must have, because the offensive segregation order got rescinded. To mollify the nativist Californians, Teddy negotiated a secret "**Gentlemen's Agreement**" with Japan to halt the flood of workers to the west coast. Lest the Japanese and the rest of the world think Americans wimpy for avoiding war, the navy painted a fleet bright white, and this "**Great White Fleet**" embarked on a round the world cruise to flex Uncle Sam's muscles and generally show off.

In the afterglow of his election in 1904, Teddy impulsively blurted out that he would not run again for another four-year term. By the time 1908 rolled around, he really regretted the outburst, but he honored his pledge and did not seek reelection. He did, however, secure the Republican nomination for his good friend, Secretary of War **William Howard Taft**. In the general election that November, Taft decisively defeated the Democrats' William Jennings Bryan who, appearing to most voters as a retread devoid of ideas and appeal, ignominiously became a three-time presidential loser. Afterwards, one cranky Democrat reportedly told Bryan to carry a picture of Henry Clay in his wallet. Satisfied his friend would carry forward his program, Roosevelt headed off to

Africa for a safari, causing folks even back then to puzzle over how hunters like Teddy could claim to love nature while at the same time wanting to shoot as much of it as possible.

President Taft weighed well over three hundred pounds, and though honest and competent, he really would have preferred napping or playing golf. He certainly was no Teddy. It is absolutely true that he got stuck in the White House bathtub and the fire department had to be called to dislodge him. Workers installed a specially designed bathtub in the executive mansion, reportedly so large it had a "deep end" and a wide ledge on the side that could accommodate soap, shampoo, and chicken wings.

Taft's stomach could handle a lot, but the Roosevelt Corollary gave him indigestion. Rather than sending in the marines to keep order, President Taft preferred to utilize economic imperialism, or **dollar diplomacy** — a foreign policy which encouraged American investors to thoroughly penetrate Latin American economies so the United States could dominate the government and control the country without the expense and international embarrassment of having to use troops. But Taft still intervened militarily when he had to, notably in Nicaragua, the Dominican Republic, Honduras and Cuba. A few Latin Americans — *caudillos* (dictators), army officers and oligarchs — loved dollar diplomacy because lots of the *dinero* ended up in the pockets of their *pantalones*. But the poor exploited masses recognized dollar diplomacy for what it was: Uncle Sam the wolf in sheep's clothing. President Taft wore a 4X Extra Large.

THE PROGRESSIVE MOVEMENT
or *My Feet Hurt — How Long Are We Marching?*

The Industrial Revolution had brought great wealth to America by the 1890s, but it was not all fresh peaches and cream. A foul rotting stench emanated from sweatshops and slums as corrupt politicians and corpulent businessmen left many Americans grasping for crumbs under the table. In yet another attempt to clean up the mess, roughly from the Spanish-American War in 1898 to the end of World War I in 1918, many reform-minded Americans created the **Progressive Movement**: a local, state and national campaign for economic, political, and social justice. You better believe the Progressive Movement had Populist roots, and even harkened back to the "Jacksonian Reform" of the early and mid-nineteenth century.

At the dawn of the twentieth century, the liberal Progressives came from many walks of American life, and both the Democrats and Republicans (yes, even the Republicans) produced their fair share. Middle class professionals resented the fact that sleazy public officials, hand in hand with corporate executives, seemed to be grabbing far more than their fair share of America's wealth. Workers in factories and mines continued to demand laws that would improve their working conditions and pay. Farmers still retained their longstanding gripes against the railroad monopolies, high tariffs and the Ebenezer Scrooge-type guys they encountered every time they went to a financial institution for a loan (imagine how infuriating it must have been when bankers said "No" and then added "Bah humbug!").

On the flip side, conservative rich types were almost never Progressives and, as they played on their private golf courses and tennis courts, frequently reassured each other that all this annoying reform talk would soon blow over. It didn't. On Saturday, March 11, 1911, 147 women and young girls died in the **Triangle Shirtwaist Company Fire** at one of the worst "sweatshops" in the heart of New York's Garment District. The nation's soul was further seared when reports revealed that, to encourage the seamstresses to stay at their machines and to inhibit stealing, company management routinely locked the exit doors.

My mother predicted that my teenage determination to travel the world as a professional surfer would turn out to be nothing but a "short lived phase." She was right — I only made it as far as the Jersey Shore. The Progressive Movement was a phase as well, but it was not short-lived, and in approximately twenty years lots of legislation passed that generally made the United States a better place.

On the city and state level, increased use of direct **primaries** allowed registered party members to choose candidates rather than party bosses. The **initiative** and **referendum** made it possible for citizens to circulate petitions and propose legislation directly to the voters in general elections. The **recall** similarly made it possible for incorrigible officials to be replaced before their terms were up...ask Arnold Schwarzenegger, who became Governor of California that way and, unless he keeps his pants on, may leave office that way as well. The **Australian ballot** offered citizens the opportunity to vote by placing their ballots in a pouch that resembled that of a kangaroo (just kidding; it was a secret ballot that gave citizens the privacy to vote without being intimidated). In some municipalities, especially in the Midwest and South, corruption so infested City Hall that disgusted voters eliminated the offices of councilman and mayor and replaced them with a **commission system** headed by a **city manager**. Presumably, they then fumigated the building.

The Progressive Movement was largely fueled by **muckrakers** — investigative journalists who continually "raked the muck" to uncover injustice and wrongdoing. Books and articles in monthly magazines such as *McClure's*, *Collier's*, and *Cosmopolitan* repeatedly called Progressives to arms (in case you're wondering, there were no lingerie-clad "Cosmo Girls" on magazine covers back then). **Ida Tarbell** tasted sweet revenge upon publication of her *History of the Standard Oil Company*, in which she documented the cold-hearted business practices of John D. Rockefeller that had destroyed the independent oil company owned by her father. **Lincoln Steffens'** *The Shame of the Cities* portrayed the symbiotic relationship between robber barons and local politicians who collectively bled city coffers dry. Theodore Dreiser's *The Financier* ripped the immorality of Wall Street executives. In *The Octopus*, Frank Norris demonstrated how the railroad industry overcharged not only farmers but all Americans, and had bribed most of the Senate to get away with it. Once, when I said to my History class that the muckrakers proved "the pen is mightier than the sword," one of my students (clearly addicted to violent video games) replied that it would be really stupid to stab someone with a pen if a sword was available. Every teacher has frustrating moments like that.

The main point here is that Progressive-era muckrakers provoked a public outrage that democratically brought about changes for the better: new laws and attitudes that moved America further away from laissez faire, and towards government action to thwart the evils of unregulated industrial growth and the poverty that sadly accompanied it.

Some progressive initiatives even made it into the Constitution. **Amendment XVI** (1913) authorized Congress to levy a federal income tax; most Progressives at the time believed it would be a "graduated" income tax that would impact more heavily upon the wealthy (Ronald Reagan, George Bush the father and George Bush the son had not been born yet, so nobody knew that ideal would go up in smoke). **Amendment XVII** (also 1913) stated, "Senators shall be elected by popular vote" rather than selected by state legislatures as had been the case up to that point. **Amendment XVIII** (1919) stated, "the sale or manufacture of intoxicating liquors is forbidden," thus inaugurating the **Prohibition** era in America. Since Prohibition was a major screw-up on the part of the Progressives, we'll discuss it later — I don't want to ruin the overall positive vibe about the Progressive movement I'm trying to put forth here.

Amendment XIX (1920) was a great one: women were guaranteed the right to vote. One by one, individual states had been granting women voting rights, but now it became a national entitlement, forcing even the chauvinistic states to comply. It had been a long campaign for women's suffrage (don't forget the Seneca Falls Convention back in 1849) but the suffragettes finally prevailed. Undoubtedly, some husbands exclaimed, "Now will you finally shut up!" Undoubtedly as well, many of these same husbands immediately regretted their outburst and realized they were the ones who should shut up.

THREE PROGRESSIVE PRESIDENTS
or *Somebody Please Wake Up President Taft*

In 1897, voters in Toledo, Ohio elected a reform-minded mayor named Samuel L. Jones, and other progressive mayors soon attacked corruption in cities such as Detroit, St. Louis, Cleveland, New York, and San Francisco. **Robert M. La Follette** of Wisconsin, doggedly running for governor for a third time against a corrupt political machine, finally won and became a progressive pit bull. Other states in which the Progressive Movement achieved notable gains included Ohio, Michigan, Oregon, California, New York, and New Jersey. Hardly any southerners could be called Progressives, busy as they were restricting African-American rights and ostracizing anyone with a modern idea.

President Theodore Roosevelt can truly be called a Progressive, and by initiating over forty anti-trust lawsuits, he rapidly gained a reputation as a "trust buster." He believed in a powerful federal government that should be honest and actively work to guarantee all Americans a **"Square Deal,"** a phrase which made for a nifty campaign slogan and was much better than his quickly discarded, "Vote for me or I'll hit you with my big stick."

As a hunter and a former cowboy, he passionately believed in preserving what was left of America's wilderness, doubling the number of national parks in his tenure. And Teddy used his bully pulpit to make most Americans aware for the first time that "conservation" was an issue our country would unavoidably need to address (ever since then, the **"bully pulpit"** refers to opportunity for Presidents, if they so choose, to use their high visibility to bring critical issues directly to the people).

In 1906, President Roosevelt read the bestselling book **The Jungle** by **Upton Sinclair**, one of the muckiest of the muckrakers. This book exposed incredibly disgusting conditions at the Chicago stockyards (slaughterhouses where cows walked in one end and got carried out the other end as a side of beef) and everybody was totally grossed out at the rat parts and vermin that routinely made it into the nation's meat supply. With the President's support, Congress rapidly passed the Meat Inspection Act (1906) and the Pure Food and Drug Act (also 1906), and finally folks could enjoy a steak without checking it first under a magnifying glass.

Teddy also became the first President to intervene in a labor dispute *on behalf* of union workers. In 1902, the United Mine Workers, representing the coal miners in eastern Pennsylvania who were thoroughly exploited by their robber baron bosses, went on strike. This was a big deal because most folks back then used anthracite coal to heat their homes and businesses. Teddy summoned both sides to the White House, whereupon the union leaders accepted arbitration but management refused. Enraged, Teddy threatened to send the army to seize and operate the mines, and browbeaten by the Rough Rider, the corporate bullies backed down. Workers eventually received modest wage increases and work hour decreases, but no official recognition of their right to organize. This was no great shakes, but Roosevelt's reaction to the coal strike stood in stark contrast to President Cleveland's dispatch of federal troops to undermine organized labor in the Pullman strike of 1894. Roosevelt emerged as a cuddly friend of the American worker; it's no wonder a company producing stuffed animals named the Teddy Bear after him. Conservatives wished the actual Theodore Roosevelt could be stuffed.

President William Howard Taft's commitment to Progressivism has sometimes been described by historians as halfhearted. In fact, the Taft Administration initiated about twice as many anti-trust suits as its predecessor, but Taft did make some mistakes and let the Progressives down. Progressives desired lower tariff rates (to bring lower prices for the consumer on imported goods, remember) and Taft did call for lower tariffs, but failed to stand up to the conservative senators who (paid off by corporate lobbyists) filled the proposed reform legislation to the brim with exceptions and loopholes. Taft signed the **Payne-Aldrich Tariff**, and infuriated Progressives by falsely proclaiming the diluted cocktail packed a punch.

Taft also managed to alienate Roosevelt. When Chief Forester Gifford Pinchot, a friend of Teddy's, sharply criticized the Department of the Interior's Secretary, Richard Ballinger, for opening some western federal land to private development (contrary to the Department's purpose), Taft fired Pinchot. Enraged and feeling betrayed, Roosevelt ripped Taft, Taft ripped back, and their friendship ruptured (basically, the President and former President descended to the level of "he's an egomaniac," and "Oh yeah, well he's a fathead").

Roosevelt grew so livid that he challenged his former friend, the sitting President, for the Republican nomination in 1912. Thus, the GOP split between the conservative "Old Guard" who loved the compliant Taft and the Progressives still under the spell of the liberal Teddy. After a bitter confrontation at the nominating convention in June, the Republicans renominated President Taft to stand for a second term. Characteristically full of umbrage and energy, Roosevelt formed his own party: the **Progressive Party**, more commonly known as the **Bull Moose Party** — an appropriate nickname since Teddy and his supporters perpetually seemed to be in heat. As the Republican Party sliced itself in half, lots of Democrats smiled, pumped their fists and yelled, "Yes!"

The Democrats nominated Governor **Woodrow Wilson** — bright, well educated, and extremely moralistic — even though he lived in New Jersey. The son of a Presbyterian minister, Wilson had been a History professor (the best), president of Princeton University, and then a successful Governor of the "Garden State." Wilson and Roosevelt both called for continued Progressive reforms, but they passionately advocated different approaches, while Taft always seemed to be on his lunch break. Roosevelt's **New Nationalism** accepted large corporations as inevitable but declared that a forceful federal government could effectively regulate them. Wilson's **New Freedom** proposed that the federal government should abolish the giant trusts in the interest of free enterprise. Taft's "More Soup" did not really catch on as a campaign slogan.

Wilson, with 6.3 million votes, won easily because the Republicans had obviously split. Roosevelt ran a decent second with 4.1 million votes, and Taft, with 3.5 million, a dismal third. With the two Progressive candidates garnering the vast majority of the votes, Americans in 1912 were still clearly in a Progressive mood. Socialist candidate Eugene V. Debs (of the American Railway Union) got 900,000 votes from naïve, misguided, mustachioed men in ugly berets who thought the government should seize all private businesses and end capitalism in America. That was the most support ever for that kind of approach in American History...thank goodness, because I still intend to get rich no matter who I need to step on.

President Wilson accomplished the most of the three Progressive presidents. He prevailed upon Congress to pass the **Underwood Tariff Act** (1913), which seriously reduced tariff rates in an attempt to allow foreign-owned businesses to enter the domestic market and force the monopolies to compete for a change. In 1914, the **Clayton Antitrust Act** strengthened the Sherman Antitrust Act and deliberately exempted unions from prosecution in antitrust lawsuits. That same year, the **Federal Trade Commission** was created to maintain impartial competition in the economy and protect consumers from unfair business practices.

At President Wilson's urging, Congress approved the **Federal Reserve Act** (1913) to create a Federal Reserve Bank, privately owned but supervised by a Federal Reserve Board, with members appointed by the President. The idea was to create an effective national banking system to monitor the amount of money in circulation, and promote financial stability by lowering interest rates in recessions and raising them in periods of rapid economic expansion to control inflation (all the big banks that operated nation-wide were required to be members, so the smaller ones generally had to go along). Economists ever since have confidently predicted "the next move of the Fed," but much of the time they've guessed wrong. Nowadays, there is suspicion in some quarters that interest rate adjustments are determined by a Ouija board.

Many historians describe Wilson's first term as the high tide of America's Progressive Movement. Maybe so, but there was lots of seaweed...some reforms worked, but others weren't enforced even though they were "on the books." High-powered lawyers donned their pinstriped suits and strode into corporate offices, brandishing loopholes and crushing antitrust legislation in their bare hands. Disgracefully, the Supreme Court struck down laws restricting child labor, stating that under the Constitution, children had the right to work as long as they wanted to. Somehow these old men slept at night. And Wilson believed (as did just about everybody) that social welfare directly for individuals should be left up to the cities and states.

Needless to say, poverty persisted unabated. So did racism...Woodrow Wilson (raised in Virginia) flat out hated African-Americans — a harsh statement but true. A delegation of black leaders met with him at the White House and the President treated them as if they were lepers. How could such a brilliant guy be so stupid about the issue of race? About a hundred years earlier the same question could have been asked about Thomas Jefferson. Likely answers: History repeats itself, the more things change the more things stay the same, and even visionaries can be blind. *Oh wow, déjà vu!*

THE MEXICAN REVOLUTION
or *It's None Of Our Business But Here We Come!*

In 1911, Mexicans led by Francisco Madero rose up in rebellion against their dictator, Porfirio Diaz, who for decades had allowed a tiny *oligarchy* (a bunch of rich Mexican families) and foreign-owned companies (mostly U.S. and British oil and mining corporations) to exploit most of the good Mexican land. In 1914, reactionary General Victoriano Huerta engineered a violent coup d'état and commandeered the Mexican Revolution. Outraged at the immorality of it all, President Wilson famously declared, "I'm going to teach the South American republics to elect good men." Mexico, of course, is not in South America, and Wilson's geographically-challenged remark illustrates how American statesmen in the nineteenth, and well into the twentieth, centuries lacked sophistication in dealing with the various regions of Latin America. Reportedly, Wilson also believed Illinois was in "Central America."

When a German merchant vessel tried to land arms in support of Huerta, the President (presumably consulting a map) moved to prevent this by ordering the U. S. Navy to seize the Mexican port of Vera Cruz. Wilson naively expected the American forces to be welcomed in the name of political and agrarian reform. But all Mexican factions — even those who hated Huerta — were Mexicans first, and resisted tenaciously before falling back; nineteen American soldiers and over 400 Mexicans were killed. If you're thinking, *gee the Mexicans reacted to American highhanded meddling the same way the Filipinos had a few years earlier*...way to go! President Woodrow Wilson, a former History teacher, should have known better. If you're also thinking, *gee the Iraqis have reacted the same way to American paternalism in Iraq*...you're right there too, but keep it to yourself because talk like that can get you wiretapped or shot in a "hunting accident."

Luckily for Wilson the *buttinski*, the "ABC" powers of Argentina, Brazil, and Chile (three nations actually in South America) stepped in to mediate, and the U.S. forces withdrew. Huerta stepped down "voluntarily" to avoid getting his head blown off by one or another of the Mexican revolutionary factions who hated him. Violent anarchy ensued as forces led by "Pancho" Villa and Venustiano Carranza battled for control. Eventually Carranza gained the upper hand and Wilson, with little choice, extended U.S. diplomatic recognition to Carranza's government.

Pancho Villa was a Mexican nationalist, but primarily a self-serving murderous thug who looked nothing like the handsome actor Antonio Banderas, who portrayed him in the HBO movie. Villa went ballistic at what he considered Wilson's betrayal, and went on a rampage. Pancho and his henchmen stopped a train in northern Mexico and deliberately murdered all sixteen Americans on board. A couple of weeks later, this thieving S.O.B. crossed into the United States, burned the town of Columbus, New Mexico, and killed another nineteen Americans.

Yellow journalists splashed banner headlines across their front pages, and this time they didn't need to lie to outrage everyone. Still reeling from the Spanish-American War in 1898, many nervous Spaniards across the Atlantic may well have muttered, "*Great, the United States will probably blame this one on us too, even though the Mexicans forced us to grant them independence way back in 1821.*" President Wilson, with no confidence that Carranza's government could capture Villa and bring him to justice, actually ordered an American force led by General John J. "Blackjack" Pershing into Mexico to capture Villa "dead or alive."

A resentful Mexico protested and threatened war, but for many months the U.S. Army determinedly galloped about the wilderness of northern Mexico. They never found the guy, though they got close (reportedly within fifty yards of a cave in which *Osama bin Villa* was hiding). But when the locals are devoted to someone they view as a hero, and they conspire to hide him in inaccessible mountainous terrain, it is extremely difficult for even a modern U.S. military force to track him down. Eventually the U.S. troops gave up and headed for another emergency in another faraway place. By the way, today there are "Mexican" restaurants in America named after Pancho Villa. There are plenty of genuine Mexican heroes to name restaurants after, so I personally will never patronize an establishment that has chosen to name itself after a mass murderer of Americans. What's next? *The Boston Strangler Steakhouse?*

The tense, forty-year peace following the Franco-Prussian War ended in 1914, when the smoldering, deep-seated rivalries in Europe erupted into fighting. In 1916, idealistic dreamer President Wilson campaigned for reelection with the slogan, "He Kept Us Out Of War!" The Democrats nominated conservative Supreme Court Justice Charles Evans Hughes, who lots of people thought was nuts for wanting to trade a guaranteed life term for four years of guaranteed headaches. Wilson won in a squeaker because most Americans, apparently, wanted to keep dreaming. But can the President keep his promises, or will the United States be jolted awake? Uh oh...stay tuned...don't touch that dial!!!

This Really Happened!

When President Theodore Roosevelt leaves office in 1909 he heads straight for a big game hunt in Africa. His many enemies hoist their drinks and toast, "Health to the lions." Others joke that some lion ought to "do his duty." But after months of tramping through the wilderness, Roosevelt emerges bearing over 3000 trophies, including 9 lions, 5 elephants and 13 rhinos. In reality, Roosevelt is much too near-sighted to be a good marksman; every time he fires his rifle, three other rifles fire at the same instant. The safari leader explains that Mr. Roosevelt had a fairly good idea of the general direction the animal was bearing down on him, but the life of a former President is far too important to take any chances.

And the rest is History....

Quiz yourself on Chapter 10

Multiple Choice (circle the correct answer).

1. Captain Alfred Thayer Mahan believed
    a. that naval power was indispensable for any nation aspiring to be "great."
    b. the Swiss had the best navy
    c. swimming lessons should be free to all Americans
    d. in Neptune, the god of the sea
    e. all of the above

2. The Spanish American War
    a. was between Britain and France
    b. was won by Teddy Roosevelt all by himself
    c. resulted in a genuine overseas empire for the United States
    d. was fought mostly in Mexico
    e. none of the above

3. The Open Door policy
    a. aimed to secure free trade in China
    b. urged men to be more polite to women
    c. complemented the Open Window Policy
    d. greatly improved trade with Latin America
    e. none of the above

4. The Roosevelt Corollary to the Monroe Doctrine
    a. made the Chinese jealous
    b. gave workers the right to bargain collectively
    c. embarrassed his wife
    d. made the United States the "policeman" in Latin America
    e. all of the above

5. The Panama Canal
    a. caused most Americans to look up the word isthmus
    b. connected the Red Sea to the Mediterranean
    c. connected the Atlantic Ocean to the Pacific Ocean
    d. replaced the Erie Canal
    e. all of the above

6. President Taft
    a. weighed over three hundred pounds
    b. got stuck in the White House bathtub
    c. favored dollar diplomacy over military intervention in Latin America
    d. loved food
    e. all of the above

7. The Progressive Movement
    a. had Populist roots
    b. was a campaign for economic, political, and social justice
    c. involved lots of irritating women
    d. resulted in lasting benefits for America
    e. all of the above

8. The muckrakers
    a. were investigative journalists who uncovered injustice and wrongdoing
    b. would have had a field day on the internet
    c. infuriated conservative businessmen
    d. provoked calls for reform
    e. all of the above

9. Prohibition
    a. came about because of Amendment XVIII in 1919
    b. was a major screw up on the part of the Progressives
    c. prohibited the sale or manufacture of intoxicating beverages
    d. provided the opportunity for the Mafia to go "big time"
    e. all of the above

10. *The Jungle* by Upton Sinclair
    a. introduced Americans to the character of Tarzan
    b. was a sexy new perfume for progressive women
    c. exposed the disgusting conditions in the Chicago stockyards
    d. exposed the disgusting conditions in Sears department stores
    e. all of the above

CHAPTER 11

THE GREAT WAR
AND THE ROARING TWENTIES

or

Enough Fighting, Let's Party!

Dreamy idealist President Wilson condemned the immorality of both Roosevelt's corollary to the Monroe Doctrine and Taft's dollar diplomacy. But his lofty words did not reflect what actually occurred during his presidency. American corporate tentacles continued to tighten their grip on Latin American economies, and when disorder threatened American interests in Haiti and the Dominican Republic, he borrowed Teddy's "big stick" and ordered the marines ashore as usual. Wilson may have sincerely desired to keep the United States out of foreign entanglements, but in the end he just couldn't resist playing Superman and swooping down into the fray in the pursuit of truth, justice, and the American way.

THE GREAT WAR IN EUROPE
or *This Was Supposed To Be Quick*

When nations spend fortunes building up their armies, all the polishing, buffing, and parades eventually become tiresome, and every egomaniacal leader gets the itch to take their "baby" out for a drag race. In 1914, all the major European powers were still infected by the "glories" of imperialism, excessive **nationalism**, and competitive **militarism**, and their **entangling alliances** had transformed Europe into a powder keg. Germany, the most militaristic of all, hungered for a war to begin so they could invade other nations, gain territory, and control Europe. All that was needed was a spark, and on June 28, 1914, a Bosnian Serb nationalist named Gavrilo Princip assassinated **Archduke Franz Ferdinand** of Austria-Hungary, who was visiting the city of Sarajevo with his wife. Diplomats dithered, and the dogs of war began to growl.

Pressured by Germany, Austria-Hungary gave Serbia a list of unacceptable demands, mobilized, and moved against them. Russia mobilized in support of Serbia. Then Germany and Ottoman Turkey (and Bulgaria) mobilized to support Austria-Hungary, causing France and then Britain to mobilize against all of them. Despite protestations from the party planner that events had gone horribly wrong, four weeks after the assassination, all the major nations of Europe were marching off to the "**Great War.**"

As usual, all sides thought they had embarked upon a short gallant adventure and certain victory. But British diplomat Sir Edward Grey famously remarked, "The lamps are going out all over Europe. We shall not see them lit again in our lifetime." Simpletons thought that lots of folks must have missed their payments to those newfangled electric companies, but what Grey correctly predicted was the end of an age of innocence and romantic notions about kings, war and heroism. The world would never be the same again.

In brief, here's how events went down. There were two groups of combatants: the **Central Powers** — Germany, Austria-Hungary, Ottoman Turkey, and Italy — against the **Allies** — France, Great Britain, and Russia. Italy later switched sides, double-crossing Germany. The Germans were furious but the Italians simply shrugged and repeated their familiar refrain, "Hey, it's nothing personal, it's just *business*. Ba Da Bing."

There were three "fronts" or "theaters of war." On the Eastern Front, the Russians won some early victories, but Germany quickly recovered and pressed deep into Russia. By 1917, Russia was in such desperate shape that food shortages (which probably would not have been so catastrophic had the supplies of vodka held out) caused riots and the abdication of **Czar Nicholas II.** For about eight months the Russians actually tried to be a republic, but they had no clue how to make democracy work. Eventually, the **Bolsheviks** (Communists) led by **Vladimir Lenin** seized control, and to consolidate the Revolution, Lenin and his minions surrendered huge chunks of Russian territory to Germany. Russia was lost to communism, and its people condemned to decades of authoritarian rule, corruption, brutality, and poverty. Most tragically, for about the next seventy years lots of hot Russian women end up spending their whole lives wearing baggy peasant dresses and smelling like cabbage.

On the Southern Front, the Italians and Austrians battled back and forth, and both sides were more of a drain than a help to the main combatants on the pivotal and much more famous Western Front, where the French and the British squared off against the Germans. Germany tried to conquer France by marching through neutral Belgium and then down through northern France to capture Paris. They almost pulled it off. But the outnumbered Belgians courageously fought for their country and slowed the Germans down just long enough for the French and the British to make a last stand at the Marne River about forty miles from Paris. It is legend that the Paris taxicabs carried 6000 French soldiers there in this desperate final chance to save France, and a few of the selfless drivers even agreed to waive the fare.

The German advance sputtered and stalled, and across northern France and into Belgium something happened that had never happened before. The warring armies burrowed deeper and deeper into trenches and neither side could dislodge the other. Trenches fortified with machine guns and barbed wire (an American invention) created conditions in which attackers invariably got beaten back: stalemate, **trench warfare**. Artillery shells rang down from the sky but the troops dug still deeper; gophers and moles that desperately tried to remain neutral were summarily shot and thrown into boiling pots of stew, wherein they tasted just like chicken.

Both sides used poison gas, and gas masks became standard equipment. Disputed territory between the enemy trenches became known as *no man's land* and it was aptly named: body parts and bomb craters devoid of any hint of greenery gave it an unearthly lifelessness resembling my dorm room freshman year. Attacks and counterattacks continually failed as infantrymen charging through exploding artillery shells and a steady stream of machine gun fire into barbed wire inevitably failed to capture the enemy trench.

For the first time in human history, the advantage in warfare shifted decisively away from the energy and courage of the offensive charge in favor of the dug-in equally determined defense. But safely behind the lines, sherry glasses in hand, unthinking, unfeeling, aging generals on both sides failed to comprehend the new tactics. For four years, in the spirit of bygone centuries, they ordered wave after wave of attacks and counterattacks, but little land changed hands, and they wiped out a generation of European men.

AMERICA TRIES TO STAY ALOOF
or *Can't We Just Sell Stuff And Watch?*

The American people were distressed at all this, and followed the war across the sea in their daily newspapers, hoping we could stay out of it. In August of 1914, President Wilson had issued a proclamation of neutrality and urged everyone not to take sides. Irish-Americans (who hated Britain) and German-Americans had a hard time with that, but they generally kept their mouths shut and didn't rock the neutral boat...an indication of how successfully they had assimilated into their adopted country. Americans with Anglo-Saxon roots (including President Wilson) favored England and the Allies. Both Germany and England tried to use propaganda to win Americans' hearts and minds, but the Brits really played dirty (or smart depending upon how you look at it) when they cut the German transatlantic cable to the United States.

Their own cable remained operational, and with journalistic scruples on the level of today's "fair and balanced" Fox News, all the "information" coming over on the British cable made Germany look bad. The most shocking revelations were the reports of German atrocities towards the citizens of neutral Belgium. Though exaggerated by the British propagandists, it was undeniably true that the German army had raped Belgium, literally and figuratively, so most Americans ended up rooting for the Allies. When a German spy cluelessly left his briefcase on a New York train and the contents revealed plans for sabotaging American factories, most Americans found it pretty hard to muster any sympathy for Kaiser Wilhelm and his "Huns."

American businessmen did not admit it publicly, but the war in Europe was a bountiful windfall for them. They started selling food and manufactured goods to any warring nation who would pay, but a British naval blockade of Germany soon ensured that most American shipments went to the Allies. An angered Germany declared that their submarines (called "**U-boats**") would sink any "neutral" merchant ships heading through the "war zone" around Britain. Americans and their President were furious. Wilson fired off a nasty warning and Germany fired back a nasty reply of its own. Wilson sent his best friend Colonel Edward M. House to act as peacemaker, but neither side wanted to make concessions, as House quickly surmised when he was continually requested to use the servant's entrance.

On May 7th, 1915, a German U-boat torpedoed the British passenger liner **Lusitania** off the coast of Ireland; 1,198 people lost their lives, including 128 Americans. The ship exploded and sank in less than twenty minutes. The German U-boat commander may well have exclaimed, "*Ach mein Gott*, that must have been some torpedo!," but the real reason the ship exploded in a fireball was that it secretly carried cases of ammunition for the Allies. Nevertheless, Americans were outraged and President Wilson sent Germany a sharp protest, demanding reparations.

Most Americans still wanted peace, but Wilson — prodded by hawkish ex-president Teddy Roosevelt and powerful Republican Senator **Henry Cabot Lodge** — decided to ask Congress to approve funds for a build-up of the army and navy. Congress, reflecting the mood of its constituents, refused and kept snoozing (Teddy reportedly tried to don his old Rough Riders outfit, but his extra pounds popped all the buttons). Then in March 1916, a U-boat torpedoed the unarmed French passenger liner *Sussex*, injuring several American citizens. Wilson now sent Germany an ultimatum: cease submarine warfare against merchant and passenger ships or the United States would sever diplomatic relations, the final step before a declaration of war. Germany, appearing to back down, issued the **Sussex Pledge** — a promise not to sink merchant ships without first attempting to save lives. Finally, Congress woke up and authorized much of the defense build-up Wilson wanted.

Americans really did want to stay out of the war and Wilson understood that, so when he ran for a second term in 1916 he touted his progressive record and hit upon the perfect slogan, "He Kept Us Out of War." The Republicans convinced progressive **Charles Evans Hughes** to resign from the Supreme Court and also run as peace candidate, but Hughes proved to be an inept campaigner who contradicted himself so often in his speeches that lots of folks came to doubt his commitment to anything. President Wilson won in a "squeaker" that November. Twelve years later, Hughes would happily return to the Court, where his boring comments fit right in.

On February 1, 1917, the Germans decided upon a desperate ploy: they would recommence their unrestricted submarine warfare — which they knew would likely bring the U.S. into the war on the side of the Allies — and simultaneously launch a final all-out assault on the western front. They gambled on defeating the British and French, who were hanging on by their fingernails, before the Americans could get their forces across the Atlantic in time to be of any help. Wilson immediately cut off diplomatic relations. Meanwhile, most Americans who said "Gesundheit" to someone who sneezed quickly corrected themselves and said, "Bless you."

Next, German Foreign Minister Arthur Zimmermann orchestrated perhaps the most inept piece of diplomacy in the history of international relations. He sent a diplomatic note to the German ambassador in Mexico City, instructing him to ask the Mexicans to side with Germany in the event of war, and upon victory be rewarded with the return of the states of New Mexico, Texas and Arizona, which they had lost way back in the Mexican War. The **Zimmermann Telegram** (or **Note**) was supposed to be a secret, but British intelligence agents intercepted it and turned it over to Wilson, who released it to the press. Americans freaked and wished they could choke the Kaiser right then and there. Then came reports of U-boats sinking four unarmed U.S. merchant ships, and news of the Czar of Russia's abdication. The Allies now totally seemed like the good guys.

Correctly concluding that German victory in Europe would one day threaten the United States, on April 2nd, 1917, President Wilson solemnly addressed a joint session of Congress (the House and Senate together) and asked (as he was constitutionally mandated to do) for a declaration of war. Four days later he got one, though fifty representatives and six senators (mostly from the Midwest and West) voted nay. One Congressmen reportedly remarked, "Hey, a submarine can't attack a cornfield, so what do I care."

President Wilson knew he couldn't sell the war to the American people by telling them that they were fighting to keep the sea-lanes open for rich industrialists. And he certainly couldn't whip up support for the war by explaining that America had loaned so much money to the Allies that a German victory would spell financial doom for lots of pinstriped rich men on Wall Street. So instead he made the war into a moral crusade — perhaps the penultimate progressive program — "The war to end all wars!" and "The war to make the world safe for democracy!"

AMERICA GOES TO WAR
or *Which Way To The Front?*

America, as usual woefully unprepared for war, immediately embarked upon a massive program of military **mobilization**. The Selective Service Act was passed to facilitate a draft, and rich guys were not allowed to buy their way out of it like during the Civil War. (One sophomore from Princeton who cried, *Please, I can't go, I'm going to be captain of the crew team!* was reportedly told by authorities that his comments were inappropriate.) This time there was little resistance to conscription, and in just months the army grew from 200,000 to three million men. Over 350,000 African-Americans served, many bravely when given an opportunity for real combat, but most were assigned menial tasks in segregated units under the command of white officers.

To pay for the war the federal government successfully sold "Liberty" and "Victory" Bonds. The "Hopefully We'll Do Okay" Bonds did not sell that well. Federal taxes were raised on incomes and imposed on certain products like tobacco and alcohol. Even some corporations were required to pay some taxes, a shock that caused uncontrollable weeping in many boardrooms. Still, even in wartime the federal government was loathe to force private businesses to do anything — that's how tenaciously the laissez faire virus still clung to its American host.

President Wilson appointed **Herbert Hoover** head of the Food Administration. Hoover was already well known to most Americans as a leader of charitable efforts to aid war-torn Belgium, and he threw himself into his new job with gusto. Thanks to increased farm output and help from everyday Americans who voluntarily observed wheatless Mondays, meatless Tuesdays, and porkless Thursdays and Saturdays, the United States vastly increased its food exports to the Allies. It has been said some wives tried to tell their husbands that there was supposed to be sexless weekends, but there is no evidence Hoover had anything to do with that.

As the country embarked upon war, an unfortunate aspect of the American character once again reared its ugly head...an intolerance of dissent. Even though the Constitution protects the rights of those who disagree with the actions of the government to speak out, the Congress somewhat hysterically passed the **Espionage Act** in 1917, mandating severe punishments for spying, sabotage and obstructing the war effort (okay so far) but also for using the mail to distribute anti-war messages (now that was way over the top). The following year, the **Sedition Act** spelled out penalties for anyone who dared to verbalize or write anything critical of the war effort. This was paranoia, a clear violation of freedom of speech, and a totally unnecessary trampling of first amendment rights. But no serious student of American History should be surprised, because this kind of stuff almost always goes on during wartime. Of course, years later, thoughtful folks invariably look back and think to themselves, *Geez, was all that really necessary?* (And now repeat after me: "*Patriot Act.*")

Stupid restrictions on our freedom notwithstanding, it is important for our government to explain to Americans why they are going to war. Given good reasons, History has shown that our nation will fight and sacrifice to the utmost...whatever it takes to win. President Wilson set up the **Committee on Public Information** to get his message out, and appointed newspaperman **George Creel** to head it. Creel was a master of propaganda who hammered home the righteousness of the American cause by flooding the land with posters, pamphlets, (silent) movies and professional speakers. Frequently, people have the idea that only evil dictators use propaganda to spread deceptive and distorted information. But propaganda is an essential and legitimate tool in any war or just cause...and Americans have tended to accept it from their own government provided they approve of the message which, at its core, must be honest and true. Of course, some of the propaganda was stupid and trite, such as when folks started calling sauerkraut "liberty cabbage" and frankfurters "hot dogs." "Liberty cabbage" never caught on, but try ordering a frankfurter at Yankee Stadium and I guarantee you the vendor will respond, *Whadaya mean...a hot dog?* (Again, repeat after me: *"Freedom Fries."*)

The American Expeditionary Force under the command of General Pershing arrived in France just in the nick of time. The navy helped out by setting up **convoys** — large groups of merchant and troop ships surrounded by submarine chasing destroyers — that zigzagged across the Atlantic, generally outfoxing and often sinking those confounded German U-boats. The Allies were exhausted and on the brink of total collapse, so it must have seemed like a miracle when into the muck and mire dashed fresh-faced American **doughboys**...a nickname for American soldiers since the Civil War, when many men had enlisted for the money, or *dough*.

So desperate were the Allies in 1917 that America rushed its youthful army across the Atlantic before a lot of our guys had a chance to figure out which end of a rifle was supposed to face outward. But their courage was ready and, suffering heavy casualties, they helped throw back German attacks at Château-Thierry and Belleau Wood in May and June of 1918, and through the rest of the summer and into the fall, they led the final Allied counter thrust at St. Mihiel and the Argonne Forest.

The Germans were just as battered as the French and the British, but no counterweight to the well-fed eager Americans arrived to prop them up. How spent was the German army at this point? **Alvin C. York**, a crack shot from the Tennessee mountains, single-handedly killed twenty of them, and then he and his men captured another 132. How did he accomplish this and become the biggest American hero of the war? Perhaps the German soldiers in the field were so hungry they simply threw up their hands and shouted, "We surrender, just get us some frankfurters." Then when York figured out they meant hot dogs, he could have easily marched his starving captives back to Allied lines, where not only did they have hot dogs but mustard and relish as well.

As they were pushed out of their trenches and back toward their own country, most German military leaders could read the handwriting on the wall (if they could find an intact wall) — they were beaten. Kaiser Wilhelm abdicated (quit) his throne and fled to Holland, where the SOB lived for another twenty-three years twiddling his stupid mustache and never apologizing for anything. On November 11, 1918, Germany signed an armistice (peace agreement) and the news rang out "**All Quiet On The Western Front**" (By the way, you should read the classic novel and see both movies — the original from the thirties and the seventies remake...all justifiably admired for their powerful anti-war message).

THE WAR TO END ALL WARS
or *The War To End All Wars Until the Next War*

On January 8, 1918, President Wilson really knocked everybody's socks off when he addressed Congress and announced to the world his vision for postwar peace, codified into fourteen points. This famous Fourteen Points speech called for (I) open treaties, (II) freedom of the seas, (III) international free trade, (IV) reduction of armaments, (V) settlement of colonial claims with the interests of the native peoples taken into account, and (VI-XIII) adjustment of European boundaries so all major nationalities could have their own independent nation. Point XIV was the most groundbreaking; it envisioned an international organization — a League of Nations — in which countries could meet to hash out their conflicts peacefully. A point XV has been rumored to been cut from the speech at the last moment when the President's advisors convinced him that world leaders would balk at mandatory hugging. Truthfully, Wilson was an idealist who almost certainly believed in his own lofty words. Most Americans did too. Suckers.

With a successful end to the war in sight, Wilson's head swelled so much that none of his hats fit him anymore. As the midterm election of November 1918 approached, the President urged Americans to vote for Democratic representatives and senators, implying that these guys would be much more devoted than the Republicans to his "Fourteen Points." Many Americans were offended that Wilson had interjected politics into a quest for world peace they had come to view as a moral crusade. When the votes were counted, the GOP gained majority control of both the House and Senate.

Many Americans felt President Wilson should have stayed home to personally attend to the domestic transition from war to peace, but President Wilson decided to personally lead the American delegation to the peace conference in Paris, thus becoming the first President to travel to Europe while in office. He further irritated people by appointing friends such as Colonel House and Secretary of State Lansing to the delegation while not including a single Republican. Henry Cabot Lodge, the powerful GOP chairman of the Senate Foreign Relations Committee (the committee which would ultimately recommend to the full Senate whether or not to ratify any peace treaty), should have been invited and heavily schmoozed by Wilson, but the swollen-headed chief executive left him behind. Henry was furious, and his refusal to send Woodrow a Christmas card that year would be just the beginning.

In Paris, President Wilson ran into a buzz saw...because the hotel he was staying at was undergoing renovations. Just kidding, the buzz saw was **Georges Clemenceau**, the Premier of France, and **David Lloyd George**, the Prime Minister of Britain, who together with **Vittorio Orlando**, Premier of Italy, and Wilson have since been called "The Big Four." Orlando was hoping to pick up some territorial crumbs for Italy, but Clemenceau and Lloyd George were obsessively determined to promote their own interests, punish Germany, and steal German colonies while holding on to their own. In other words, they wanted a peace *with* victory...and balloons and noisemakers paid for by the defeated Germans.

Wilson negotiated his idealistic butt off for months, but gradually the British and French wall of intransigence forced him to make numerous concessions. Republican potshots from back home didn't help, either. Eventually what emerged from the "peace" conference was the very imperfect **Treaty of Versailles**. Germany was harshly punished, and over Wilson's objections lost territory, its overseas colonies, and had to pay huge reparations (damages) for the war. Germany was further humiliated by being forced to sign a "war guilt clause" accepting all blame for the costly conflict. As the dust cleared, astute observers worried about how long the rabid German Shepard would stay tethered to its leash (less than twenty years it turns out, but we'll get to that).

Wilson saw the formation of a League of Nations, but in one of the most disgraceful episodes in our American experience, the country refused to join, with Henry Cabot Lodge playing a pivotal role as spoiler. Senator Lodge desperately wanted to be President Lodge, and let everyone know how much he loathed Wilson. The President was a bit more circumspect; whenever someone asked him about Lodge he would simply grasp his own throat and make a gagging sound.

A small group of thickheaded isolationist senators, dubbed the "irreconcilables," followed Lodge around like a lap dog. Their biggest problem with the League of Nations — aside from the fact that it wasn't their idea and Wilson would go down in History for it — was the clause mandating that all member nations must come to the aid of any member nation under threat of "external aggression." Congress, they argued, should have the ultimate war-making authority as guaranteed in the Constitution, as well as the final say on trade issues such as tariffs and regional foreign policy exemplified by the good ol' Monroe Doctrine.

Reasonable men, through negotiations and amendments to the League charter, could have satisfactorily addressed all of these concerns. But neither Wilson nor Lodge was reasonable. The showboating Lodge sardonically announced *fourteen* "reservations" to the Treaty of Versailles. Ironically, a solid majority of Republicans and Democrats in the Senate (not to mention the American people) favored U.S. membership in a League of Nations, but the bitter domestic politics dragged on.

To garner support for *his* League of Nations, President Wilson embarked on a nationwide speaking tour. Accounts of his spellbinding speeches confirm that Wilson was still the idealist devoted to his dream of a future world living in justice and peace. Unfortunately, when the President left a city, one or another of senatorial Lodge stooges would blow into town and call Woodrow a weenie or words to that effect. In Pueblo, Colorado, suffering from physical and nervous exhaustion, the President collapsed, and a few days after returning to Washington, he suffered a stroke that paralyzed his left side. Lodge was actually happy with this turn of events, and in November, 1919, Lodge and his party line Republican Senators voted down the pristine Wilsonian version of the Treaty.

Next, Lodge engineered a Senate vote on a new version of the Treaty with his reservations included. From his sickbed, President Wilson — reportedly drifting in and out of consciousness — told his wife to urge all loyal Democratic Senators to vote against this new Treaty draft (remember, a two-thirds vote in the affirmative is required for approval of a treaty). He still hoped it could somehow be ratified *his* way, with at most a few mild changes by friendly Democrats. At the President's behest, Democratic Senators defeated Lodge's modified Treaty.

The public was so outraged that the Senate had little choice but to vote again on the Treaty of Versailles, and a vote was scheduled for March 19, 1920. By this point it was obvious that the Treaty (including American membership in the League of Nations) could only gain Senate ratification with the Lodge amendments attached — obvious to everyone, that is, except the President. Wilson stubbornly asked Democratic Senators to again vote no, and enough of them robotically followed orders to defeat the Treaty for the third and final time.

Many historians believe that Wilson's stroke affected his judgment, and made an already obstinate and proud man irrational at a critical moment in American History. They are probably correct. Mrs. Wilson and the White House physician conspired for weeks to successfully hide the true extent of the President's illness from the country. This charade could not have been easy for Edith Wilson to pull off, particularly since it has been said that while delirious, Woodrow continually called out the name of his late first wife, Ellen.

The League of Nations came into being, but the United States, by then the most powerful industrial nation in the world, did not join. Who was to blame? Our invitation did not get lost in the mail, so blame both Wilson and Lodge for their stupid selfish stubbornness. But ultimately the American people, who drifted into uncertainty and indifference, should never have allowed the Republicans and the Democrats to play politics over such a crucial issue.

POSTWAR TRANSITION TO PEACE

or *Conservatives...They're Back!*

The end of the war buffeted the economy; wages dropped, prices and profits fell, and lots of private companies went belly up. No longer restrained by patriotism, many unions called strikes. But the American public still associated labor unions with communism — especially after the 1917 Bolshevik Revolution in Russia — so the workers still received little popular support. A big shipyard strike in Seattle in January 1919 collapsed hard when the Mayor called in federal troops. Steelworkers in Indiana met the same fate. For example, when the police in Boston went on strike, Massachusetts Governor **Calvin Coolidge** received national acclaim for calling in the National Guard. In most Americans' minds, organized workers were all "Reds," and out of this grew the postwar **Red Scare** of 1919-20. There was also a brief "green scare" in 1920, but when everyone realized it was St. Patrick's Day they just joined the party.

In truth, there were relatively few communists in America after World War I, and they were virtually all harmless and law abiding, but too many mainstream Americans, prodded by headlines and self-serving politicians, allowed themselves to be duped into lashing out irrationally. There were book burnings, and loyalty oaths for public officials to sign to keep their jobs. In New York, five duly elected members of the state legislature were denied their seats simply because they professed to be socialists (you might expect this kind of thing in Kansas...but not New York!).

Attorney General **A. Mitchell Palmer** went even further, orchestrating "Palmer Raids" across the country, in which accused communists and radicals were rounded up without warrants and denied access to a lawyer. The raids netted lots of pamphlets but few weapons, and Americans quickly realized they had better refresh their memories with a quick read of the Constitution. Palmer, who dreamed of being called "President Palmer," was undeterred, however. Completely full of himself, he predicted a massive communist demonstration for the socialist holiday, May Day, in 1920. Deliberately blowing off the Bill of Rights, he put the police and the army on alert the night before, but when no demonstration occurred he looked like the overzealous imbecile he was, and Americans' red hysteria rapidly faded to pink.

Public suspicions of vague "radical" threats did remain, though, particularly after a terrible September 1920 bomb blast on Wall Street (still unexplained) which killed thirty-eight people and wounded hundreds. The question of the hour was *who are these radicals anyway?*, and for many Americans the answer was *they must be those crazy, swarthy sausage-eaters from the hinterlands of Europe.* Congress would respond a few years later with the **Immigration Act** of 1924, severely restricting immigration via a quota system blatantly favorable to western Europeans, and discriminatory toward eastern and southern Europeans, where radical types supposedly came from. White western-European-descended Americans applauded this, and actively discriminated against immigrants from countries viewed as radical spawning grounds: mainly Russia, Poland, Greece, and Italy.

The presidential election of 1920 gave no clear indication of what most folks wanted. The Democrats nominated Governor James M. Cox of Ohio, who strongly supported American membership in the League of Nations and followed Wilson's advice to make the race a "great and solemn referendum" on the League. The Republicans finally settled on the friendly and likeable Senator Warren G. Harding (also from the swing state of Ohio). A dutiful conservative, Harding waffled masterfully on the League while insisting that America should return to its traditional commitment to isolationism, and pretend the Progressive Movement and the Great War never happened.

Harding declared that Americans wanted a return to *normalcy* (making up a word that should have been properly expressed as *normality*). He correctly sensed that most mainstream Americans were fed up with the angst of war and muckraking, and in November, Harding creamed Cox 16,143,407 to 9,130,328 in the popular vote and 404 to 127 in the Electoral College. Socialist candidate Eugene V. Debs garnered over 900,000 votes, the most ever for a radical left-wing party in this country (Debs was in jail for the entire campaign for violating the Espionage Act of 1917, so obviously his "get out the vote" rallies were extremely lonely affairs). It should be noted that women, taking advantage of the Nineteenth Amendment, voted nationally for the first time.

Was the election essentially a referendum on the League of Nations? No; voters were also mad at Cox and the Democrats for the economic downturn which had set in (briefly it turned out), and even more fed up with highbrow Wilsonian platitudes. Safely elected, President Harding declared that America had spoken out against membership in the League and that was that. Woodrow Wilson died in 1924, a broken and bitter man. Americans mourned his passing, but not too deeply. It was time to party.

Harding assumed the Presidency in March of 1921 and immediately proved to be adept at poker and womanizing. It is legendary (and apparently true) that his wife caught him in a White House closet with his mistress when the smoke from his cigar wafted under the door. Reportedly, Mrs. Harding was further enraged when her husband blurted out, "I swear I was just showing her some of my new suits."

Harding was handsome and debonair, but his mind was a bit haggard. A few solid cabinet appointees made him look like a genius at first, though, particularly Secretary of the Treasury **Andrew W. Mellon**. Mellon believed (as did Harding after it was explained to him with simple charts and graphs) that high taxes were driving down the economy, and by cutting taxes for the wealthy, the wealthy would in turn invest in new businesses and create jobs. This remains the classic conservative economic doctrine often called "trickle down theory" (sadly, at many junctures in our History, underprivileged Americans have died of thirst waiting opened mouthed at the end of the spigot).

In the early twenties, this shift of the tax burden from the rich to the middle class and poor appeared to work, largely because Congress created a Bureau of the Budget, and Harding appointed Charles G. Dawes to head it. Ever since, the President has been required to submit a federal budget to Congress, whereupon members bicker for months, make lots of changes to benefit their states and districts, and wind up ignoring the whole thing anyway. But back then, Congress stayed *within* the budget(!) and responded effectively to Mellon's calls for real cuts in federal spending. Lo and behold, there was soon a budget *surplus*, and by the end of 1922 the American economy was back on its feet and "roaring"(sorry Liberals, I'm just reporting the facts here). It has been said that, when informed of all the good economic news, Harding simply clapped his hands and headed off to his favorite closet.

The sound from farmers, though, was more like an angry snarl. Wartime demand had boosted the market price of farm commodities, but after the war the happy "ho down" ended. Congress erected high tariff walls around the country; thriving manufacturers relished the protection from foreign competition, but as usual the Europeans responded by cutting back their purchases of the food overflowing in American warehouses. Ironically, tractors now powered by gasoline had helped produce the record crop surpluses that contributed to the low farm prices. And around this time the first pickup trucks appeared on the scene, allowing some farmers to tear around the country-side terrifying the poor unemployed horses.

Despite the booming economy, Harding's presidency was headed for a fall, due to handsome Warren's poor administrative habits. Instead of choosing the best people for important government positions, he tended to appoint his poker buddies — a big presidential *no-no* (I guess it's hard to see from inside a closet).

One by one, these pals got busted robbing the country blind. Harry M. Daugherty, the Attorney General, could supposedly be bribed with as little as a free piece of cheese-cake. Colonel Charles R. Forbes, head of the Veterans Bureau, also loved cheesecake, and could buy lots of it with the millions he stole taking kickbacks in connection with the building of veterans' hospitals. The worst scandal occurred when Secretary of the Interior Albert B. Fall accepted bribes from private businessmen to allow them access to government oil reserves at Elk Hills, California and Teapot Dome, Wyoming. This **Teapot Dome Scandal** shocked a law-abiding public already amazed at just how far greedy public officials would go to stuff their bellies and bank accounts.

Unlike today, when scandal hits news channels in minutes, it took weeks for bad news to spread across the nation. Harding learned of the scandals as he was embarking upon a nationwide speaking tour and, betrayed and heartbroken, he realized that very soon his public popularity would turn to scorn. On his way back from Alaska, the depressed President collapsed, and his personal physician told him he had food poisoning from eating some bad crabs. In reality, Harding had suffered a heart attack, and he died in San Francisco on August 2nd, 1923. Americans deeply mourned him at the time and cut back on their crab consumption, but within a few weeks everyone started to realize Harding had been the worst President since Ulysses S. (bring me another drink) Grant.

Harding's vice president, the uptight, stuffy New Englander Calvin Coolidge, has always been described as aloof; it's been rumored that upon Harding's death, he had to be reminded to take over. He was a man of few words, earning him the nickname "Silent Cal." The quintessential conservative Republican, Coolidge was utterly devoted to laissez-faire and minimal government, as was illustrated when he strung together the eight words he is most famous for: "The business of the United States is business." He also said, "The man who builds a factory builds a temple," which a few Americans tried to use as an excuse to blow off church services on Sunday morning.

Coolidge had been untouched by the Harding scandals, so the Republicans unhesitatingly chose him as their standard bearer for the 1924 presidential election. It was a hot summer that year, and "Keep Cool With Coolidge" seemed the perfect slogan. The Democrats, squabbling amongst themselves, finally nominated a conservative Wall Street lawyer named John W. Davis.

Dismayed at this, progressive-minded folks formed a new Progressive Party and nominated one of their own, Senator Robert La Follette of Wisconsin. La Follette still clung to liberal (and by this time nostalgic) ideas; he wanted more aid to farmers, legal protections for organized labor, government ownership of railroads and some electric companies, and (as Shakespeare said, here's "the rub") higher income taxes.

La Follette polled a respectable five million votes, but the country was undeniably in a conservative mood; Davis got 8.5 million, and Coolidge won with 15 million. Victorious and now President on his own, the federal budget and taxes plummeted as Coolidge vetoed every government spending plan he could get his hands on. Finally, he had to relent a bit when someone told him the White House was running low on toilet paper.

THE JAZZ AGE
or *Wow, I Can See Her Legs!*

The Progressive Movement had exhausted itself by the end of World War I, but women's groups, joined by lots of protestant Christians, managed one last gasp. Prohibition, a ban on the "sale or manufacture of intoxicating liquors," was added to the Constitution as Amendment XVIII in 1919. White southerners hoped to keep alcohol away from blacks lest they develop troublesome "beer muscles," and many Anglo-Saxon-descended protestants relished the chance to slap the beloved beer and wine out of the hands of the "socially inferior" (and generally Catholic) Irish, German, and Italian Americans. "Decent" women, traditionally excluded from neighborhood taverns, wanted their men sober and home. Little wonder, when America's fighting men returned from Europe really thirsty and furious...even more so when they went to parties and all the girls wanted to do was play charades.

Immediately, lots of folks completely blew off the law. The Italian **Mafia**, which had been in the gambling, prostitution, and extortion rackets in big cities since the 1890s, now went big time. They "bootlegged" booze (can you guess where they hid the bottles?) from the West Indies or Canada to a thirsty public, and made a fortune. Local police, federal agents (hopelessly understaffed), politicians, and judges were frequently paid off, and "speakeasies" (illegal bars) opened on street corners across the land. If you knew the password you could get in, and once inside, the mayor or the chief of police would be happy to buy you a drink. When I was a kid, my grandfather told me he met my grandmother in a speakeasy...but then denied it when he sobered up.

Americans have a long custom of resisting laws they don't believe in — something King George III learned the hard way. Americans also have a long tradition of fondness for alcohol (many of my own underachieving ancestors are evidence of that). In the case of Prohibition, these traditions trumped an ill-conceived, poorly enforced law which contradicted another long held value — that the government should stay out of citizens' personal lives. Thus the Eighteenth Amendment became an exercise in national hypocrisy, and (for the most part) a failure. But if you are tempted to believe that this presents a precedent for the legalization of marijuana, think again. It took more effort to find a drink during Prohibition, and studies have shown that overall alcohol consumption went *down*, individuals' savings accounts rose, and employers reported fewer employee absences and hangovers. Food (or if you are a pothead, Doritos) for thought.

In the 1920s, women made up nearly a quarter of the workforce, mostly on assembly lines, in mills, or in clerical jobs subservient to men. Women did not receive equal pay for equal work — only about sixty percent — a discrepancy not fair then or now. But our sisters finally threw away their corsets. Dubbed **"flappers,"** these progressive ladies bobbed their hair, pulled their hemlines above their knees, wore rouge and lipstick, and smoked cigarettes in public, raising many an eyebrow. Elderly men bemoaned that there had been no flappers around in their Victorian day, while most younger guys kept quiet with dumb smiles on their faces.

On the dance floor, young couples also raised eyebrows by gyrating wildly to **jazz**. Jazz became the music of the age as black musicians — notably **"King" Oliver**, **Louis Armstrong**, and composer **W.C. Handy** — mixed African rhythms with a cornucopia of American sounds, and brought the melodious concoction with them north from New Orleans to Kansas City, St. Louis, and then Chicago and New York. Smaller towns that were passed over had to make do with the polka.

The lives of many African-Americans were also changing. Beginning in 1917, more and more decided to forsake dead-end southern sharecropping for a chance at a new life in the rapidly expanding industrial north. By the end of the 1920's, about one million had migrated to cities like Chicago, Detroit, and Cleveland, taking poorly paid jobs whites did not want. Excluded from most conventional opportunities, many blacks also went into business on their own, including Garrett Morgan, the first to mass produce the traffic light, reportedly after he got fed up with all the accidents he was having on his way to work. The Harlem area in New York City produced a veritable explosion of African American literature. **Langston Hughes'** poetry and prose contributed much to this flowering of black culture and pride. Black huckster **Marcus Garvey** rose and fell, but his calls for Black Nationalism caused many Americans of all stripes to examine their own attitudes on race.

Predictably, though, northern whites resented their new neighbors and the competition for jobs, and as a result the Ku Klux Klan experienced a wicked resurgence in the 1920s *in the North*. But the Klansmen and Klanswomen did not only hate blacks; they also hated Catholics, Jews, immigrants, and most of the new ideas percolating in the big cities such as women's rights and birth control. The backbone of the Klan consisted of fundamentalist white Protestants, who stretched and twisted their Christian faith into a social movement that resolved to tell everyone else how to live their lives. Dismissive of freedom, diversity, and separation of church and state, the super conservatives of the Klan were afraid of the unstoppable tide of modernity sweeping across the land, and by 1925 there were about five million proud public members. But when their leader was exposed as a sexual pervert and convicted of manslaughter, and other Klan executives were caught stuffing members' dues money into their underwear, membership diminished rapidly. By the end of the decade the KKK had faded back to its usual status as a fringe movement for the offspring of close relatives. Curiously, the Ku Klux Klan had a fetish for making up words that started with the letter "K," such as kloran, klaliff, and kleagal. What a bunch of kreeps.

Public education, like many things in the 1920's, was experiencing an evolution — literally. A forward-thinking philosopher, **John Dewey**, pioneered the idea that schools should go beyond the mere memorization of facts and give young people an opportunity to "learn by doing," preparing them for a future as good citizens and critical thinkers who could work to improve society. Dewey's ideas included the teaching of modern science, and by the twenties, many progressive Christians had found it possible — even inspiring — to embrace both modern science *and* the great moral lessons of the Bible. This did not sit well, however, with Fundamentalist "Christians," who couldn't stand Dewey because modern education included the verifiable fact of human evolution. Uneducated and unsophisticated, these conservative Christians clung to the medieval view. And boy did they flip out when modern professional educators taught Darwinian theory in public schools.

In 1925, Tennessee science teacher **John C. Scopes** was arrested in the small town of Dayton and put on trial for teaching evolution. Americans avidly followed newspaper coverage of what was soon dubbed the "Monkey Trial." William Jennings Bryan (yup, that same three-time presidential loser Bryan) prosecuted, hotshot Chicago lawyer **Clarence Darrow** defended Scopes, and a titanic legal battle ensued. Darrow famously put Bryan himself on the stand to testify as an expert on the Bible, but the old man came across as childlike, silly, and just plain stubborn. Scopes was eventually convicted — he had broken some ridiculous Tennessee law — but folks in the big cities and progressives all over America collectively sneered at the small town southern "hicks" like they were living in the Dark Ages. And rural fundamentalists scowled back at progressive city dwellers like they were (literally) an army of Satan worshippers.

Tension between generally conservative country folk and generally progressive city folk has been a constant part of American life, as I personally found out when I was pulled over in Georgia with New York license plates. But back then conservatives hadn't incorporated "intelligent design" (a euphemism for *faith*) into the curriculum of public schools. My recommendation: when someone says something ignorant like "I ain't descended from no monkey," don't respond — just tell them a rerun of *Dukes of Hazzard* is on television and they'll slither away.

The continued growth of electric power kept the 1920s booming; by the end of the decade about seventy percent of the nation's homes were wired, housewives kept frozen foods in their new refrigerators, and thanks to Clarence Birdseye's company, everyone in America learned the word *niblet*. The chemical industry also took off, due to the growing use of plastic instead of iron or steel. Many plastic household objects became available, though they would break much more often and need replacing — a headache for consumers ever since.

The automobile industry expanded rapidly, too, with numerous manufacturers such as Chevrolet and Dodge flooding the streets with their rolling wares. Many dirt roads got paved, and soon the landscape was dotted with diners, gas stations, and other attractions that could attract customers if they offered a bathroom. **Henry Ford** figured out how to use the **assembly line** and **mass production** to turn out a Model T that could sell new for less than three hundred bucks...a price the average American worker could afford.

The automobile age also changed the nature of "courtship" in America. Instead of "paying a call" on a woman at her house with her parents present, a gentleman could pick up his date in his car and go somewhere private (cars would naturally run out of gas at the local lovers' lane). With this new-found freedom, attitudes regarding sex loosened up. A red-blooded all-American guy finally had a chance — but now he had to pay for dinner.

Books became old news for lots of people as radio stations began to beam entertainment directly into the living room, and movies soared to new heights of popularity when the flickering images added sound in 1928. "Talkies" made cinematic entertainment grander than ever before, causing attendance to shrink at live stage productions. Vaudeville was virtually wiped out. Movie stars rose to godlike status, and in some places, church attendance fell as preachers found it hard to compete with the handsome "Sheik" **Rudolph Valentino**, America's sweetheart **Mary Pickford**, and that funny little tramp, **Charlie Chaplin**. Movie stars became full of themselves and behaved stupidly in their personal lives...Mel Gibson et al would have been right at home.

Americans worshipped their heroes. Boxer **Jack Dempsey**, tennis star **Helen Mills**, golfer **Bobby Jones**, and football player **Knute Rockne** (a Native-American who persevered) all helped popularize their respective sports. Baseball's mighty slugger **"Babe" Ruth** generated enormous publicity; he remains one of the greatest athletes of all time despite the old newsreels that make him look like those fat guys who play weekend softball and run the bases carrying beer cans.

By far the greatest sensation of the twenties was the young pilot who became the first person to fly solo across the Atlantic Ocean from New York to Paris. Twenty-five-year-old **Charles Lindbergh** climbed into his single-engine plane *Spirit of St. Louis* and stayed awake for almost thirty-four hours to make it. Lots of man-eating sharks felt cheated, but Americans idolized him. Lindbergh was given the very first ticker tape parade down Broadway, which everyone enjoyed — except the sanitation workers, who were mad about cleaning up the mess after everyone else had gone off to find another party.

The roaring twenties was a bigoted, hedonistic, self-destructive time when many white Americans boozed, danced all night, indulged in silly fads like flagpole sitting, and tore about the countryside in spiffy new cars trying to convince themselves everything was hunky-dory in the United States of America. Some groundbreaking writers, including novelists **Jon Dos Passos** and **Sinclair Lewis** and dramatist **Eugene O'Neill**, confronted this shallowness and materialism. **Ernest Hemingway** and **F. Scott Fitzgerald** proved particularly effective in evoking the nature of the time, perhaps because it takes one to know one. Both these guys could write wondrously, but they were also habitually whacked out of their skulls.

Yup, the roaring twenties was a heady time all right. The stock market soared all day and the revelry soared through the night. But was there anything to worry about? Most Americans didn't seem to think so, and anyone who said something like, "What goes up must come down" was looked upon as a party pooper. But will the good times roll forever? Uh oh...stay tuned...don't touch that dial!!!

This Really Happened!

To keep America's highest court above politics, Supreme Court judges are appointed for life. "The Great Dissenter" — Justice Oliver Wendell Holmes, Jr. — took that to heart. Appointed in 1902 by President Theodore Roosevelt, he served until 1932, when he was nearly ninety-one years old. For more than thirty years his salty wit, white hair and flowing mustache were a fixture in the nation's capitol. In his final year on the bench, old Justice Holmes was taking his daily walk with fellow justice Louis Brandeis when a gorgeous woman walked by. Holmes gazed at her then turned to Brandeis and said: "Oh, what I wouldn't give to be seventy again!"

And the rest is History...

Quiz yourself on Chapter 11

Multiple Choice (circle the correct answer).

1. World War I
    a. began at Fort Sumter in 1861
    b. began in Europe in 1914
    c. occurred right after War One-Half
    d. was over after six months
    e. none of the above

2. When Belgium refused to allow Germany to march troops through its territory into France
    a. Germany replied, "Okay, no problem."
    b. Germany decided to go through Poland
    c. Germany immediately cut off beer exports to the small nation
    d. Germany brutally occupied the small nation
    e. None of the above

3. During the presidential election campaign of 1916, President Wilson
    a. promised to bomb Iraq
    b. promised to send American boys to fight in Europe
    c. promised to keep America out of the war in Europe
    d. confused the nations of Switzerland and Sweden
    e. all of the above

4. Fresh American troops entering the Great War
    a. turned the tide in favor of the Allies
    b. turned the tide in favor of the Central Powers
    c. turned the tide in favor of the New York Yankees
    d. started teaching both sides English
    e. all of the above

5. The United States
    a. did not join the League of Nations
    b. joined the League of Nations but never showed up
    c. got lost on the way to the first meeting of the League of Nations
    d. formed its own League with other countries
    e. all of the above

6. According to the U.S. Constitution, the President negotiates treaties and
   a. the Senate tries to understand them
   b. the Senate takes its cut under the table
   c. the Senate must ratify them
   d. the House of Representatives feels left out
   e. a, c and d

7. The Red Scare
   a. eventually made Attorney General A. Mitchell Palmer look like an idiot
   b. eventually faded to pink
   c. resulted in many unconstitutional actions by the federal government
   d. was immediately followed by an Orange Scare
   e. a, b and c

8. During the twenties, Americans
   a. generally loosened up
   b. generally partied hard and made lots of money
   c. generally ignored folks who remained poor
   d. generally thought the good times would last forever
   e. all of the above

9. During the twenties, lots of conservative fundamentalists
   a. joined the Ku Klux Klan
   b. resisted new ideas
   c. hated folks who lived in big cities
   d. were ignorant and narrow minded
   e. all of the above

10. George Herman "Babe" Ruth
    a. was a great athlete who helped popularize baseball
    b. loved hotdogs and beer
    c. hit home runs like nobody else
    d. became a ballerina after he retired from baseball
    e. a,b, and c

CHAPTER 12

DEPRESSION AND WORLD WAR II

or

The Greatest (and Most Full of Themselves) Generation

During the Golden Twenties many American consumers embraced an enticing innovation...buying on credit. James Cash Penney founded Sears (just kidding, JC Penney) and chain stores quickly spread from coast to coast. Advertising became a big (and crass) business, selling everything from appliances to cars to furniture to beanies with propellers on them. There were signs the good times would not last forever, but it was hard for folks to see anything as they staggered down Main Street loaded with packages shouting, "Charge it!"

THE BIG CRASH ON WALL STREET
or *You Only Loved Me When I Was Rich*

In the summer of 1927, Calvin Coolidge announced, "I do not choose to run for president in 1928." Americans were stunned because this was the longest sentence they had ever heard from the tight-lipped New Englander. The Republicans scrambled and quickly enlisted a suitable replacement: Iowa-born Herbert Hoover. The GOP bubbled with optimism as the campaign commenced. After all, there were few discontented voices across the land in the summer of 1928 (grumbling from those pesky farmers could easily be tuned out) and prosperity still seemed to be on an endlessly upward spiral.

Hoover was a Quaker and a familiar figure to most Americans, who viewed him as the embodiment of the American Dream; he had started life as a poor orphan boy, put himself through Stanford University, and achieved success as a mining engineer and businessman. Widely acclaimed as a leader of charitable efforts to aid war-torn Belgium, President Wilson appointed him head of the Food Administration. Next, he enjoyed considerable renown as Secretary of Commerce under Harding and Coolidge. His core values were individualism, efficiency, unfettered capitalism, and small government. In person he was stiff and shy, and usually sported a high, starched collar behind a fat ruddy face that sometimes made it look as if his head would explode at any moment.

The Democrats nominated Hoover's exact opposite: Governor **Alfred E. Smith** of New York, a cigar-chomping, brown-derby-wearing son of poor Irish immigrants. Smith was a "wet" (opposed to Prohibition) while Hoover was a "dry" (no fun at all). Smith was a product of Tammany Hall, the Democratic "machine" in New York City. Hoover repeatedly fired salvos at corrupt city bosses. On the radio, Smith's New *Yawk* accent really grated on the ears of country folk. Hoover — with no discernable accent at all and the charisma of a dust mop — sounded clear and distinguished. Most notably, Smith was a Roman Catholic, and this scared the devil out of many Protestants, who still comprised most of the country.

Herbert Hoover never disparaged Smith's religion, but he was just about the only one. Republican campaign workers on both state and local levels continually mocked Smith's Roman Catholicism, and bigoted Democrats, mainly in the South and West, did the same. Protestant groups conjured up all manner of incendiary rhetoric, but the fundamentalists were the most extreme and cruel. Their basic message: elect Smith and he will destroy all public schools, and then secretly smuggle the Pope into the country to take over the government. It was all just plain stupid and irrational, but many prejudiced and unsophisticated Americans actually bought all that nonsense (if one more pinhead tells me Barack Obama is secretly a Muslim, my head will explode).

Needless to say, Hoover creamed Smith, largely due to the Governor's association with immigrants, the big city, and his Catholic faith. Smith carried most of the big cities in the North — the first time a Democrat had done that since before the Civil War —

but he also lost five states in the supposedly "solid" Democratic South. In 1928, most Americans were just not ready to accept a Catholic as president.

The twenties kept roaring on as President Hoover was sworn in on March 4, 1929. A **bull market** enthralled Wall Street, and the good times seemed like they would last forever (a bull market is when investors generally believe stocks will continue to move upward; a **bear market** is the opposite and what always happens when I try to invest...I thought for sure bell-bottoms were going to come back). But on **Black Tuesday**, October 29, the dominos fell, the house of cards collapsed, and the you-know-what hit the fan. The 1929 stock market crash started the **Great Depression** in America — by far the most severe economic downturn the country has ever seen before or since.

What the heck happened? It does seem clear the economy was seriously out of whack. In a time before any government financial regulation, lots of folks bought stocks with money borrowed from stockbrokers, who in turn had borrowed money from banks. All this made good sense as long as stocks were going up, but when stocks fell, all those loans got called in, and many banks soon failed. The federal government did not guarantee bank deposits back then, so lots of people lost their entire life savings. As usual at the onset of a depression, American factories had produced more than consumers could buy, so lots of companies — needing to reduce inventories — cut back and fired workers. Less money in circulation only made the downward spiral steeper and faster. Hoover kept making optimistic statements, and it was rumored that after blabbering something for the hundredth time like, "Come on folks, just keep smiling...," someone lobbed a rotten tomato over the White House fence that almost nailed him. If you have any more questions, ask your economics teacher because all this financial gobbledygook gives me a headache.

"PROSPERITY IS JUST AROUND THE CORNER"
or *Who Is This Guy Kidding?*

In 1930, Hoover supported a protective tariff that completely backfired. The President urged Congress to raise import duties to protect hard-hit farmers, but the self-interested legislators produced the **Hawley-Smoot Tariff**, which erected a super high tariff wall against virtually all goods from abroad. Europeans found they could not sell their products in America, so they stopped paying back their loans from World War I. Our former Allies argued that the loans should have been considered part of the cost of the war and forgiven, but most Americans — cheapskates at heart — shouted *pay it back or we'll break your legs* or other unkind remarks to that effect. There was considerable bitterness on both sides at the time, especially because when the Allies defaulted on their loans, American banks ceased loaning money to Germany, causing that country to stop making its war reparations payments to the Allies...all of which spread what was initially an American depression across the Atlantic and quickly around the world. If this idiotic financial cycle — instituted in 1924 and known as the **Dawes Plan** — sounds stupid to you, that's because it was stupid. In addition, the Hawley-Smoot Tariff debacle provides a History lesson that demonstrates the risks of protectionism and argues in favor of free trade. Plenty of unemployed American factory workers may disagree, but don't blame me — I always try to "buy American" except, uh, for my Toyota Prius.

The Great Depression was much worse than any of the periodic recessions we currently deal with. Most Americans survive a recession with minor concessions such as forgoing their season tickets to their favorite team. I recently gave up my tickets to the New York Knicks, but they stunk so I didn't mind. But this depression was no joke. Unemployment skyrocketed, in some places to around thirty percent. Many Americans simply could not afford adequate food, clothing and shelter. Even folks with professional skills could not find work. Families suffered and many broke apart. A few of the *uber* wealthy floated obliviously above it all, but regular Americans really suffered...especially the children. Many men, humiliated by their economic impotence, got psychologically depressed and gave up even looking for jobs. Encampments of homeless living in cardboard boxes or tin shacks aptly became known as **Hoovervilles**. Meanwhile, the President slept snugly in the White House.

Hoover kept making cheerful pronouncements but he realized the economy was in serious distress. The trouble was he didn't know what to do about it. As a conservative, Herbert Hoover was fundamentally against direct government relief (to be fair, no president had ever advocated it), lest rugged American individualism be corrupted forever. Some city and state governments and private charities sprang into action — they set up "soup kitchens" that literally saved lives — but they lacked resources and barely dented the suffering. Meanwhile, Americans' anger mounted as Hoover "fiddled while Rome burned" (no, the President was not over in Italy...look it up if you have to).

Hoover did ask for voluntary actions on the part of labor unions (*Please don't ask for wage increases right now...*), and corporate executives (*Please don't cut workers' wages right now...*), and reportedly his wife (*Please don't let your mother visit right now...*). He also begged Congress for public works projects to stimulate the economy. The normally feckless lawmakers understood they better not dither this time, so they approved funding for new waterways and harbors, roads, public buildings, and a dam on the Colorado River eventually named the Hoover Dam — ironic because most people had gotten used to saying, "Damn Hoover."

All these efforts were not nearly enough, however. Unemployment climbed from 500,000 at the time of the crash to more than four million a year later. Former Wall Street big shots sold apples on the sidewalk. Prices fell and farmers shook their heads in disbelief. A couple of years later Mother Nature kicked the prairie farmers and their families while they were down, forcing them to endure a prolonged drought that turned their fields into desolate patches of bone-dry dirt. This "Dust Bowl" forced many to load their belongs into rattling old trucks and head to California for a new start...though none of these folks had any interest in surfing. Known as "Okies" (many came from Oklahoma), these tenacious people suffered much but persevered; their ordeal is eloquently portrayed in John Steinbeck's classic novel *The Grapes of Wrath*, which was made into a classic Hollywood movie starring Henry Fonda.

As cities, states, and private charities ran out of money, Hoover continued to cling to the classic conservative doctrine that direct welfare payments to people in need creates dependency and destroys individual initiative. This is a hugely important issue worthy of debate today, but as the decade of the thirties dawned the human tragedy was off the scale. Americans were starving, and bold moves were required — bold moves Hoover would not, or could not, make. Finally, in 1932, he supported the creation of the **Reconstruction Finance Corporation** (RFC), and Congress authorized the Emergency Relief and Construction Act, allocating $300 million to the RFC for loans to struggling cities and states. But it was all too little too late; hungry men, women, and children simply said, "I just need a meal and a place to sleep." Comedian Eddie Cantor cracked, "These days, when somebody goes into a hotel and asks for a room, the clerk asks, '*For sleeping or jumping?*'" A funny line, but a few Americans sadly lost all hope and decided to check in and then "check out."

In 1924, Congress had approved pensions for World War I veterans to be paid in 1945. Starving and out of work in the summer of 1932, many veterans demanded the payment immediately, and a large contingent of them trekked to Washington, D.C. to drive home their point. They moved into abandoned buildings or set up shacks and refused to leave until they got their money. The House of Representatives approved a payment but the Senate voted it down (obviously, that meant no bonus since both chambers must approve a measure for it to go through). Some in this "**Bonus Army**" left, but thousands remained under increasingly unsanitary conditions so bad that men would scavenge for old newspapers, not to read but to sleep under — so-called "Hoover blankets." The thicker Sunday editions were presumably called "Hoover comforters." The President, bowing to pressure to restore law and order, directed the army to clear the capital of, well, the former army. **General Douglas MacArthur** (psyched to have somebody to push around during peacetime) commanded troops that violently evicted the veterans with bayonets and tear gas. The nation watched in horror, the Depression kept getting worse, and there seemed to be no end in sight to all the misery.

THE FAILURE OF COLLECTIVE SECURITY
or *We'll Just Stick Our Heads in the Sand*

In the 1920's, the United States pretended it was all alone in the world by refusing to join the League of Nations or the World Court, restricting European immigration, passing high tariffs on European goods and refusing to share any of our beach toys. America was not hostile to the League — we did cooperate with several League humanitarian agencies — but our nation would have nothing to do with any of the international volleyball tournaments. In 1921, the U.S. did sponsor the **Washington Naval Conference** in which nine major powers pledged to respect the independence and territorial integrity of China. In addition, nations agreed to partial naval disarmament by limiting the size of their navies based upon the following ratio: United States — 5, Great Britain

— 5, Japan — 3, France — 1.67, Italy — 1.67. If you are thinking the U.S. and Britain gained the advantage here...gotcha. Japan needed to cover only one ocean (the Pacific) and clearly had an edge over the U.S. and Britain whose two ocean navies also needed to project power into the Atlantic. At the **London Conference** in 1930, Japan gained an agreement for a 10:10:7 ratio (even better for them) and five years later they demanded parity. When the U.S and Britain refused, Japan (cheating all along anyway) started building the biggest navy they could. So much for "international agreements."

The United States and France sponsored a conference in 1928 that really takes the cake. Secretary of State Frank B. Kellogg (sick of all the free Corn Flakes his family in Battle Creek, Michigan kept sending him) and Foreign Minister Aristide Briand orchestrated a meeting in Paris whereupon sixty-two nations signed a treaty to outlaw war. The diplomats all stood around in their formal garb, sipping champagne, posing for photographs, congratulating themselves that — thanks to their Herculean efforts in signing a piece of paper — there would never ever be another war. How could there be? The **Kellogg-Briand Pact** made war illegal. Even at the time, many critics ridiculed the agreement as the ultimate paper tiger and nothing more than an "international kiss." But for the diplomats — fearful of another world war but unwilling to spend the money or make the effort to maintain the military strength to truly deter aggression — the crepe Suzettes in Paris were absolutely scrumptious.

Latin America continued to receive periodic spankings from Uncle Sam even though Washington wished those nations would behave themselves. Troops remained in Haiti but Harding finally pulled the soldiers out of the Dominican Republic in 1924, and Coolidge withdrew the marines from Nicaragua the following year. Unfortunately, our forces needed to rush back into Nicaragua in 1926 when rebels tried to overthrow the dictator friendly to American interests. You may be saying, *Hey, these third world conflicts were internal struggles and none of our business.* You're right, but America has intervened in developing nations — time and again — throughout the twentieth century and beyond. Why? Because we can, that's why. American business and strategic interests (almost always connected at the hip) have always been our government's priority, and friendly dictators can be counted on to dance to our tune...a tune that to me always sounds like an obnoxious country western song.

In 1927, skillful diplomacy prevented Mexico from expropriating (or nationalizing) American-owned oil fields. Expropriation means "take back," such as when a developing nation wants to exert sovereignty over its own resources. International corporate owners hate expropriation because they never feel they receive adequate compensation for their lost properties. Sometimes these bigwigs wake up screaming in the middle of the night, whereupon their wives (or mistresses) tell them, *Go back to sleep dear, it was only that expropriation nightmare again.*

President Hoover genuinely wanted to improve relations with Latin America, and in 1930 his Administration issued a memorandum written by Undersecretary of State J. Reuben Clark. The **Clark Memorandum** canceled the Roosevelt Corollary to the Monroe Doctrine by stating that the United States did not have the right to intervene militarily in the internal affairs of our southern neighbors. Incredulous Latin Americans asked, *What's the catch? There is no catch*, Uncle Sam replied, crossing his fingers behind his back.

FRANKLIN ROOSEVELT AND THE NEW DEAL
or *Let's Try Something...Anything*

The Republicans knew Hoover smelled like rotten eggs to most Americans, but in 1932 they renominated him anyway. The Democrats gleefully staged a convention at which Al Smith was rudely pushed aside in favor of the current governor of New York, **Franklin Delano Roosevelt**. A "man of the thirties," Roosevelt broke tradition by flying to Chicago to personally accept the nomination and address the delegates ("man of the twenties" Al Smith — cursing his former friend — took the train home). With great courage and every ounce of his strength, the new Democratic standard bearer managed to get up out of his seat and maneuver in a standing position to the podium, where in a strong voice he promised a "new deal" for the American people. Nobody including FDR was sure what the **New Deal** would be, but committing to doing something even if it didn't work seemed better than the empty platitudes the conservative Hoover had to offer. Republicans meanwhile sneered that Roosevelt was planning to use the federal government to give "free stuff" to poor people who were not supposed to have "stuff" because they were poor.

Born to a wealthy landowning family on the shores of the Hudson River, everyone called him Franklin or FDR (not Frank or Frankie) as befitting a Protestant patrician attending the snobby Groton prep school, Harvard University, and Columbia Law School. He served in the state legislature and President Wilson appointed him Assistant Secretary of the Navy. Not a Republican like most wealthy "silver spooners," FDR embraced the progressive movement and fit comfortably into the Democratic Party. He advocated for American entry in the League of Nations and ran for Vice President in 1920 to no avail, but his natural charm made him nationally popular.

The following year, when he was paralyzed by an attack of polio it appeared his political career was over. Today, we get vaccinated for polio, but Roosevelt never again regained the use of his legs. To his credit, he maintained his positive outlook and vigor and, confined to a wheelchair, ran successfully for the New York State Governorship. When the Depression hit, Roosevelt remained popular in his state by advocating for assistance for the unemployed and elderly. He was a distant cousin of Theodore Roosevelt and FDR proudly carried Teddy's progressive mantle, but in personal style the two men deviated. During arguments Teddy would bellow; Franklin would smile and schmooze. FDR also allowed people he disagreed with to use the bathroom.

Hoover received a dose of his own landslide medicine in November when he carried only Vermont and Maine (where the voters obviously let too much maple syrup go to their heads) while Roosevelt creamed him everywhere else. Back then the new president was not sworn in until four months later in March. Lame duck Hoover was power-less to do anything, and the Depression sank to new depths as Roosevelt paced (actually rolled) about in the wings. Appalled by all this but too late to be of any help at the time, the new heavily Democratic Congress successfully sponsored the **Twentieth Amendment** to the Constitution, requiring elected presidents and federal legislators to be inaugurated two months earlier in January. In late 1933, fully realizing the mess Hoover had bequeathed him, Roosevelt really needed a stiff drink, so he requested, and Congress and then the states approved, the passage of the **Twenty-first Amendment** to repeal the Eighteenth Amendment. Taverns reopened, Prohibition drowned to death, and the government began happily taxing every gallon of legalized "hooch."

In his inauguration address, President Roosevelt tried to rally the nation by declar-ing, "The only thing we have to fear is fear itself...and monsters under our beds." Just kidding, he didn't mention monsters. But many folks did wonder what he meant by fearing fear and whether by extension it could be possible to fear a fear of the fear. Anyway, it was clear — like Presidents Teddy Roosevelt, Abe Lincoln, and Andy Jack-son before him — Franklin Roosevelt planned to be a proactive and powerful chief executive.

Americans worried their own banks would be the next to fail, so lots of depositors rushed to withdraw their money. These bank "runs" exhausted cash reserves and caused some banks to simply go out of business. People lost their life savings, and back in those days their only recourse was to pound on padlocked doors...and all the janitor inside could do was shrug. President Roosevelt immediately shut down all banks by declaring a **bank holiday**; institutions were not allowed to reopen until treasury officials had exam-ined their assets and declared them "solvent." Supposedly, one ex-banker who told an-gry former customers that they might find loose change in their sofas found himself wedged head-first into the night deposit slot.

Impressed by the arguments of economist **John Maynard Keynes**, who argued that increased government spending would offset declines in private spending and help the economy recover, FDR immediately proposed many new initiatives. Congress passed every one of them so quickly that this early period of the New Deal became known as the "**Hundred Days**." To this day every new president and Congress is judged by their performance in their first one hundred days. No one has ever topped the accomplish-ments of Roosevelt, probably because the economy has never again been in such dire straits. After his first one hundred days, President George W. Bush reportedly remarked, "Gee, I guess I should get started."

Roosevelt explained the New Deal would entail the three R's: **Relief, Recovery, and Reform**, and he proposed the creation of agencies Americans got used to calling by their initials: the *alphabet agencies* (Republicans generally referred to the agencies with nasty hand gestures). *Relief* entailed direct aid to the hungry and homeless with direct payments if necessary...though with one quarter of the population unemployed the Presi-dent preferred the creation of emergency public jobs. The **Civilian Conservation Corps** (CCC) gave jobs to young people who lived in camps, received free food and in return cleaned up forests and planted trees. The **Works Progress Administration** (WPA) hired writers, artists, and musicians who responded with creative accomplishments reflecting their newly found self-respect. The **Public Works Administration** (PWA) put Americans to work building roads and bridges we still use today.

Recovery entailed the creation of the **National Recovery Administration** (NRA) that asked businesses to voluntarily adhere to codes setting prices, production limits, and a minimum wage. Lots of greedy storeowners displayed the NRA's "blue eagle" symbol but completely refused to modify their business practices. Philadelphia named its football team the "Eagles" but that did not help the hungry masses. Here once again History demonstrates that volunteerism never works in America as a response to economic problems. The **Agriculture Adjustment Act** (AAA) paid farmers to produce less so that the resulting scarcity in commodities would help farm prices and farmers' incomes rise. The basic idea made sense, but lots of hungry Americans found it to tough to comprehend fields deliberately unsown and hogs slaughtered and left to rot.

Reform brought about institutional changes to ensure that another depression could not happen again. The **Federal Deposit Insurance Corporation** (FDIC) insured bank deposits and continues in effect today, so if you hear on the radio that your bank has failed, hit the snooze button and go back to sleep because the federal government has got you covered. The **Securities and Exchange Commission** (SEC) was supposed to regulate the stock market and prevent fraud; over the decades, its results have been spotty, but once in a while we do get the pleasure of watching dirtbag Wall Street types doing the "perp walk" on the TV news.

The **Wagner Act** *finally* gave workers the legal right to join unions and bargain collectively. Skilled and unskilled workers continued to feud, but under the leadership of former mine worker **John L. Lewis**, president of the **Congress of Industrial Organizations** (CIO), union membership soared in the thirties. Labor by children under the age of sixteen was forbidden, forty cents an hour became the minimum wage, and the forty-hour week became a recognized national standard. Wealthy industrialists moaned about their lost profits and cursed "that damned cripple in the White House." The **Social Security Act** protected workers by providing insurance for unemployment and old age. Of course, Social Security is still a cornerstone of our nation's economy today; young people don't think about it much, but try to tell an older American you want to change the system and you'll get hit with a cane faster than President George W. Bush used to say, "Let's privatize it!"

In 1933, Congress authorized the creation of the **Tennessee Valley Authority** (TVA), a government-owned entity designed to improve economic conditions in the region through the development of hydroelectric power. Most Americans (including FDR) supported the creation of this public power company to compete with the private power companies that had been gouging Americans for decades. Conservatives claimed that this was unfair competition for private companies, while the liberal New Dealers said a public option would keep the private power companies from overcharging. Just north of the border in Canada, public utilities provided their customers with electric power for a much lower rate. If you think this sounds like our modern health care debate, you would be right. The TVA has been controversial and imperfect but largely successful, and it remains popular in the areas it serves. Citizens of the Tennessee Valley have not been transformed into communistic drones. But fanatical conservative opposition has prevented the spread of the Tennessee Valley Authority idea to other parts of the country. Is that a good thing? Next time you get your electric bill and your eyes bulge out, think about it and you decide.

Not surprisingly, FDR got criticized from both sides. Wealthy conservative types (with the assistance of Al "Sour Grapes" Smith) formed the **American Liberty League** to help recruit golf foursomes but also launch a mean-spirited attack that equated FDR with Marx and Lenin, and accused him of contaminating "the clear, pure, fresh air of free America" with the "foul breath of communistic Russia." Roosevelt, who couldn't play golf, thought they were a bunch of selfish rich jerks. Attacks also came from the left, as radical extremists accused the New Deal of not going far enough. A loudmouth Catholic priest in Michigan, Father **Charles Coughlin**, broadcast anti-New Deal (also fascist and anti-Semitic) diatribes on the radio, until word came down all the way from the Vatican ordering him to pipe down and stick to scripture.

The "Share Our Wealth Society" — propagated by Louisiana Senator **Huey "King-fish" Long** — called for the wealthy to pay more taxes so every family in America could receive an annual payment of five thousand dollars. Long hoped to ride his populist wave into the White House in the next election, and who knows how far this demagogue would have surfed had not one of his many enemies fatally shot him in the back. An elderly retired doctor in California, **Francis E. Townsend**, called for every senior citizen over sixty to receive two hundred dollars a month provided they spend all of it in that same month. This would have bankrupted the country, but the desperate times produced desperate (and crackbrained) schemes.

President Roosevelt promoted himself and the New Deal through the radio; his over the air "fireside chats" gave average folks hope for better days ahead and a sense that he respected and cared about them. The President radiated warmth and trust, and he played the game of politics like a grand master. He cultivated newspaper and radio reporters assigned to the White House by inviting them into the Oval Office (a tight fit) and cheerfully calling individuals by name. The media responded with a class unimaginable today. His paralysis was never written about, he was virtually never photographed in his wheelchair, and with his leg braces painted black many regular Americans never even knew he was physically challenged. Imagine today: FDR's paralysis would be ridiculed by shock jocks, and when he was carried on to the presidential train like a baby in the arms of a secret service agent, paparazzi looking for a fat check from the likes of the *National Enquirer* would jump out of the bushes and yell, "Say Cheese!" It was a different time...in many ways a more refined and classy time.

A SECOND TERM FOR FDR

or *We'll Never Go Back To Laissez-Faire*

Roosevelt proved adept at listening to many sides of an issue and then acting on his best instincts, and he was a smart guy who made sure he was surrounded by advisors even brighter than he was. This group of elite college professors was dubbed the "Brain Trust" by the newspapers, while conservatives called them the "Gang of Communist Idiots With Bad Breath Who Hate Puppies." The President also had another ace in the hole: his wife, Eleanor. They did not have a traditional relationship. Early in their marriage she found incriminating love letters he had written to someone else (history lesson for today: delete your emails). Rather than demand a divorce — a great scandal back then that would have finished FDR's political career — Eleanor agreed to stay married for appearances, but never again did they share the same bedroom or bed or...you know. As the years passed, she became his best friend and his eyes and ears at events he couldn't attend. Fortunately for her wayward husband, Eleanor Roosevelt possessed great character and intellect. Truly a classic liberal, she continually advocated for the "Forgotten Man" <u>and</u> woman regardless of their race. Franklin could not always take her advice — he was a politician who needed to compromise to survive — but Eleanor continually thrust her moral compass in his face. She traveled and spoke out publicly much more that any president's spouse ever had before, and she remains to this day America's greatest First Lady.

Everyone close to Roosevelt urged him to run for a second term, and the President was more than happy to comply. He knew he had assembled a formidable coalition: northern white liberals, traditional southern democrats, urban ethnic groups, union members, farmers, the rural poor, and African-Americans. Roosevelt and the New Deal reached out to Blacks as government never had before, so in the thirties African-Americans who could vote (it was still difficult down South) shifted their allegiance wholesale from the Republicans to the Democrats. The President did not, despite Eleanor's urging, advocate for a national anti-lynching law because he could not afford to alienate southern white voters (lynching specifically refers to murder by a mob). Even so, when the Republicans tried to remind African-Americans about the Civil War, most of them thought to themselves, *Yeah, but what have you done for me lately? Besides, half a loaf is better than none.*

The Republicans nominated Governor **Alfred M. Landon** of Kansas, but he never had a chance. Alf was a lousy campaigner, and everyone still remembered Hoover and the nationwide economic orgy that had imploded under his watch. The Depression kept rolling on, but New Deal programs had made somewhat of a positive impact, particularly by reaching out to individuals and groups heretofore ignored by the federal government. Thus FDR engendered fierce loyalty; those who loved him really loved him and those who hated him (mostly conservative rich types who had no use for his tax-raising New Deal social programs) wished someone would roll him off a cliff. Fortunately, the poor and middle class outnumbered the rich, and Roosevelt earned his second term with a smashing electoral victory. It has been rumored that the next day, home alone and reading the papers, Herbert Hoover's head finally did explode, whereupon it was sewn back together and several journalists paid off to keep the incident quiet.

It is really difficult for American presidents to pull off a better second term than their first — I can't think of a single one who did — probably because they are running out of favors to dole out and rapidly becoming old news. FDR tanked in his second term. Workers went on strike in important industries such as textiles, shipbuilding, steel, oil, and rubber, and when Roosevelt refused to call out federal troops to crush the unions (a key component of his coalition), lots of folks worried irrationally that the country was lurching towards communism and soon everyone (including women) would be required to wear a goatee.

Franklin's biggest gaffe involved his ill-fated plan to change the make up of the Supreme Court. Serving for life, the conservative justices had in 1935-36 ruled both the NRA and the AAA unconstitutional on grounds the federal government had exceeded its authority. Flushed with feelings of power and infallibility following his smashing reelection, the President proposed a plan to increase the number of justices on the court from nine to sixteen...an action requiring a change (an amendment) to the Constitution. Since presidents nominate Supreme Court justices (pending approval by the Senate in yet another good ol' example of checks and balances), FDR wanted to guarantee all the new judges would be liberals who would block the Court's annoying judicial interference with his "baby"...the New Deal.

Boy, did he screw up. The President did not comprehend how much most Americans of all stripes deeply respected the Constitution and did not want it messed with for purely political purposes. Republicans were outraged, and even friendly Democrats started to find excuses to decline luncheon invitations to the White House. One Congressman reportedly pointedly remarked he wanted to take his sandwich "to go" so he could go back to his office to reread the Constitution. At this point, Roosevelt lucked out because the Supreme Court — perhaps intimidated by the President's histrionics — started to *uphold* (affirm the constitutionality of) several New Deal laws, including Social Security. Then one justice retired and FDR was able to appoint a friendly liberal without reorganizing the whole judicial shebang. Eventually, thoroughly chastened, Roosevelt in effect said of the court packing scheme, *Never mind*...yet another chief executive to receive a lesson in just how seriously Americans take that "separation of powers" stuff in the Constitution.

The "court-packing" brouhaha really cost FDR politically. To many his fireside chats started to seem like a blast of hot air. Then, in late 1937, the economy stopped its slow rise out of the Depression and slumped badly. Roosevelt — never fully comfortable with government deficits — had reduced federal spending. Unemployment grew, businesses cut back, and the economy started to march backwards. The President reversed course the next year; Congress approved $1.5 billion for the WPA and about $1 billion for the PWA, and the economy began to inch forward again. But FDR was about to learn that besides "fear itself" he also had to be wary of cranky American voters.

In the 1938 midterm elections, the Democrats received a thorough hammering even though they still clung to their majorities in the House and Senate. Republicans joined with conservative southern Democrats to prevent Roosevelt from pushing any further New Deal legislation through Congress, though they could not muster the votes to unravel the New Deal itself. It was a standoff...a legislative stalemate similar to the muck and mire our contemporary politicians often find themselves stuck in, and the country suffered for it.

Did the New Deal end the Great Depression? Nope. Unemployment still stood at eight million in 1939. But the New Deal was an unparalleled success. It reduced unemployment by five million, improved the economic status of most Americans, and the work relief programs provided not only self-respect, but roads, bridges, buildings, dams and parks still in use today. It brought us many invaluable laws and agencies to regulate the unbridled laissez-fare of an American capitalism that paradoxically made so many prosperous while leaving so many in the dust. Best of all, it made conservative overstuffed country club types bust their buttons...a few of which flew into their bouillabaisse. The New Deal was the beginning of the big government we have today. Bureaucracies are always imperfect — improving their efficiency remains one of our central challenges to this day — but to deny that the enormity of the Great Depression demanded forceful action is to be blind to History. Americans today who, in the midst of economic crisis, view the federal government as the enemy of free enterprise while clamoring for tax cuts and deregulation should be ashamed of themselves...they have learned nothing.

STORM CLOUDS ON THE HORIZON
or *Can't the Rest of the World Behave Themselves?*

As Americans lost interest in increasing the scope of the New Deal, they found themselves increasingly fixated on events overseas. Woodrow Wilson's "War To End All Wars" clearly was not to be. In Italy in 1922, dictator **Benito Mussolini** and his Fascist Party had seized power. Like communism, **fascism** was a *totalitarian* system, meaning the government controls everything and there was no political freedom. The difference was that under communism the government owned all businesses, while under fascism wealthy capitalists could continue to operate as long as they danced precisely to the dictator's tune. Fascists and communists hated each other, while over in America, folks hated both sides and assumed all of them had greasy hair and bushy mustaches.

Germany tried democracy in the 1920s — a government called the **Weimar Republic** — but the economy remained in the tank, and the government rashly printed so many German marks (their unit of currency) that a wheelbarrow full of them could not buy a loaf of bread unless the baker could also keep the wheelbarrow. Amidst this chaos, an undistinguished World War I veteran named **Adolf Hitler** was inspired by Mussolini's fascism to join the Nazi party.

Both communists and fascists tried to take over and fought in the streets. While in jail, Hitler wrote a book he called *Mein Kampf* (My Struggle) in which he clearly delineated what a misguided son of a bitch he was. Nonetheless, despondent Germans responded positively when he told them they were destined to get revenge for the Treaty of Versailles and gain *Lebensraum* (living space) for a German "master race." By 1933 Hitler's Nazi Party controlled the *Reichstag* (Germany's parliament) and Hitler seized total power as "Chancellor." The *Fuhrer* (leader) wore a mustache with the sides trimmed off in a style that, for obvious reasons, virtually no one has adopted since.

Hitler needed a scapegoat to help unify his followers, so he focused on the Jews, who were assimilated into German society and had done nothing wrong...except perhaps be successful while many unemployed were marching around waving swastikas. Relentless persecution ensued, and on the night of November 8th, 1938 — "Kristallnacht" — thousands of Jewish homes, synagogues, businesses, and schools were destroyed. Much more was yet to come: ghettos...deportations...death camps...and a Holocaust the world must never forget. Incidentally, in the 1936 Olympics, African-American sprinter **Jesse Owens** ran rings around Hitler's supposedly "superior" athletes. An embarrassed Hitler reportedly tried to blame Jews for sabotaging the Germans' running shoes, but the world knew he was just a sore loser.

In 1934, the Senate's **Nye Committee** announced the results of its inquiry into the reasons for American entry into World War I. The general conclusion was that American arms manufacturers, together with Wall Street tycoons, had orchestrated the whole shebang. The public was outraged, and Congress passed the **Neutrality Act of 1935** authorizing the President to ban arms shipments to *belligerents*...nations at war.

The **Neutrality Act of 1936** made it illegal for American banks to make loans to belligerents. This worked out great for **Francisco Franco**; he and his fascist followers ignited a civil war in Spain by trying to overthrow the left-leaning (but legally elected) government in Madrid. Germany and Italy sent Franco lots of help and had a field day testing out new tanks, planes and tactics, while the United States, France and Britain did nothing, so deep were their isolationist heads buried in the sand. Private American volunteers journeyed across the Atlantic to fight against Franco, but the fascists finally took over because idealism and bravery alone are not enough to win wars. They do make for great stories, though. You should read Ernest Hemingway's *For Whom the Bell Tolls*...a terrific book that was made into a really good movie. Turn off the television...no, don't turn on the computer...put down the cell phone...drop the iPod...oh, never mind.

In 1937, the Congress passed a third Neutrality Act that was still aimed at keeping us out of war, but could at least allow American companies to make some money off the world crisis. Though arms sales and loans to belligerents were still banned, any foreign nations could purchase other supplies here as long as they paid in cash and carried the goods away in their own ships. **"Cash and Carry"** — posted prominently on the walls of so many shops across the country — now became official U.S. foreign policy. To many, it seemed like a "Two For One Special" would come next.

Events were also going down the tubes in the Far East. In Japan, a cadre of military officers gained power over the civilian government, and these oriental thugs believed that Japan — rich in population and industry but poor in land and raw materials — needed to gain control over much of China. Shinto teachings had contributed to a belief among many Japanese that they were superior to other Asian peoples, and destined to rule the region in what they called a "**Co-Prosperity Sphere.**"

It became clear that joining with the Japanese would not be voluntary when, in September of 1931, Japanese troops swiftly invaded and occupied the northern Chinese province of Manchuria. Subsequently, these militarists commenced building up their army and naval fleet. All this violated the Open Door Policy, the Kellogg-Briand Pact, naval disarmament treaties, and the League of Nations Covenant, of which Japan had been a signatory. Diplomats around the world were aghast, and a few reportedly gasped, "But they promised and they signed all the papers!"

American Secretary of State **Henry L. Stimson** huffed and puffed and sent a letter of protest: the United States would not "officially recognize" any territory Japan had stolen by force. But this "Stimson Doctrine" was mere words; in actuality the United States did nothing. Japanese leaders simply shrugged, quit the League, and continued to scheme for an empire. Paradoxically, these events caused many Americans to look more favorably on the Soviet Union, a nation also concerned about Japanese expansionism. Unaware of, or more likely choosing to ignore, Stalin's violent purges that were brutally destroying the lives of millions of Russians, in 1933 the State Department conferred *diplomatic recognition* upon the Soviet government. Clearly, expediency trumped morality...kind of like when we cheer for lying baseball players who use steroids as long as they help our team to win.

In 1937, the Japanese invaded eastern China and committed untold atrocities, most notoriously the slaughter of innocent civilians in the city of Shanghai (now called Nanking). President Roosevelt, acutely concerned about the spread of militarism in both Asia and Europe, decided to brave isolationist sentiment and gave a stern speech warning the nation against "the present reign of terror and international lawlessness." Roosevelt's awareness of this was way ahead of the curve compared to most Americans and Congress. He cited a real threat to the United States, comparing these events to an epidemic of disease, and called for a "quarantine" of the offending nations.

Outraged isolationists charged he was rocking the boat of neutrality. Newspaper editorials accused him of being a "warmonger," a resolution of impeachment was discussed on the floor of the House of Representatives, and some really gullible Americans wondered if the polio had spread to his head. The reaction to his **Quarantine Speech** caused Roosevelt to tone down his rhetoric, and he continued to fret over how he could get his complacent fellow citizens to wake up and smell the coffee.

On December 12, 1937, Japanese warplanes bombed the **U.S.S. Panay** as it was evacuating American citizens from China. The Japanese apologized and offered to pay damages for what was almost certainly a deliberate act, and most Americans were relieved when the crisis passed and we could continue to stay out of war.

Hitler, meanwhile, continued to push the envelope and get away with it. Back in 1935, with nary a peep from Britain or France who both still had military superiority, Hitler built up his armed forces and occupied the Rhineland, a border region between France and Germany. Three years later, Hitler invaded and annexed Austria. Many ethnic Germans in Austria had no objections to *Anschluss*, the union of Germany and Austria — lucky for them since they were not given a choice.

Next, Hitler demanded possession of the Sudetenland, a Czechoslovakian region bordering Germany and inhabited mostly by German-speaking people. Czech officials refused, and counted on their allies Britain and France to back them up. British Prime Minister **Neville Chamberlain** and French Premier **Edouard Daladier** flew to Munich for a big conference with Hitler. Amidst lots of Bavarian cream pie and strudel, Hitler promised that the Sudetenland was the last territorial claim he planned to make in Europe...and they believed him. Had he told them he could turn water into wine they probably would have believed that too. The **Munich Agreement** was signed, and Neville Chamberlain announced to the world that, "We have achieved peace in our time."

In fact, he had achieved nothing at all — Hitler was merely buying time to build up his forces. Laughing at the weak-kneed British and French, six months later the Führer's troops invaded and annexed all of Czechoslovakia. Reportedly, Chamberlain tore down the framed copy of the Munich Agreement he had put up in his bedroom and demanded that Hitler send back his friendship ring. Giving in to dictators is known as **appeasement**, and Neville Chamberlain will always be remembered as the ultimate sucker.

Any glance at a map revealed that Hitler's next obvious target would be Poland, so the British and French — finally realizing they were facing a rabid German shepherd which had wriggled loose of its tether — pledged to jointly protect Poland if Hitler attacked. Hitler giggled, clapped his hands and dreamed of a champagne brunch in Poland's capital, Warsaw. He half thought the Allies were bluffing, and even if they weren't, he believed his forces were ready for any contingency. There was just one more loose end to take care of...

In August, 1939, the world was stunned to learn that Germany and the Soviet Union had agreed to a non-aggression treaty. What? Everyone assumed the Soviet Union and Germany were hostile to each other. But Hitler and Stalin shared a lust for power and territory, and the **Russo-German Non-Aggression Pact** contained a secret clause dividing Poland between the two dictators. Hitler could thus capture half of Poland while not having to worry about an eastern front in the event of war against Britain and France. Many Poles, who had only been granted their own independent country since the end of World War I, wondered: *why us?* Talk of sending Hitler a nice basket of *kielbasa* to get him to change his mind was quickly shot down.

On September 1, 1939, Germany attacked Poland with dive-bombers, fast-moving tanks, and armored personnel carriers, introducing the world to *blitzkrieg,* or "lightning war." Britain and France declared war two days later, but were unable to stop the onslaught. After a month of courageous resistance, Poland surrendered, and Stalin seized its eastern half plus the Baltic states of Latvia, Estonia, and Lithuania. In Finland, valiant resistance maintained that country's independence despite a loss of territory. The war had officially begun, and everyone started calling it World War II because there had been a World War I a scant twenty years earlier. Besides, World War A and World War B just didn't sound right.

THE UNITED STATES STAYS OUT OF THE FIGHTING
or *War...What War?*

Most Americans rooted for Britain and France and against Italy and Germany, but hardly anyone wanted to get involved in the actual fighting. A well-meaning (but dead wrong) peace organization named **America First** (fronted by Charles Lindbergh) continued to plead for isolation at all cost...deaf, dumb and blind to the fact that bullies exist, and if all else fails they need to be punched.

Fortunately, FDR knew the score and called a special session of Congress — the president can do that, and the members are required to cancel their golf games and show up. He wanted an amendment to the Neutrality Act to allow the U.S. to sell arms to the Allies. For six weeks the debate raged, and many worried the next logical step would be American boys heading for the battlefields of Europe. Roosevelt promised no U.S. forces were going to head abroad, though he must have had his fingers crossed behind his back. If he could have crossed his toes he would have. Congress finally allowed the arms shipments, but they still had to be purchased "cash and carry" because all American ships were forbidden to enter the dangerous sea lanes bordering on the warring nations.

In the winter of 1939-40 there was not much action on the ground in Europe. Both sides glared at each other and mobilized during what the newspapers dubbed the "**Phony War**." Britain's navy tried to enforce a blockade on Germany and Germany launched submarines (much improved since World War I) against any merchant ships heading for its enemies' shores. Americans welcomed the uptick in factory production due to rush orders from the Allies, and sprang into action by listening in increasing numbers to entertainment on the radio...the *Jack Benny Show* was a big hit. Edgar Bergen was also a big radio star...something I've never understood because he was a ventriloquist. Think about it...a ventriloquist on the radio...I'm not making this up...

Hitler ratcheted the action up a notch in April when German forces overran Denmark and Norway. Next, the Netherlands and Belgium (raped again) fell. The French thought their defenses were ready, but remember we are talking about the French here. The Germans simply outflanked the vaunted **Maginot Line** fortifications by storming through the supposedly impenetrable Ardennes forest to get behind the French positions. One French general reportedly remarked, "Gee, too bad these big guns can't swivel." Overwhelmed and demoralized, France fell in about six weeks, and about 340,000 French and British troops found themselves trapped on the northern French coast at **Dunkirk**. A motley flotilla of British naval ships, fishing boats and private yachts rushed across the channel and evacuated the stranded men in the nick of time. Meanwhile, across the Atlantic, Americans listened raptly as the Lone Ranger and his trusted Indian sidekick Tonto galloped about the Wild West outwitting dastardly villains.

Germany occupied the northern part of France (including Paris) and allowed French traitors to govern the southern half. This region became known as **Vichy France** since, lead by Marshal Pétain, these collaborators — cowardly dirtbags all of them — were headquartered in the town of Vichy. The real French (with pride and guts), under General **Charles de Gaulle**, made themselves a headquarters in an office building in London.

At this moment in History, Britain stood alone in Europe. It has been said that the following joke made the rounds: *Why do trees line most of the streets in France? Because the Germans like to march in the shade.* But it did not seem so funny when in August, 1940, Hitler's *Luftwaffe* (German Air Force) began to bomb Britain in preparation for a land invasion. Prime Minister **Winston Churchill**, a tireless firebrand who had replaced the appeasing Chamberlain four months earlier, rallied the British people. In London, as the bombs rained down and the populace scrambled for shelter, the Royal Air Force (RAF) rose to the challenge. In their *Spitfire* planes, aided by the invention of radar, the out-numbered British pilots perished in great numbers but turned the tide. The *Luftwaffe* suffered losses it could not sustain, and by the late fall Hitler was forced to give up on the idea of invading Britain.

The **Battle of Britain** was over and Churchill, commemorating the valor of the British pilots in what he called his country's "Finest Hour" said, "Never in the field of human conflict have so many owed so much to so few." It is rumored that the Prime Minister, who loved his champagne and brandy, actually said, "Never in the few fields of many, have so few owed so little to a lot. Hic." But what he meant will always be remembered in History.

These were truly some of the most critical times in the history of America and the world, and in the summer of 1940 President Roosevelt decided to run for a *third* term. Nobody had ever done that before. Two terms had always been the accepted limit — a kind of "gentlemen's agreement" since Washington had stepped down voluntarily in 1796. The Constitution said nothing about term limits, and Roosevelt — bowing to both duty and ambition — let it be known to the Democratic delegates at their nominating convention in Chicago that he would run again if so called. He tried to camouflage his intense desire for a third term — there were a host of other qualified potential nominees — but there is no doubt FDR wanted to go for it.

The Republicans passed over crusading New York District Attorney Thomas E. Dewey and conservative Ohio Senator William H. Taft (son of the former president), and somewhat quixotically settled on a big-business Wall Street lawyer named **Wendell Wilkie**, who had supreme self-confidence and a wisecracking sense of humor. During the campaign, however, Wilkie had difficulty finding issues on which to oppose FDR, and Roosevelt coasted to victory, crushing Wilkie in the Electoral College 449 to 82, and in the popular vote 27 million to 22 million.

In America, folks *finally* started to get concerned about the war in Europe, even though there was this really cool crime fighter on the radio named *The Shadow* who could make himself invisible through the power of hypnosis. At Roosevelt's urging, Congress approved a vast military buildup and passed the 1940 Selective Service Act, America's first peacetime draft.

German submarines hunting together in the North Atlantic — called *wolf packs* — torpedoed so many British ships that Roosevelt concocted the **Destroyer-Naval Base Deal** (September 1940) in which the United States would lend Britain fifty "over-age" destroyers in exchange for military bases on British territory from Canada to South America. In January 1941, Roosevelt proposed lending or leasing goods to any nation whose defense he deemed necessary for the defense of the United States. The **Lend-Lease Act**, Roosevelt said, would maintain America as the "arsenal of democracy," and even though Britain's cash had run out, allow continued aid "by all measures short of war."

The President also ordered the U.S. Navy to convoy British merchant ships part way across the Atlantic. Isolationists squealed but Congress went along, especially after vacationers on the East Coast complained about all the German periscopes just beyond the lifeguards' ropes. FDR gave an especially crackling fireside chat in which he declared the war was being fought for **Four Freedoms**: freedom of speech, freedom of religion, freedom from want and freedom from fear. Most Americans were relieved to learn FDR had trimmed down his rhetorical dreams from Wilson's fourteen to four. But most people were unaware that when German submarines fired, American warships fired back, and in the summer and fall of 1941 an undeclared naval war raged in the Atlantic.

Frustrated, Hitler turned his back on the British, wrongly assuming that though they were still standing they were nonetheless crippled. Craving still more territory and raw materials, he ignored the Non-Aggression Pact and launched a surprise *blitzkrieg* against the Soviet Union on June 22, 1941. Stalin was shocked to learn that Hitler was even more of a crazed, lying sociopath than he was. The Nazis drove deep into Russia but were never able to capture Moscow, Leningrad, or Stalingrad. As fall turned into winter, the Red Army fought back fiercely and, remembering Napoleon's butt-kicking at the hands of the Russians, astute students of History recognized that the frostbitten **Wehrmacht** (German Army) had bitten off far more chicken *kiev* than they could chew.

In August 1941, Roosevelt and Churchill had a secret meeting aboard a U.S. destroyer anchored off Newfoundland. They told the world they were going fishing, which fooled no one since neither man brought poles or bait. Over four days, the two leaders drafted a statement of postwar goals called the **Atlantic Charter**: neither the United States nor Britain sought territorial gain, citizens of all countries had the right to freely choose their governments, every single person in the world should be free from want and fear, and nations should abandon the use of force and seek collective security in a new international organization. Everyone took great pains to avoid using the word "League" for obvious reasons.

Meanwhile, Hitler's conquests in Europe gave Japan the opportunity it needed. With France and Holland defeated and Britain barely hanging on, Japan decided the time was ripe to take over European colonial possessions in Asia, so they invaded French Indochina. In September 1940, Japan had signed the **Tripartite Pact** with Germany and Italy formalizing a military alliance known as the Rome-Berlin-Tokyo **Axis** (now this was the original "Axis of Evil"...absolutely the bad guys in World War II and much creepier than Bush's lame Iran-Iraq-North Korea spinoff).

American diplomats protested and told the Japanese they were violating the Open Door Policy, but the Japanese basically said they had never heard of it. Roosevelt embargoed American sales to Japan of iron, chemicals and other strategic materials, including oil (hard to believe, but back then the United States was an oil underlin/exporter, not the tapped-out oil addicts we are today). The two nations opened formal diplomatic talks to address their grievances, but the meetings went nowhere as one side reportedly refused to eat cheeseburgers while the other gagged on raw octopus.

While this was going on, American intelligence experts cracked Japan's secret diplomatic code. They learned an attack was coming but did not know exactly where...the best guess was probably American-owned Guam or the Philippines. Then in late November, 1941, naval intelligence lost track of the Japanese fleet. It was out at sea...but where? Then on Sunday, December 7, 1941, Japanese planes launched from aircraft carriers swooped down on the Pacific Fleet at **Pearl Harbor**, Hawaii.

American forces were completely surprised and vulnerable: ships at anchor and planes lined up on the airfield. In a couple of hours, two battleships were destroyed, six others heavily damaged, and nearly a dozen smaller ships knocked out of action. More than 150 planes were torn apart, over 2300 soldiers and sailors killed and 1100 wounded. Returning to their carriers, jubilant Japanese pilots celebrated, probably high-fiving then bowing over and over again until they got dizzy. But the architect of the sneak attack, Admiral **Isoroku Yamamoto**, did not join in the revelry even though his plan had played out perfectly.

Yamamoto had been educated in the United States at Harvard. He had a sense of what the American people might be capable of, and he was worried, famously saying, "I fear we have awakened a sleeping giant." Some of his subordinates thought he had been nipping at the *saki*...certainly no one could have slept through all the excitement. But they had missed the point; Yamamoto was right on target yet again. With one dastardly sneak attack, the Japanese had taken the United States from mostly isolationist and determined to stay out of the war to...one hundred percent pissed. Nobody was an isolationist on December 8th — the bastards attacked our territory — and a unified America would proceed to mobilize and lead the Allies to a defeat of both Japan and Germany *at the same time*. Thus the perfectly executed attack on Pearl Harbor was perhaps the biggest strategic mistake in military History. The Axis powers had no idea what they were in for.

THE HOME FRONT

or *Does Anyone Have Any Extra Gas Coupons?*

President Roosevelt, visibly shaking in anger, addressed the nation the next day, and Congress declared war on Japan. Germany and Italy honored their treaty agreement with Japan and declared war on the United States. America was suddenly fully involved in yet another war and, as usual, utterly unprepared. But that would change. The isolationists collectively said: *Whoops...never mind.* It is fun to talk about strategy, battles and heroes, but the real story behind America's success in World War II is what happened at home. Everyone put their backs behind the war effort and mobilization. The nation's enlistment of men and creation of weapons of war, on a scale of one to ten, was an eleven. From 1941 to 1945 American factories and farms churned out enough "stuff" to simultaneously deliver a crushing knockout of Germany in Europe and Japan in the Pacific. The sleeping giant awoke indeed after that early morning attack on Pearl Harbor, and it quickly became clear that Uncle Sam was not a morning person.

President Roosevelt really rose to the occasion (though he did not literally stand up) and forcefully, confidently lead the country through the crisis. He created lots of government agencies (something the New Deal had made him really good at) to manage the war. The **Office of War Mobilization** (OWM...sorry, more alphabet agencies), headed by former South Carolina Senator **James Byrnes**, oversaw everything. Byrnes had so much responsibility that some called him the "real president." But if you said that in front of Roosevelt, he'd ram you with his wheelchair.

The **War Production Board** (WPB) helped factories shift from peacetime to wartime production. It became virtually impossible to get a new car because auto plants now churned out tanks and planes. New plants sprang up to produce aluminum and synthetic rubber...an invention which meant American importers no longer needed to get real rubber from rubber trees in the Amazon, and risk taking a blow dart in the neck.

The **War Manpower Commission** (WMC) drafted about ten million men into the regular army, while another six million volunteered for the navy, marines and army air corps. Using family connections to get into the National Guard to stay out of real danger did not work back then because all units were likely to fight. Lots of women volunteered for noncombat roles in the uniformed services, and they proved invaluable in freeing up more men for combat roles. About 900,000 African Americans served in all-black units commanded by white officers. Disgracefully, not much had changed since the Civil War, but as usual, when given the chance the black soldiers fought hard and died just like the white units.

Due to the war, the federal government was hiring and unemployment virtually vanished. The Great Depression finally became a memory. Labor unions — for the most part — patriotically refrained from strikes. The **Office of Price Administration** (OPA) regulated both prices and wages, and even rationed scarce items such as sugar, shoes, coffee, meat, butter, cheese, nylon, and gasoline. Americans did need to sacrifice, but this was minor compared to the shortages across the rest of the world. In the United States, your neighbor always seemed able to spare a cup of sugar or coffee or something stronger.

To pay the huge costs of the war, the federal government raised taxes on individuals and corporations. Not surprisingly, the wealthy complained, since being materialistic and self-centered is what made them wealthy in the first place. The government needed the money sooner rather than later, so employers were required to deduct taxes from workers paychecks and send it in right away. That neat trick is still with us today — a *withholding tax* — but if you are clever with your deductions you can get a lot of it back (don't do what I did and get flagged by the IRS for trying to write off the cost of dinner at a Hooters restaurant as a business expense).

Movie stars and popular athletes all pitched in to help with massive war bond drives, and Americans eventually purchased $100 billion worth. Victory gardens sprang up across the land, youth groups organized scrap iron drives, and Hollywood churned out movies bashing the "Nips" and the "Krauts." Walt Disney produced a film called *"Der Führer's Face,"* but it is doubtful the Nazi's were frightened by Donald Duck who, if you think about it, is naked from the waist down.

Along with men, women stepped up and really put out...come on, you know what I mean...really contributed to the war effort. Inspired by posters of a fictional "Rosie the Riveter" — a muscle-bound yet somehow still attractive female version of, well, myself — women picked up blow torches and jackhammers and helped construct everything our warriors needed. Though scant attention was paid to these ladies' needs ("Daycare? What's daycare?"), they and their children sacrificed to the utmost.

Civil rights during the war were a mixed bag. With white men going overseas to fight, hundreds of thousands of African-Americans moved north to take jobs in the defense industry. Whites often resented blacks moving in to their neighborhoods, and there were severe race riots in some *northern* cities, particularly Detroit. Mexican-Americans faced the same treatment in the southwest. Young Latinos proudly sported suits, making them perfect targets for drunken sailors on liberty in the 1943 **Zoot Suit riots** in Los Angeles.

Americans panicked after Pearl Harbor and, fearing an imminent attack on the mainland, questioned Japanese-Americans' loyalty. In one of the sorriest episodes in our nation's History, Japanese-Americans on the West Coast were actually rounded up and sent to internment camps inland. They lost their homes and businesses but, amazingly, some Japanese-American men served honorably in our army while their families remained in plywood prisons in the desert. German and Italian Americans, by contrast, had assimilated to a greater extent and thus faced no such persecution. There's a lesson to be learned from this. If — God forbid — there is another attack on the United States by evil Muslim fanatics, we should not condemn all Muslim-Americans. We should all stick together, and if someone must be blamed, then let's blame annoying folks who really deserve it...like Glenn Beck and Sarah Palin.

ALLIED STRATEGY AGAINST THE AXIS

or *Battles That Would Be Really Cool Except For All the Death And Destruction*

Churchill convinced Roosevelt the situation in Europe was even more dire than in the Pacific. In the fall of 1942, in what was dubbed **Operation Torch**, the Allies embarked upon a campaign to liberate North Africa from Axis occupation. British forces under the command of **General Bernard Montgomery** moved east, and defeated General **Irwin Rommel** and his *Afrika Korps* at **El Alamein** (Rommel was nicknamed the "Desert Fox" because of his strike-and-retreat tactics...it had nothing to do with his physical appearance). American, British and Canadian forces commanded by **General Dwight Eisenhower** advanced from the west. Fierce desert warfare led to the emergence of a determined American tank commander, **General George S. Patton**, ultimately resulting in an Academy Award for Best Actor in 1971 for actor George C. Scott. Patton was a great strategist, drove his troops relentlessly, won victory after victory, and was completely off his rocker (see the movie *Patton!*). Eventually, North Africa was unshackled from the Nazis' grip.

Meanwhile, the Russians were giving the Germans more than they could handle. In early 1943, they obliterated a 300,000-strong Nazi army at Stalingrad and then counterattacked. The Germans fought fiercely, but their Eastern Front became a nightmare; the Soviets (who knew the terrain and were used to the severe winters) surged westward, blowing everything to smithereens, liberating their own lands, and then forcing the Nazis out of Romania, Bulgaria, Hungary, Yugoslavia, Austria, Czechoslovakia, and Poland. Captured *Wehrmacht* officers lamented their failure to at least bring an extra sweater.

In January 1943, Roosevelt and Churchill met at the **Casablanca Conference**, where they reportedly interrupted the work of Humphrey Bogart who was trying to make a classic film. Churchill convinced FDR that they were not ready to invade France, but an attack on the "soft underbelly" of Europe could work. The only alligators Roosevelt had ever seen were on shirts at the country club, but he grasped the metaphor. In 1943, the Allies crossed the Mediterranean and attacked the island of Sicily, and in thirty-nine days of bloody fighting the German and Italian defenders were routed. Interestingly, the local populace laid low during the fighting and generally did not resist the Americans, thanks in part to New York Mafia Don "Lucky" Luciano. Lucky was incarcerated in Sing Sing prison for tax evasion, and out of pure patriotism (and for a reduction in his sentence) he put the word out for all Sicilians not to hassle the invading U.S. soldiers. It turned out that the Mafia — always the real authority in Sicily — was rooting for America in the war. Democracies (with their constitutions, human rights, and the rule of law) are by far the best places to be a criminal; dictators will just have you shot.

With Allied planes bombing Rome, the Italian people concluded the bloom was definitely off the Mussolini rose. Let's just say they deposed his government and his naked corpse ended up dangling from a meat hook...another obvious lesson that brutal dictators often get a dose of their own vile medicine in the end. In September 1943, American troops under General Mark W. Clark hit the beaches in southern Italy and headed for the town of Salerno. The Germans fought fiercely as the Allies advanced mile by mile, sometimes yard by yard. Fierce fighting would characterize the entire campaign to liberate the Italian peninsula, which continued with enormous casualties until nearly the end of the war. The Allies battled the enemy from Salerno to Naples to Anzio to Rome, and up into the mountainous north. Some priceless ancient and medieval relics were spared; others were bombed into oblivion. Italy became Hitler's open sore, requiring him to divert increasingly scarce resources to try and staunch the bleeding. The Italian army quickly surrendered and became a nonfactor...they simply put down their shells and ordered some ziti.

In November 1943, Roosevelt and Churchill flew to Tehran, Iran, to meet with Stalin. At the **Tehran Conference**, FDR tried to get chummy with his wartime ally and called him " Uncle Joe." But jokes and drinks could not deter Stalin from pointing out that the "Americans and the British seem to be willing to fight to the last drop of Soviet blood." FDR and Churchill did not see anything wrong with that, but did not say so out loud; instead they acquiesced to Stalin's demand that the Allies open another front in northern France to take the pressure off Russia. The operation was codenamed "**Operation Overlord**" and slated to take place as soon as the weather improved the next spring. Stalin also promised to join the war against Japan as soon as the Nazis were defeated...which seemed like a good idea at the time.

FIGHTING BACK AGAINST THE JAPANESE
or *You Can Take Your Rice and Shove It!*

In April 1942, a little over four months after Pearl Harbor, the U.S. Army and Navy loaded sixteen B-25 bombers onto the newly-built aircraft carrier *USS Hornet* and headed off in the direction of Japan. Not wanting to risk the priceless carrier, the planes launched at a distance of over 600 miles from Tokyo. They reached their target, dropped their bombs and, despite not doing much damage, shocked the heck out of the Japanese citizenry, who had assumed they were invulnerable to American retaliation. The pilots did not have the fuel to return to their carrier, so they kept going across the Sea of Japan in the hopes of landing in a friendly Chinese-occupied area rather than crashing in a decidedly unfriendly Japanese-occupied one. They wore leather bomber jackets with maps sewn into the lining and Chinese writing on the back reportedly saying things like "PLEASE HELP ME," "FRIEND NOT FOE," and "WHERE IS THE RESTROOM?" Under the command of General James H. Doolittle, America's **Doolittle Raid** buoyed American spirits and made its point...*we're really mad and you will rue the day you decided to bomb us at Pearl Harbor and start this fight.*

Americans felt good about the Doolittle Raid, but in reality the American position in the Pacific was desperately weak. In the wake of the attack on Pearl Harbor, the

Japanese war machine conquered the American-held islands of Guam and Wake; Singapore and Hong Kong then fell, as did Burma and Thailand. By mid-1942, the Japanese empire stretched all the way from Manchuria down to the Malay Peninsula on the Asian mainland, plus hundreds of Pacific islands and countless tiki bars.

The U.S. Army heroically tried to defend the Philippines but were hugely outnumbered, and General Douglas MacArthur, commander of American forces in Asia, was forced to retreat to the Bataan Peninsula. He set up his headquarters on a nearby island named **Fortress Corregidor** and put up a fierce three-month stand, but could not hold out, and under direct orders from the President, MacArthur was evacuated on a small patrol boat. He dramatically promised the Filipino people he would return, and there are unsubstantiated rumors that at this point, the small boat lurched forward and he almost fell overboard. His troops were taken prisoner and forced to endure a brutal 61-mile march to a Japanese prisoner of war camp. Thousands died en route from disease, starvation, dehydration, heat prostration, and untreated wounds; those who fell behind were usually executed or left to die. The **Bataan Death March** proved that behind all the smiling and bowing, the Japanese military were truly barbaric and uncivilized.

Japanese hubris next led them to scheme for an attack on Australia, and in preparation they sent a fleet of ships into the Coral Sea near New Guinea. An outnumbered American fleet intercepted them, and an intense two-day battle raged as the two sides launched carrier-based planes against each other...the first naval battle in History in which neither side's ships came within sight of each other (some of the Japanese sailors wondered why they had even bothered to iron their uniforms.) The U.S. Navy actually suffered more damage than the Japanese, but the enemy fleet withdrew and their advance toward Australia stalled. Australians celebrated the Americans' victory in the **Battle of the Coral Sea** by *throwing another shrimp on the barbie.*

Like many Americans, Roosevelt feared the Japanese might invade America's West Coast...that's how desperate the situation was in the spring of 1942. These fears were well-founded — the Japanese next intended to capture the small island of Midway in the central Pacific to use as a base for attacking Hawaii and then the mainland. Fortuitously, navy code breakers figured out where the Japanese fleet was heading (back then our intelligence experts got it right, as opposed to the "Iraqi weapons of mass destruction are a slam dunk" crew we're saddled with today.)

Admiral **Chester W. Nimitz**, commander of the Pacific Fleet, made sure his forces were in position to meet the Japanese attack on Midway, which commenced on June 4th. Our planes fought through enemy planes and swooped down on enemy ships, and the heroism of the American airmen and sailors carried the day. Our losses were heavy, but the Japanese navy was devastated, losing four of its best carriers and 275 planes. The **Battle of Midway** was the turning point of the Pacific war; from then on, the Rising Sun was on the defensive.

General MacArthur and Admiral Nimitz disagreed on what to do next. MacArthur wanted to fight up through the South Pacific, liberate the Philippines, and then push on to Japan. Nimitz wanted to plow through the Central Pacific and crush the Japanese fleet. At their meeting, MacArthur reportedly stamped his feet and cried, "But I promised the Filipinos I would return." Nimitz reportedly replied, "Not my problem." FDR the politician stepped in and, characteristically, gave both men what they wanted. But to minimize casualties, not every Japanese-held island would be attacked. An ingenious "island hopping" strategy evolved, in which American forces would liberate an island and skip over another before attacking the next enemy position. The isolated Japanese-held islands, with the Japanese fleet in retreat, would become strategically irrelevant and "wither on the vine."

This strategy worked, but the Japanese resisted fanatically and our guys endured enormous casualties. The enemy suffered far greater losses, however, (usually in a 20- to 30-1 ratio), and in the Central Pacific — from Tarawa to the Marshall Islands to Saipan, and Guam in the Mariana Islands — the Japanese were dislodged from their defenses. In the South Pacific, MacArthur's forces landed on Guadalcanal and took the rest of the Solomon Islands. Next, they liberated New Guinea and headed for the island of Leyte (pronounced "lay-tay") in the Philippines. In the Battle of **Leyte Gulf**, the largest naval battle in History, the U.S. Navy decimated the enemy. MacArthur waded ashore (a couple of times so the photographers could get lots of photos) and declared, "I have returned." One Filipino who mumbled, "It's about damn time..." was edited out of the newsreels.

After four months of ferocious fighting, the entire Philippines was liberated, and U.S. forces pushed on to two more islands, Iwo Jima and Okinawa, both of which were really close to the Japanese homeland. The enemy contested every inch, but our heroic soldiers and marines pushed them back, and the Japanese became so desperate that they unleashed a terrible new weapon...the suicide pilot, or *kamikaze*. Kamikaze attacks inflicted heavy damage, though they did not turn the tide of war as some Japanese commanders had hoped. Pilots who had second thoughts while flying their mission quickly realized they had been given only enough gas for a one-way trip.

With great fortitude and taking huge casualties, the army, navy and marines took everything the Japanese could throw at them and prevailed. The Japanese navy was rendered irrelevant, as were their air forces. From Iwo Jima and Okinawa as well as the Marianas, American B-29s could now take off from landing strips and bomb Japan directly, and planning commenced for a land invasion of Japan to, hopefully, end the war in the Pacific once and for all.

CRUSHING THE NAZIS TO A PULP
or *Hurry Up Before the Russians Get There First!*

The Battle of the Atlantic turned better for the Allies in late 1943. The invention of sonar (a kind of an underwater radar that continually goes beep beep or boop boop depending on the model) made it possible for destroyers and planes to locate U-boats and nail them with depth charges and bombs. Merchant ships in huge convoys also got better at zigzagging without ramming into each other, so enormous amounts of supplies from the U.S. reached Britain. Allied bombers targeted military bases, factories and cities inside Germany, causing lots of Germans to begin to wonder (secretly to themselves) if the Führer knew what the hell he was doing.

In southern Britain, the Allies assembled a mighty invasion force: 176,000 troops, 4,600 ships, 11,000 aircraft, and an angry German shepherd who wanted revenge for all the rotten borscht it had been fed. Only a few Allied commanders knew precisely where on the northern French coast the landing would be, so the Germans had to keep guessing and fortify the entire coastline. One Nazi military analyst who predicted an attack on the French Riviera was reportedly sent back to Berlin for a "rest."

The Allies (mostly Americans and British, but we should not forget the Canadians, Australians, New Zealanders and others) were ready to go in late May, but the weather remained foggy and rainy. Eisenhower, who had been made Supreme Allied Commander, was finally told by meteorologists the skies would soon lighten, and he was especially pleased because it was **D Day**. On June 6, 1944, he gave the command, and the mighty flotilla crossed the English Channel and surprised the Nazi defenders at Normandy. On some of the beaches resistance was relatively light, but at Omaha Beach in particular, American casualties were near sixty percent. Hitler was convinced the attack would come farther north and west at Calais, so he personally held back reinforcements for Normandy until it was too late to stop the heroic troops from getting ashore and punching through the German defenses to get inland. Tom Hanks got through, intent on *Saving Private Ryan*.

Once they failed to stop the Allies on the Normandy beaches, the *Krauts* were toast, though they would fight on fiercely for nearly another year. Within about a month the Allies advanced inland, pivoted to the west, and started beating back the German occupation of France, city by city, town by town, croissant by croissant. On August 25, 1944, Paris was liberated amidst wild celebrations in which American GIs had more luck with French women than they ever had before or since. Lots of French people declared they had been in the "Underground" all along, had never heard the word "Vichy," and proudly marched as "Free French" under the command of General Charles DeGaulle, who was thrilled to go back home once the Americans and the British had done all the heavy lifting. Soon all of France was liberated, along with Belgium and Luxembourg…a tiny country most U.S. soldiers did not even know existed and kind of wanted to skip.

As the Allies drove inexorably towards German territory, the Germans mustered one last desperate counterattack in the Ardennes Forest of Belgium. It caught the GIs off guard and the American lines got pushed (bulged) back about fifty miles in this aptly named **Battle of the Bulge**. In the little town of Bastogne, the Germans encircled the Americans and bombarded for six days. When the German commander demanded surrender, General Anthony C. McAuliffe sent a defiant reply that simply read, "Nuts!" The Germans took that as a "No" and concluded that McAuliffe had a lot to learn about how to curse. American reinforcements soon arrived, liberated Bastogne, and reversed the German advance. The Nazis were spent.

American presidential elections arrive like clockwork every four years even in the midst of crisis...Lincoln needed to run for reelection in 1864, and so did Roosevelt in 1944. Believing the U.S. should not change horses at such a critical time, FDR stood for an unprecedented fourth term. The Republicans nominated the scrappy Governor of New York, **Thomas E. Dewey**, a former racket-busting district attorney with slicked back dark hair and a pencil-thin mustache; critics sneeringly pointed out that he resembled "that little tuxedo man on top of the wedding cake." Dewey had a reputation for honesty and integrity, but found it difficult to campaign against Roosevelt; the Governor reportedly fired a speechwriter who wrote: "The economy is improving, inflation is under control, the war is going well, so it's time for change." To no one's surprise, Roosevelt won a solid victory in November. His new Vice-President was Senator Harry S. Truman of Missouri, placed on the ticket because Vice-President Henry Wallace had irritated the conservative wing of his own Democratic party by being too friendly to the Soviet Union and refusing to brand all Russians as minions of Satan.

With the war in Europe coming to an end, Roosevelt, Churchill, and Stalin decided to hold another summit at Yalta, an ancient Russian resort town on the Black Sea. At this **Yalta Conference** they discussed how the postwar world would be configured. Stalin reportedly cried, "I want everything!" but was told to sit down and negotiate seriously. The leaders agreed to divide a conquered Germany into four zones of occupation: American, Russian, British and (what a gift) French. Stalin demanded some of Poland's eastern territory, claiming this was historically where most attacks on Russia had come from, and Franklin and Winston let him take it. The dictator promised that democratic elections would be held in the rest of Poland and in the other eastern European nations the Soviets had occupied on the way to crushing Germany. Roosevelt seems to have believed Stalin's promises, but today we know the President was weak and deathly ill (with congenital heart failure and other maladies) after a debilitating twelve-plus years in office.

By early 1945, Germany was caught in a vise. Russia closed in from the east. In March, Allied troops crossed the Rhine River from the west into German territory. And that's when they started to see it — the results of the **Holocaust**. As the Army advanced they came across death camps (such as Auschwitz, Bergen-Belsen, Dachau, and Buchenwald) in which prisoners had been starved, tortured, shot, gassed and had their bodies cremated in specially designed ovens. Hitler wanted to destroy all Jews, and he succeeded in killing about one-third of those living in Europe...over six million in total. This was genocide — the attempted murder of an entire ethnic group — and evil in its purest form. Hitler had championed a deliberate lie — the false science that proclaimed a master German "Aryan" race — and he also presided over the extermination of another six million "undesirables" including many Slavic people, gypsies, homosexuals, and the physically and mentally challenged. Today, "Holocaust deniers" are either degenerate liars or leaders of radical Muslim theocracies or both.

American and British troops advanced as far as the Elbe River, where on April 25, 1945, they met and eyed the Russian troops with suspicion. Still, everyone raised a glass (or canteen) in celebration because they were all supposed to be allies and friends. As the Soviets stormed into Berlin, Hitler retreated to an underground bunker and — by this time completely insane — married his mistress Eva Braun and then promptly killed her and himself. Their honeymoon was far less romantic than what Eva had always dreamed it would be...their bodies were tossed into a bomb crater, doused with gasoline and burned.

On May 8, 1945, what was left of the German High Command surrendered unconditionally, and the United States celebrated **V-E Day** (Victory in Europe Day). Franklin Roosevelt did not live to see it; he had died on April 12th of a cerebral hemorrhage while posing for a portrait at his retreat in Warm Springs, Georgia. His mistress was sitting right next to him at the time, but historians tend to gloss over this. Most of us like FDR and recognize that with all his great power he remained an intensely lonely man. Our Constitution tells us what to do in such situations, so Vice-President Harry Truman was immediately sworn in as President. FDR did live long enough to understand victory was a *fait accompli* so, when Truman fretted that he wasn't sure what to do next, nobody panicked because a favorable outcome to the war was already in the bag. Supposedly, it was a little awkward when Harry froze and they had to nudge him in the direction of "that big White House on the end of Pennsylvania Avenue."

THE DECISION TO USE THE ATOMIC BOMB
or *You Started It, We'll Finish It!*

With Truman replacing FDR, the Allies held the **Potsdam Summit** in July, 1945, in a bombed out suburb of Berlin. Hard to believe but, before the presidency was thrust upon him, Truman had only met Roosevelt six times. FDR never had much sense of his own mortality and had failed to keep his own Vice-President "in the loop." Thus, Harry was completely floored when on July 17th he was handed a confidential report that a super-secret (and money is no object) **Manhattan Project** had split the atom and put the United States in possession of a gigantic "atomic bomb" that could utterly destroy an entire city in one fell boom. He was really relieved when his generals told him they were not carrying the bomb with them; one had tested successfully at Los Alamos, New Mexico and the two other in existence were still out in the desert.

The President quickly realized that Japan could be forced to surrender without a costly land invasion that, according to some estimates, might produce as many as one million U.S. casualties. Furthermore, the United States could now defeat the Japanese alone, so Soviet help — and a share of the occupation — would not be necessary. Nobody wanted a North (controlled by the Soviets) and South (controlled by the U.S.) Japan. The big bomb would also surely keep the grasping, expansionist-minded Russian bear in check. Incredibly, Truman informed Stalin of the invention of this new weapon — we were still Allies after all — and the Soviet Premier faked a surprised smile, even though he had already learned of its existence through Russian spies, identified by some sources as Boris Badunov and Natasha Fatal.

A **Potsdam Declaration** demanded that the Japanese immediately surrender or face "prompt and utter destruction," obviously without describing the details of the new weapon. The Japanese generals, covertly working on their own atomic bomb project, refused to allow their government to reply to the Allied ultimatum. With virtually no high-level dissenting views save for Dr. **Robert Oppenheimer**, civilian director of the Manhattan Project, and a few other scientists who were starting to feel "creators' remorse," President Truman ordered the atomic bomb dropped on Japan.

On August 6th, 1945, a bomber nicknamed *Enola Gay* (after pilot Colonel Paul Tibbet's mother) dropped the A-bomb on the Japanese industrial city of **Hiroshima**. There were military and industrial targets in Hiroshima, but the final choice of target actually came down to where the weather was clearest that day. In a blinding flash, over eighty percent of the city was destroyed, 68,000 people killed instantly, and in the aftermath, thousands more would perish from radiation poisoning. Over the next three days Japan made no overt attempt to surrender, so another bomb was dropped on **Nagasaki** with similar results.

Finally, on August 14, Japanese leaders agreed to an unconditional surrender; they did so formally the next day on the deck of the battleship *Missouri,* which had docked in Tokyo Bay. Diminutive Emperor Hirohito — who will forever have to answer for his "willful impotence" during the war — appeared, dressed in top hat and tails, looking like the banker on a Monopoly board. The United States had agreed to treat him with respect and allow him to remain symbolically in office. Finally, the greatest conflict in world History was over.

Whether or not the United States was "right" to utilize such a horrible weapon remains hotly debated. Some people today simply ignore historical reality, wring their hands and start to sing, "Where Have All the Flowers Gone?" whenever the subject comes up. Of course the death and destruction was unspeakable, but the alternatives were worse. A land invasion may well have cost hundreds of thousand of American lives — the issue Truman was ethically and constitutionally mandated to prioritize above all — and there would have been a much greater loss of Japanese lives. But why not drop a demonstration bomb? (It might not work, and we only had two.) Why not wait longer before dropping the second bomb? (A valid question that deserves further research, though there is scant evidence that Japanese generals were ready to fall on their samurai swords after the first detonation.) Point of fact: the dropping of the atomic bomb saved lives. It was the right thing to do...horrible as it was, it had to be.

I must include a disclaimer here: your author's father was stationed in Okinawa at the time, and involved in the planning for a land invasion. He always said the atomic bombs probably saved his life, thus making my birth possible. This may influence my opinion on the matter, so you should consider the arguments carefully before agreeing with me.

The devastation from World War II was enormous, but the United States fared better than much of the rest of the world. In America, 322,000 had died, compared to five million in Germany and twenty-five million in the Soviet Union. Hungry and homeless people roamed much of Europe. Only two nations emerged stronger from the war — the United States and the Soviet Union. And with their common enemies in ruins, the preeminent reason for their alliance evaporated. Will these two new "superpowers" be able to coexist? Will there finally be a lasting world peace? Will vodka remain popular across the U.S.? Or will a World War III waged with nuclear weapons threaten to spill everyone's drinks and destroy the earth? Uh oh...stay tuned...don't touch that dial!!!

This Really Happened!

It is 1906, and the murder of renowned architect Stanford White exposes the details of a scandalous love triangle that shocks a nation still clinging to Victorian virtue. Sensational and immoral behavior is revealed, as the killer, millionaire playboy Harry Thaw, is brought to court. Newspaper circulations soar as the tabloids thrive on stories such as White's swinging his naked mistress from a red velvet swing in his Madison Square Garden penthouse. In rural areas, people trudge through the snow to buy big-city papers that carry every word of the scandalous testimony. President Theodore Roosevelt is so shocked he threatens to prosecute the reporters covering the trial for promoting obscenity. When the trial finally ends, Americans breathe a sigh of relief and most don't imagine the "trial of the century" they have just witnessed will be just the first of many sensational trials.

And the rest is History…

Quiz yourself on Chapter 12

Multiple Choice (circle the correct answer).

1. The stock market crash on October 29, 1929
   a. started the Great Depression in America
   b. was the most severe economic downturn the country has ever seen
   c. proved you are crazy to put all your money in stocks
   d. probably could have been avoided with some sensible regulations
   e. all of the above

2. Herbert Hoover responded to the Depression
   a. by telling everyone everything was going to be okay
   b. calling for the ill-fated Hawley-Smoot Tariff
   c. blaming Teddy Roosevelt
   d. by acting like a deer in headlights
   e. all of the above

3. Franklin Delano Roosevelt
   a. believed in the active use of the federal government to aid the economy
   b. believed states and private charities should handle the crisis
   c. called for a "New Deal"
   d. was really hated by wealthy conservatives
   e. a, c and d

4. The New Deal's "3 R's" stood for
   a. Relief, Recovery and Reform
   b. Rum, Romanism, and Rebellion
   c. Reading, 'Riting, and 'Rithmetic
   d. Railroads Run Regularly
   e. None of the above

5. Roosevelt's "Court Packing" scheme
   a. was his plan to increase the number of justices on the Supreme Court
   b. required a constitutional amendment
   c. failed utterly
   d. even dismayed his own fellow Democrats
   e. all of the above

6. The Kellogg-Briand Pact
    a. was an international treaty to outlaw war
    b. really scared Hitler and Mussolini
    c. guaranteed free Corn Flakes for the poor and unfortunate
    d. failed to keep the peace
    e. a and d

7. Pearl Harbor
    a. was a great vacation spot before December 11, 1941
    b. brought a united United States into World War II
    c. proved the Japanese government could not be trusted
    d. resulted in the devastation of America's Pacific Fleet
    e. all of the above

8. American mobilization during World War II was
    a. on a scale of one to ten… eleven
    b. incredible… enough to fight on two fronts at the same time
    c. aided immeasurably by women and African-Americans
    d. something Germany and Japan could not dream of matching
    e. all of the above

9. D-Day
    a. really boosted the acting career of Tom Hanks
    b. followed C-Day
    c. was June 6, 1944
    d. was the Allies successful cross-channel invasion of France
    e. a, c and d

10. Japan surrendered
    a. after the dropping of two atomic bombs
    b. after the U.S. agreed to nominally respect the office of the Emperor
    c. and was occupied by the United States
    d. and was occupied by the United States and the Soviet Union
    e. a, b and c

CHAPTER 13

THE COLD WAR
AND THE AMERICAN CENTURY

or

The Russians Are Coming, the Russians Are Coming!

The Great Depression and World War II had certainly been mighty inconvenient, so after the "Big One," folks wanted to get on with their lives. There were businesses to create! Money to be made! Neighborhoods to build! Families to raise! Minorities and poor to be exploited! The economy was poised to grow like it had never grown before. What a wave! Let's catch it! It sure was a real downer when those Russians, who we never trusted anyway, seemed determined to take over the world.

STARTING A COLD WAR

or *What Do You Mean the Russians Won't Leave?*

As a direct result of dropping the atomic bombs, the United States alone occupied Japan under the command of General Douglas MacArthur. All of its conquered lands were taken away and its armed forces disbanded, causing some former Japanese generals to fall on their swords and commit hara-kiri (ritual suicide) — which is what I would do when faced with eating sushi.

In 1952, the occupation officially ended and Japan became sovereign again, with a democratic constitution that denied it the right to have any serious military forces. How they found all those tanks and bazookas to fire at Godzilla I'll never know. Anyway, Japan has been a loyal ally of the United States ever since. Relieved of the necessity of providing for its own security (the U.S. to this day protects Japan from exterior threats), the Japanese focused their resources on rebuilding their industrial base. By the 1970s many of their new modern factories could produce better and cheaper products than our American companies. Can you say Honda, Nissan, and Toyota? Question: How many televisions are manufactured in the U.S. today? Answer: None. As Americans embraced Japanese products, many domestic manufacturing sectors sputtered. Meanwhile, our own products and foodstuffs (especially rice grown in the USA) were kept out of Japan through its deliberate policy of protectionism. From the Japanese point of view, if you have to be defeated and occupied, the United States is the best option. The Americans help you rebuild, leave peacefully, and then allow you to exploit them.

In the months after the war, the Allies joined together and established the **Nuremberg Trials** to charge top Nazis of "crimes against the laws of war and humanity." Twenty-two top Nazis squirmed uncomfortably in the prisoner's dock, and when given the chance to explain themselves, most feigned ignorance or claimed they were "just following orders." "Let's let bygones be bygones" just didn't fly, given the magnitude of the evil these guys had perpetrated on the world. Field Marshall Hermann Goering poisoned himself with a secret cyanide capsule just hours before he was to be hanged, and many around the world were justifiably bummed that the SOB had been able to control the circumstances of his death.

During the final weeks of the war, representatives from over fifty countries met in San Francisco to participate in the **United Nations Founding Conference**. A rough outline had been discussed by the Allies in August, 1944, at **Dumbarton Oaks**, a wooded estate conveniently near Washington D.C. but still remote enough to allow for wife swapping (just kidding — I have no proof, but let's start a juicy rumor anyway). Roosevelt died two weeks before the San Francisco Conference, but the delegates pressed forward, reassured by Truman's pledge that he would carry on FDR's policies. They all agreed they wanted to create a powerful entity that would not disintegrate like the ill-fated League of Nations. Angling for postwar advantage and hoping for a continuation of lend-lease aid after the war, even the Soviet Union seemed outwardly cooperative.

All participating countries would be equal members in a **General Assembly**, but to give the **United Nations** a strength the League had lacked, there was general agreement that there should be a **Security Council** with enforcement power, containing fifteen members: five permanent and eleven (now fifteen) with rotating two-year terms. The permanent members were (and remain to this day) the United States, Soviet Union, Great Britain, France, and China. Those choices reflected "realpolitik," the practical and undeniable fact that those five nations had the most power and influence in the world. It wasn't necessarily fair but it was reality, so if you lived in Brazil, Egypt, India or someplace else where everyone felt they deserved to join the "Big Five," you just got over it.

Another debate focused on whether or not the Security Council — with its power to implement economic embargoes or even authorize armed force — could compel member nations to comply with its directives. The United States (not ready to throw all in with an untested world organization) and all the other members of the "Big Five" were not willing to go that far. Therefore, the U.N. Charter contained an article granting any of the five permanent members veto power in the Security Council, preserving their foreign policy independence while greatly weakening the power of the United Nations. For the next fifty years the United States and Soviet Union would disagree on almost everything. But at least all the ambassadors got to sit behind a nice nameplate and wear cool headphones providing translations of every single language.

In 1944, economic ministers from forty-four nations had met at a resort in New Hampshire called **Bretton Woods**. While devouring stacks of pancakes dripping with maple syrup, they created the **International Monetary Fund** to encourage world trade and at least try to keep exchange rates stable. The International Bank for Reconstruction and Development (now called the **World Bank**) would offer aid and loans to rebuilding and developing nations. Both of these agencies later became part of the United Nations and continue to be controversial to this day. Why? Because nobody ever feels they are being treated fairly, and everyone — including me — hates paying back loans.

The UN quickly created an Atomic Energy Commission, and the U.S. representative **Bernard Baruch** put forth a plan to outlaw atomic weapons. He was thrilled when everyone started calling it the **Baruch Plan**. They should have called it the "Dream On Plan" because a world without the threat of nuclear destruction never had a chance. The U.S. was willing to support peaceful use of atomic energy and even share the technology, provided it was coupled with universal inspections of nuclear facilities. But the Soviet Union would have none of it. In Stalin's police state, nobody could trust even their own shadow, so there was no way they were going to trust the United States to destroy its nuclear stockpile. Secretly, the Soviets started working on their own atomic bombs and the Baruch Plan went down the tubes.

After Russia's recent historical experience of being attacked from the west twice in the last fifty years, Stalin desperately wanted to guarantee his country's security from what he now saw as a hostile world dominated by the United States. By 1946, it became crystal clear the Soviet Union intended to create a buffer zone of puppet (or satellite) states in Eastern Europe. Winston Churchill, voted out of office the previous year by a "but what have you done for us lately" British electorate focused on its devastated domestic economy, astutely proclaimed: "An **Iron Curtain** has descended across the continent." At this point it was not really iron — mostly barbed wire and Soviet guards reeking of vodka and cabbage at military checkpoints — but rhetorically Churchill hit his mark perfectly. What could the United States do about it? Nothing really. Nobody wanted to even contemplate a World War III.

Pretty soon everyone realized we were in a "**Cold War**" against the Soviet Union. No direct fighting took place, but neither side understood the other very well and both nations eyed each other with suspicion. It did seem to Americans like the Soviets wanted to spread their dominance across the world.

After the war, the Soviets had refused to withdraw their troops from oil-rich Iran, and most observers believed the Russians planned to take it over. UN Security Council resolutions aimed at curbing the Russian machinations met with scowling Soviet vetoes. Reportedly, after it was explained to him that the names Persia and Iran could refer to the same territory, Truman, furious, acted unilaterally and demanded that the Soviet Union "get the hell out of whatever you call it." The President even sent a U.S. naval fleet into the eastern Mediterranean to emphasize his point. The Soviet Union, not willing to provoke a direct military confrontation, backed down and pulled its troops out. When Truman heard this, it was said, he started shadow boxing and muttering, "I sure showed them."

A policy of **containment** began to evolve. From his post as chargé d'affaires (a fancy term for second in command) at the U.S. Embassy in Moscow, **George F. Kennan** wrote an 8000-word cable, famously dubbed the "Long Telegram," and sent it to his bosses in the State Department. At first he was identified only as Mr. X, but everybody knew it was him and his fake Groucho Marx mustache fooled no one. Kennan, who definitely could have benefited from some sedatives, expressed in alarmist tones that the United States must adopt "a policy of firm containment designed to confront the Russians with unalterable counterforce, at every point where they show signs of encroaching upon a peaceful and stable world." The Soviet leadership, Kennan implied, would only respond to power and force. President Truman, who'd already declared he was "sick of babying the Soviets," loved the Long Telegram.

Kennan's testosterone-laden language seemed to make sense, especially since Stalin had demanded possession of two Turkish provinces and bases on the Bosporus and the Dardanelles that would give Russia its long craved for access to the Mediterranean through the Black Sea. In Greece, American policymakers believed the Soviets were aiding communist rebels in a civil war to overthrow the pro-western government. The British, who had been trying to restore the Greek monarchy, told the United States they could no longer afford to do so (Great Britain had emerged from World War II an exhausted and considerably diminished world power — and a place where most people referred to sausage and potatoes as "bangers and mash"). What would happen in Greece and Turkey was entirely up to the United States.

President Truman appeared before Congress and pleaded for $400 million in foreign aid to strengthen the governments of those two nations. To make sure the lawmakers would approve the money, he scared the bejesus out of them by implying that if Greece and Turkey fell to communism, it would be only a matter of time before American democracy would be enveloped by communistic hordes that would take away everyone's country club memberships. Congress quickly approved the funds, and the **Truman Doctrine** — American financial aid to help Greece and Turkey avoid communist takeovers — worked.

CONTAINMENT IN ACTION
or *Why Won't These Darn Communists Give It A Rest?*

Realizing that the desperate, starving people of Western Europe might be tempted to surrender their political freedom to the false promises of a communist dictator, Secretary of State **George Marshall** came up with a truly great idea. He proposed the best way to prevent such a scenario would be to rebuild the devastated economies in that region. He urged the United States to spend billions of dollars on a coordinated financial program to help Europe recover from the war — a lot of bling, but far less than the cost of an all-out "shooting war" if the Soviets kept trying to expand their influence. President Truman requested the funds from Congress, and the perfect timing of a pro-Moscow coup in Czechoslovakia convinced the legislators to go along.

The **Marshall Plan**'s primary purpose — to stop the spread of communism — dovetailed perfectly with a genuine humanitarian effort to rebuild shattered lives. The plan specified that the foreign aid dollars could only be spent on American goods and services, benefiting our own economy and drawing recipient nations more tightly into an American economic web. The Soviet Union did not let any of its Eastern European puppet states participate, so their economies continued to limp along. In short, the Marshall Plan was a huge success; by the early fifties the factories of Western Europe were humming again. Talk about a slam dunk!

In June 1948, the U.S., Britain, and France agreed to merge their German zones of occupation into one western zone, including Berlin, which was located 117 miles inside the Soviet's eastern zone. Threatened by all of this (the idea of a resurgent Germany sent chills up the Russian spine), Stalin decided to starve the Allies out of West Berlin by cutting off land and rail transportation routes. In response, President Truman decided to break the Soviet blockade with what became known as the **Berlin Airlift**. The United States and Britain jointly flew in food and medical supplies, keeping West Berlin alive and free. The Soviets, unwilling to provoke a military confrontation, did not dare to fire on the planes, which at times landed every three minutes with coordination rivalling our modern day airlines (and they didn't charge for pillows).

After eleven months, the Soviets relented and lifted the blockade in May, 1949. The West German Federal Republic (**West Germany**, aligned with the West) came into existence, and the Russians countered by creating the East German Democratic Republic (**East Germany**, a puppet of the Soviet Union). **East Berlin** became the capital of East Germany, while **West Berlin** survived as a precarious outpost of democracy in the middle of Stalin's latest conquest.

Stalin's shenanigans convinced American policymakers of the necessity for a defensive military alliance with the friendly nations of Western Europe. In April, 1949, at a meeting in Washington, twelve nations agreed to form **NATO** — the **North Atlantic Treaty Organization**. The United States, Britain, France, Belgium, Luxembourg, the Netherlands, Italy, Canada, Portugal, Norway, Denmark, and Iceland all agreed that "an armed attack against one or more of them in Europe or North America shall be considered an attack against them all" (when an Icelandic delegate reportedly asked if an armed attack against all of us shall be considered an attack against one of us, he was handed some hot cocoa and told to sit by the fireplace).

Greece and Turkey joined NATO in 1952, and West Germany joined in 1955. Stalin obsessively needed to counter everything the United States did, so the Soviet Union and seven of its puppets soon established a rival alliance, the **Warsaw Pact** (consisting of little more than the Soviet military, though they did open up offices and put up signs). The Russians also created **COMECON** — the **Council of Mutual Economic Assistance** — to provide aid for Marshall Plan-deprived Eastern Europe, though the agency never had much money to put where its communist mouth was.

Besides attending to the military security of Europe and Asia, the Truman Administration put forth an ambitious aid program for the Third (developing) World. (Professors in corduroy jackets with elbow patches began referring to communist nations as the Second World and the "free" countries as the First World.) The **Point Four Program** was designed to export American "know-how" to poor nations trying to raise their standard of living. There was clearly not enough money to bring the Marshall Plan everywhere, but sharing technical knowledge was cheaper and just might help to improve lives and keep the communist bear at bay. In practice, western technical aid did improve agriculture and public health around the world, and spread good will. Knowledge flowed in both directions as Americans interacted with their new Third World friends. Of course, the first thing local villagers asked for were projectors and Hollywood movies starring Marilyn Monroe.

In 1948, the United Nations carved the country of Israel out of Palestine as a refuge and homeland for the displaced Jews of Europe. Palestine was slated to be shared by the Arabs and the Jews, and Jerusalem, a holy place to Islam, Judaism, and Christianity, was to be an international city administered by the United Nations. The Jews accepted this plan, but the Palestinians who lived there — supported by the rest of the Arab world — went ballistic, and the the two sides have been at each other's throats ever since. President Truman immediately offered diplomatic recognition to Israel, cynically remarking that he had never heard of a single instance in which the Arab vote had swayed a U.S. election.

Supplied mainly by the United States, Israel has forcefully protected itself through the decades and, ironically, all the fighting has garnered the Palestinians less than what they were offered in the original U.N. mandate. Don't hold your breath for the Israelis and the Palestinians to come together for gefilte fish and shish kebab any time soon. Both sides appear trapped in an eye-for-an-eye and a tooth-for-a-tooth mode, and it will be up to future generations to come to a lasting settlement. Back in the late forties, the United States worried about losing Arab friendships, and the always opportunistic Soviets tryed to stick their paws into the critically strategic region.

In September, 1949, Americans lost a peace of mind they'll never get back again when they learned the Soviets had exploded their own atomic bomb. American "intelligence" experts who'd predicted that this would take decades put on sunglasses and muttered, "No comment." A thorough reexamination of America's foreign policy strategy seemed in order, and Truman turned to the N.S.A. — the **National Security Agency** (the NSA had been created in 1947 to work out of the executive branch, give the President a "second opinion," and generally run amuck in the basement of the White House. Not surprisingly, officials in the State and Defense Departments often butt heads with the N.S.A.). In April 1950, the NSA produced a report creatively titled **NSC-68**, which built upon George Kennan's ideas and exaggerated the Soviet threat to bolster a claim that the U.S. desperately needed an immediate upgrade of its military forces. Truman believed in containment, but even he had his doubts about the drastic costs of such an endeavor. Then events spun out of his control.

China's decades-old civil war finally came to a head. Since the 1920s, communist forces led by **Mao Zedong** had been grappling against conservative Nationalist forces led by **Chiang Kai-Shek**. Chiang was a corrupt right-wing dirtbag, but the Truman administration felt it had no choice but to support him as an alternative to the communist Mao. Billions of dollars failed to prop up the unpopular Chiang, and in 1948 the U.S. cut off financial aid that some in the State Department admitted had been "money down a rat hole" all along. In 1949, the inevitable happened and Mao seized power. Chiang and the Nationalists fled to the island of **Taiwan** (also known as Formosa) where they deluded themselves into believing one day they would take back the mainland.

Acting tough, the United States refused to engage or even offer diplomatic recognition to Mao's "Red Chinese" government, and the State Department continued relations with the Nationalists on Taiwan as if they were still the "real" Chinese. A generation of American students (myself included) grew up looking at maps that left the name of the most populous nation in the world blank. Even today some of us slip and say "Red China" instead of simply China. Back when all this went down, the Republicans predictably tried to take political advantage of the situation by charging that President Truman and his newly appointed Secretary of State **Dean Acheson** had allowed "the loss of China."

OUTBREAK OF WAR IN KOREA
or *Darn, My Old Uniform Is Too Tight*

After World War II, the Soviet Union and the United States, unable to agree on one government for a unified Korea, divided the peninsula at the 38th parallel; the North received a communist dictator and the South was bequeathed its own right-wing dictator friendly to the United States. On June 24, 1950, North Korean forces — confident of support from both the Soviet Union and Mao's China — swarmed down into the South. The South Korean army was completely caught off guard and retreated down to the bottom of the peninsula, where they were able to establish a shaky perimeter around the city of Pusan (the accusation that many South Korean soldiers had left their posts to participate in a karaoke contest is false, since karaoke had not been invented yet).

President Truman blew his top. Believing the communist attack a further validation of containment theory, and without requesting a Declaration of War from Congress, he ordered U.S. forces into action to support South Korea. At the time, the Soviet Union was boycotting the Security Council (supposedly to protest the U.N.'s refusal to seat the new government of "Red" China), and as a result of this huge diplomatic blunder, the Soviet representatives (probably sipping vodka at a café down the street) were not present to cast their usual veto when the rest of the Security Council member nations voted to authorize armed force to roll back the incursion. Thus, the "Korean War" officially became a United Nations operation, though the United States provided the vast majority of men and materiel. General Douglas MacArthur, sick of the occupation of Japan and a postwar peace that denied him the opportunity to make headlines, was thrilled to take command of the international force and get his name back in the newspapers.

MacArthur was a huge prima donna, but when it came to military tactics he really knew his stuff. He ordered U.S. forces to execute an amphibious landing behind North Korean lines at **Inchon**. Many of his subordinates thought the attack too risky, but MacArthur overruled them, and his gamble paid off. The Americans pushed inland, retook the South Korean capitol of Seoul, and forced the North Koreans to scamper back up the peninsula as fast as they had come down. President Truman flew to Wake Island in the Pacific to meet with MacArthur who, luckily, had been reminded several times by his aides that a president outranks a general, so he should at least try to be nice.

Truman faced a dilemma. The original mission had been to roll back the invasion and contain communism by reestablishing South Korea, and that had been accomplished. But at their meeting, MacArthur asked the President to expand America's goals and liberate the entire Korean peninsula. Against his better judgment, Truman gave in.

U.S. air forces held complete command of the skies, so at first, American infantry advanced up into the north with relative ease. On October 19, Pyongyang, the capitol of North Korea, fell and MacArthur proclaimed to reporters that "American boys would be home by Christmas," even though it was more important for everyone to remember his own birthday was January 26th. But as American forces got closer and closer to the Yalu River, the border with China, the Chinese government freaked out. They sent eight divisions of Chinese troops down into Korea and attacked. The Americans were completely surprised to encounter waves of Asian soldiers who looked sort of the same but sounded different and wore different uniforms. General MacArthur had guaranteed President Truman the Chinese would never dare do such a thing. Outnumbered and having outrun their supply lines, the U.S. forces had no choice but to retreat — under enormously difficult conditions that nonetheless further illustrated their bravery and fortitude. After fighting back and forth, eventually a relatively stable defense line was established near the 38th parallel (where everything started in the first place), and a protracted stalemate ensued. Negotiations with the Chinese formally opened in July 1951, but the fighting and dying would continue well into 1953.

Truman blamed himself for approving MacArthur's recommendation to widen the war into the North, and MacArthur blamed everyone but himself. The General publicly criticized the President for being weak, and demanded the U.S. attack China and even use atomic bombs if necessary. Truman, worried that such an approach might bring Soviet nuclear weapons into play and result in a World War III that could, uh, destroy the world, ordered General MacArthur to pipe down and support his Administration's strategy for a negotiated peace. But MacArthur popped off once too often, particularly in a public letter to the House Republican leader in which he stated, "There is no substitute for victory."

Truman finally had enough, picked up the phone and fired the bombastic commander. This is perhaps the most vivid example in our history that the President — a civilian — commands the American military. MacArthur enjoyed wide public support at the time; he came home to parades and gave a speech before a joint session of Congress in which he proclaimed, "Old soldiers never die, they just fade away." Luckily, the Constitution had not faded away, and as the months went by and the facts behind his dismissal became known, most Americans quietly realized that President Truman had been right to give this egotistical popinjay the boot.

AMERICA UNDER TRUMAN
or *What Would Franklin Have Done?*

Many Americans worried the Depression would return with the end of war. That did not happen, but the economy did have a bumpy ride as it converted to peacetime. The **Servicemen's Readjustment Act** (1944), better known as the **G.I. Bill**, offered tuition grants and low-interest mortgage loans to returning veterans who attended college and bought homes — veterans who in turn contributed so much back to the country that the G.I. Bill still stands out as one of the most successful examples of progressive legislation ever. Fears that many servicemen had been trained to be psychopathic killers who couldn't readjust to peacetime never materialized; anyone with a compulsive need to see offenses and defenses injure each other simply became a fan of the increasingly popular National Football League.

With the war over and most Americans looking to spend some savings, inflation took hold. Persistent shortages of food, consumer goods and housing inconvenienced just about everyone. The cost of living climbed steadily, workers needed more money, and this resulted in labor unrest that had been patriotically deferred during the war. When railway workers went on strike, President Truman threatened to use the army to run the trains and draft the strikers into the military. Union workers were furious and anyone singing, "I've been working on the railroad all the live long day..." risked getting assaulted. The strike collapsed.

In the 1946 midterm elections, cranky voters took out their frustrations on the party in power and sent Republican majorities to the House and Senate. Conservative Republicans and conservative southern Democrats set about attacking the New Deal. Truman, a liberal Democrat like Roosevelt, loved the New Deal and wanted to put his own stamp on it with new initiatives and a new name, the "**Fair Deal**." He called for civil rights legislation, an anti-lynching law, an anti-poll tax law, a Fair Employment Practices Commission, compulsory health insurance, and federal aid to education. Conservatives in Congress refused to pass any of it. Like today, they claimed that progressive legislation costs too much and is a violation of states' rights. Liberals charged that conservatives were just looking for an excuse not to do the right thing. Working on behalf of their corporate benefactors, and to show workers who was still the boss, conservatives in Congress passed the **Taft-Hartley Act** to weaken the power of labor unions. Truman vetoed Taft-Hartley but was overridden. Presidents hate that, and the salty Harry reportedly cursed so much his wife had to tell him to sit down and shut the you-know-what up.

As the presidential election of 1948 approached, Truman announced he wanted to earn the presidency in his own right. He wasn't very popular — polls showed him with only about a thirty-three percent approval rating — so no doubt about it, his scrappy stubbornness had put a lot of folks off. The Democrats nominated him in July at their convention in Philadelphia, but factions from both the right and the left broke away. Conservative southern "Dixiecrats" were repelled by the President's relatively strong stand on civil rights, which included Executive Order 9981 integrating the armed forces. These rednecks formed the **States' Rights Party**, combined populism and bigotry (eerily resembling the contemporary Tea Party movement), and nominated North Carolina's segregationist Governor **Strom Thurmond**. Lefty Democrats created the **Progressive Party** and nominated FDR's former Vice-President **Henry Wallace**, who believed that America was being too tough on the poor little misunderstood Ruskies. Truman thought to himself "next to those two clowns, I stack up pretty well."

With the Democrats split three ways, the Republicans were psyched to pick off the presidency. At their convention, they bypassed a doctrinaire conservative, Ohio Governor **Robert Taft**, and decided to give moderate New York Governor Thomas E. Dewey another shot. Everyone — politicians, pollsters, and pundits alike — figured Truman had no chance. Dewey and his staff were definitely overconfident, and just a couple of days into the campaign they reportedly debated whether geraniums or petunias should dominate the centerpieces at their inaugural ball. But feisty little Truman did not give up. He boarded the presidential train and started giving fiery speeches at "whistle-stops" before ever-increasing crowds across the country. He largely ignored Dewey and ripped into an easy target, the "do-nothing eightieth Congress!" Some guy in the crowd yelled out, "Give 'em hell Harry!" and that perfect slogan really caught on. Meanwhile, Dewey coasted on automatic pilot, never took off his jacket or rolled up his sleeves, and delivered bland speeches full of platitudes. "That's kind of interesting, Thomas" never caught on as a slogan.

Scientific polling was in its infancy back then, and smug pollsters, thinking the election a done deal, stopped asking questions with about two weeks to go. But Truman had saved his kick for the home stretch. He pulled together Roosevelt's coalition and added independent voters who, as it turned out, did not want the fundamentals of the New Deal rolled back. On Election Night, Dewey snuggled under the covers believing he had been elected President, but the news the next day gave him morning sickness. Truman bounded out of bed and said, "No kidding?" Famously, the Chicago Tribune printed the headline "Dewey Defeats Truman," ensuring that generations of journalism students would be told by generations of professors to nail down the facts before running with the story. A few would even take the lesson to heart.

Truman's own term in office proved to be rough sledding; the Democrats regained control of Congress in 1948, but conservatives in both parties prevented any progress on the President's Fair Deal. Correspondingly, Truman's veto pen prevented any serious dismantling of the liberal programs that already existed. And as the Cold War continued to expand, a genuine Red Scare materialized (technically a **Second Red Scare**, considering what had transpired after World War I).

In the first five years after World War II, the Soviets had aggressively set up puppet states in Eastern Europe, facilitated the division of Germany, maneuvered to take advantage of postwar chaos in Iran, Greece, Turkey and elsewhere, and attempted to starve the Allies out of Berlin. But the greatest impact on the national psyche occurred in 1949, when the Russians exploded their own nuclear warhead. For the first time, Americans looked up at the sky and realized that Russian bombers could wipe entire cities off the map. That same year China fell to communism, and the following year North Korea attacked South Korea, so it is understandable that many Americans felt traumatized and insecure. It was just one thing after another. The fact that many folks had purchased televisions and now spent their Tuesday nights watching comedian Milton Berle dressed in drag only added to the confusion.

The United States had every reason to be concerned about the Soviet Union. Stalin and his minions would have been happy to paint the entire world red if they could. A forceful foreign policy of containment appears in hindsight to have been both sensible and effective. But the communist threat inside the country got blown all out of proportion. True, an American Communist Party did exist. Particularly since the Russian Revolution of 1917, a relatively small number of Americans had become infatuated with

Soviet-style communism. But the party never wielded significant influence, and American communists did not intend to overthrow the government. They were mostly left-wing wackos churning out pamphlets that hardly anybody read; Superman and Batman comic books were infinitely more popular.

Folks also found out that the Soviet Union had for decades maintained an extensive spy network in America. It is undeniable that traitors **Klaus Fuchs** and **Julius Rosenberg** passed classified information to the Soviets that had helped them get their A-bomb years before they would have otherwise. Obviously, the United States government could not ignore spies and the FBI and other agencies conducted aggressive counterespionage. Unfortunately, they tossed the law and civil liberties overboard, exaggerated the threat of domestic communism to increase their budgets and power, and ultimately caused many mainstream Americans to start thinking that even Grandma's red sweater looked suspicious.

THE RISE OF JOSEPH McCARTHY
or *What Sewer Did This Guy Crawl Out Of?*

In 1947, Republicans in Congress created the **House Un-American Activities Committee** (HUAC) to try and prove the Democrats had been sympathetic to communist subversions. HUAC first went after Hollywood, and most people in the movie business quickly fell all over each other trying to prove how patriotic they were. Several key senators supposedly received free lifetime passes to the movies, but since popcorn wasn't included, the bribe was not enough. A few brave writers and producers, dubbed the **Hollywood Ten**, refused to be cowed into revealing their political views or informing on others and wound up in jail for contempt. Others, including actors, who insisted upon their constitutional right to remain silent, found themselves out of work and on a "blacklist." A young congressman from California, **Richard Nixon**, used HUAC to make a national name for himself by enthusiastically helping to expose the communist ties of **Alger Hiss**, a high-ranking State Department official. Hiss always denied he had been a spy until his death in 1996, but there was lots of cool evidence (like microfilm hidden in a hollowed out pumpkin) that sure made him look guilty.

Fearing Republican attacks would make his Administration look soft on communism, President Truman responded by instituting the Federal Loyalty Program. This unnecessary "Constitution-busting" legislation would over the next few years result in the firing of hundreds of officials and the resignation of more than 2000. The Attorney General announced a list of subversive organizations and encouraged FBI Director J. Edgar Hoover to have all the fun he wanted harassing them. Worst of all was Congress' **McCarran Internal Security Act,** which required all "subversive" organizations to register with the government and publicize their records. Truman sensibly vetoed this bill but again was overridden. All this nonsense ultimately revealed that communist-leaning groups in America were weak, disorganized, and in many cases in their death throes.

But nobody was thinking logically. Hoover reportedly clicked his high-heeled pumps every time the FBI charged a law-abiding citizen with communist sympathies.

As usual, an ambitious politician would come along and try to exploit the national mood for his own personal benefit. Hardly anyone outside Wisconsin had ever heard of first-term Republican Senator **Joseph McCarthy** until February, 1950, when during a speech in Wheeling, West Virginia he whipped out a sheet of paper and claimed he had a list of 205 communists working in the State Department. Over the next couple of years he attacked many government agencies and waved his ever-growing list of communists around, all the while never providing tangible proof of any of his charges. He always put the list back in his pocket and never showed it to anyone. According to one rumor, it was a bill for all the liquor he'd charged at his hotel.

Conservative Republicans in particular, and perhaps at one point even a majority of Americans, succumbed to his rhetoric and supported his antics. Chairing a Senate subcommittee, McCarthy had a forum from which to rant against any target he desired, eventually even including former Secretary of State George Marshall! For nearly four years, hardly anyone had the guts to stand up to this smarmy witch-hunting SOB, and a panicked nation turned inward on itself. Many schools and universities, state and local governments, labor unions, and plain old community organizations placed themselves on the lookout for "Reds." Sometimes, if they couldn't find any real commies, the unpopular or vulnerable (gays and minorities in particular) were targeted and framed. Many innocent lives were ruined. To illustrate what was going on in his present day America, playwright Arthur Miller wrote *The Crucible*, a drama (on one level) about the Salem witch trials. It was never censored because McCarthy and his ilk never figured out what the play was really about.

A NEW PRESIDENT FOR A NEW DECADE
or *We All Like Ike!*

In 1951, the Congress and three-fourths of the state legislatures approved **Amendment XXII** to the Constitution, to make sure no president could ever again serve more than two terms, and that filling in for a deceased president for more than two years counted as one term. President Truman was fine with that; he was exhausted and didn't want to run again anyway. The Democrats turned to Illinois Governor **Adlai Stevenson** — intellectual, eloquent, nuanced — exactly the kind of guy too many Americans tend to reject when they crave simple answers to complicated questions. The Republicans found an exact opposite to run for their side — former General Dwight David Eisenhower, who had been marking time in civilian life serving as president of Columbia University and playing lots of Scrabble (he insisted that "D" alone should count as a word). Called "Ike" by his friends, Eisenhower had always been nonpolitical and was so popular that both parties courted him, but he chose the dark side...uh...I mean the Republicans. To his credit, and unlike most modern Republicans, Ike was never hyper-partisan, didn't believe his party was always right, and he was respectful of the Democratic opposition.

During the campaign, Eisenhower came across as the reassuring nice guy while Stevenson seemed a bit of an egghead. To keep the extreme right-wing in his own party happy, Ike tossed them some red meat by choosing conservative California Senator Richard Nixon as his running mate. During the campaign, Nixon was accused of accepting illegal campaign gifts, but he saved his bacon by going on live television to declare in a self-pitying but effective performance that the only gift he ever accepted was for his daughters...a cocker spaniel named "Checkers." Lots of Americans felt nauseous (even Eisenhower drank a glass of Alka-Seltzer), but after the **"Checkers Speech"** he kept Nixon on the ticket. When Ike promised he would personally put an end to the Korean conflict, his political victory was assured. He creamed Stevenson in November, the Republicans took control of both Houses of Congress, and the GOP did a victory dance it had almost forgotten how to do since the twenties.

Peace talks in Korea had bogged down for two years; North Korea and South Korea found themselves relegated to the sidelines as two Cold Warriors, the United States and China, glared at each other across the line of scrimmage. China was especially embarrassed that thousands of its soldiers held prisoner by the U.S. did not want to return to their hovels in Mao's supposed communist paradise, and America refused to force them. Frustrated, Eisenhower let it be known through diplomatic channels that he might be willing to use the atom bomb to end the war (though despite what you may have heard, he never said, "Ask China if they feel lucky today").

In reality, China was sick of the war, and received signals from the Soviet Union to make peace. Stalin had finally croaked and the new Soviet leadership was anxious to improve ties with the West. Emerging from a scrum of vodka-soaked conspirators, former World War II general **Nikita Khrushchev** actually denounced the excesses of the Stalin era and appeared for a brief time like he might be just a big cuddly Russian bear. Unfortunately, this bear would soon turn out to have rabies. Anyway, the United States and China agreed to an armistice...a truce, not an official end to the war. The two Koreas were divided roughly at the 38th parallel, where the whole mess started in the first place (to this day, the demilitarized zone in between remains one of the tensest places in the world), but containment had worked. A communist invasion had been turned back, and we avoided World War III. The cost was high, though — over 54,000 Americans killed and 100,000 wounded in what is today sometimes called the "Forgotten War."

President Eisenhower could not stand Joseph McCarthy but did not personally attack him, confiding to his aides that he did not want to "get into the gutter with that guy." Remarkably, in late 1953, the Senator's subcommittee expanded its investigations to include the United States Army, making charges in hearings that were broadcast on live television. For thirty five days, millions of Americans watched a sweat-drenched McCarthy expose himself as a shameless witch hunter. When he faced off against the Army's lawyer, **Joseph Welch**, who was obviously a decent man, the television cameras made the contrast between the two palpable. A television news program called "See It Now," hosted by **Edward R. Murrow** (the kind of courageous anchorman we don't have anymore), also revealed McCarthy's cruel tactics. Collectively, most Americans realized, "Uh oh, we've really gone too far here." Almost overnight, McCarthy went from heroic communist fighter to embarrassing fanatic, and nobody wanted to admit they'd ever paid any attention to him. FOX News did not exist back then, so no network offered him a job as a commentator. Shunned by his Senate colleagues, and a pariah to all but the most wacky right-wingers, his heavy drinking rotted out his liver and he died about three years later.

A DECADE OF PROSPERITY
or *Let's Go To Disneyland!*

During the fifties, inflation and unemployment generally remained under control, and despite periodic mild recessions the American economy boomed. Many farmers, however, missed out. Innovations in fertilizer, seeds, and equipment improved their productivity so much that increased crop yields contributed to a drop in the price of their products. It's a recurring irony in American History: farmers produce more and their profits go down...so much for efficiency. But most everybody else went on a shopping spree, snapping up deals on automobiles, televisions, washers, dryers, dishwashers, record players, and annoying electric can openers that constantly broke when you were the most hungry. With the large-scale air conditioning of factories now practical, many traditional industries in the Northeast and Midwest pulled up stakes and headed for a "sunbelt" that spread from Florida to Southern California, offering cheaper land and a lower cost of living. A swath of Northern industrial towns left behind with abandoned factories are to this day called the "rustbelt." I'm sure the folks in Allentown, Pennsylvania, are pleased Billy Joel wrote a song about them, but you can bet they'd much rather have the jobs back.

Starting in 1946, couples who'd put off having children during the Depression and the war got busy in their bedrooms, producing a "baby boom" that lasted well into the sixties. **Dr. Benjamin Spock** wrote a bestselling child-rearing book emphasizing love and nurturing, which some conservative types still believe contributed to the hedonistic behavior many baby boomers have continually engaged in. They are wrong and deserve a "timeout." My parents used to spank me all the time, and I'm self-absorbed anyway. So there.

Population trends that were present before the war accelerated in the fifties. Besides the migration from the Northeast to the South and West, young families in particular moved from the cities to the suburbs. They wanted a less crowded neighborhood and a detached house with a backyard their 2.3 children could play in (I've always felt sorry for that pathetic .3 of a child). Dad could drive to work and Mom could drive to a "supermarket" grouped with other stores in newly constructed "shopping malls." For the first time thoughtless idiots could ram shopping carts into their neighbors' cars.

African-Americans — always disproportionately poor in America due to prejudice — found themselves left behind in the inner cities. Middle class whites fled beyond the city line ("white flight") and paid their taxes to their new suburban communities, leaving urban municipalities pinched for funds and straining to maintain services. Most large American cities (especially in the North and East) began a decades-long period of "urban decay." White suburbanites who drove into the city for a night of partying constantly glanced over their shoulders for fear of being mugged. Ignorant bigots blamed "those people": African Americans and the increasing numbers of Puerto Ricans fleeing the economic stagnation of their island to start a new life in the eastern big cities. But as usual in American History, poverty was the root of the problem, not race or ethnicity.

Automobiles became much fancier in the fifties, and models now came in two- and three-tone finishes with power steering, power brakes, air conditioning, and tail fins on the back. Lots of shallow guys believed the cooler the car they had, the more sensual they would appear to women. Lots of shallow women bought into that and preened frantically as guys "cruised" up and down Main Street, U.S.A. Americans now demanded improved roadways, and influenced government at all levels to cater to this car culture by building thousands of miles of new highways. So what if some old communities had to be bulldozed aside...so what if mass transportation in the cities had to be neglected...it was only "those people" riding the subways and buses anyway.

Congress passed, and President Eisenhower signed, the **National System of Defense Highways**, authorizing the federal government to provide ninety percent of an initial $50 billion outlay for forty thousand miles of additional roadway. How did the lawmakers justify the expense? Some said, "Walt Disney just opened a really cool theme park just south of Los Angeles that people need to get to fast, with diners and motels along the way." Others added, "Don't forget... all these new interstate highways will make it easier to evacuate the big cities in the event of a nuclear war with the Soviet Union." Yes, this was the fifties. Cars were the bomb, gas was cheap, and anyone could get their kicks on Route 66.

Lots of Americans had to find new jobs when they were supplanted by **automation**. After all, machines never ask for a raise or take a sick day, so many businesses loved them. Industries that had been around since the nineteenth century declined as ever resourceful Americans found even better ways to make a buck; mining, steel, railroad, and textile corporations became old news with the advent of plastic, chemical, aviation, drug, and electronics companies. Kmart, Walmart and Target discount department stores can all trace their roots to the fifties, ultimately making it possible (if you connect the dots) for all of us today to buy incredibly cheap bath towels made in Chinese sweat shops. The McDonald's Corporation started up in the fifties, demonstrating that Americans were happy to gulp down unhealthy food as long as it was served fast...with fries and a Coke to go. Despite some success organizing government workers, unions remained unpopular during the decade. The old "organized workers are really commies" idiocy lingered, and then real, organized labor connections to organized crime hit the papers. Mafia goons were drawn to the enormous sums in union pension funds like flies to...uh...like mice to cheese.

America experienced a religious revival in the fifties — a twentieth century Great Awakening. All the rapid change and uncertainty drew folks to the comfort of church, as did a deliberate response to the militant atheism of the Soviet Union. Karl Marx said God is dead — yeah, well, we'll show those Reds how to pray. President Eisenhower's first inaugural parade led off with a "Float to God" and a hyped-up Congress cast aside our founders' precious notion of "separation of church and state" to add "under God" to the Pledge of Allegiance and "In God We Trust" to our money. Note to insightful progressives: obviously our founders belief in freedom of religion also encompassed freedom from religion, but let the Pledge thing and the money thing go. They are relatively harmless and you've got to pick your battles. Try to look at "In God We Trust" and "Under God" episodes in the fifties as a quaint part of our History...kind of like hula hoops and yo-yos.

After World War II, societal leaders and the media emphasized traditional gender roles; women were expected to get married, have children, and subordinate their own needs to the needs of their family. Dinner needed to be ready when the husband — the sole breadwinner — returned home from work. No wonder so many women who felt trapped in their roles as wives and mothers devoured newly-available tranquilizers by the handful. On the television shows of the period, female characters were shown cleaning the house dressed in a skirt and high heels. Absurd — who vacuums in high heeled pumps? I do...but it's none of your business what I do on weekends.

In 1953, Dr. **Alfred C. Kinsey** published his scientific study entitled *Sexual Behavior in the Human Female* to complement his earlier study on men. As it turned out, both men and women were enjoying a wide variety of sexual acts before marriage, and basically being private about it. Uptight people refused to believe the findings, though some of them read the report over and over again late at night. Homosexuals continued to face discrimination from the general public; lots of idiotic "homophobes" refused to drink milk until it was explained to them that the word "homogenized" on the bottle did not mean drinking milk would make them gay. **Hugh Hefner** launched *Playboy* magazine in December 1953, making him in my mind one of the greatest Americans of all time. The magazine immediately became wildly popular among millions of men who wanted to fantasize about sex without any responsibilities. I myself found the fold out "centerfolds" really hot, though the staples across the model's stomach could be a turnoff.

Popular music in the early fifties was mostly boring and unchallenging. Think about it...you rarely hear a disc jockey say something like, "Here's another great tune from 1951." But a change was in the air(waves). African American and white musicians, particularly in the South, heard each other's jazz, folk, country, blues, and gospel music on records and on the radio, and their sounds began to intermingle. African American "race music" powerfully vibrated and intrigued whites, who named it rhythm and blues, or R&B. In 1952, Cleveland disc jockey **Alan Freed** started calling the new music "rock 'n' roll" which for decades had been slang for sex. As an ever-increasing audience of white teenagers became enthralled with the black music, record companies scrambled to find a white performer who could deliver and sell the black sound. Thus arose **Elvis Presley**, whose slicked back hair, swiveling hips and provocative snarl captivated young people and panicked parents. Other artists — white and black — followed, and music has never been the same since. Elvis, of course, is still alive.

Even though on the surface the fifties appeared to be a decade of family values, prosperity, and wholesome fun, there were critics who saw through the facade. A small group of writers challenged the mindless conformity and outraged mainstream society by scorning the Cold War, materialism, Christianity, the nuclear family, and even those ugly skinny ties men always seemed to be wearing. **The Beats** — their followers became known as beatniks — wore black turtlenecks, sprouted goatees, and sipped cappuccino in Greenwich Village cafes in a foreshadowing of the social upheaval soon to follow in the sixties. Famous Beat novelist **Jack Kerouac** wrote *On the Road*, chronicling a cross-country hitchhiking odyssey wherein he meets all kinds of weirdos along the way. It's a terrific book, but when I travel I still prefer to make reservations.

In September, 1955, President Eisenhower, a smoker, suffered a serious heart attack. He resumed work about a week later, but everyone wondered whether he would run again. Then the following June he got hit with a nasty attack of ileitis, a colon disorder that required surgery. But his recovery was swift and he announced he would seek a second term. The Democrats nominated Adlai Stevenson again, and the perceptive guy made some very valid points about ending open-air testing of the hydrogen bomb, suspending the draft, the lack of a national health insurance program, and the federal government's refusal to help fund public education. But the public still loved the comforting style of the grandfatherly general-turned-president, and Eisenhower creamed Stevenson by an even greater margin than in '52. The public, however, liked Ike much more than his party, and the Democrats actually strengthened their hold on the Senate and the House. Meanwhile, many GOP conservatives did not think he was conservative enough, and constantly followed him around begging him to cut domestic spending, increase defense spending, and make everyone in the nation wear buttons saying, "God Loves Republicans Best!"

Eisenhower infuriated the right wing of his own Republican party because he was a moderate at heart. He had no real desire to expand the New Deal, but he did not want to roll back the reforms already in place. He did not believe the Republicans were "good" and the Democrats "bad" like so many of today's political simpletons in both parties. He respected the opposition and cooperated well with a Congress controlled by Democrats for six of the eight years he was in office. An examination of his foreign policy will reveal he was a moderate in that realm as well. He believed communism needed to be contained, but he loathed the prospect of an all-out war. He was — and this is a well deserved compliment — a general who had seen enough of war and hated it.

PRESIDENT EISENHOWER'S FOREIGN POLICY
or *You Can Destroy Us But We Can Destroy You, So What's the Point?*

John Foster Dulles, President Eisenhower's Secretary of State, viewed the Cold War in stark terms: a great moral battle between good and evil, God and the Devil, Superman and Lex Luthor. Luckily, the much more level-headed Ike kept him on a short leash. Dulles wanted to save money, so he orchestrated cutbacks on America's costly conventional forces and emphasized nuclear weapons for defense. By 1953, both the United States and the Soviet Union had developed the much more powerful hydrogen bomb, and consequently found themselves in an escalating nuclear arms race. Dulles called his policy the "doctrine of massive retaliation." The newspapers dubbed it, "More Bang for the Buck!" Both nation could obliterate each other, and if either side attacked, the whole planet would be irradiated toast. This was called a "balance of power" — we still live under this arrangement today — and it is so scary that most of us delude ourselves into believing we'll be safe in the basement with some bottled water and ninety-seven cans of tuna.

In 1954-55 and again in 1958, Red China threatened to attack Quemoy and Matsu, a comedy team on Taiwan infamous for doing bad impressions of Dean Martin and Jerry Lewis. Just kidding. Quemoy and Matsu were two islands off the Chinese coast from which the Nationalists had been launching commando raids against the mainland. When China began shelling the islands, the United States threatened nuclear retaliation. To save face, the Red Chinese seized a couple of smaller islands instead and the crisis abated, but it became clear that American nuclear "brinksmanship" was not appropriate for every small "brushfire" conflict that might erupt around the world. Furthermore, by the close of the fifties, nuclear bombs and missiles had proven to be every bit as expensive as conventional forces. Thus, the American buildup of nuclear stockpiles that the Soviets scrambled to keep up with turned out to be a costly blunder for both sides. The decade ended with the U.S. and the Russians armed to the teeth with nukes and glaring at each other, daring the other side to "go ahead, make my day."

During World War II, Japan had siezed control of Indochina — a region of Southeast Asia including Vietnam, Laos, and Cambodia — from France. After the war, France reclaimed her colonies, but a group of Vietnamese nationalists, led by **Ho Chi Minh**, declared their independence. These guys were also communists, which caused the U.S. great concern. According to the newly popular **domino theory**, once Vietnam fell to communism, so would Cambodia, Laos, Thailand, and then New Jersey.

France tried to crush the nationalists (known as Vietminh), and the United States volunteered to pay for about eighty percent of the war. But Ho Chi Minh's indigenous forces bedeviled the French army, and in the spring of 1954, 20,000 French forces found themselves surrounded near the town of **Dien Bien Phu**, in the hills of northwest Vietnam. Dulles wanted to send U.S. air support and parachute in ground forces to help, but President Eisenhower overruled him and (reportedly) asked his Secretary of State to look up the word quagmire in the dictionary. After a nearly two-month siege, the French army at Dien Bien Phu surrendered — something they were very good at. One French general reportedly cried "Dien Bien Phooey!"

The Soviet Union, France, Britain, and China got together at a conference in Geneva, Switzerland, to sort everything out (the Swiss, being officially neutral, love to host peace conferences because their hotels and restaurants get a real boost). Even though we were not directly involved, the United States sent "observers" to constantly butt in and remind everyone who was really the "big cheese" in the world. Laos, Cambodia, and Vietnam gained their independence, and Vietnam was divided at the 17th parallel to "temporarily" create a North Vietnam, led by communist Ho Chi Minh, and a South Vietnam under a pro-western dictator, Ngo Dinh Diem.

All nations agreed that an election would be held in one year to unify the country. But when it became clear the popular Ho Chi Minh was going to win, the United States — fearing the loss of all of Vietnam to communism (and a cascade of dominos) — urged the South not to participate in the voting. Diem happily complied and held on to power, and Vietnam was not unified. The United States started sending money to prop up the anticommunist South Vietnamese government, and the Vietminh (with clandestine support from China and the Soviet Union) began plotting to take over the South. Switzerland announced, "Hey, any time you folks want to hold another conference, we'll give you a discount."

In 1955, the United States and the Soviet Union again rented lots of hotel rooms in Geneva...easy to do because everyone knew the front desk clerks by their first names. President Eisenhower wanted to ease Cold War tensions, and Nikita Khrushchev, the big brute of a man who had finally emerged as the Russian leader after Stalin's death two years earlier, seemed to be on the same page. Khrushchev would soon dare to admit to his own people that perhaps Stalin's murder of millions of Soviet citizens had been a bit excessive. Rumors that Ike and Nikita strolled hand in hand along the Rhône River were of course absurd — both men we already married — and even though nothing concrete came out of the meeting, folks around the world allowed themselves to hope an international thaw was in the wind.

No soap. Lesson in history: when dictators loosen up even a little, the oppressed crave even more. In June of 1956, Polish patriots demanded more autonomy, and Khrushchev granted it while still making sure to maintain ultimate military control over the puppet nation. Inspired, Hungarian nationalists denounced Soviet rule the following fall and demanded independence. Not willing to offer concessions and appear weak, Nikita sent Soviet tanks rolling into Budapest, crushed the rebellion like a gnat, thereby sending a message to the rest of "his" Eastern Europe not to get any more ideas. The United States denounced the Soviet use of force against the Hungarians but did not want to risk going to war. The more restrained President Eisenhower reportedly had to say, "Down Boy!" and keep Secretary of State Dulles tethered to his leash.

Meanwhile, trouble was brewing in the Middle East. The flashpoint was Egypt and its ambitious President, **Gamal Abdel Nasser**, who wanted to make himself a "Pan-

Arab" leader of the entire region. To win over the public, he planned to build the Aswan Dam (a huge project that would increase the amount of arable land in Egypt by one-third). Unfortunately, Egypt didn't have the money for such a huge project, so he negotiated a loan with the United States. But then he checked with the Soviets to see if he could get a better loan deal from them, and at the same time offered diplomatic recognition to Mao's China. Secretary Dulles lost his temper and said, in effect, "To hell with you, build your own damn dam." Infuriated, Nasser gave a big speech in which he railed against western influence in the Arab world and announced that Egypt would immediately nationalize (seize control of) the Suez Canal from the French-British company that owned it. Canal revenue would then pay for Aswan's construction. The public cheered, and Arabs across the region were galvanized — but so were Britain and France, who immediately started scheming to get their canal back. After all, it connected the Mediterranean Sea to the Red Sea, and was critical for the shipment of Middle Eastern oil to Europe.

Both Britain and France desperately wanted to maintain their influence in the Middle East, and they enlisted the aid of an opportunistic Israel, which welcomed the chance to strengthen its southern border and weaken its hostile neighbor, Egypt. In late October, 1956, Israel attacked Egypt and occupied the Sinai Peninsula. Simultaneously, Britain and France launched their own offensive and took back the canal. The United States had been kept out of the loop, and to the surprise of the British and the French, Eisenhower and Dulles were furious. The United States had been trying to walk a middle course in the region — supporting Israel and simultaneously cultivating various Arab States — so this sudden military maneuver, from the American point of view, did nothing but gum up the works. The Soviet Union — constantly sucking up to the oil-rich Arabs — also condemned the fighting. On this rare occasion, both sides agreed, and were opposed to the British/French/Israeli offensive, which they found...well...offensive.

The U.S. sponsored a U.N. resolution calling for a cease fire and withdrawal, and the Soviets made noises about sending in troops to help Egypt. Under intense pressure, Britain and France pulled out of the Suez Canal, their humiliation complete. The Israelis fortified their border with Egypt (from which Nasser had been launching attacks), withdrew from the Sinai, and — pleased with the opportunity to demonstrate their tenacity to the Arab world — likely considered the whole exercise worthwhile. Nasser became a nationalist hero in much of the Arab world, started acting real cool by wearing sunglasses all the time, and strutted about like he was going to be the next Saladin (you remember...Saladin was the Muslim leader who sent the Crusaders packing back in the Middle Ages, before sunglasses had been invented).

Eisenhower, concerned about the threat of increasing Soviet influence in the Middle East, swiftly announced a policy that soon became known as the **Eisenhower Doctrine**; declaring the United States would use armed force to come to the aid of any nation in the region threatened by the demons of international communism. He showed his resolve in 1958, when a revolt threatened to topple the pro-western regime in Lebanon. Ike sent in 5000 Marines, though the regime managed on its own, and by the time they landed the conflict had died down. Sunbathers on the beaches of Lebanon complained loudly about all the men and tanks storming ashore kicking up sand and blocking the sun. There were even reports that U.S. troops confiscated all the beach umbrellas to keep them out of the hands of the commies.

America's southern neighbors continued to complain the United States had been ignoring them in favor of Europe and Asia. Latin Americans had welcomed the Good Neighbor policy (continued by Presidents Roosevelt and Truman) and lined up like ducks behind the United States during World War II (Argentina had briefly been an ugly duckling and tilted toward the Axis, but that all changed when it became clear Germany was going to lose and Eva Peron started singing "Don't Cry For Me, Argentina" from her balcony every night). By the fifties, Latin Americans were loudly clamoring for the economic support they had been led to believe would be coming their way after the war. But all the United States government really cared about was keeping communism out the region, so what aid the U.S. sent tended to be military aid, aimed at strengthening right-wing dictators in power who in return pledged to resist communism. The masses of Latin America received virtually no assistance and remained mostly landless and poor. Little wonder they hated their dictators, and the United States for supporting them. Americans today who cluelessly say things like, "Why do they hate us?" would do well to study this bit of History.

In 1950, the U.S. had joined with the other nations of the Western Hemisphere to create the **Organization of American States** (OAS) so they could come together in an emergency to maintain peace and security in the neighborhood. The U.S., of course, successfully pressured the OAS to be staunchly anti-communist. In 1951, Guatemala had the temerity to legally elect a left-of-center government that took steps to implement land reform — the expropriation of privately owned land for redistribution to the impoverished and landless. Much of the land slated to be seized belonged to America's United Fruit Company, which made a fortune growing and then importing bananas. High-ranking members of the Eisenhower Administration were shareholders in United Fruit and loved bananas on their Rice Krispies in the morning, so they made exaggerated claims that the Guatemalan reformers were bent on bringing Soviet-style communism to Latin America. President Eisenhower bought into it, and authorized the Central Intelligence Agency (CIA) to stage a coup d' tat — an overthrow of the government.

Eisenhower embraced America's new spy agency because covert operations were much cheaper than sending in troops to depose communist leaders, and U.S. involvement could (hopefully) be kept a secret. The CIA did it's job efficiently in Guatemala; in the summer of 1953 a right-wing Guatemalan general was recruited to become dictator, and about one thousand handpicked (and paid and armed) "freedom fighters" bullied and bluffed their way to power. Most Guatemalans hated the new *caudillo* (military strongman) who subsequently canceled land reform and instituted repressive rule, but he was America's "bought and paid for boy" who could be counted on to keep communism out of Guatemala and allow American-owned companies like United Fruit to do pretty much as they pleased. Hardly anyone believed the coup had just happened "naturally" with no U.S. involvement...especially when the CIA started handing out free bananas to all its employees.

In 1958, Vice President Nixon embarked on a "goodwill" visit to several Latin American nations. The dictators tried to welcome him but the masses turned out to heckle, spit, protest and, well, kill him if they could get close enough. In Caracas, Venezuela, crowds surrounded the American embassy where Nixon was staying, and the President was concerned enough to put army units on alert in case they needed to rescue the "veep" and get him out of Latin America in one piece. Nixon managed to escape without the army — though his secret service detail was sorely taxed — and Americans began to realize our relations with Latin America were severely out of balance (rumors that Nixon made a secret exit dressed in drag as "Carmen Miranda" were false). Luckily, American travel agents insisted there was no need to postpone beach vacations down there, so everyone relaxed. But the Eisenhower Administration took note, and cooperated in the formation of the Inter-American Development Bank, with $500 million appropriated to improve living conditions in Latin America. As it would turn out, however, these belated efforts would be way too little way too late.

In January, 1959, Cuban rebels led by **Fidel Castro** overthrew the right-wing anti-communist government of dictator **Fulgencio Batista**, another one of America's "boys" in Latin America. At first, Americans hoped Castro might actually be a good guy who would set up a democracy, and President Eisenhower even offered diplomatic recognition to the new government. But once again, no soap. Castro proceeded to expropriate large Cuban- and foreign-owned plantations and businesses, curb civil liberties, jail opponents, and close the hotels and casinos that had helped make Havana a real "sin city" before Las Vegas even existed. When Castro signed a trade deal with the Soviets, the U.S. placed an embargo on Cuba, and the beautiful island just ninety miles from Florida swung closely into a Russian orbit. Luckily, the Corleone family didn't invest in cuban casinos...but let's not confuse a classic movie with reality.

Nobody in America was happy with any of this, especially the Mafia, which lost its entire take of the gambling action it used to control in Havana. Many wealthy Cubans fled to Florida, where they remain to this day, united in their obsessive hatred of Castro and the communist government of Cuba, yet refusing to admit that as repressive as the left-wing Castro became, the right-wing dirtbag he overthrew was probably worse. Cubans fleeing the poverty and repression of their island nowadays are generally detained by the Coast Guard and sent back...unless the Yankees need them to pitch.

In October, 1957, the Soviets launched **Sputnik** — the first artificial satellite to orbit the earth — and gave all Americans a shock. Sputnik was certainly no threat, just a basketball-sized hunk of metal going round and round, but it appeared the Russians were ahead in the realm of space exploration. A month later, the Soviets launched a dog into space, which caused animal lovers in the U.S. to gasp when they found out there were no plans to bring the pooch back. During the Cold War, the idea that "Ivan" would be superior to "Uncle Sam" in anything except vodka production was unthinkable, and a cause for panic. How could such a thing have happened? Some hyper-patriots blamed everything on our schools: supposedly Russian students were studying hard while all our kids were doing was reading *Mad Magazine* and lusting over girls. That description fits me perfectly, but it certainly not everyone.

Congress reacted by passing the **National Defense Education Act**, which provided $280 million for the states to spend specifically on the teaching of math, science, and engineering. The humanities and social sciences were neglected — but what help would historians and writers be if there was a future war in outer space? Under pressure, Eisenhower ordered the launching of an American satellite as soon as possible. This effort was a bit rushed, and the first civilian Vanguard rocket blew up on the launchpad on live television. Lots of kids exclaimed, "Cool!" but most grownups were not amused and dubbed the entire debacle "Flopnik." Several months later a military rocket successfully launched an American satellite into orbit, and the "Space Race" officially commenced. Ike successfully urged Congress to create the **National Aeronautics and Space Administration** (NASA), a civilian agency which would direct a U.S. space program tasked with bettering their Soviet counterparts.

Soviet Premier Nikita Khrushchev continued to be unpredictable. In late 1958, he demanded that the United States, Britain and France remove their forces from West Berlin. U.S. aid and capitalism had turned West Berlin's postwar recovery into a rousing success, while on the other side of the barbed wire, East Berlin remained sullen and economically deprived. Since the city had been divided, over three million East Germans had fled their black-and-white world for the technicolor of the West, and for Stalin that was just plain embarrassing.

Ike refused to abandon West Berlin, and the whole situation remained a real sticking point. But when Khrushchev traveled to the U.S. for another summit meeting in June of the following year, he and Ike got along quite well. The two strolled about Camp David (the presidential retreat in the mountains of Maryland named for the President's brother) and agreed that they should try to settle disagreements peacefully, rather than destroy the world. The Secret Service would not allow a disappointed Khrushchev to visit Disneyland (apparently they feared a would-be assassin might disguise himself as Goofy), but other than that, the visit went swimmingly. The world applauded the "Spirit of Camp David" and the two leaders agreed to meet again in May, 1960 to address a mutual ban on above-ground nuclear testing.

Plenty of suspicions remained, though, and as the date for the next summit in Paris approached, Eisenhower wanted to know exactly what cards the Soviet dictator was holding. At that time, the U.S. relied on **U-2** spy planes, which could take photographs at altitudes over 80,000 feet — a height at which, the CIA assured the President, Soviet missiles could not shoot them down. A number of flights were successful, but on the eve of the summit, Eisenhower decided on one more — a pivotal, fateful decision. This time, the Russian missile hit its target, and the plane fell out of the sky (reportedly, Ike had to be restrained from striking one C.I.A. official who called it a "lucky shot").

Our crack "intelligence" agency then assured Eisenhower there was no way the wreckage could be identified, and no way the pilot could have survived, so the President went on television and (presumably with his fingers and toes crossed) announced to the world that an American weather balloon had strayed off course. The Soviets, however, identified the wreckage and captured the pilot, **Francis Gary Powers** — alive. Eisenhower's deception was exposed (in his memoirs, Ike admitted he was never more depressed while serving in office), and when he arrived in Paris for the summit, Khrushchev displayed wreckage photos and demanded a public apology. The President, naturally, refused. The meeting broke up before it began and the Cold War suddenly seemed more frigid than ever. It was reported that as Khrushchev was boarding his flight back to Moscow, he murmured "...and I hope Disneyland catches on fire."

Before he left office, The President delivered **Eisenhower's Farewell Address**. Delivering another president's farewell address would have made no sense. In his speech, he said, "Farewell!" and that was that. No, actually there was much more to it. Pulling no punches, Ike told the nation to beware of the threat of the "military industrial complex." Everyone's first reaction was, What is that...another communist nation? But Eisenhower was referring to an alliance between the military and industrial corporations that conspired to appropriate an outsized amount of America's wealth by wielding a disproportionate amount of political influence. He did not name any names, and though most agreed his admonition made good sense, there was no consensus on what to do about it. To this day, Ike's insight has been shown to be right on the money time after time, as defense contractors continue to grab much more than their fair share of the American pie. Like Halliburton...there, I named a name.

The fifties had been pretty good for the white wealthy and middle class in the United States. But an important book — **The Other America** by Michael Harrington — revealed that at some point, thirty percent of all Americans had lived in poverty. For African Americans, Hispanics, and the elderly, the situation was even worse. Poverty had different faces — from the slums of New York City to the mountains of West Virginia — but wherever they were, those visages often portrayed hopelessness, disease, and even hunger. For these disadvantaged folks, the Cold War seemed far away and irrelevant.

Most Americans back then averted their eyes from unpleasant sights, and to this day they remember the fifties fondly...a family-friendly time watching Lucy and Desi on TV, hula hoops, roller skates, coonskin caps, movie stars like Marlon Brando and James Dean, parking at the drive-in, dances at the church, really cherry cars and new fangled rock 'n' roll on the radio. Toward the end of the decade you could travel on a jet, and in 1959 the new states of Alaska and Hawaii joined "the lower forty-eight." On the Mickey Mouse Club television show, Annette Funicello began as a child star and, well, blossomed. Will the sixties bring more of the same? Will young people toe the line? Uh oh... Stay tuned... don't touch that dial!!!!

This Really Happened!

Frenchman Henri Matisse is identified with a group of avant-garde artists called the fauves, or "the wild beasts," who are among the first painters to use color for its own sake rather than as a means to render reality accurately. Throughout his long life Matisse paints with stunning pigments unrelated to the real colors of the subject, believing that art is more significant as the expression of emotion rather than the representation of facts. He dies in 1954, recognized as a master of modern art. Six years later, Americans demonstrate how sophisticated they are when his picture Le Batteau is exhibited for forty-six days at the Museum of Modern Art in New York City. Over one hundred thousand people pass in front of it and admire it, but not a single one of them reports the painting is hung upside down.

And the rest is History...

Quiz yourself on Chapter 13

Multiple Choice (circle the correct answer).

1. After World War II
    a. the U.S. agreed to join the United Nations as long as it was not called the League of Nations
    b. the Allies occupied the western part of Germany
    c. the Soviet Union occupied the eastern part of Germany
    d. the U.S. and the Soviet Union emerged as the world's two superpowers
    e. b, c and d

2. The U.S. policy of containment
    a. was originally articulated by diplomat George F. Kennan
    b. declared that all the Soviets understood was power and force
    c. led to an arms race between the Soviet Union and Portugal
    d. led to an arms race between the U.S. and the Soviet Union
    e. a, b and d

3. The Truman Doctrine
    a. made General Eisenhower jealous
    b. consisted of American financial aid to help Greece and Turkey avoid communist takeovers
    c. actually worked really well
    d. demonstrated American determination to halt the spread of communism
    e. all of the above

4. The Marshall Plan
    a. was named after George Kennan
    b. aimed to land a man on the moon within ten years
    c. really helped East Germany
    d. had a primary purpose to stop the spread of communism that dovetailed perfectly with a humanitarian effort to rebuild shattered lives
    e. none of the above

5. NATO
    a. stood for North Atlantic Treaty Organization
    b. members agreed "an armed attack against one or more of them shall be considered an attack against them all."
    c. included the Soviet Union
    d. kicked out Italy after it ordered a hit on Spain
    e. a and b

6. China's decades-old civil war
    a. was won in 1949 by communist forces under the command of Mao Zedong
    b. was won in 1949 by nationalist forces under the command of Chiang Kai-shck
    c. was won in 1865 by Union forces under the command of Ulysses S. Grant
    d. gave ownership of Taiwan to the communists
    e. none of the above

7. President Eisenhower
    a. threatened to use nuclear weapons to end the Korean War
    b. offered to trade Vice-President Nixon for American POWs
    c. offered to give General MacArthur back his command
    d. eventually agreed to a cease fire right about where it all started
    e. a and d

8. The Servicemen's Readjustment Act (1944) better known as the GI Bill
    a. offered tuition grants and low-interest mortgage loans to returning veterans who attended college and bought homes
    b. contributed much back to the country
    c. remains one of the most successful examples of progressive legislation ever
    d. proves the federal government can get some things right
    e. all of the above

9. The Second Red Scare after World War II
    a. proved Americans had not learned much since the First Red Scare
    b. brought notoriety to Wisconsin Senator Joseph McCarthy
    c. turned Americans inward against each other
    d. was used by politicians for selfish purposes
    e. all of the above

10. In both foreign policy and domestic policy, President Eisenhower
    a. rarely paid attention
    b. asked Fidel Castro for advice
    c. backed down to Soviet Premier Nikita Khruschev
    d. was basically a moderate
    e. none of the above

CHAPTER 14

NEW CHALLENGES FOR A CHANGING AMERICA

or

Cut Your Hair And Turn Down That Music

For most Americans, the fifties ended with the American Dream very much in their grasp. But change was in the wind, along with a lot of incense that could be really annoying if you were allergic. Many young people began to view the world much differently from their parents and "the authorities." The first birth control pill went on the market in 1960, a portent of greater empowerment for women. "Baby Boomers" with time and their parents' money began to experiment with life and love and sought out new ways to have fun. More than ever before, marginalized folks of all types started to stand up and declare, "I am who I am and I'm proud." But this was the sixties, so often their next words were, "Come on let's party!"

A NEW PRESIDENT BUT THE SAME OLD COLD WAR
or *I Swear the President Just Winked At Me!*

As the sixties approached, President Eisenhower appeared a bit tired and detached. He had allowed himself to be photographed playing way too much golf, and in late 1957 he suffered a mild stroke that caused him to slur his words even though his mental faculties remained intact (the upside was that he could substantially increase his alcohol intake without anyone noticing). As far as Eisenhower and the nation were concerned, the presidential election of 1960 arrived none too soon.

Vice-President Nixon won all the GOP primaries unopposed, so the Republicans had their man. The Democrats held a scrappy convention in Los Angeles and a surprise candidate emerged: Senator **John Fitzgerald Kennedy** (JFK) of Massachusetts...only forty-three, handsome, Irish Catholic, and an inveterate skirt chaser even though he had married the glamorous Jacqueline Lee Bouvier. JFK grew up the second son in a large and wealthy family headed by its patriarch, Joseph Kennedy. Joe had made a fortune in the liquor importing business, definitely engaged in some illegal shenanigans during Prohibition, and eventually used his connections to get appointed Ambassador to the Court of St. James (Great Britain) before World War II. His pro-German sympathies to this day remain a family embarrassment, and reportedly, all the photographs of him in his underwear wearing a Nazi helmet have been destroyed. His life-long dream to get one of his sons elected president would be fulfilled by John: Harvard graduate, dashing naval hero wounded in World War II, congressman and then senator with as much testosterone as a bull elephant. Lots of whiskey-soaked Kennedy money, sometimes strategically placed under the table, continually propelled young JFK towards the finish line.

John Kennedy represented himself as a member of a new generation that would bring energy and change to Washington. Jack, as his friends called him, was a liberal on domestic issues and a proud Cold Warrior like any American back then who ventured outside during daylight. Throughout the campaign, he and Nixon sparred over who would be tougher on the Soviets and nicer to the elderly. Nixon, as Vice-President, was better known and thus possessed an early advantage, but all that changed when the two candidates agreed to meet in America's first televised national debates. Kennedy grasped television's vast new power and influence. Nixon did not. JFK prepped and got plenty of rest right beforehand, hired a Hollywood make-up artist, and looked plenty spiffy in a perfectly tailored suit. Nixon, campaigning nonstop, was tired, rumpled, sweated a lot, sprouted a five o'clock shadow, and resembled a lot of guys in their mug shots after they've been arrested for drunk driving. Both candidates held their own on the substantive issues, but Kennedy looked more "presidential" and many Americans began to get comfortable with the idea of this attractive young senator moving into the White House. A poll of folks who listened to the debates on the radio believed Nixon had prevailed, but radio was old news, so the gleaming white knight from Cape Cod won the joust.

The Roman Catholic Kennedy assured everyone he would follow the Constitution first before the Pope. Despite continuing prejudice from conservatives, America had become much more accepting of Catholics since 1928 when Al Smith had been nailed to a Protestant cross. JFK won in November but it was super close: 34,226,731 to 34,108,157 and 303 to 219 in the electoral college. Commendably, Nixon patriotically accepted defeat and did not launch divisive legal challenges. President Kennedy's inaugural address proved memorable; it was frigid outside, he wore no overcoat just to prove how tough he was, and he uttered the famous words, "Ask not what your country can do for you — ask what you can do for your country." Americans who worried he wanted to cut their Social Security benefits completely missed the point. Kennedy's ad-libbed final remark — "Let's get the hell inside, I'm freezing" — luckily was not picked up by any of the microphones.

Even though his election had been by the thinnest of margins, President Kennedy wanted to do big things. Like Roosevelt with his "Brain Trust"; JFK surrounded himself with snooty Ivy League advisors who became known as the "Best and the Brightest." No community college faculty — much more in touch with mainstream America — were included, and that would later prove to be the President's loss. Yes, I am biased on this.

President Kennedy, a liberal Democrat in the mold of FDR, wanted to expand the New Deal and in effect "out Roosevelt" Roosevelt. He called his program the **New Frontier**, and though it did achieve modernization of some existing social programs, additional progressive legislation pending in Congress remained blocked by conservative Republicans and southern Democrats. Kennedy wanted government health insurance for the elderly and the poor, federal funding for education, economic aid to rural regions, government intervention to halt a stubborn recession, and federal civil rights legislation. Meanwhile, conservatives worried that increased greens fees at private golf courses could constitute a threat to national security.

Another one of the new frontiers Kennedy wanted to tackle was outer space. Perhaps he fantasized that extraterrestrial chicks could be really hot. In a national address, the President proclaimed America was capable of "landing a man on the moon <u>and returning</u> him safely to the earth" before the decade was out. This was a direct challenge to the Soviet Union, and an indirect tribute to the Russian space dog who was currently a frozen ball of fur hurtling through the Milky Way. NASA officials — with dollar signs racing toward them like a meteor shower — launched themselves into the task. Soon "Gemini" capsules were orbiting the earth, followed by an "Apollo" program aiming to prove once and for all that the moon was not made out of green cheese.

One of the best things Kennedy ever did was create the **Peace Corps**: selfless volunteers who brought American technical know-how to the Third World and in so doing improved both living standards and international understanding. The Peace Corps still exists today, remains an American gem, and many returning volunteers admit they got more than they gave. We should give them a lot of credit because overseas they sometimes had to eat weird food that was still moving.

Kennedy also inherited the tense situation with Castro in Cuba, and understood that much of Latin America remained a powder keg, with impoverished masses resenting their pro-American dictators. To try to soothe some of the anger, he proposed a program called the **Alliance for Progress** in which nations in the region would receive $80 billion in economic aid...kind of like a Marshall Plan for Latin America. Once again, American officials hoped humanitarian assistance would dovetail with not-so-subtle push-back against communism, but the Alliance flopped. Latin American economies could not be revived the way the Western European economies had been; they needed to be rebuilt from scratch, diversified, and weaned off of dependence on single "monocrops" and the dominance of foreign corporations. Land reform was needed, and democracy reinvigorated through real elections, but the dictators and their oligarchic minions remained determined not to let that happen. Thus the Alliance lost its focus; there was massive corruption, most of the money ended up as military aid that strengthened the dictators against their own people, and the vast majority of the people in Latin America continued to hate our guts. Despite this, lots of Americans remained oblivious and continued to book vacations down there to take advantage of the great snorkeling.

Bearded revolutionary Fidel Castro continued to consolidate his authority in Cuba and make it very cool to wear green army fatigues, smoke Cuban cigars and lust after sultry Latinas. Conditions did improve — particularly in health care and education — so he was popular with most Cubans, who had known nothing but misery under Batista. Cubans had also never known democracy and Fidel never had any intention of bringing it to them. President Kennedy also lusted after sultry Latinas, particularly when the First Lady was out of town, but he hated the communist Castro and agreed with most Americans who thought the Cubans had traded a dirtbag right-wing dictator for a dirtbag left-wing dictator. Well-off Cubans who had thrived under the old regime lost their homes and businesses, fled for their lives, and ended up in South Florida, where they continued to eat their pork sandwiches and snarl at the mere mention of Castro's name.

President Kennedy's eyes lit up when CIA officials informed him that Eisenhower had authorized planning for a covert military operation to remove Castro. The plan was finished and in place and all they needed was a presidential thumbs-up. They implied success was a sure thing, though it is unclear whether they used the words, "slam dunk." No U.S. forces would be directly involved, and it would appear to the world that patriotic Cubans had materialized on the island to bring the people freedom and democracy. Kennedy enthusiastically gave the go ahead, while none of his advisors possessed the fortitude to suggest to the ginned-up chief executive that it might be a good idea to take a breath and reconsider.

Virtually everything went wrong in the **Bay of Pigs Invasion**. Castro learned they were coming and had his army ready. Secretly trained and equipped by the CIA, the Cuban "freedom fighters" got pinned down on the beach and about 1200 out of 1500 soon surrendered. The President declined to order American air support, hoping U.S. involvement could be kept hidden. The Cuban people — predicted to rise up and support this "spontaneous" invasion — did not because Castro was popular. The U.S. role soon leaked out, and our country was condemned as "invaders" even by countries that were supposedly our friends. The Soviets chortled to the world, "We told you so!" President Kennedy took personal responsibility for the debacle in a nationally televised address, but he confided to close associates that he thought the CIA was out of control and he wouldn't mind cutting the "intelligence" agency down to size. Significantly, he took CIA Director Allen Dulles off his Christmas card list. Even more significantly, the Soviets resumed above-ground nuclear tests, the United States responded likewise, and the nuclear arms race ratcheted up.

JFK soon grasped that events around the world could not always be easily manipulated. In June 1961, he traveled to Vienna, Austria, to meet with Khrushchev, who thought he could bully the young president. The Soviets were embarrassed that free passage from East Berlin into West Berlin was allowing thousands of East Germans to escape to the West. Nikita issued an ultimatum that the Americans, British, and French had to pull their troops out of West Berlin within six months. President Kennedy said "No way!" with confidence, perhaps bolstered by his success in seducing the most beautiful woman in the world...Marilyn Monroe. He returned to Congress and requested a large increase in defense spending.

The Soviets started building the **Berlin Wall**: a barbed wire and concrete barrier replete with guards and searchlights intended to keep the East Germans entombed in their Marxist-Leninist hell. The West condemned the wall, but it actually diffused the crisis and Khrushchev softened his demands. A couple of years later Kennedy traveled to West Berlin and before a huge cheering crowd dramatically declared, *"Ich bin ein Berliner"*— "I am a Berliner." His Boston accent caused him to slightly mispronounce his German, so some thought he said, "I am a jelly doughnut." But everyone knew what he meant...the United States would not abandon West Berlin.

President Kennedy next asked the C.I.A. to secretly assassinate Castro. In a comedy of errors known as Operation Mongoose, agents with all the competence of Austin Powers tried to spear him as he snorkeled, plant explosives in his cigars, and sprinkle depilatory powder in his boots. Nothing worked, and the C.I.A. briefly considered hiring the Mafia to kill Castro...reasoning that at least the "wise guys" knew how to do a hit. The idea was abandoned when everyone realized a fleet of black limousines arriving in Havana would be mighty conspicuous. An alarmed Castro asked the Soviet Union for protection.

Then came the most trying and dangerous episode of the Kennedy administration. Khrushchev snuck some medium-range nuclear missiles onto Cuba that could strike as far as Washington, D.C. Then, when he realized just storing them on the island would be pointless, he ordered the construction of launching sites. American U2 spy planes captured unequivocal photographic evidence of the Soviet machinations and President Kennedy — determined not to appear weak after the Bay of Pigs failure — demanded the missiles be removed. He ordered a *quarantine* — a blockade — around Cuba, and commanded the U.S. Navy to stop and search any Soviet ships heading for the island and turn back any carrying offensive weapons. He explained the situation to the nation in a televised address and Americans held their breath. A Soviet military response could lead to war...possibly a nuclear war that would destroy the world. For several days no one knew what would happen, and reportedly the situation was so tense the President lost interest in chasing women. Suddenly, Soviet ships steaming toward Cuba stopped dead in the water. Khrushchev, it appeared, had "blinked."

The Soviets agreed to remove the missiles and dismantle the launch pads, and the **Cuban Missile Crisis** passed into History. Kennedy looked like a steadfast leader who had stood up to Soviet bullying. It was not revealed at the time that the U.S. had agreed to remove its nuclear missiles deployed in Turkey, and to cease its attempts to depose or assassinate Castro. The two nations also agreed to install red "hotline" phones so leaders on both sides could immediately communicate in the event another disagreement threatened to spiral into Armageddon (pink phones supposedly didn't look right). Humiliated, Khrushchev realized he would never get a chance to chance to visit Disneyland, and Russian rivals deposed him a year later. Kennedy, enjoying the high point of his presidency, started dating again, with the assistance of Secret Service agents who would warn him when his wife, Jackie, pulled into the White House driveway. President Kennedy got some action in the White House closet President Harding had used for the same purpose. Maybe that closet should be displayed at the Smithsonian. Maybe not.

President Kennedy picked up where Eisenhower had left off in Vietnam — propping up an anticommunist dictator even his own staff couldn't stand. South Vietnam's President Diem was a Catholic in a predominantly Buddhist country who presided over an incompetent army and corrupt government, and additional American aid failed to induce any improvements. In protest, a Buddhist monk immolated himself (doused himself with gasoline and lit himself on fire) in the middle of a busy Saigon intersection; caught on film, his ritual suicide was broadcast around the world. Most Americans watching the evening news had no idea where Vietnam was. Disgusted, they gagged and pushed away their TV dinners — newly-invented frozen meals on foil trays that could be heated and eaten in front of the television for nonstop viewing.

Kennedy, who previously supported Diem, gave the okay for the dictator to be deposed; dissident South Vietnamese generals obliged, and in the process Diem was murdered. The President, shocked at the brutality, realized Vietnam would be a tough nut to crack, but he remained determined to appear tough and prevent the communist North Vietnam from taking over the South. By November of 1963, there were 16,000 American military "advisors" in the country, who were doing a heck of a lot more than advising. What Kennedy's ultimate approach to Vietnam would have been we'll never know. Maybe he would have recognized we were heading straight into quicksand and pulled back. Maybe not.

ADVANCES IN CIVIL RIGHTS
or *I'm Not Leaving Until I Get My Hamburger*

African-Americans had been making slow but steady progress in civil rights since World War II. In 1947, **Jackie Robinson** joined the Brooklyn Dodgers and became the first black player in the major leagues. A true American hero, he persevered through lots of racism and resentment from beer-bellied white ballplayers who realized their competition to make the team would soon get a lot tougher. The following year, President Truman banned segregation in the armed forces through a gutsy executive order that outraged a lot of bigots in and out of uniform. They bitched a lot but had to follow orders, and as blacks proved their worth, the issue soon subsided. Obviously, the same thing will occur now that our nation has finally jettisoned the gutless "don't ask don't tell" policy and integrated gays into the military to (1) do what is right and (2) ensure that future foxholes won't be so drab.

NAACP lawyers continued to argue that the "separate but equal" Jim Crow laws in the South violated the "equal protection of the law" provisions of the 14th Amendment. Certainly they were right; separate was inherently unequal and facilities for whites were always better, though blacks held an advantage in the areas of cuisine, music, and (obviously) dancing. In 1954, the Supreme Court issued the landmark **Brown v. Board of Education of Topeka, Kansas** ruling that overturned the segregationist Plessy v. Ferguson decision of 1896. The case applied to public schools and the Court ruled that they should be integrated "with all deliberate speed." African-Americans felt that meant *immediately* while white southerners figured, *we'll get to it in a century or two.*

Southern state and local governments, controlled by white bigots, made no move to implement the decision. Blacks realized they would have to physically show up and press the issue to make the integration of schools a reality. In September, 1957, nine black students enrolled in Central High School in Little Rock, Arkansas. Governor Orval Faubus — you can't make up a name like that — called up the Arkansas National Guard to keep the black kids out. A hostile white mob surrounded the school in a disgraceful spectacle beamed coast to coast on television. President Eisenhower, who much preferred to watch old war movies, decided to act.

Though not a big supporter of the civil rights movement, he was appalled that the southern states were flouting American law as determined by the Supreme Court. He took command of the Arkansas National Guard away from Governor Faubus and ordered the soldiers to turn around and <u>protect</u> the incoming African-American students. Integration clearly was going to be rough. Some clueless white girls and their parents cried, "Does this mean they're allowed to be cheerleaders, too?"

On December 1, 1955, a middle-aged black seamstress named **Rosa Parks** was on her way home from work when the bus she was on filled up, and she was ordered to give up her seat to a white person. Her feet hurt, so on the spur of the moment she refused, and she was arrested for breaking an Alabama Jim Crow law requiring segregation on buses. The NAACP saw this as a perfect test case, and counterattacked with a legal challenge in the courts and a boycott against the Montgomery city buses.

Reverend Dr. Martin Luther King, Jr., a twenty-seven-year-old African-American Baptist minister from Atlanta, quickly became the recognized leader of the **Montgomery Bus Boycott** due to his superlative oratorical and organizing skills. Terrorists — fanatical southern white racists, in this case — bombed churches and even King's home, but for a year blacks and some sympathetic white liberals refused to ride the buses. In November, 1956, the Supreme Court overturned the Alabama bus segregation law, and with the bus company riled about all the money it was losing, the Montgomery authorities caved, the buses were integrated, and the successful boycott became history. Martin Luther King, Jr. would go on to become the greatest civil rights leader the United States has ever known, working tirelessly...and never taking off Martin Luther King Day because it didn't exist yet.

King had studied Thoreau and Ghandi, and firmly believed in nonviolent civil disobe-dience: a deliberate but peaceful refusal to obey unjust laws. Among those he influenced were four young African-American men who sat down at a department store lunch counter in Greensboro, North Carolina, and, denied service, refused to leave (yes, the food was lousy, but that was not the point). Hundreds of similar sit-ins by blacks and sympathetic whites spread across the South. Interracial groups of activists deliberately took bus trips to challenge segregation in interstate travel and at all the bus stations along the way, and became known as "freedom riders." They were frequently attacked by white mobs, and the local police either looked the other way or joined in. In 1962, **James Meredith**, a black veteran of the Air Force, attempted to enroll at the University of Mississippi. As I'm sure you can imagine, a riot broke out, two people died, hundreds were injured, and federal troops had to remain on campus until Meredith graduated.

King's protests in Birmingham, Alabama did not set well with the chief of police, "Bull" Connor — a fat southern sheriff who really looked the part of the ignorant south-ern cracker. He ordered his officers to use clubs, firehoses, and attack dogs to disperse the protesters. Most Americans watching on television were appalled — especially when they realized they were not watching a TV series filmed in Hollywood.

President Kennedy knew something had to be done, so he sent federal troops to Birmingham and really worked the phones to get all sides to calm down. Local busi-nesses, worried all the violence would damage profit margins, generally agreed to deseg-regation. On June 11, 1962, the President gave a conciliatory speech in which he prom-ised to ask Congress for civil rights laws to ban discrimination in employment and public accommodations such as hotels and restaurants. The very next day, NAACP leader **Medgar Evers** was shot dead as he entered his home in Jackson, Mississippi. Rioting broke out in Jackson, and demonstrations spread to most major cities across the nation. Kennedy reportedly shook his head and muttered, "Didn't anybody see my speech?" He knew that when it came to civil rights, both he and the country faced rough seas.

Martin Luther King, Jr. kept marching into the headwinds. President Kennedy defi-nitely sympathized, but he had a political problem: he needed to carry southern states to win reelection in 1964. If he moved too fast on civil rights, he risked alienating white southern Democrats. The President's younger brother, Attorney General **Robert Kennedy** (gee, how did he get that job?), asked black leaders for a cooling-off period of a few months so tempers could subside. James Farmer, the Executive director of the Congress of Racial Equality (CORE) replied in exasperation, "We've been cooling off for one hundred years." Reportedly, Robert offered free rides on the Kennedy family yacht but that didn't work, either. The protests continued.

F.B.I. Director **J. Edgar Hoover** obsessively hated King, and wiretapped him to prove he was a communist. It turned out that King was no communist, but he did enjoy the company of a variety of women. Attorney General Robert Kennedy wanted to fire Hoover but didn't dare, because the Director possessed audio tapes of a youthful JFK unknowingly in bed with a German spy during World War II (honest...you can't make this stuff up).

In August 1963, African-American leaders organized the **March on Washington**. Over 300,000 people — mostly black but many whites — turned out on the mall facing the Washington Monument. Martin Luther King, Jr. delivered a speech that raised his game to another level. His "I Have a Dream" speech will always be an inspiring part of American History. I especially admire the part where he said, "I have a dream that my four little children will one day live in a nation where they will not be judged by the color of their skin but by the content of their character."

President Kennedy found King inspiring, but continued to worry that his support of the Reverend and civil rights had angered a lot of white southern bigots whose votes he needed. His thick Boston accent was no help, either; half the time southerners couldn't even understand him, and it was impractical to invite all of them to go sailing off Cape Cod. In the fall of 1963, Vice President Johnson invited the President to visit Texas to do some fence-mending, and Kennedy gladly accepted. Reportedly, before leaving he practiced saying, "Howdy Y'all."

He received a warm reception from a pro-business group in Austin, and was relieved nobody made fun of him when the hot sauce on the ribs made him gasp for a glass of water. In Dallas, riding in an open convertible limousine with Jackie, Texas Governor John Connolly and his wife, the President waved to enthusiastic crowds. Suddenly shots rang out. Bullets struck Kennedy twice, first in the throat and then in the head. He was rushed to the hospital, but doctors could not revive him and he was pronounced dead at 12:22 pm on November 22, 1963. Vice President **Lyndon Baines Johnson** (LBJ) was sworn in as President two hours later on Air Force One as Jackie Kennedy looked on, still splattered in her husband's blood.

Later that day, authorities arrested an oddball named Lee Harvey Oswald, who had killed a policeman and taken refuge in a movie theater. A couple of days later, when Oswald was being transported to another jail, Americans watching the live TV coverage saw a man step forward and shoot him point blank in the abdomen — incredible reality television before there ever was such a thing. Oswald died, but the questions and the doubts have lived on. It did not help that Jack Ruby, Oswald's murderer, claimed he was simply distraught over Kennedy's murder, but then turned out to have connections to the Mafia.

There was evidence that Oswald had fired at the President from a sixth floor window of the Dallas book depository building. President Johnson appointed a high level committee — the **Warren Commission** — in the hopes that its findings would calm the public and offer a measure of emotional closure, but the exact opposite occurred. The committee's work seemed rushed and incomplete, and raised more questions than it answered. Did a "magic bullet" hit both JFK and Governor Connolly, or were more than three shots fired? Why were they riding in an open limousine when the Secret Service had gotten wind of threats? Were there other shots from the "grassy knoll?" Were extra-terrestrials involved? Obviously, some people completely lost it over all this.

The truth may never be known. It is difficult to accept that such an incredible tragedy could have been perpetrated by a lone gunman, and at times a majority of Americans have believed there was a conspiracy to assassinate the President. Legitimate questions remain unanswered, and the list of people who wanted the President dead was certainly long: (1) pro-Castro Cubans angry about the Bay of Pigs and Operation Mongoose, (2) anti-Castro Cubans angry that Kennedy was blocking further attempts to murder or depose Castro in the wake of the Cuban Missile Crisis, (3) rogue elements of the Central Intelligence Agency concerned that Kennedy planned a decrease in their power and resources in retaliation for the Bay of Pigs debacle, (4) the Mafia angling for a quick end to the aggressive prosecution of organized crime orchestrated by Attorney General Robert Kennedy, (5) Lyndon Johnson looking for a quick promotion, (6) the Soviets willing to risk taking the Cold War to an even scarier level, (7) the Military Industrial Complex worried that Kennedy would find the wisdom to cut our losses and pull America out of their made-to-order financial windfall, the war in Vietnam, and, of course, (8) jealous husbands.

My money is on a rogue element of the C.I.A.; supremely confident as a result of their successes in the fifties, in the sixties our spies couldn't seem to get anything right. They set up Oswald to be the patsy. No, I can't prove any of this. But do you really believe that John Kennedy — a leader whose youth and vigor inspired so many hopes and dreams that his Administration earned the nickname "Camelot" — could be murdered by one crazed gunman for no clear reason?

President by assassin's bullet, Lyndon Johnson reassured everyone he would continue JFK's policies and readied himself to run for a term of his own in 1964. The Republicans jettisoned New York Governor **Nelson Rockefeller** and the eastern liberal wing of their party and nominated conservative Arizona Senator **Barry Goldwater**. Goldwater can be considered the father of modern conservatism and the GOP has been heading in that direction ever since. Today, if you are looking for a liberal Republican, you might find one — stuffed — in the Museum of Natural History. Goldwater came across as an extremist (because he was one) and Johnson effectively used attack ads on television to make Americans believe that if elected, Goldwater would get us into a nuclear war with the Soviets. Largely in tribute to the deceased Kennedy, Johnson won in a landslide.

THE NEW PRESIDENT FIGHTS FOR EQUALITY IN AMERICA

or *Why Are We Giving All This Free Stuff to Poor People Who Should Just Work Harder?*

Elected to the House in 1937, the Senate in 1948, and serving as Majority Leader for the last six years of the Eisenhower Administration, LBJ was a progressive New Dealer like JFK. But the similarity ends there. Lyndon grew up poor in rural Texas and graduated from Southwest Texas State Teachers College, a school that never had the opportunity to play Harvard in football. Snooty Ivy League types left over from Kennedy's team resented him and deliberately performed poorly. Still, Johnson had some big ideas. In yet another example of the human dichotomy — the good and bad sides of people — LBJ wanted to advance African-American civil rights for two reasons: first, he genuinely believed it was the right thing to do and, second, he wanted to bind African-American voters even more closely to his Democratic Party and himself.

Amendment XXIV, outlawing a fee for voting — the insidious poll tax still used by five states in the South — was ratified in January, 1964. During the "Freedom Summer" of that year, three civil rights workers were murdered with Mississippi law enforcement officials in cahoots. One year later, a racist sheriff in Selma, Alabama, led the police on a brutal rampage against demonstrators that resulted in two deaths. Television networks beamed the violence into Americans' living rooms and most were appalled. President Johnson jumped on his chance to advocate the most sweeping civil rights legislation in American History, and he received the solid support he needed (outside the South) to get it passed through Congress. The **Civil Rights Act of 1964** prohibited discrimination in voting, employment and places of public accommodation. The **Voting Rights Act of 1965** outlawed discriminatory voter registration tests and gave the federal government the authority to send officials down into the southern states for actual enforcement. Three years later, the **Civil Rights Act of 1968** banned discrimination in the sale and rental of housing. But the event that really illuminated African-American progress occurred when Bill Cosby received a starring role in a really cool television drama, *I Spy*.

President Johnson fervently believed that Americans — if they worked together — could end war, vanquish poverty and racial injustice, provide excellent education and health care to all, rebuild decaying urban centers, and ultimately create the conditions for (to use FDR's words) "freedom from want." LBJ enjoyed large Democratic majorities in the House and Senate, so he pushed through progressive legislation on a scale that rivaled the New Deal of his mentor. He called his vision the **Great Society** and, of course, conservatives hated it. Most of them already had most of what they needed and in no way wanted their taxes increased to help the less fortunate. Reportedly, even though the Republicans did not have the votes in Congress to block the Great Society, at the last moment they did strip out a provision for free ice cream.

Medicare (1965) provided federal health insurance for the elderly and **Medicaid** (1966) offered federal medical assistance to the poor. **Head Start** (1965) promoted school readiness by enhancing the social and cognitive development of children through the provision of educational, health, nutritional, social and other services that included the creation of the PBS television show, *Sesame Street*. The **Office of Economic Opportunity** oversaw a panoply of innovative education, housing, and employment programs.

Affluent Republicans decried "more big government" and rooted for the Great Society to crash and burn, so they applauded when costs spiraled and programs failed to meet their goals. Some of them even said bad things about Elmo and Big Bird. To this day, conservatives point to the Great Society as proof that the federal government should refrain from trying to address social issues and the general welfare, and the states alone should provide the "safety net" for the needy. But there is absolutely no historical precedence to expect the states can handle such a task, and it is particularly instructive to remember how the states were virtually helpless in dealing with the Great Depression. Heck, today most states can barely handle snow removal without crying for federal aid... except for Florida and Hawaii.

The truth was that the Great Society was a rousing success. Millions of elderly and poor received invaluable assistance they would not have otherwise, and poverty was significantly reduced. But with a goal to completely eliminate poverty and inequality, perhaps it was inevitable there would be disappointment. The programs were sometimes mismanaged, rife with corruption, and lacking in input from the poor folks they were supposed to help. Most notably, because of the rising costs of the Vietnam War they were drastically underfunded. But at least the Johnson Administration *tried* to do the right thing. Progressives continue to believe — to their credit — that the federal government should bring its full power and scope to bear to address society's challenges: making federal programs run efficiently remains the true task, and giving up should not be an option. Conservatives in the sixties labeled Johnson and his liberal supporters "commies," while liberals dubbed their conservative critics "fascists." Neither charge made the slightest bit of sense, but it did allow everyone to blow off steam.

The Supreme Court under **Earl Warren** did its part to further not only civil rights but also civil liberties. President Eisenhower had appointed California's Governor Warren to the post of Chief Justice in 1954, thinking he would continue to be conservative, but once into his lifetime appointment, the conservative leopard not only changed his spots but actually morphed into a liberal zebra. Ike confessed it was "the biggest damn fool mistake I ever made"...quite a statement from a man who had asked Richard Nixon to be his Vice President.

In **Engel v. Vitale** (1962), the Court ruled that prayer in schools was unconstitutional, outraging the Christian conservatives continually unable to fathom the separation of Church and State. In **Gideon v. Wainwright** (1963), felony defendants who could not afford an attorney were granted the right to an overworked and underpaid public defender unable to hook up with a prestigious private firm. **Escobedo v. Illinois** (1964) gave defendants the right to have their lawyers present during questioning and frustrate the police on *Law and Order* by "lawyering up." In **Miranda v. Arizona** (1966), the police were required to inform a suspect of their rights upon arrest. That's why on so many television dramas we watch the arrest and hear the words, "You have the right to remain silent. Anything you say can and will be used against you in a court of law. You have the right to an attorney... " Then comes the commercial. By the end of the decade, many Americans believed the courts had done too much to help the criminals and not enough to support victims. Earl Warren voluntarily stepped down in 1969, and since then more conservative Courts have chipped away at — but not dismantled — these basic protections.

THE VIETNAM WAR ESCALATES
or *What Do You Mean I'm Drafted?*

Safely reelected in 1964, President Johnson decided to take the gloves off and really kick some butt in Vietnam. In breathless tones reminiscent of President Polk's exaggerated claims prior to the Mexican War, he announced that U.S. Navy ships had been attacked by North Vietnamese patrol boats (later, it was reported our destroyers had fired blindly in the dark and possibly hit some whales). This time a compliant Congress responded, not with a formal declaration of war, but the **Gulf of Tonkin Resolution,** granting what the President interpreted as a blank check to "take all necessary measures" to protect American forces and "prevent further aggression" in the region. He sent more and more American troops over there, until by the end of 1967 there were over 500,000 trying to prop up South Vietnam by driving out the invading North Vietnamese army and crushing the Vietcong (South Vietnamese guerrillas fighting for North Vietnam). American bombers dropped their payloads on targets in the North and South relentlessly.

Nothing seemed to work, and Murphy's Law — whatever can go wrong will go wrong — kicked in. The Vietcong guerrillas knew their terrain and used hit and run tactics to bedevil our GIs, ironically the exact opposite of the situation during the Revolution, when we were the guerrillas and the British were the modern army. American attempts to deny sanctuary to the Vietcong by burning villages and defoliating farmland with Agent Orange only turned South Vietnamese peasants against the U.S. and recruited more Vietcong. Bombing raids alerted the enemy the Americans were coming, allowing them time to take sanctuary in their extensive underground tunnel networks.

The U.S. forces adopted a strategy of "attrition" designed to wear down the enemy, but relying on "body counts" only invited lying on reports and the shooting of innocent civilians, who were impossible to tell apart from the guerrillas. The North Vietnamese, believing this was their war for independence, seemed to have an endless supply of soldiers and will to fight. China and the Soviet Union secretly sent lots of aid to the North, and peasants carried it down into the South on foot and by bicycle on the **Ho Chi Minh Trail** (roller blades had not been invented yet). The Americans continually tried to disrupt the Ho Chi Minh Trail, but it was difficult to find in the jungle, and the

North cheated by snaking parts of it into the adjoining countries of Laos and Cambodia where our guys were supposedly not allowed to go. And the more fighting and dying our soldiers did, the more the corrupt and incompetent South Vietnamese Army stayed in their camps watching John Wayne movies.

Back home, legal means to avoid being drafted included staying in college or convincing the local draft board you were a conscientious objector (someone deeply opposed to war on religious or philosophical grounds), or just a really good liar. Pinocchio never could have pulled it off, but middle and upper class young men (like future President George W. Bush and future Vice President Dan Quayle) were much better equipped to game the system, so a higher percentage of minorities and the poor found themselves trying to stay alive in the jungle. Once over in Vietnam, many men used drugs and alcohol to deal with the horrific conditions, lack of leadership and clear goals. As always in war, brutality begets more brutality; South Vietnamese society was ripped apart and there were horrible reports of atrocities on all sides. The Army tried but failed to cover up the **My Lai Massacre** in which over five hundred unarmed South Vietnamese villagers, mostly women and children, were murdered by rampaging American troops. Nightly newscasts made this a "living room war" and Americans had increasing difficulty reconciling the rosy reports of General William Westmoreland and the Johnson Administration with the bloody and senseless stalemate they could see with their own eyes on their TV screens.

As casualty counts mounted in 1967, increasing numbers of Americans turned against the war, and the nation split between "doves" who opposed the war, "hawks" who supported it, and "pigeons" who did not want to get involved and just pooped a lot. Public antiwar activism that year resulted in the "Vietnam Summer" in which thousands took to the streets. A wide variety of prominent figures turning against the war included Arkansas Senator and Chair of the Foreign Relations Committee J. William Fulbright, Rev. Martin Luther King, Jr., former Secretary of State Dean Atchesen, Robert F. Kennedy (now a Senator from New York), and even George Kennan, who argued Vietnam was a distraction from more strategically important regions, notably Europe.

In November, discouraged and disheartened, Secretary of Defense **Robert McNamara** resigned. Hawks in the Administration continued to call for an escalation of the war and General Westmoreland asked for another 206,000 men. Angrily, President Johnson denied the request. He communicated to the North Vietnamese that he would order a halt to bombing if they would agree to open negotiations. The North Vietnamese, sensing time was on their side with the growing opposition to the war in the United States, turned him down.

On January 30, 1968, on the Vietnamese Lunar New Year holiday of Tet, North Vietnamese forces and the Vietcong launched a coordinated attack against dozens of major cities and towns across South Vietnam. Nineteen Vietcong guerrillas on a suicide mission blasted through the wall of the U.S. Embassy in Saigon and held off the Marines for six hours. Caught off guard, American forces quickly recovered, and over six weeks inflicted a crushing blow to the enemy (many in the South Vietnamese Army, supposedly on our side, reportedly had difficulty finding their boots and helmets). But the damage had been done.

On the *CBS Evening News*, the country's most trusted anchorman, Walter Cronkite, shocked his viewers by taking off his glasses in disgust and declaring — live on the air — "What the hell is going here? I thought we were winning this war." Many Americans were wondering the same thing and started to ask pointed questions: Is the government of North Vietnam really any worse than the government of the South? Is this really just a local civil war we should have stayed out of? Does the fate of Vietnam really make any difference in the worldwide Cold War? Where is Vietnam, anyway? The **Tet Offensive** was a <u>military</u> defeat for the North Vietnamese and the Vietcong but a <u>political</u> victory... the point of no return for public opinion as more and more Americans became convinced this was the wrong war in the wrong place against the wrong enemy.

In the weeks after the Tet Offensive, President Johnson's popularity rating tumbled precipitously to around 35 percent. Nineteen-sixty-eight was a presidential election year, and a little known senator from Wisconsin felt emboldened to challenge the sitting president for the Democratic nomination. With the rabid support of college students and antiwar activists, **Eugene McCarthy** nearly won the first primary in New Hampshire, shocking LBJ and the political establishment. Sensing the President could be beat, Robert Kennedy quickly declared his candidacy and — given his stature and resources — effectively snatched the liberal antiwar mantle away from McCarthy.

On the evening of March 31st, President Johnson addressed the nation on television. He unilaterally announced a partial halt to the bombing of North Vietnam in the hopes of getting peace talks going. Then he startled everyone (he had told only his wife) by announcing he would not be a candidate for reelection. My father, a hawk on Vietnam who never cursed in front of his children, let loose with a torrent of four letter words. At age fourteen, I just sat there and tried to figure out what was going on. But I did resolve to stop cutting my hair and get a pair of those new bell bottom pants. Truly, the hopes and dreams of Johnson's presidency and the Great Society drowned in the rice paddies of Vietnam.

A SOCIAL REVOLUTION SHAKES THE NATION

or *We're Going To Protest Until Our Demands Are Met... Whatever They Are!*

College students in 1962 formed **Students for a Democratic Society** (SDS) and issued a proclamation of beliefs: the **Port Huron Statement,** a clarion call for a generation of young people to cast off their apathy and work to make America truly a participatory democracy. This was progressive thinking at a time when "kids" could fight and die in Vietnam but not vote until the age of twenty-one. Radical student movements eventually began to be referred to under an umbrella term: the **New Left**. They objected to the rigidity of their educational institutions and demanded college policies more appropriate to the times. Campus restrictions on free expression tumbled hard, so did dress codes, antiquated course requirements, and the age-old tradition that college administrators could not be challenged. Most importantly of all, we can thank the New Left for coed dormitories.

As the decade wore on, the students of the New Left increasingly opposed the Vietnam War and the draft. Sit-ins, marches, and student strikes roiled most campuses across America. A tiny extremist offshoot of SDS called the "Weathermen" — after a line in a Bob Dylan song — disgraced the New Left by engaging in bombing and arson that claimed several innocent lives. Another tiny offshoot of the SDS — named the "Puff the Magic Dragons" after a song by the folk trio Peter, Paul, and Mary — held sing-alongs around bonfires but garnered far less attention.

At the same time the New Left was taking its first steps, a new youth movement — a genuine *counterculture* — took root. Openly scornful of middle class values, traditional no-questions-asked patriotism, and obsessive dedication to the pursuit of personal wealth, "hippies" donned tie-dyed clothing and wore flowers in their ever lengthening hair (some had so much dirt in their hair that when watered the flowers would stay alive for months). They embraced recreational drugs and premarital sex and deliberately tried to differentiate themselves from their parents' generation.

Rock music evolved throughout the sixties and provided essential nutrients for the counterculture. The **Beatles**, a band from the slums of Liverpool, England, first caught on with some bouncy up-tempo love songs. The "Fab Four" made a triumphant appearance on the Ed Sullivan show in 1964, just as Elvis Presley had in the fifties, and the "Beatlemania" that swept America inspired many other British and American bands to expand upon the "Beatle Beat" and create a cacophonous kaleidoscope of melodies and vibrations. The folk music of Bob Dylan and Joan Baez sounded almost quaint as musicians like the Rolling Stones, the Jefferson Airplane, the Doors, Jimi Hendrix, and others utilized the power of their electric guitars and uninhibited song lyrics to promote both themselves and the "Revolution."

Most young Americans were not hippies, but by the end of the decade they were wearing their clothes, playing their music, and engaging in pastimes their parents had only dreamed of. In the summer of 1969, the **Woodstock** music festival, on a farm in upstate New York, drew hundreds of thousands for three days of peace, love, recreational drugs and inspirational music. Woodstock remains an emblem of the age, but it was a once in a lifetime magical event, as the Rolling Stones soon proved when their free concert near San Francisco turned into an orgy of drunkenness and violence...and the crowd was also very unruly.

Just as the spirit of change so alive in the sixties propelled the movement for African-American equality, other long-downtrodden minorities were inspired to turn up the volume and demand redress of their grievances. Ever since the Dawes Act of 1887, the federal government had generally facilitated the division of tribally held lands into individually owned parcels so the Indians could be "Americanized." The "allotment" strategy never worked; priceless tribal culture was eviscerated and Native Americans continually faced discrimination. "Termination" laws passed in 1953 intensified the destruction of tribal identity and resulted in cries of outrage by many of those affected. President Kennedy gave up on the termination policy, but radicalized Native Americans continued to protest in favor of increased federal aid to reservations and self-determination for tribes (they even occupied Alcatraz Island in San Francisco Bay, the abandoned federal prison they soon realized was a pretty creepy place with very poor recreational facilities). The **Indian Civil Rights Act** of 1968 guaranteed Native Americans all freedoms contained in the Bill of Rights, and recognized some tribal laws within reservations. But progress for Native Americans to this day has been painfully slow. Indian-owned casinos have been a stunning success — idiots like me lose lots of money there — but most reservations continue to struggle with inordinately high rates of poverty, substance abuse, diabetes, and suicide.

Hispanics are folks who can claim heritage from a Spanish-speaking country, and during the sixties the population of "latinos" and "latinas" legally resident in the United States rose from three to nine million. Ever since then their legal population has grown dramatically, and they have made up the largest share of illegal immigrants, estimated in 2010 to range as high as twelve million. Hispanics have continually faced discrimination and as a result have consistently been among the poorest of Americans. But Cuban Americans have made great progress in South Florida, Mexican Americans are pulling themselves up by their bootstraps in the Southwest, and Puerto Ricans are claiming their just place in New York and the other cities of the Northeast (don't ever ask a Puerto Rican person if they are an American; Puerto Rico remains a territory of the United States and folks from there are just as American as anyone else).

In the late sixties, an American-born migrant worker, **Cesar Chavez**, organized Mexican seasonal workers in California and called national attention to their starvation wages and cruel treatment. Back East, liberal white guys like me boycotted grapes because we were told it would somehow help. Hey, sometimes you need to sacrifice.

On July 12th, 1969, police raided the Stonewall, a gay bar in New York City. The establishment offended the authorities simply because it catered to gay men and lesbians. To the cops' astonishment, the patrons and neighborhood bystanders fought back. Drag queens wielded six-inch heels like Arab scimitars. Reportedly, several "off duty" officers drinking in the bar at the time the melee broke out had a lot of explaining to do. Emboldened by the "spirit of the sixties," street riots raged over several nights, and the gay liberation movement was born. Gay men, lesbians and the transgendered have struggled mightily for acceptance and equal rights in subsequent decades, but it has been a difficult fight against ignorance and prejudice. Enormous progress has been made as each younger generation proves to be generally more tolerant than their homophobic elders.

The sixties reawakened a women's movement that had been largely dormant since the Nineteenth Amendment had passed back in 1920. In 1963, Betty Friedan authored **The Feminine Mystique** to directly challenge the notion that women were best suited to work inside the home as wives and mothers. In 1963, the Kennedy Administration helped secure passage of the **Equal Pay Act** to make it illegal to pay women less than men for the same work. In 1966, Friedan and other women founded NOW, the **National Organization For Women,** to lobby on behalf of women's issues and make men feel guilty for enjoying Playboy magazine. Radical feminists rejected marriage and even heterosexuality; most women were not willing to go that far, but there was lots of agreement that women had the right to reach their full potential on an equal footing with men. Thanks to this reawakened women's movement, Americans today are much more informed on the issues of rape and abuse, contraception, childcare, and sexual harassment. And any male business owner who gets caught shortchanging his female employees risks getting a beating from the women on *The View*.

The emphasis placed on expanding women's rights in the sixties led directly to a groundbreaking Supreme Court decision in the seventies. The justices ruled in **Roe v. Wade** (1973) that a pregnant woman has the uninhibited right to an abortion during the first trimester. They based their decision on the novel idea that the Constitution provides a zone of "privacy" for every American...the question of when life begins had nothing to do with it. Conservative "pro lifers" have been apoplectic ever since and demand the right to tell everyone what do, and subsequent Republican Presidents have tilted the court rightward to the extent that Roe versus Wade may be overturned in the near future. Abortion remains the most controversial and emotional issue facing our nation today — second only to the judges' decisions on *American Idol*.

The sixties also gave birth to a movement to protect our environment. First Lady "Lady Bird" Johnson called attention to the garbage alongside interstate highways in particular, and the degradation of the land by rapid industrialization in general. **Rachel Carson** penned a powerful book, **The Silent Spring**, exposing the dangers of pesticides and how the bug-killing poisons were entering into our own food supply. Lake Erie caught on fire — that's right, sections of the lake erupted into flames. Some of the fish undoubtedly exclaimed, "How can you cook me? I haven't even been caught yet?" The pollution was undeniable, and some Americans proclaimed themselves *environmentalists* dedicated to the protection of our natural resources. Previous generations of nature lovers had called themselves *conservationists* — Teddy Roosevelt was a prime example — but now a new science was born — ecology, with focus on the interconnectedness of the natural world and the interaction of people with their environment.

Pioneer environmentalists organized **Earth Day** on April 22, 1970, and millions of folks, especially young people, participated all across America. It was actually one giant teach-in intended to spread awareness of the threats to our environment. Congress responded to the public mood, and in the early seventies created the **Environmental Protection Agency** to enforce anti-pollution laws. The **Clean Air Act** (1970) and the **Clean Water Act** (1972) also passed. The Sierra Club, the National Wildlife Federation and other environmental organizations enrolled lots of new enthusiastic members and suddenly found reporters willing to take their calls. "Green Power" has been a potent political force in our nation's discourse ever since the sixties. Then and now, powerful conservative forces in the service of large industrial corporations regularly object to environmental legislation, on the grounds that it is costly and makes American businesses less competitive abroad. They paint all common sense environmentalists as extremists or "tree huggers." I hugged a tree once but a squirrel bit me.

AMERICANS TURN TO A MORE CONSERVATIVE PRESIDENT

or *Love It or Leave It You Stinkin' Freaks!*

The Democratic nomination in 1968 came down to Senator Robert F. Kennedy, who favored American disengagement from Vietnam, and Vice President **Hubert H. Humphrey**, a Minnesota native and progressive who nevertheless remained a hawk on the war. Humphrey had the support of Johnson and party leaders but Kennedy demonstrated rank and file support by winning several primaries (it didn't help the Vice President that his last name could be shortened and rhymed in the unflattering chant, "Dump the Hump"). This race was going to go down to the wire.

On April 4, 1968, Martin Luther King, Jr. was killed by an assassin. King, who had traveled to Memphis, Tennessee to show his support for striking sanitation workers, was shot when he stepped onto his second-floor motel balcony. Riots erupted in sixty American cities and forty-three people died. **James Earl Ray** was arrested two months later in England and charged with the crime. He died in prison in 1998 at the age of seventy, still refusing to admit guilt. Ray was almost certainly the shooter, but evidence indicates he was likely hired — by whom, it is frustrating to say, we may never know. In the fictional world of television back then, a super hero like Batman or the Green Hornet could crack any case in about half an hour, and if you were lucky to have a new expensive TV set, you could watch them zap the bad guys in "living color." But this was the real America of the late sixties, and with the Vietnam War, social upheaval, and now another assassination, many feared the nation was coming apart at the seams.

On June 4th, Robert Kennedy won the critical Democratic presidential primary and seized the momentum heading into his party's nominating convention in Chicago. After midnight, he delivered a rousing speech to his supporters at the Ambassador Hotel in Los Angeles. As he left the podium to head to his car, the front entrance was so crowded with well-wishers that he and his bodyguard decided to duck out the back way. As he was walking through the hotel kitchen, **Sirhan Sirhan**, a Palestinian angry about the Senator's support for Israel, stepped forward and shot him three times at point blank range. Robert slumped to the floor, and after being rushed to the hospital, clung to life for nearly twenty-six hours. Sirhan Sirhan, still serving life in prison, continues to claim he has no memory of his actions, which were clearly witnessed by bystanders (he also has no good explanation for why his first name is the same as his last name). Sad to say, we may never learn what really went down here, either. But in my view this one was definitely a conspiracy, probably orchestrated by the same group that murdered JFK and King. Back in the summer of '68, America reeled and many went numb.

Protesters descended upon Chicago as the Democratic convention opened July 23rd, and a small but unruly minority aimed to be as disruptive as possible. Mayor Richard Daly — the epitome of the intransigent authority figures young people rebelled against — authorized the police to use virtually any level of force to keep "his" streets orderly. The cops obliged and went on a vicious rampage against both the demonstrators and innocent bystanders unfortunate to get caught in the rain of nightsticks. Americans stared at their televisions in disbelief. Inside the hall, anxious Democratic delegates bestowed the nomination upon Vice President Humphrey. Outside amidst the mayhem, Mayor Daly reportedly remarked, "Hey, it's not my fault these punks forgot to bring helmets."

The Republicans held their convention in Miami and nominated former Vice-President Richard M. Nixon, and in doing so heaped more dirt on Governor Nelson Rockefeller and the mouldering corpse of the GOP's liberal wing. Fewer protesters showed up at this convention, and it has been theorized that wild beach parties at night caused a lot of them to oversleep. Nixon's resurrection was impressive; after losing both the presidency in 1960 and a contentious race for Governor of California in 1962, he had dedicated himself to crisscrossing the country, attending local Republican functions, courting party leaders, and out of necessity eating a lot of the "rubber" chicken dinners they often serve at political functions. His determination (and lots of Alka-Seltzer) paid off with a second chance to go for the Oval Office gold.

During the campaign, Nixon held a consistent lead over Humphrey as his calls for smaller government, a return to "basic" American values, and a negotiated peace in Vietnam resonated with many mainstream Americans who simply craved stability in tumultuous times. An even more conservative candidate than Nixon ran as a third party candidate: Governor **George Wallace** of Alabama. Wallace railed against proactive civil rights legislation, federal programs and regulations, and called for law enforcement officials to be tougher on crime (he clearly meant African Americans here) and antiwar demonstrators.

Most Americans — Republicans and Democrats alike — recoiled at the extremism of Wallace, but political change was in the wind. Nixon claimed most regular folks wanted an end to the social turbulence swirling about the land. It turned out he was right. Humphrey closed the gap in the final weeks and the popular vote was close, but Nixon won solidly in the electoral college and took office believing he had a mandate to put the brakes on all the sex, drugs, and rock'n roll and, unfortunately, the growing acceptance of diversity in America. Unable to fathom the true meaning of the youth movement, Nixon viewed people with long hair and bellbottoms as the spawn of Satan or, worse, communists.

NIXON'S FOREIGN POLICY

or *Trust Me, I Have a Plan*

Americans rejoiced on July 21, 1969 when astronaut **Neil Armstrong** stepped onto the surface of the moon and declared, "That's one small step for a man, one giant leap for mankind." Reportedly he had been offered millions to yell, "I'm going to Disney World!" but wisely stayed on the high road. But as folks returned to earth, they remembered that during the campaign Nixon had promised he had "a plan" to end the war in Vietnam. After a few months it became clear he had no plan...or even an inkling. The President knew he had to put an end to the unpopular war in Vietnam if he wanted to be reelected in four years. But because he believed a surrender would damage America's standing around the world, unconditional withdrawal was out of the question. He demanded "peace with honor," reasoning correctly that "peace with humiliation" would not keep him popular with conservative supporters of the war.

Paradoxically, Nixon withdrew ground forces in the hopes of reducing U.S. casualties and quieting dissent at home, while at the same time he increased aerial bombing in order to bludgeon North Vietnam into making concessions at the bargaining table. The President also called for "**Vietnamization**" of the war: a hand off of the ground fighting from U.S. troops to their South Vietnamese comrades at arms. But, as had been the case since the early sixties, the South Vietnamese army resisted taking the baton, shying away from fighting and performing horribly when they did engage the enemy. Despite the bombing and horrific casualties, North Vietnam deliberately dithered at the ongoing peace talks in Paris because they knew they were winning, and their hand was being strengthened by the growing antiwar movement in the United States.

Nixon tapped Harvard professor **Henry Kissinger** to be his National Security Advisor, and he soon held the President in such thrall that Secretary of Defense Melvin Laird and Secretary of State William Rogers found few people in the West Wing willing to take their calls. Kissinger concurred with Nixon's escalation of the war and convinced the President to allow U.S. troops to cross into Cambodia and Laos to get at the clandestine North Vietnamese supply lines in the jungle — the infamous Ho Chi Minh Trail.

This news revitalized the antiwar movement and produced the most virulent protests to date. At Kent State University in Ohio, National Guard troops panicked, killing four demonstrators and injuring nine. Congress jumped off the sinking sampan and repealed the Gulf of Tonkin Resolution. Former defense official **Daniel Ellsberg** leaked a classified study of the Vietnam War, prepared by the Department of Defense, to the *New York Times*. The so-called **Pentagon Papers** revealed officials had long known the war could not be won and issued false reports claiming progress. President Nixon appealed to the Supreme Court to stop publication, but the Justices ruled in favor of "freedom of the press." To prevent further leaks and harass opponents, top aides to Nixon created the "Plumbers," a clandestine group of operatives charged with harassing and intimidating Americans who opposed the President's policies. One of their first schemes entailed a break-in of Ellsberg's psychiatrist's office to find information to discredit him. If you are wondering what kind of a man Nixon must have been to surround himself with such people, you are on the right track.

On October 26, 1972, Kissinger reported that negotiations with the North Vietnamese had been fruitful and "peace was at hand." Peace was not at hand, but the presidential election was a few days away and the announcement made the President look good. In reality, the U.S demanded further concessions and sent wave after wave of B-52 bombers over North Vietnam to apply further pressure. This "Christmas Bombing" had little effect and on January 27, 1973, the United States and North Vietnam signed a formal cease fire. Finally! The terms were little changed from what President Johnson had been willing to accept in 1968. American troops withdrew and North Vietnam released several hundred U.S. prisoners — supposedly all of them, unless you are a fan of Chuck Norris movies. North Vietnamese troops were allowed to remain in the South, and some vaguely defined "committee" was supposed to sort everything out in the future.

Almost immediately, the Paris Peace Accords collapsed. In March 1975, the North launched an all out offensive, and the South Vietnamese army — now completely on it's own — performed like the Chicago Cubs in a pennant race. Many soldiers simply stripped off their uniforms and tried to blend in with the rest of the population. Those who in their haste forgot to put on other clothing were easily identifiable. At the end of April, the North Vietnamese Army marched into Saigon and renamed it Ho Chi Minh City. Americans watched their televisions in horror as helicopters lifted off from the roof of the U.S. Embassy at the last moment, leaving behind panicked throngs of South Vietnamese allies who would face retribution. A cargo plane leaving Saigon crashed on takeoff, killing 155 of 328 on board, including 98 South Vietnamese orphans. It was bad — a national humiliation — but mercifully our long nightmare in Indochina was over. What a waste...over 58,000 patriotic Americans ordered by their government into this ill-advised war died, and over 300,000 were injured. Over 1.2 million Vietnamese soldiers lost their lives and no one has ever been able to accurately count the civilian casualties.

In another part of the world, President Nixon sought detente — a lessening of tensions — with the Soviet Union. The Nixon Administration conducted several years of Strategic Arms Limitation Talks (SALT) with the Soviets, and negotiated a marginal reduction in nuclear weaponry. Issues remained thorny, but Nixon met twice with Soviet Premier **Leonid Brezhnev** and there was a palpable thawing in the Cold War. In perhaps his greatest achievement, Nixon traveled to China and set the United States on a course towards a normalization of economic and political relations with the world's most populous nation. He walked on the Great Wall and remarked, astutely, "Wow, this truly is a great wall." Then he supposedly remarked to his wife, Pat, "Look, honey, not a single long-haired hippie protester as far as the eye can see!"

Nixon and Kissinger had no respect or understanding of movements in the Third World against oppressive dictatorships. They reflexively believed the uprisings were communist-inspired and anti-American, and they often proffered U.S. aid to prop up the right-wing dictators. When the citizens of Chile democratically elected leftist President **Salvador Allende**, Nixon approved a coup by right-wing Chilean generals, successfully orchestrated by the CIA, that resulted in Allende's murder. Kissinger to this day refuses to accept any responsibility for what happened, and some of his frustrated critics have been reduced to chanting, "Liar. Liar. Pants on fire."

On Yom Kippur in 1973, combined forces from Egypt and Syria launched a coordinated surprise attack on Israel. The United States pledged supplies to Israel and the tide soon turned. Kissinger energetically negotiated a cease fire by flying from capital to capital in what the press dubbed "shuttle diplomacy." Reportedly, negotiations nearly broke apart when an exhausted Kissinger, now Secretary of State, forgot where he was and whispered "Shalom" as he hugged Egyptian President **Anwar Sadat**. The military disengagement was a significant achievement, but a lasting peace in the region remained elusive, and an embargo of oil exports to the U.S. by the Organization of Petroleum Producing Countries (OPEC) to protest American support for Israel served notice that the world had entered into a new economic era. Dominance by the United States could no longer be taken for granted.

President Nixon embarked upon his reelection campaign in 1972 in a strong position. His diplomacy with both the Soviet Union and China made him appear statesman-like, and it looked like the war in Vietnam was finally winding down. Hubert Humphrey, George Wallace, and South Dakota Senator **George McGovern** contested for the Democratic nomination. In May, a gunman shot Wallace at a rally in a shopping center; paralyzed from the waist down, he had to drop out. Liberal Democrats gained control at the convention in Miami and secured the nomination for McGovern, a dove on Vietnam and a liberal on social and economic policy.

Mainstream Americans, exhausted and exasperated by the excesses of the sixties, wanted no part of McGovern's message. His campaign misfired from the start when it was revealed his running mate, Missouri Senator Thomas Eagleton, had received electroshock treatment for depression. Had he just taken tranquilizers and kept his mouth shut like everyone else there would have been no problem, but an embarrassed McGovern was forced to replace him. Nixon spouted about "law and order" and a return to the values of an older America, claiming that a "**silent majority**" agreed with him. Again, he was right. He crushed McGovern on Election Day, winning forty-nine states. Soon bumper stickers would proclaim, *DON'T BLAME ME, I'M FROM MASSACHUSETTS!* But we are getting ahead of ourselves.

Nixon considered himself a solid conservative, and he dismantled much of the Great Society, including Johnson's coveted Office of Economic Opportunity. He pandered to his conservative base by ordering the Department of Health, Education, and Welfare to stop withholding federal funds from school districts that failed to integrate. But he was surprisingly progressive in some respects; he supported the creation of the Environmental Protection Agency, and advocated for a program of national health insurance and a federally guaranteed income for all Americans. Modern day FOX-watching-Republicans would have fainted.

The American economy sputtered and stalled during the Nixon Administration because of changes in the world economy the United States could no longer control. Nations in Europe and Asia now produced competitive manufactured goods, causing our manufacturing base — virtually unchallenged since the end of World War II — to decline. Factories closed and manufacturing jobs were lost, a trend that continues to this day. Rising oil prices and then an OPEC boycott led to double-digit inflation.

The President responded by cutting spending and raising taxes, and by placing conservatives on the Federal Reserve Board, he successfully maneuvered for high interest rates and a tight money supply to keep a lid on inflation. There was actually a modest budget surplus in 1969. But the inflation stubbornly persisted, and in August 1971, the President announced a ninety-day wage and price freeze. Still, in late 1971 a recession loomed, so interest rates were allowed to fall and government spending increased, producing the largest budget deficit since World War II. Educated Americans learned a new word in the early seventies — **stagflation** — a combination of inflation and a stagnant economy. Others simply complained about the rising cost of their beer and cigarettes.

THE WATERGATE SCANDAL BRINGS DOWN A PRESIDENT
or "I Am Not a Crook."

President Nixon, an insecure and deceitful man, never grasped that Americans who disagreed with him had a constitutional right to do so. He equated dissent with a lack of patriotism. He surrounded himself with staff willing to use aggressive and illegal means to discredit his enemies, whom he presumed lurked everywhere. He politicized the F.B.I., C.I.A., and even the I.R.S. and used them to harass his opponents. Navy Seals were never utilized...as far as we know. On June 17, 1972, as part of a regular pattern of dirty tricks, five burglars hired by members of Nixon's White House staff were arrested as they attempted to break into the Democratic National Committee headquarters, located in the **Watergate** office building in Washington, D.C. Two reporters for the *Washington Post*, **Bob Woodward** and **Carl Bernstein**, relentlessly pursued the story and uncovered that high-ranking White House officials had been involved in both the burglary itself and a coverup, in which the burglars were paid not to reveal their connections to the Nixon Administration.

Nixon called the break-in a "third rate burglary," and throughout the '72 election campaign, McGovern's best efforts were unable to get the electorate to pay much attention to the affair. In the last couple months of that year, however, public interest spiked as the burglars went on trial, and a special Senate committee opened an investigation. The skeptical federal judge presiding over the trial, the prickly **John J. Sirica**, did not believe the prosecutors' claims that the caper only involved a few low level officials. He succeeded in getting one burglar to talk, and the entire tangled web of lies began to unravel.

The Senate Watergate Committee was chaired by North Carolina Senator **Sam Ervin**, an old, self-described "simple country lawyer" with a thick southern drawl (and a Harvard Law degree) who was as sharp as a tack. Throughout the late spring and early summer of 1973, Ervin and his committee grilled White House officials who, with Americans watching on live television, squirmed and sweated and proved to be terrible liars. The man who had organized the coverup, White House Counsel **John Dean**, became afraid he was going to be made the fall guy and decided to spill everything he knew.

Top-ranking officials from the Committee to Reelect the President (appropriately assigned the acronym, CREEP) and the Administration resigned as Nixon continued to proclaim his complete innocence. Wanting to at least appear on the side of justice, the President appointed a "Special Prosecutor" to investigate the Watergate break-in: Harvard law professor **Archibald Cox**. Then, one of the defendants revealed that Nixon had taped all his conversations in the Oval Office in hopes of memorializing himself post-presidency. Judge Sirica, Ervin's Senate Watergate Committee, and Cox all subpoenaed the tapes. Nixon, knowing what was on them, refused, citing "executive privilege" — the right of the President to keep his communications private on the grounds of national security.

Cox took the matter to court, and Nixon concluded the Special Prosecutor wasn't so special anymore. He ordered Attorney General **Elliot Richardson** to fire him. Richardson, a man of integrity, declined, so Nixon fired the Attorney General. Deputy Attorney General **William Ruckelshaus**, also incorruptible, refused to fire Cox, so Nixon sacked him, too. Third in command at the Justice Department, conservative lawyer Robert Bork, did the dirty work. Newspaper headlines dubbed Nixon's firing of the Attorney General, the Deputy Attorney General, and the Special Prosecutor the "Saturday Night Massacre." Luckily for the press, these events had actually taken place on a Saturday night, or they would have been really embarrassed. Even Americans inclined to cut Nixon some slack were shocked by this turn of events. Under pressure, the President appointed another Special Prosecutor, Leon Jaworski, who kept going after the tapes. Calls for impeachment rang loud and clear in the halls of Congress.

Late in 1973, as Watergate fever gripped the country, it seemed almost surreal when Nixon's Vice President, **Spiro Agnew**, was busted for taking kickbacks (bribes) when he had been Governor of Maryland, and even after he had become Vice President. Agnew pleaded no contest to a lesser charge and resigned in a deal to avoid jail time. Amendment XXV, adopted in 1967, entitled Nixon to appoint his new Vice President, and he chose House Minority Leader **Gerald Ford**, an undistinguished congressman from Michigan whose incurious mind had served him well as a member of the Warren Commission. Ford had virtually no foreign policy experience and Nixon calculated Congress would hesitate to remove him from office and replace him with someone who could barely identify continents, let alone countries.

In April 1974, Nixon attempted to release edited transcripts of the tapes. Nobody bought into that ploy. In July, the Supreme Court ruled unanimously that Nixon had to stop trying to hide behind his warped interpretation of executive privilege and turn over the actual tapes in their entirety. Nixon finally relented and surrendered the tapes. Incredibly, one tape of a meeting with a top aide on the subject of Watergate contained an eighteen minute "gap" that the President pathetically claimed was due to an accidental erasure. Still, there was plenty of evidence on other tapes to prove that Nixon had been actively involved in the coverup of the Watergate burglary (whether or not he had prior knowledge of the actual burglary remains unclear and controversial).

His support, even among Republicans, collapsed, and with impeachment in the House and conviction in the Senate a sure bet, Nixon brooded for three days. Much of the time he was drunk and irrational...not the best condition for a man in control of a nuclear arsenal. Finally, on August 8, 1974, he announced he would resign the following day at noon. Gerald Ford was sworn in as President and Nixon flew home to California.

Most Americans at the time were simply relieved, and the Watergate crisis continues to have a mixed legacy. Lots of folks, already skeptical about our elected officials, soured forever on politicians and government. But ironically, our system of checks and balances had worked. Once it became incontrovertibly clear the President had committed gross violations of the law — and tried to justify himself by claiming the President is, in effect, above the law — both Democrats and Republicans called for his impeachment. This impeachment threat was not borne of the political partisanship that had befallen President Andrew Johnson or would befall future (horny) President Bill Clinton. Our Founding Fathers who wrote the Constitution showed great wisdom and foresight when they created a government with power separated amongst three distinct branches... a government in which no one is above the law. It took 187 years, but James Madison and the boys deserve the ultimate credit for taking down Richard Nixon.

A PRESIDENT WHO WAS NOT ELECTED
or *Watch Your Head!*

Gerald Ford had been appointed Vice President and not elected, but rules are rules, so he became President number thirty-eight. He immediately needed to confront an economy that had slipped into recession in 1974 and a populace shaken by the twin disasters of Watergate and defeat in the Vietnam War. Everyone agreed Ford was a nice enough guy, but he never demonstrated he was up to the enormous tasks he faced. To curb inflation, he called for voluntary efforts, as if businesses would cut their prices and profits just to be nice. OPEC kept raising the price of oil and the American economy kept heading south. Boldly, Ford wore a button that said "WIN" — whip inflation now. Actually, the button seemed ineffectual, and looked especially ridiculous when he accidentally wore it upside down, causing it to say, "NIM"... an obscure Asian curse word.

The President also had the unfortunate propensity to trip and hit his head a lot in front of the television cameras. Comedian Chevy Chase had a field day imitating a stumbling and bumbling Ford on the original *Saturday Night Live*. Just when it seemed the jokes had run their course, the President would bang his head again and keep the laughs going. He really needed a helmet, but that idea was rejected as "unpresidential."

About a month after he took office, President Ford addressed the nation on television and granted Nixon an "absolute pardon" for any crimes he may have committed during his presidency. Totally in character, the former President accepted the pardon but refused to admit guilt, claiming only that "mistakes had been made" during the Watergate affair. The President showed some guts in pardoning Nixon; many Americans were outraged and his popularity crumbled. Others believed the nation would benefit by being spared the painful saga of a debilitating public trial of a former President who had already faced the justice of being forced into a humiliating resignation. Still others worried President Ford would hit his head again.

President Ford kept Secretary of State Kissinger on the job, and Henry continued a policy of detente with the Soviet Union. He also induced Israel to return to Egypt some occupied land in the Sinai Peninsula, and gently nudged those two nations toward a mutual rejection of armed conflict to settle their differences. Looking at a map, Ford reportedly muttered, "So that's where the Sinai is."

Ford was instinctively a middle-of-the-road kind of guy...a genuine moderate Republican that today has gone the way of the Dodo Bird. He appointed Nelson Rockefeller as his Vice President, infuriating conservative Republicans. By the time 1976 rolled around, the President faced strong attacks from the left (the Democrats, naturally) and the right (his own Republican party). A former movie actor turned Governor of California, **Ronald Reagan**, mounted a serious challenge for the Republican nomination. Ford barely beat back the efforts of the conservative Governor at the convention in Kansas City by promising to dump his liberal Vice President, stop all that arms control nonsense with the Soviets, and withdraw his support for the proposed treaty to return the Panama Canal to the people we'd stolen it from. Reportedly, the Governor's support really crumbled after President Ford's campaign manger arranged for late night screening of the film, **Bedtime for Bonzo**, in which Reagan had been out-acted by a chimp.

The Democrats wanted to capitalize on the public anger against the Republicans in general, and Ford's pardon of Nixon in particular. At their convention in Atlanta, they deliberately reached outside the despised world of Washington D.C. and tapped former Georgia Governor **Jimmy Carter.** A peanut farmer by trade and an evangelical Christian, Carter adopted moderate positions, stoked the public's economic concerns and general frustration with President Ford, and never failed to remind his audiences he was *not* a Washington insider. In one of the televised presidential debates, President Ford mistakenly stated that Poland and Hungary were not under communist domination behind the iron curtain. As cameras cut to Carter breaking into a toothy grin resembling piano keys, junior high students across America said to their parents, "Gee Mom and Dad, of course Eastern Europe is communist...we learned that in Social Studies." Carter eked out a narrow victory over Ford and was sworn in as President on January 20, 1977. During his inaugural address, an audible crunching sound could be heard from all the free peanuts handed out.

THE PRESIDENT'S MIDDLE POSITIONS
PLEASE NOBODY
or *He Must Stand for Something*

President Carter and his staff from Georgia frequently rubbed people the wrong way. Despite the free peanuts, Speaker of the House "Tip" O'Neill was offended when he was assigned a bad seat at the inauguration...the last person you wanted to tick off if you were hoping to get your program through Congress. Carter also had a tendency to micromanage; he kept the schedule for the White House tennis court on his desk and obviously had a problem delegating authority. Jimmy also reportedly put up a sign next to the courts that said, "Whites Only" — causing quite a stir until folks figured out he was just requesting traditional white tennis attire.

The centrist Carter soon found that it could be lonely in the middle. He tried to appease both sides in the abortion debate — an impossible task — and ended up angering them both. In **University of California Board of Regents v. Bakke** (1978), the Supreme Court addressed **affirmative action**: a policy in job hiring or educational admissions that gives special treatment to traditionally disadvantaged groups to address the present effects of past discrimination. The decision allowed for affirmative action but disallowed rigid quotas; neither supporters nor opponents were pleased, but the President seemed to embrace the ambiguity when he ordered federal agencies to follow a ruling nobody really understood. In another example of trying to please everyone, one time when the White House tennis court was accidentally double booked, President Carter ordered everyone involved to play doubles.

Jimmy Carter entered office in the midst of a recession and responded by calling for increased federal spending to fight unemployment and lower taxes to jump start the economy. But OPEC kept sticking it to us and inflation kept going up and up. To put the brakes on the rising prices, President Carter pushed for high interest rates, and boy did they go high — over 20 percent at times. Some folks shopping for home loans had to be sedated. In 1979, Middle Eastern instability resulted in a fuel shortage, and OPEC deliberately made things worse with another gigantic price increase.

Carter sprang into action by heading to the presidential retreat in the Maryland mountains, Camp David, to ruminate for ten days. When he returned to the White House he made some sensible policy proposals, but what was most notable were his statements that America was indeed in a crisis and citizens needed to snap out of their doldrums and have faith in their government. Remembered in History as the "National Malaise Speech," it convinced even more folks that the President was ineffectual and misguided. The country actually was in a national malaise, but it was politically really dumb for the President to say so. A lot of other politicians in the same predicament would have just said everything is wonderful and blamed immigrants.

In the realm of foreign policy, to his credit, President Carter denounced human rights violations around the world. He forcefully pressured the Soviet Union to allow

Jews to emigrate and condemned South Africa's policy of **apartheid** — deliberate segregation based upon race. In a few select cases, aid was cut to right-wing dictators who violated human rights, although there was no wholesale shift in the traditional U.S. policy of propping up foreign leaders who could be reliably counted on to be anti-communist. Teddy Roosevelt rolled over in his grave when Carter approved a treaty that would return the Panama Canal to Panama in 1999, even though terms would require it to be open equally to all nations of the world. Some reported that right after he signed, the President clapped his hands and said, "Bully!" Also give President Carter some credit on this one… he immediately followed through on his campaign promise and offered a complete pardon to all who had used hook or crook to dodge the draft during the Vietnam War. His intention was to heal some deep wounds, but conservatives freaked and made it clear they would do their best to keep the wounds festering.

President Carter built upon Nixon's efforts at rapprochement with China, and in 1978, formal diplomatic relations were reestablished. He also continued to seek detente with the Soviets, but when he negotiated a "SALT II" treaty to further reduce nuclear missiles, posturing Senators from both parties, seeking political gain, resisted approving it. In 1980, relations really took a hit when the Soviet Union invaded Afghanistan in a blatant attempt to curtail the growing influence of Afghani Muslim extremists and keep their neighbor under a puppet government. President Carter reacted decisively, and in a huge show of force pulled the United States out of the 1980 Summer Olympics scheduled to be held in Moscow. To really show the Soviets who's boss, Carter also reportedly considered closing down the Russian Tea Room in Manhattan.

President Carter's greatest foreign policy achievement occurred when he successfully shepherded Egypt and Israel into signing a peace agreement. Egyptian President Anwar Sadat had initiated discussions with Israeli President **Menachem Begin**, but the negotiations stalled, so President Carter corralled the two men for two weeks at Camp David. Carter's aggressive mediation paid off when on March 26, 1979, Begin and Sadat joined the President at the White House for the signing of the **Camp David Accords**. In return for getting back the Sinai Peninsula lost in 1973, Egypt acknowledged Israel's right to exist, and the two nations renounced violence as a means for settling future differences. It was an amazing moment when Begin and Sadat shook hands and Carter joined in. Few noticed that the two former enemies quickly wiped their hands on their jackets. What really counts, though, is that Egypt and Israel have been at peace ever since.

Back in 1953, a CIA-inspired coup had elevated **Shah Reza Pahlavi** to power in Iran. With enormous amounts of American aid, the Shah proved for more than three decades to be a dutiful puppet. Not everyone in Iran appreciated the Western influences, particularly Islamic fundamentalists, but the Shah's army and secret police wielded an iron fist. Resistance grew, and in January 1979, Muslim extremists forced the Shah to flee and installed Ayatollah Ruholla Khomeini as "Supreme Leader." When Carter allowed the deposed Shah to enter the United States for cancer treatment, resentment boiled over, and on November 4th, Muslim radicals stormed the U.S. Embassy in Tehran, seizing about seventy hostages. A furious President Carter froze Iranian assets in the U.S. and, grumbling about "American honor," declared he wouldn't leave the White House until the hostages were released.

Initially, Carter's popularity rose; Americans love to criticize their President, but don't react too well when Muslim fanatics burn him in effigy on the evening news. As the days, weeks, and then months passed, though, Carter realized there were no moderate Iranian leaders left with any influence, and the radicals had no intention of negotiating for the release of the hostages. Yellow ribbons sprang up all over the place to honor the hostages, and eventually Tony Orlando would record a sappy love song called *"Tie a Yellow Ribbon..."* but that is beside the point. President Carter seemed stuck in the White House, and for a lot of Americans the sickening feeling returned that this guy was just not up to the job.

Plenty of conservative types who were not deep thinkers groused that American honor required the United States to nuke Iran into oblivion. Carter, although sometimes indecisive, nevertheless was a decent human being who wanted to get the hostages out unharmed. He accepted the advice of National Security Advisor Zbigniew Brzezinski and ordered a risky rescue mission. Eight helicopters lifted off a carrier, headed to a nighttime rendezvous in the Iranian desert. They ran into a dust storm, causing three of the helicopters to malfunction. The mission needed to be aborted, but as the remaining force withdrew, another helicopter collided with a refueling plane, killing eight servicemen. Carter reported the failure to a depressed and frustrated nation. Defense Secretary Cyrus Vance, who had opposed the mission all along, resigned in protest. Others simply wondered why the designers of our helicopters had seemingly failed to account for the existence of sand in the desert.

Carter eventually had to leave the White House to campaign for a second term, but he was so unpopular, even among his own party, that he had to beat back a strong nomination challenge by hard-partying Senator **Edward Kennedy**, the baby of the famous clan. The Republicans nominated Governor Ronald Reagan, a dyed-in-the-wool conservative in the mold of Barry Goldwater. Carter's advisors initially believed Americans would reject Reagan out of hand for being too right-wing. They worried as much about a moderate third party candidate, former Republican Congressman John Anderson. But America had been swinging from left to right during the seventies, so much so that the dynamic rock n' roll of the sixties had been supplanted by disco — vacuous pop music with a regular base beat intended to engender dancing and not thinking.

In the presidential debates, the telegenic Reagan asked point blank, "Are you better off then you were four years ago?" For most folks the answer was "Hell No!" and besides, the President had still not been able to get the hostages released from captivity. Voters devoured Reagan's charm, compliments, and call for a return to happier times minus all the annoying talk about sacrifice. He creamed Carter on Election Day, 51% of the popular vote to forty-one percent.

The Iranians really stuck it to the vanquished President Carter. They waited until Inauguration Day to release the hostages — one half hour after Ronald Reagan was sworn in as our 40th President. He delegated now-former President Carter to fly to an American military base in Germany to greet them, bringing along his own peanuts to save taxpayer money. The hostages had been abused, but they were alive. Honors, celebrations, and seemingly endless spools of yellow awaited them at home. Some historians today believe Reagan's operatives secretly offered the Iranians an arms deal so they would hold onto the hostages long enough to ensure Carter's defeat. Sadly, American politics is such a cutthroat business it is entirely possible.

THE REAGAN REVOLUTION

or *Cut Taxes, Increase Spending, and Let Our Children Worry About It*

Ronald Reagan grew up poor in rural Illinois and in his twenties became a fervent New Dealer. He found a job as a local sports announcer, and when he visited Hollywood in 1937, he aced a screen test and began a successful film career that lasted nearly two decades. Ronnie was no Cary Grant or Clark Gable, but he was a pretty good actor. The famous phrase, "Win one for the Gipper!" derives from Reagan's role as George "the Gipper" Gipp in the film *Knute Rockne, All-American*. Most young people today have no idea what it means, and some think it must have something to do with the Jewish high holy day, Yom Gipper.

As president of the Screen Actors Guild from 1949 to 1952 and again in 1959, Reagan collaborated in the FBI's efforts to rid the movie business of communists, and began sliding to the right. His second wife, Nancy Davis, also pushed him in a conservative direction, and as a spokesman for General Electric, Ronnie started to believe the pro-business pep talks he had been hired to deliver. In 1962, Reagan formally joined the Republican party, and two years later made speeches in support of Goldwater...speeches so seemingly heartfelt and uplifting, only a seasoned actor could have pulled them off. Goldwater certainly couldn't. In 1966, wealthy supporters helped him upset Democratic incumbent Pat Brown to become Governor of California. Reagan's conservative rhetoric sometimes belied a pragmatic approach to governing, but even so, when he left office in 1974, lots of conservatives viewed him as the Second Coming.

Ronald Reagan added a new dimension to what it meant (and continues to mean) to be a Republican in America. Since Roosevelt's New Deal of the 1930s, Democrats had generally favored a forceful role for government while Republicans had desired less government and unbridled capitalism. Now Reagan aligned the GOP with his positions on social issues — against gun control, abortion, welfare for the poor, and gay rights, but in favor of prayer in schools, the death penalty, and American flag lapel pins. The rapidly expanding evangelical Christian movement loved him, even though Reagan himself could best be described as a "sleepest"... someone who believed in sleeping in on Sundays. In response, Democrats adopted opposite views and generally championed diversity and keeping the government out of peoples' personal lives.

Just a two months into his presidency, walking to the presidential limousine after a speech, a waving President Reagan was shot under the arm by a deranged gunman who claimed he did it to impress the actress Jody Foster (guys: some advice here — if you want to impress a woman, try flowers, candy or jewelry; trying to assassinate the President is a huge turnoff). To his credit, Reagan showed great fortitude and a sense of humor, and Americans were reassured when he appeared to recover quickly.

Reagan's economic program took America on a sharp right turn. Some called it "supply-side" economics or "Reaganomics;" his critics called it "trickle down" economics, because his approach called for reducing taxes and regulations on businesses and the wealthy in order to generate wealth that would "trickle down" to the poor. Rich folks loved it, and Reagan's sunny disposition and optimism convinced most of white middle America to go along. Hey, who doesn't want their taxes cut? Unfortunately, as far as poor folks could tell, the spigot stayed dry.

President Reagan worshipped at the altar of "deregulation" and, taking their cue from their boss, some federal agencies dutifully sat on their hands. The Department of the Interior in particular became a den of corruption, turning its back on much of the federal land it was supposed to protect. Reportedly, Secretary of the Interior James Watt tried to sell the Washington Monument to the Mobil Oil Corporation. Meanwhile, deregulation of the Saving and Loan industry resulted in such chaos that to avoid disaster, the federal government had to step in with a taxpayer bailout of half a trillion dollars. Hmmmm...lack of regulation of the stock market leads to the Great Depression of the 1930s, and lack of regulation of the mortgage industry leads to the Great Recession that began in 2008. Do you see a pattern here?

President Reagan pushed huge tax cuts through Congress that favored the wealthy, but he never succeeded in cutting spending nearly enough to make up for the loss of revenue. He did reduce spending on welfare and disability programs, but could not convince legislators to touch the two big kahunas, Social Security and Medicare, because most Americans liked and counted on those programs. Costs for both skyrocketed. Reagan also drastically increased the defense budget, in keeping with his view that America should maintain a forceful role abroad to promote U.S. interests and thwart communism. In 1982, America sank into the deepest recession since the 1930s, but eventually Reagan's tax cuts and overall increases in spending pushed the economy upward. Both the federal deficit and debt exploded, and foreign-owned banks were more than happy to make loans to Uncle Sam that would take generations to repay. You think college loans are tough to pay off? Boy, are our grandchildren going to be mad at us when this bill comes due!

REAGAN ON THE WORLD STAGE

or *America Gets Its Mojo Back*

President Reagan believed it was the duty of the United States to be the world's defender of democracy, freedom, and big American corporations. He called the Soviet Union "an evil empire," which ramped up Cold War tensions but pleased conservatives and fans of Star Wars movies. Reagan also endorsed the development of a nuclear shield over North America to be implemented through the use of satellites and lasers. The Soviets felt threatened by this **Strategic Defense Initiative** (SDI) and relations deteriorated further. In response, mass demonstrations sprang up in the United States and Europe calling for a "nuclear freeze." Not coincidentally, the Reagan Administration moderated its rhetoric in 1983 and publicly broached the idea of restarting arms control negotiations.

Reagan also decided that since Presidents Truman and Eisenhower had doctrines named after them, he should too. The **Reagan Doctrine** proclaimed that the United States would not just contain communism but would proactively roll it back by aiding anti-communist "freedom fighters." In El Salvador, the pro-American right-wing government received critical military and economic aid and used it to (brutally) beat back determined left-wing revolutionaries. In Nicaragua, the government had already fallen to the communist "**Sandinistas**" so Reagan authorized aid to an anti-government guerrilla militia called the **Contras**. The Contras never received mass support in their own country, but American guns and training kept their war going. In October 1983, a leftist government on the tiny Caribbean island of Grenada struck up a close friendship with the Soviet Union. Fearing another Russian puppet in the Western Hemisphere, President Reagan sent in military forces. After Vietnam and Watergate, the U.S. really needed a win, and the easy butt-kicking of tiny Grenada allowed lots of Americans to congratulate themselves as if they had just won a homecoming football game.

Throughout the eighties, Americans began to take note of how conventionally weak extremist groups could resort to suicide bombings, often with devastating results. One of the worst attacks came in 1983, when U.S. troops were stationed in Beirut as peacekeepers during the Lebanese civil war. Terrorists blew up a marine barracks at Beirut International airport, killing 241 servicemen. Wanting to avoid additional casualties, Reagan withdrew remaining American forces. Libyan leader Muammar al-Qaddafi was a major sponsor of international terrorism, and after a nightclub bombing in Berlin that injured scores of off-duty U.S. soldiers, President Reagan ordered U.S. planes to drop some bombs on his tent. Qaddafi survived, and the President claimed somewhat implausibly the bombs were not deliberately intended to kill him. Perhaps they were just trying to wake him up.

Ronald Reagan served as President during the critical years that the Soviet Union irrevocably began to break apart. Partisans today who claim Reagan "singlehandedly won the Cold War" grossly ignore History; the nearly fifty-year-long struggle was actually won by the steadfast efforts of generations of Americans, Democrats and republicans alike. The bullying Soviets were contained, and in the end, capitalism buried communism. President Reagan does deserve credit for seizing the moment and hastening the fall. In 1985, the sputtering Russian economy convinced Soviet leader Mikhail Gorbachev that the Soviet Union could no longer afford the cost of its iron fist. He started to pull Soviet forces out of their quagmire in Afghanistan and proposed **perestroika** (reform) and **glasnost** (greater openness) at home. In a significant breakthrough, Gorbachev and Reagan negotiated a dismantling of all intermediate-range nuclear missiles in Europe. With a perfect sense of timing, President Reagan visited West Berlin and declared, "Mr. Gorbachev, tear down this wall!" Most people on both sides knew it was just a matter of time and were encouraged — except for a few fanatical handball players.

SECOND TERM BLUNDERS
or *"I Had No Idea They Were Doing That."*

With the economy heading upward, and the public not yet comprehending or caring about the exploding long-term debt, Reagan commenced his reelection bid from a position of strength. The Democrats, failing to grasp how far America had leaned to the right, nominated Carter's former Vice-President **Walter Mondale,** whose sad, tired demeanor and hangdog expression failed to excite mainstream voters. Even some liberals admitted that the ever-cheerful Reagan, whose cheeks were getting rosier by the day, was going to get their vote. On Election Day, the Gipper cruised to victory, while Mondale only managed to carry his home state of Minnesota and the District of Columbia. The Democrats, though, gained seats in the Senate and held their own in the House.

Describing Ronald Reagan as a hands-off administrator would be putting it mildly, though it's unclear how much time he spent watching old movies starring himself. The President preferred to give those working for him broad guidelines and then let them "do their thing." Unfortunately, their "thing" sometimes turned out to be downright illegal, and scandal engulfed several executive departments including Labor, Justice, and Housing and Urban Development. But by far the worst was the "arms for hostages" deal, which became known as the **Iran-Contra Affair**.

Reagan was outraged when Congress, realizing America's proxy war in Nicaragua was doing more harm than good, prohibited further aid to the anti-communist Contras there. His foreign policy team deliberately schemed to get around the law, and came up with a truly cockamamie plan. At the time, Islamic terror groups with strong ties to Iran were holding several American hostages in the Middle East. The President's cronies tried to have Israel secretly sell U.S. arms to the terrorists, who in "exchange" would "work to free the hostages;" Israel would purchase replacement arms from the U.S., which would then illegally funnel the proceeds to the Contras. The plan rapidly deteriorated, with administration officials selling the arms to Iran directly (in violation of our own embargo). Then a plane carrying the clandestine aid money crashed in Nicaragua, and when the captured pilot spilled the beans, the scheme began to unravel.

Congressional investigations soon revealed the extent of the skullduggery, and several high-ranking officials were convicted. Much of the legwork in the caper had been carried out by bombastic young Lieutenant Colonel Oliver North, who to this day still doesn't get what he did wrong. In one television appearance, an unrepentant North pulled out a copy of the Constitution that he claimed to always carry with him. Perhaps rather than carry it, he should read it — especially the part about how Congress makes the laws and you follow them no matter how enthralled you are with your own right-eousness.

President Reagan basically stated he had no idea what was going on. His political opponents had been saying that for a long time, but in this case the President was claiming that his subordinates had been running wild without his knowledge. He eventually made a national television address in which he admitted that, although the facts might indicate otherwise, in his heart he had never meant to trade arms for hostages or violate the Constitution. Many Americans watching were relieved and thought, *Well, I guess he really didn't know what was going on...good ol' Gipper.* Public outrage faded quickly, and Reagan weathered a scandal that had revealed a presidential misuse of power arguably more extensive than Watergate. He justly earned the nickname the "Teflon President" because nothing negative seemed to stick to him.

Most Americans felt comfortable with their genial laid-back President. The economy performed well for the middle and upper class, and the poor and disadvantaged waiting in vain for opportunities to trickle down could easily be tuned out in favor of patriotic country and western songs. So could an emerging AIDS epidemic, which appeared at first to affect only "others," meaning gays and impoverished Haitians. The bull ran loose on Wall Street, the Soviet Union faltered live on CNN, and Michael Jackson danced the "moonwalk." It was the go-go eighties...author Tom Wolfe decried a "Splurge Generation" of status seekers. Billionaires rose and fell on hostile takeovers, leveraged buyouts and mega-mergers. Many Americans believed "greed is good," obsessed over labels and engaged in "conspicuous consumption." Ronald Reagan left office in January 1989 with a sixty-three percent approval rating — the highest since Franklin Roosevelt.

PICKING UP WHERE REAGAN LEFT OFF
or *"Read My Lips, No New Taxes...Not."*

Vice President **George H. W. Bush** ran for the presidency, promising to continue Reagan's policies and dramatically declaring, "Read my lips, no new taxes!" The Democrats, still unable to admit they needed a moderate to have any chance of winning, chose the liberal former Governor of Massachusetts, **Michael Dukakis**. It was a depressing election cycle. Bush, having none of Reagan's charm, ran a seemy campaign, while Dukakis ran on a record of competence but was cold and unconnective with voters. Dukakis' claim that Bush looked like Mr. Rogers didn't stick after the Vice President stopped wearing buttoned down sweaters at campaign stops. Dukakis had an early lead in the polls, but by Election Day it had evaporated, and Bush blew him away.

George H. W. Bush entered the presidency with a heck of a resume. Son of a U.S. Senator from Connecticut, George became a decorated fighter pilot in World War II, graduated from Yale, and then moved to Texas to make a fortune in the oil business. He served two terms as a Republican in the House of Representatives and then received appointments as Ambassador to China and Director of the CIA. Those who said this proved he could not hold a job were just jealous.

In the realm of foreign policy, President Bush really knew what he was doing In his first test in office, he used military force to oust the corrupt military dictator of Panama, Manuel Noriega, who was trafficking drugs into the U.S. Desperate, Noriega tried to take refuge in the Vatican's Panamanian embassy. U.S. forces surrounded the building... and blasted him with heavy metal music; Noriega reportedly surrendered, but only after the soldiers started playing Barry Manilow songs.

Bush also presided over a number of successful initiatives. One of the most significant of these was the ratification of the START I (Strategic Arms Reduction Talks) Treaty with the Soviets, which reduced the two nations' strategic nuclear stockpiles by 35 percent and land-based missiles by 50 percent. Many Americans were relieved that the the two nations could only destroy the world half as many times...at least it was a "start."

The Cold War truly ended — the Soviet Union completely collapsed — during President Bush's watch. The Berlin Wall literally toppled live on CNN, and East and West Germany were reunited, causing some in the CIA to privately admit, *Gee, we probably should have predicted that.* The Soviet Union ceased to exist when its constituent republics declared independence and joined the newly created and loosely constructed **Commonwealth of Independent States.** Russia kept control of the nuclear weapons and Bush aggressively pursued further arms reduction. Americans were thrilled by all these goings on and they appreciated their quietly reassuring President, who had gone back to wearing buttoned-down sweaters.

At this point, Iraq's brutal dictator **Saddam Hussein** screwed up big time. Wanting to get his grasping hands on the oil wealth of the tiny neighboring country of Kuwait, he calculated that the world would stand by if he, well, just invaded and took over the place. Big mistake. President Bush, noting that the Iraqi thug stood poised to next go after the huge oil reserves of Saudi Arabia, declared publicly that "This invasion will not stand."

Following the terms of the War Powers Act, he sought permission from Congress to send American Forces into harm's way. It was clearly necessary for the good of the country and Congress approved, but many Democrats voted no, demonstrating that both parties are at times capable of craven partisanship. With all the skill of a seasoned diplomat, Bush approached the UN Security Council and asked for resolutions demanding the removal of Iraqi forces from Kuwait, through an economic embargo if possible and by force if necessary. He got them. The Soviet Union, in its death throes, was looking to increase its participation in the world economy and did not cast its usual vetoes in opposition to the United States. A couple of years earlier the Soviets might have gummed up the UN, but Saddam had failed to comprehend how fast the world was changing. He was about to find out. President Bush may have resembled a mild-mannered librarian, but he now had the support of the United Nations and American military might at his disposal. And Saddam had lost his library card.

President Bush wisely gave command of the mission to remove the Iraqis from Kuwait to the talented General **Norman Schwarzkopf**, and thankfully did not micromanage him. Schwarzkopf patiently built up his coalition forces on Saudi Arabian soil; on January 17, 1991, American jets began pounding Iraqi targets and on February 23rd American troops attacked. They chased Iraqi forces out of Kuwait and halfway to Bagdad in about one hundred hours. Lots of other countries contributed forces and resources, and the ghost of bygone Secretary of State John Hay must have exclaimed, "Now that's really a splendid little war!"

Two hundred twenty three coalition forces died in **Operation Desert Storm**, most through accidents and "friendly fire." Uncounted thousands of Iraqi soldiers perished. With Iraqi troops scampering back to Bagdad and being killed like fish in a barrel — mission accomplished — President Bush called off the massacre and justly declared victory. The President's son, George W. Bush, wondered why he didn't just finish the job, depose Saddam Hussein and occupy Iraq. His father patiently explained that it would be folly to place American troops in the middle of such a volatile nation divided by Sunni and Shiite Muslims, and besides, as unsavory as a defanged Saddam Hussein might be, he and Iraq could still serve as a counterweight to expansion-minded Iran. Apparently, "Dubya" dozed off during this explanation. President Bush's approval rating soared to an astronomical ninety percent and his reelection seemed assured.

In 1991, Congress passed a really terrific piece of legislation: the **Americans With Disabilities Act**, outlawing discrimination against folks with disabilities in the areas of public accommodations and employment. You didn't think all the increased accessibility was because companies decided on their own to be nice, did you? As we've seen, the rule of law is most often necessary to get most Americans to do the right thing. Hey, you've got to love those huge handicapped accessible toilets.

Despite his foreign policy acumen, President Bush did not cooperate well with the Democratic Congress, so he was unable to fulfill his pledges to improve education, increase the battle against drug abuse, and demonstrate greater empathy for the poor and disadvantaged. His hands remained tied by the exploding deficit and debt and — willing to face embarrassment for the good of the country — he ate his "no new taxes" words and agreed to an increase. When the economy entered recession in late 1990 and continued to worsen, the President took most of the blame. Desert Storm was a helpful distraction and helped maintain Bush's popularity, but after the war, lots of Americans realized once again that the cost of beer and cigarettes — or now a video cassette player or a SONY Walkman — were still going up.

The fundamental problem was that President Bush lacked any passion for a domestic agenda. Wealthy all his life, he could not relate to the everyday challenges of regular

Americans. Folks were appalled when President Bush and his wife Barbara staged a shopping trip for the press and George appeared bemused at the cashier's newfangled scanning device that beeped. Most Americans who shopped all the time had known about these devices for years. Bush looked really out of touch because, well, he was really out of touch. As the recession persisted, President Bush's patrician bearing, genuine indifference to the travails of the economy, and that stupid sweater increasingly grated on people.

President Bush convinced himself he would handily win reelection in 1992. He declared that with the fall of the Soviet Union there existed a "New World Order"... certainly true, though the wording grossed out lots of folks because it sounded like the way Hitler used to talk. Yes, the United States was the world's only remaining superpower, but at home, the economy remained listless and President Bush didn't seem to have a clue. One upstart Democratic candidate for the presidency started telling folks, "I feel your pain." He told attractive women, "I really really really feel *your* pain."

So the big bad Soviet Union is finally toast — who can we blame next for all our problems? And now there is a "New World Order" — but what does that mean? Will there be a new era of international peace? Will we be able to cut back on military expenditures and spend the savings on helping the unfortunate and modernizing our country? Will Republicans and Democrats moderate their incessant partisanship? Will new, more powerful computers and networks really make the world a better place, or just a faster place? Actually, now it is time to touch that dial, turn it off and look outside the window. Care. Get involved. Vote and make a difference. Get out there and shape your own History!

This Really Happened!

In 1989, Colorado inventor Gay Balfour comes up with one of the most creative uses for a vacuum cleaner ever — suctioning pesky prairie dogs out of their burrows. This unique vacuum system does not harm the animals at all; it deposits them in a large tank on the back of a truck — alive and "somewhat confused." What happens to the prairie dogs next? Balfour believes America can tackle its trade deficit by selling the animals as pets...in Japan. Who says the United States is not ready for globalization?

And the rest is History...

Quiz yourself on Chapter 14

Multiple Choice (circle the correct answer).

1. President Kennedy represented himself to the public as
    a. one of a new generation that would bring energy and change to Washington
    b. a proud Cold Warrior
    c. a liberal on domestic issues
    d. a real stud
    e. all of the above

2. Kennedy's "New Frontier"
    a. failed to make much headway in Congress
    b. aimed to expand the New Deal
    c. was despised by conservatives
    d. helped him meet Marilyn Monroe
    e. a, b and c

3. The Bay of Pigs invasion
    a. went perfectly as planned
    b. was welcomed by most Cubans
    c. showed the world how professional the CIA could be
    d. failed when the pigs were warned in advance
    e. none of the above

4. The Cuban Missile Crisis
    a. was actually between the United States and the Soviet Union
    b. forced the Cubans to give us back the missiles they stole
    c. nearly resulted in nuclear war
    d. showed the Soviets that President Kennedy was no push over
    e. a, c and d

5. During the March on Washington in 1963
    a. over 300,000 blacks and whites called for civil rights
    b. the Rev. Dr. Martin Luther King, Jr. delivered his "I Have a Dream" speech
    c. Kennedy watched on TV and was impressed by King
    d. Kennedy watched on TV then switched over to *The Flintstones*
    e. a, b and c

6. The Warren Commission
   a. reassured most Americans Oswald had acted alone
   b. whitewashed the whole affair
   c. gave birth to countless conspiracy theories
   d. explained Earl Warren had died from a "magic bullet"
   e. b and c

7. President Johnson's Great Society
   a. greatly expanded the New Deal
   b. created Medicare, Medicaid, Head Start, and Big Bird
   c. worked really well considering it was vastly underfunded
   d. caused tantrums at exclusive golf clubs
   e. all of the above

8. The Vietnam War
   a. diverted needed funds from the Great Society
   b. galvanized protests by the "counterculture"
   c. was poorly conceived, planned, and executed
   d. caused lots of folks to try to find Vietnam on a map
   e. all of the above

9. Watergate
   a. resulted in the resignation of President Jimmy Carter
   b. resulted in the resignation of President Ford
   c. resulted in the resignation of President Richard Nixon
   d. convinced a young George W. Bush that anyone could be President
   e. none of the above

10. President Reagan's domestic policies
    a. were basically continued by President George H.W. Bush
    b. resulted in huge deficits and debt
    c. were classic conservative "let the poor fend for themselves" doctrine
    d. were confusing even to Reagan
    e. all of the above

Epilogue

A NEW GLOBAL AGE

or

Why Are You Texting Me When I Am Standing Right Here?

Boy, have things been changing these days. The Internet, email, Facebook, Twitter, smart phones, instant messaging...finding an old fashioned phone booth is almost impossible. For those of us who are nostalgic, will any company ever take a chance and produce a cell phone with a rotary dial? With all the technological, economic, and environmental developments continually percolating out there, what will become of America? Will we be okay? Or will our country disintegrate and make us all feel like we are living inside one giant reality television show?

A NEW GENERATION AND A NEW CENTURY
or *Why Are We Still Arguing So Much?*

Democratic President Bill Clinton presided from 1993-2001, and his economic policies bore fruit. By the time he left office, business profits and unemployment were at historic highs and the federal government produced a series of budget surpluses. He pushed the North American Free Trade Agreement through Congress. When Serbian nationalists attempted the "ethnic cleansing" of Muslims in Kosovo, President Clinton pushed for the use of NATO forces to bomb Serbia and put a stop to the killings. He even chastised China for its human rights abuses, but backed off when American consumers complained such talk might jeopardize the availability of cheap towels at Wal-Mart.

Conservatives hated Bill Clinton with a talk-radio-fueled passion that was irrational, given the general peace and prosperity that prevailed during his two terms in office. Clinton — who could have accomplished so much more — proved to be all too human, and unable to keep his outsized libido in check. An independent prosecutor learned the President had lied under oath about a sexual liaison with a White House intern (if you are over eighteen, you've probably heard all the details; if you are under eighteen, ask your parents about it and then watch their faces turn red). The House of Representatives impeached the President, but the Senate fell short of the two-thirds vote required to remove him from office. In the throes of excessive partisanship, Republicans wanted his head, while Democrats and most independent voters, though dismayed by his irresponsible behavior, did not feel it rose to the level of impeachment. In short, the Clinton impeachment was politics at its worst, an embarrassment for the nation, and one big waste of time. Meanwhile, office holders in both parties let their guard down and turned a blind eye to the growing threat of radical Muslim terrorism.

The presidential election of 2000 will always be remembered as controversial and heart-rending. Vice-President Al Gore won the popular vote over Texas Governor George W. Bush, the son of the former President. But it all came down to Florida as to who would win the electoral college, and down in the Sunshine State, charges and counter-charges of voter fraud flew fast and furious. Ultimately, the Supreme Court decided the issue in favor of Bush — legal under the Constitution, but a bitter pill for Gore and his supporters. Al Gore was like that annoying smart kid in elementary school who would remind the teacher that she forgot to assign homework. George W. Bush was more like "let's forget the homework and go have a beer".

"Dubya" initially appealed to lots of folks because he promised big fat tax cuts and proudly boasted of his Christian faith. With support from conservative Republicans in Congress, he facilitated the deregulation of Wall Street and big banks, encouraged federal inspectors of all stripes to take a permanent coffee break, and pushed through huge tax cuts that favored the wealthy. The phrase, "What's a little pollution among friends?" was reportedly cut from his inaugural address at the last moment. President Bush would have tried to eliminate the Departments of Interior and Education if he thought he could get away with it. But this crop of Republicans, as during the Administrations of Reagan and his father, had no stomach for cutting other government spending so, naturally, the national deficit and debt shot through the roof.

Bush had been in office less than eight months when the attacks of September 11, 2001 stunned the nation and defined the rest of his presidency. Most people will always remember that day as if it was frozen in time — just like earlier generations recall the assassination of John F. Kennedy or the attack on Pearl Harbor (I remember the day actor Erik Estrada fell off his motorcycle taping an episode of *CHIPS*, but maybe I'm overly sensitive). The world changed forever. Americans must now be ever-vigilant against terrorists willing to kill themselves and take the lives of innocents to further their cause. Fortunately, most have learned a lesson from the World War II-era internment of Japanese-Americans, and are not blaming all Muslims for the hideous acts of a small number of radical extremists who have chosen to pervert their own faith.

President Bush responded by first attacking the right country and then the wrong one. Afghanistan, controlled by fundamentalist Muslims known as the Taliban, was where Osama Bin Laden and his terrorist Al Qaeda had been granted sanctuary to scheme and train. U.S. forces deposed the Taliban and hunted for Bin Laden but, reminiscent of Pancho Villa in a faraway place and time, the architect of 9/11 received support from the locals in the mountains and remained elusive.

Then on March 20, 2003, the United States attacked Iraq, supposedly because unsavory dictator Saddam Hussein was developing "weapons of mass destruction" for use against the United States. But then it turned out there were no weapons of mass destruction. Next, the President informed Americans that Iraq had somehow conspired with Al Qaeda on the 9/11 attacks. That turned out not to be true, though Vice President Dick Cheney, like the Nazi propagandists, believed that lies repeated over and over again could somehow make everyone believe it. Since there needs to be *some* reason (or excuse) for a war, President Bush (who apparently cut his History classes that covered Wilson and the aftermath of World War I), then told us America was fighting to make the Middle East safe for democracy.

Bush won reelection against Senator John Kerry of Massachusetts, mainly because the Republicans were able to scare Americans into thinking the Democrats would be weak in the fight against terrorism. Besides, the tax cuts had temporarily spurred the economy and John Kerry did not go to church enough. In his second term, however, Dubya's chickens came home to roost.

American forces got caught in the midst of sectarian fighting between Iraq's Sunnis and Shiites, and like the war in the Philippines nearly a century earlier, the aftermath of the war proved much more costly than the war itself (that was another History class George had cut). Corruption abounded, true democracy remained exasperatingly elusive, and worst of all, Iran — a country ruled by radical Muslim theocrats that really was developing weapons of mass destruction — gained influence over a demolished Iraq, its traditional enemy and diplomatic counterweight. Meanwhile, the military effort in Afghanistan — where the real enemy was — remained underfunded and poorly managed.

The wars — in reality there were two separate wars, one necessary, one pure folly — cost America trillions of dollars at the same time the Bush tax cuts resulted in greatly reduced government revenue. Even so, Congress proved it was completely craven by caving to lobbyists working for big drug companies and approving a costly Medicare drug benefit that continues to hemorrhage the nation's treasury.

In December 2007, the nation dipped into a severe recession, the worst financial crisis since the Great Depression of the thirties. Finally, average Americans diverted their eyes from their new flat screen televisions and realized something was very wrong... the Bush Administration's foreign and domestic policies seemed to be working for the wealthy but not for them. Angry voters returned Democratic majorities to Congress in 2008. President Bush stood around looking like Alfred E. "What me worry?" Newman, causing *Mad Magazine* to consider a lawsuit for copyright infringement.

Then the interlinked housing and banking crises hit. Deregulated, banks had sold "subprime" mortgages to consumers who could never hope to pay them back, and greedy Wall Street creeps had promoted them as can't-miss investments. The house of cards naturally came tumbling down, and even the Bush Administration recognized the federal government needed to bail out failing financial institutions, simply to avoid tipping America and the world into the abyss of another Great Depression. Regular taxpayers were left holding the bag and nobody bailed them out when the recession hurt their livelihood.

The financial crisis and two mismanaged wars created a climate that allowed America to elect its first African American president, Barack Obama. The strong support in the Democratic primaries for former President Clinton's wife, New York Senator Hillary Clinton, demonstrated the nation may have been ready for a female president had Barack not come along. We've come a long way, baby! President Obama inherited a devastated economy and two difficult wars, so his presidency has continued to be a tough slog forward. He has achieved health care reform and killed Osama Bin Laden, and his heart and considerable mind seem to have put the United States — slowly but surely — on the right track. But will his soaring eloquence ever be matched by deeds? Will the super conservative Tea Party, reminiscent of the nativist Know-Nothing Party that reared its ugly head in the mid-nineteenth century, succeed in pushing America off a cliff? Only the future will tell.

THE AGE OF GLOBALIZATION

or *Isn't Anything Made In America Anymore?*

The United States began as an agricultural nation, but then industrialized farther and faster than any other nation on the planet. But in recent years, the U.S. has been moving towards what some call a "post-industrial" economy, in which we manage capital and information and let low paid factory workers in foreign countries do the actual manufacturing. Will the decline of domestic manufacturing permanently hurt America? Nah. We've had to adjust before. Just ask our ancestors, who lived through the Embargo Act and the War of 1812 and then headed west to start from scratch.

This is an age of globalization...a process of interaction and integration among the people, companies, and governments of different nations driven by international trade and investment and aided by information technology. It is transforming our world and our neighborhoods. The products we buy come from all over. Ethnic identities are undermined as the world becomes increasingly homogenized. Will this globalization one day destroy all that is uniquely American? Nah. We've held tight to our national identity before. Just ask our ancestors who had to fight off the British — twice.

America today faces challenges no one could have predicted just a couple of generations ago: terrorism, uncontrolled illegal immigration, unchecked drug trafficking, global warming, and the continued popularity of Lady Gaga. Will we rise to meet the challenges? Of course. Just ask our ancestors, who fought to preserve the Union or tamed the frontier or pushed back the Germans — twice.

The point here is that our History has shown us we'll be okay. It is sadly true that the collapse of the Soviet Union did not result in a new era of world peace and prosperity. Should we be surprised? Nah. Just ask our ancestors, who longed for Shangri-La after President Wilson's "War To End All Wars" or hoped Woodstock would usher in an age of peace and love. America survived the Redcoats burning of Washington, Pearl Harbor, and now 9/11. We rebounded after the San Francisco Earthquake, the Dust Bowl, and Hurricane Katrina. Heck, we even survived Presidents Grant, Harding, Nixon, and Bush (both of them).

Be optimistic. Our History is filled with many more successes than failures, even though the failures sell more papers and get higher ratings. Never forget those who have gone before. Their legacy is nothing less than breathtaking and it offers hope that next time things will be different. And don't forget to laugh once in a while. Taking this stuff too seriously will drive you crazy...just look at the Republicans lately. Most important of all — always remember.

THE DECLARATION OF INDEPENDENCE

When in the Course of human events, it becomes necessary for one people to dissolve the political bands which have connected them with another, and to assume among the powers of the earth, the separate and equal station to which the Laws of Nature and of Nature's God entitle them, a decent respect to the opinions of mankind requires that they should declare the causes which impel them to the separation.

We hold these truths to be self-evident, that all men are created equal, that they are endowed by their Creator with certain unalienable Rights, that among these are Life, Liberty and the pursuit of Happiness. That to secure these rights, Governments are instituted among Men, deriving their just powers from the consent of the governed, That whenever any Form of Government becomes destructive of these ends, it is the Right of the People to alter or to abolish it, and to institute new Government, laying its foundation on such principles and organizing its powers in such form, as to them shall seem most likely to effect their Safety and Happiness. Prudence, indeed, will dictate that Governments long established should not be changed for light and transient causes; and accordingly all experience hath shewn, that mankind are more disposed to suffer, while evils are sufferable, than to right themselves by abolishing the forms to which they are accustomed. But when a long train of abuses and usurpations, pursuing invariably the same Object evinces a design to reduce them under absolute Despotism, it is their right, it is their duty, to throw off such Government, and to provide new Guards for their future security.

Such has been the patient sufferance of these Colonies; and such is now the necessity which constrains them to alter their former Systems of Government. The history of the present King of Great Britain is a history of repeated injuries and usurpations, all having in direct object the establishment of an absolute Tyranny over these States. To prove this, let Facts be submitted to a candid world.

He has refused his Assent to Laws, the most wholesome and necessary for the public good.

He has forbidden his Governors to pass Laws of immediate and pressing importance, unless suspended in their operation till his Assent should be obtained; and when so suspended, he has utterly neglected to attend to them.

He has refused to pass other Laws for the accommodation of large districts of people, unless those people would relinquish the right of Representation in the Legislature, a right inestimable to them and formidable to tyrants only.

He has called together legislative bodies at places unusual, uncomfortable, and distant from the depository of their public Records, for the sole purpose of fatiguing them into compliance with his measures.

He has dissolved Representative Houses repeatedly, for opposing with manly firmness his invasions on the rights of the people.

He has refused for a long time, after such dissolutions, to cause others to be elected; whereby the Legislative powers, incapable of Annihilation, have returned to the People at large for their exercise; the State remaining in the mean time exposed to all the dangers of invasion from without, and convulsions within.

He has endeavoured to prevent the population of these States; for that purpose obstructing the Laws for Naturalization of Foreigners; refusing to pass others to encourage their migrations hither, and raising the conditions of new Appropriations of Lands.

He has obstructed the Administration of Justice, by refusing his Assent to Laws for establishing Judiciary powers.

He has made Judges dependent on his Will alone, for the tenure of their offices, and the amount and payment of their salaries.

He has erected a multitude of New Offices, and sent hither swarms of Officers to harrass our people, and eat out their substance.

He has kept among us, in times of peace, Standing Armies without the Consent of our legislatures.

He has affected to render the Military independent of and superior to the Civil power.

He has combined with others to subject us to a jurisdiction foreign to our constitution, and unacknowledged by our laws; giving his Assent to their Acts of pretended Legislation:

For Quartering large bodies of armed troops among us;

For protecting them, by a mock Trial, from punishment for any Murders which they should commit on the Inhabitants of these States;

For cutting off our Trade with all parts of the world;

For imposing Taxes on us without our Consent;

For depriving us in many cases, of the benefits of Trial by Jury;

For transporting us beyond Seas to be tried for pretended offences;

For abolishing the free System of English Laws in a neighbouring Province, establishing therein an Arbitrary government, and enlarging its Boundaries so as to render it at once an example and fit instrument for introducing the same absolute rule into these Colonies;

For taking away our Charters, abolishing our most valuable Laws, and altering fundamentally the Forms of our Governments;

For suspending our own Legislatures, and declaring themselves invested with power to legislate for us in all cases whatsoever;

He has abdicated Government here, by declaring us out of his Protection and waging War against us.

He has plundered our seas, ravaged our Coasts, burnt our towns, and destroyed the lives of our people.

He is at this time transporting large Armies of foreign Mercenaries to compleat the works of death, desolation and tyranny, already begun with circumstances of Cruelty & perfidy scarcely paralleled in the most barbarous ages, and totally unworthy the Head of a civilized nation.

He has constrained our fellow Citizens taken Captive on the high Seas to bear Arms against their Country, to become the executioners of their friends and Brethren, or to fall themselves by their Hands.

He has excited domestic insurrections amongst us, and has endeavoured to bring on the inhabitants of our frontiers, the merciless Indian Savages, whose known rule of warfare, is an undistinguished destruction of all ages, sexes and conditions.

In every stage of these Oppressions We have Petitioned for Redress in the most humble terms: Our repeated Petitions have been answered only by repeated injury. A Prince whose character is thus marked by every act which may define a Tyrant, is unfit to be the ruler of a free people.

Nor have We been wanting in attentions to our British brethren. We have warned them from time to time of attempts by their legislature to extend an unwarrantable jurisdiction over us. We have reminded them of the circumstances of our emigration and settlement here. We have appealed to their native justice and magnanimity, and we have conjured them by the ties of our common kindred to disavow these usurpations, which, would inevitably interrupt our connections and correspondence. They too have been deaf to the voice of justice and of consanguinity. We must, therefore, acquiesce in the necessity, which denounces our Separation, and hold them, as we hold the rest of mankind, Enemies in War, in Peace Friends.

We, therefore, the Representatives of the united States of America, in General Congress, Assembled, appealing to the Supreme Judge of the world for the rectitude of our intentions, do, in the Name, and by Authority of the good People of these Colonies, solemnly publish and declare, That these United Colonies are, and of Right ought to be Free and Independent States; that they are Absolved from all Allegiance to the British Crown, and that all political connection between them and the State of Great Britain, is and ought to be totally dissolved; and that as Free and Independent States, they have full Power to levy War, conclude Peace, contract Alliances, establish Commerce, and to do all other Acts and Things which Independent States may of right do. And for the support of this Declaration, with a firm reliance on the protection of divine Providence, we mutually pledge to each other our Lives, our Fortunes and our sacred Honor.

United States Constitution

We the People of the United States, in Order to form a more perfect Union, establish Justice, insure domestic Tranquility, provide for the common defence, promote the general Welfare, and secure the Blessings of Liberty to ourselves and our Posterity, do ordain and establish this Constitution for the United States of America.

Article I

Section 1

All legislative Powers herein granted shall be vested in a Congress of the United States, which shall consist of a Senate and House of Representatives.

Section 2

1: The House of Representatives shall be composed of Members chosen every second Year by the People of the several States, and the Electors in each State shall have the Qualifications requisite for Electors of the most numerous Branch of the State Legislature.

2: No Person shall be a Representative who shall not have attained to the Age of twenty five Years, and been seven Years a Citizen of the United States, and who shall not, when elected, be an Inhabitant of that State in which he shall be chosen.

3: Representatives and direct Taxes shall be apportioned among the several States which may be included within this Union, according to their respective Numbers, which shall be determined by adding to the whole Number of free Persons, including those bound to Service for a Term of Years, and excluding Indians not taxed, three fifths of all other Persons. The actual Enumeration shall be made within three Years after the first Meeting of the Congress of the United States, and within every subsequent Term of ten Years, in such Manner as they shall by Law direct. The Number of Representatives shall not exceed one for every thirty Thousand, but each State shall have at Least one Representative; and until such enumeration shall be made, the State of New Hampshire shall be entitled to choose three, Massachusetts eight, Rhode-Island and Providence Plantations one, Connecticut five, New-York six, New Jersey four, Pennsylvania eight, Delaware one, Maryland six, Virginia ten, North Carolina five, South Carolina five, and Georgia three.

4: When vacancies happen in the Representation from any State, the Executive Authority thereof shall issue Writs of Election to fill such Vacancies.

5: The House of Representatives shall choose their Speaker and other Officers; and shall have the sole Power of Impeachment.

Section 3

1: The Senate of the United States shall be composed of two Senators from each State, chosen by the Legislature thereof,3 for six Years; and each Senator shall have one Vote.

2: Immediately after they shall be assembled in Consequence of the first Election, they shall be divided as equally as may be into three Classes. The Seats of the Senators of the first Class shall be vacated at the Expiration of the second Year, of the second Class at the Expiration of the fourth Year, and of the third Class at the Expiration of the sixth Year, so that one third may be chosen every second Year; and if Vacancies happen by Resignation, or otherwise, during the Recess of the Legislature of any State, the Executive thereof may make temporary Appointments until the next Meeting of the Legislature, which shall then fill such Vacancies.

3: No Person shall be a Senator who shall not have attained to the Age of thirty Years, and been nine Years a Citizen of the United States, and who shall not, when elected, be an Inhabitant of that State for which he shall be chosen.

4: The Vice President of the United States shall be President of the Senate, but shall have no Vote, unless they be equally divided.

5: The Senate shall choose their other Officers, and also a President pro tempore, in the Absence of the Vice President, or when he shall exercise the Office of President of the United States.

6: The Senate shall have the sole Power to try all Impeachments. When sitting for that Purpose, they shall be on Oath or Affirmation. When the President of the United States is tried, the Chief Justice shall preside: And no Person shall be convicted without the Concurrence of two thirds of the Members present.

7: Judgment in Cases of impeachment shall not extend further than to removal from Office, and disqualification to hold and enjoy any Office of honor, Trust or Profit under the United States: but the Party convicted shall nevertheless be liable and subject to Indictment, Trial, Judgment and Punishment, according to Law.

Section 4

1: The Times, Places and Manner of holding Elections for Senators and Representatives, shall be prescribed in each State by the Legislature thereof; but the Congress may at any time by Law make or alter such Regulations, except as to the Places of choosing Senators.

2: The Congress shall assemble at least once in every Year, and such Meeting shall be on the first Monday in December, unless they shall by Law appoint a different Day.

Section 5

1: Each House shall be the Judge of the Elections, Returns and Qualifications of its own Members, and a Majority of each shall constitute a Quorum to do Business; but a smaller Number may adjourn from day to day, and may be authorized to compel the Attendance of absent Members, in such Manner, and under such Penalties as each House may provide.

2: Each House may determine the Rules of its Proceedings, punish its Members for disorderly Behaviour, and, with the Concurrence of two thirds, expel a Member.

3: Each House shall keep a Journal of its Proceedings, and from time to time publish the same, excepting such Parts as may in their Judgment require Secrecy; and the Yeas and Nays of the Members of either House on any question shall, at the Desire of one fifth of those Present, be entered on the Journal.

4: Neither House, during the Session of Congress, shall, without the Consent of the other, adjourn for more than three days, nor to any other Place than that in which the two Houses shall be sitting.

Section 6

1: The Senators and Representatives shall receive a Compensation for their Services, to be ascertained by Law, and paid out of the Treasury of the United States.6 They shall in all Cases, except Treason, Felony and Breach of the Peace, be privileged from Arrest during their Attendance at the Session of their respective Houses, and in going to and returning from the same; and for any Speech or Debate in either House, they shall not be questioned in any other Place.

2: No Senator or Representative shall, during the Time for which he was elected, be appointed to any civil Office under the Authority of the United States, which shall have been created, or the Emoluments whereof shall have been encreased during such time; and no Person holding any Office under the United States, shall be a Member of either House during his Continuance in Office.

Section 7

1: All Bills for raising Revenue shall originate in the House of Representatives; but the Senate may propose or concur with Amendments as on other Bills.

2: Every Bill which shall have passed the House of Representatives and the Senate, shall, before it become a Law, be presented to the President of the United States; If he approve he shall sign it, but if not he shall return it, with his Objections to that House in which it shall have originated, who shall enter the Objections at large on their Journal, and proceed to reconsider it. If after such Reconsideration two thirds of that House shall agree to pass the Bill, it shall be sent, together with the Objections, to the other House, by which it shall likewise be reconsidered, and if approved by two thirds of that House, it shall become a Law. But in all such Cases the Votes of both Houses shall be determined by yeas and Nays, and the Names of the Persons voting for and against the Bill shall be entered on the Journal of each House respectively. If any Bill shall not be returned by the President within ten Days (Sundays excepted) after it shall have been presented to him, the Same shall be a Law, in like Manner as if he had signed it, unless the Congress by their Adjournment prevent its Return, in which Case it shall not be a Law.

3: Every Order, Resolution, or Vote to which the Concurrence of the Senate and House of Representatives may be necessary (except on a question of Adjournment) shall be presented to the President of the United States; and before the Same shall take Effect, shall be approved by him, or being disapproved by him, shall be repassed by two thirds of the Senate and House of Representatives, according to the Rules and Limitations prescribed in the Case of a Bill.

Section 8

1: The Congress shall have Power To lay and collect Taxes, Duties, Imposts and Excises, to pay the Debts and provide for the common Defence and general Welfare of the United States; but all Duties, Imposts and Excises shall be uniform throughout the United States;

2: To borrow Money on the credit of the United States;

3: To regulate Commerce with foreign Nations, and among the several States, and with the Indian Tribes;

4: To establish an uniform Rule of Naturalization, and uniform Laws on the subject of Bankruptcies throughout the United States;

5: To coin Money, regulate the Value thereof, and of foreign Coin, and fix the Standard of Weights and Measures;

6: To provide for the Punishment of counterfeiting the Securities and current Coin of the United States;

7: To establish Post Offices and post Roads;

8: To promote the Progress of Science and useful Arts, by securing for limited Times to Authors and Inventors the exclusive Right to their respective Writings and Discoveries;

9: To constitute Tribunals inferior to the supreme Court;

10: To define and punish Piracies and Felonies committed on the high Seas, and Offences against the Law of Nations;

11: To declare War, grant Letters of Marque and Reprisal, and make Rules concerning Captures on Land and Water;

12: To raise and support Armies, but no Appropriation of Money to that Use shall be for a longer Term than two Years;

13: To provide and maintain a Navy;

14: To make Rules for the Government and Regulation of the land and naval Forces;

15: To provide for calling forth the Militia to execute the Laws of the Union, suppress Insurrections and repel Invasions;

16: To provide for organizing, arming, and disciplining, the Militia, and for governing such Part of them as may be employed in the Service of the United States, reserving to the States respectively, the Appointment of the Officers, and the Authority of training the Militia according to the discipline prescribed by Congress;

17: To exercise exclusive Legislation in all Cases whatsoever, over such District (not exceeding ten Miles square) as may, by Cession of particular States, and the Acceptance of Congress, become the Seat of the Government of the United States, and to exercise like Authority over all Places purchased by the Consent of the Legislature of the State in which the Same shall be, for the Erection of Forts, Magazines, Arsenals, dock-Yards, and other needful Buildings;—And

18: To make all Laws which shall be necessary and proper for carrying into Execution the foregoing Powers, and all other Powers vested by this Constitution in the Government of the United States, or in any Department or Officer thereof.

Section 9

1: The Migration or Importation of such Persons as any of the States now existing shall think proper to admit, shall not be prohibited by the Congress prior to the Year one thousand eight hundred and eight, but a Tax or duty may be imposed on such Importation, not exceeding ten dollars for each Person.

2: The Privilege of the Writ of Habeas Corpus shall not be suspended, unless when in Cases of Rebellion or Invasion the public Safety may require it.

3: No Bill of Attainder or ex post facto Law shall be passed.

4: No Capitation, or other direct, Tax shall be laid, unless in Proportion to the Census or Enumeration herein before directed to be taken.

5: No Tax or Duty shall be laid on Articles exported from any State.

6: No Preference shall be given by any Regulation of Commerce or Revenue to the Ports of one State over those of another: nor shall Vessels bound to, or from, one State, be obliged to enter, clear, or pay Duties in another.

7: No Money shall be drawn from the Treasury, but in Consequence of Appropriations made by Law; and a regular Statement and Account of the Receipts and Expenditures of all public Money shall be published from time to time.

8: No Title of Nobility shall be granted by the United States: And no Person holding any Office of Profit or Trust under them, shall, without the Consent of the Congress, accept of any present, Emolument, Office, or Title, of any kind whatever, from any King, Prince, or foreign State.

Section 10

1: No State shall enter into any Treaty, Alliance, or Confederation; grant Letters of Marque and Reprisal; coin Money; emit Bills of Credit; make any Thing but gold and silver Coin a Tender in Payment of Debts; pass any Bill of Attainder, ex post facto Law, or Law impairing the Obligation of Contracts, or grant any Title of Nobility.

2: No State shall, without the Consent of the Congress, lay any Imposts or Duties on Imports or Exports, except what may be absolutely necessary for executing it's inspection Laws: and the net Produce of all Duties and Imposts, laid by any State on Imports or Exports, shall be for the Use of the Treasury of the United States; and all such Laws shall be subject to the Revision and Control of the Congress.

3: No State shall, without the Consent of Congress, lay any Duty of Tonnage, keep Troops, or Ships of War in time of Peace, enter into any Agreement or Compact with another State, or with a foreign Power, or engage in War, unless actually invaded, or in such imminent Danger as will not admit of delay.

ARTICLE II

Section 1

1: The executive Power shall be vested in a President of the United States of America. He shall hold his Office during the Term of four Years, and, together with the Vice President, chosen for the same Term, be elected, as follows

2: Each State shall appoint, in such Manner as the Legislature thereof may direct, a Number of Electors, equal to the whole Number of Senators and Representatives to which the State may be entitled in the Congress: but no Senator or Representative, or Person holding an Office of Trust or Profit under the United States, shall be appointed an Elector.

3: The Electors shall meet in their respective States, and vote by Ballot for two Persons, of whom one at least shall not be an Inhabitant of the same State with themselves. And they shall make a List of all the Persons voted for, and of the Number of Votes for each; which List they shall sign and certify, and transmit sealed to the Seat of the Government of the United States, directed to the President of the Senate. The President of the Senate shall, in the Presence of the Senate and House of Representatives, open all the Certificates, and the Votes shall then be counted. The Person having the greatest Number of Votes shall be the President, if such Number be a Majority of the whole Number of Electors appointed; and if there be more than one who have such Majority, and have an equal Number of Votes, then the House of Representatives shall immediately choose by Ballot one of them for President; and if no Person have a Majority, then from the five highest on the List the said House shall in like Manner choose the President. But in choosing the President, the Votes shall be taken by States, the Representation from each State having one Vote; A quorum for this Purpose shall consist of a Member or Members from two thirds of the States, and a Majority of all the States shall be necessary to a Choice. In every Case, after the Choice of the President, the Person having the greatest Number of Votes of the Electors shall be the Vice President. But if there should remain two or more who have equal Votes, the Senate shall choose from them by Ballot the Vice President.

4: The Congress may determine the Time of choosing the Electors, and the Day on which they shall give their Votes; which Day shall be the same throughout the United States.

5: No Person except a natural born Citizen, or a Citizen of the United States, at the time of the Adoption of this Constitution, shall be eligible to the Office of President; neither shall any Person be eligible to that Office who shall not have attained to the Age of thirty five Years, and been fourteen Years a Resident within the United States.

6: In Case of the Removal of the President from Office, or of his Death, Resignation, or Inability to discharge the Powers and Duties of the said Office,9 the Same shall devolve on the VicePresident, and the Congress may by Law provide for the Case of Removal, Death, Resignation or Inability, both of the President and Vice President, declaring what Officer shall then act as President, and such Officer shall act accordingly, until the Disability be removed, or a President shall be elected.

7: The President shall, at stated Times, receive for his Services, a Compensation, which shall neither be increased nor diminished during the Period for which he shall have been elected, and he shall not receive within that Period any other Emolument from the United States, or any of them.

8: Before he enter on the Execution of his Office, he shall take the following Oath or Affirmation:—"I do solemnly swear (or affirm) that I will faithfully execute the Office of President of the United States, and will to the best of my Ability, preserve, protect and defend the Constitution of the United States."

Section 2

1: The President shall be Commander in Chief of the Army and Navy of the United States, and of the Militia of the several States, when called into the actual Service of the United States; he may require the Opinion, in writing, of the principal Officer in each of the executive Departments, upon any Subject relating to the Duties of their respective Offices, and he shall have Power to grant Reprieves and Pardons for Offences against the United States, except in Cases of Impeachment.

2: He shall have Power, by and with the Advice and Consent of the Senate, to make Treaties, provided two thirds of the Senators present concur; and he shall nominate, and by and with the Advice and Consent of the Senate, shall appoint Ambassadors, other public Ministers and Consuls, Judges of the supreme Court, and all other Officers of the United States, whose Appointments are not herein otherwise provided for, and which shall be established by Law: but the Congress may by Law vest the Appointment of such inferior Officers, as they think proper, in the President alone, in the Courts of Law, or in the Heads of Departments.

3: The President shall have Power to fill up all Vacancies that may happen during the Recess of the Senate, by granting Commissions which shall expire at the End of their next Session.

Section 3

He shall from time to time give to the Congress Information of the State of the Union, and recommend to their Consideration such Measures as he shall judge necessary and expedient; he may, on extraordinary Occasions, convene both Houses, or either of them, and in Case of Disagreement between them, with Respect to the Time of Adjournment, he may adjourn them to such Time as he shall think proper; he shall receive Ambassadors and other public Ministers; he shall take Care that the Laws be faithfully executed, and shall Commission all the Officers of the United States.

Section 4

The President, Vice President and all civil Officers of the United States, shall be removed from Office on Impeachment for, and Conviction of, Treason, Bribery, or other high Crimes and Misdemeanors.

ARTICLE III

Section 1

The judicial Power of the United States, shall be vested in one supreme Court, and in such inferior Courts as the Congress may from time to time ordain and establish. The Judges, both of the supreme and inferior Courts, shall hold their Offices during good Behaviour, and shall, at stated Times, receive for their Services, a Compensation, which shall not be diminished during their Continuance in Office.

Section 2

1: The judicial Power shall extend to all Cases, in Law and Equity, arising under this Constitution, the Laws of the United States, and Treaties made, or which shall be made, under their Authority;—to all Cases affecting Ambassadors, other public Ministers and Consuls;—to all Cases of admiralty and maritime Jurisdiction;—to Controversies to which the United States shall be a Party;—to Controversies between two or more States;— between a State and Citizens of another State;10 —between Citizens of different States, —between Citizens of the same State claiming Lands under Grants of different States, and between a State, or the Citizens thereof, and foreign States, Citizens or Subjects.

2: In all Cases affecting Ambassadors, other public Ministers and Consuls, and those in which a State shall be Party, the supreme Court shall have original Jurisdiction. In all the other Cases before mentioned, the supreme Court shall have appellateJurisdiction, both as to Law and Fact, with such Exceptions, and under such Regulations as the Congress shall make.

3: The Trial of all Crimes, except in Cases of Impeachment, shall be by Jury; and such Trial shall be held in the State where the said Crimes shall have been committed; but when not committed within any State, the Trial shall be at such Place or Places as the Congress may by Law have directed.

Section 3

1: Treason against the United States, shall consist only in levying War against them, or in adhering to their Enemies, giving them Aid and Comfort. No Person shall be convicted of Treason unless on the Testimony of two Witnesses to the same overt Act, or on Confession in open Court.

2: The Congress shall have Power to declare the Punishment of Treason, but no Attainder of Treason shall work Corruption of Blood, or Forfeiture except during the Life of the Person attainted.

ARTICLE IV

Section 1

Full Faith and Credit shall be given in each State to the public Acts, Records, and judicial Proceedings of every other State. And the Congress may by general Laws prescribe the Manner in which such Acts, Records and Proceedings shall be proved, and the Effect thereof.

Section 2

1: The Citizens of each State shall be entitled to all Privileges and Immunities of Citizens in the several States.

2: A Person charged in any State with Treason, Felony, or other Crime, who shall flee from Justice, and be found in another State, shall on Demand of the executive Authority of the State from which he fled, be delivered up, to be removed to the State having Jurisdiction of the Crime.

3: No Person held to Service or Labour in one State, under the Laws thereof, escaping into another, shall, in Consequence of any Law or Regulation therein, be discharged from such Service or Labour, but shall be delivered up on Claim of the Party to whom such Service or Labour may be due.

Section 3

1: New States may be admitted by the Congress into this Union; but no new State shall be formed or erected within the Jurisdiction of any other State; nor any State be formed by the Junction of two or more States, or Parts of States, without the Consent of the Legislatures of the States concerned as well as of the Congress.

2: The Congress shall have Power to dispose of and make all needful Rules and Regulations respecting the Territory or other Property belonging to the United States; and nothing in this Constitution shall be so construed as to Prejudice any Claims of the United States, or of any particular State.

Section 4

The United States shall guarantee to every State in this Union a Republican Form of Government, and shall protect each of them against Invasion; and on Application of the Legislature, or of the Executive (when the Legislature cannot be convened) against domestic Violence.

Article V

The Congress, whenever two thirds of both Houses shall deem it necessary, shall propose Amendments to this Constitution, or, on the Application of the Legislatures of two thirds of the several States, shall call a Convention for proposing Amendments, which, in either Case, shall be valid to all Intents and Purposes, as Part of this Constitution, when ratified by the Legislatures of three fourths of the several States, or by Conventions in three fourths thereof, as the one or the other Mode of Ratification may be proposed by the Congress; Provided that no Amendment which may be made prior to the Year One thousand eight hundred and eight shall in any Manner affect the first and fourth Clauses in the Ninth Section of the first Article; and that no State, without its Consent, shall be deprived of its equal Suffrage in the Senate.

Article VI

1: All Debts contracted and Engagements entered into, before the Adoption of this Constitution, shall be as valid against the United States under this Constitution, as under the Confederation.

2: This Constitution, and the Laws of the United States which shall be made in Pursuance thereof; and all Treaties made, or which shall be made, under the Authority of the United States, shall be the supreme Law of the Land; and the Judges in every State shall be bound thereby, any Thing in the Constitution or Laws of any State to the Contrary notwithstanding.

3: The Senators and Representatives before mentioned, and the Members of the several State Legislatures, and all executive and judicial Officers, both of the United States and of the several States, shall be bound by Oath or Affirmation, to support this Constitution; but no religious Test shall ever be required as a Qualification to any Office or public Trust under the United States.

ARTICLE VII

The Ratification of the Conventions of nine States, shall be sufficient for the Establishment of this Constitution between the States so ratifying the Same.

done in Convention by the Unanimous Consent of the States present the Seventeenth Day of September in the Year of our Lord one thousand seven hundred and Eighty seven and of the Independence of the United States of America the Twelfth In witness whereof We have hereunto subscribed our Names, ...

AMENDMENTS TO THE CONSTITUTION

Congress Of The United States
begun and held at the City of New-York, on Wednesday the fourth of March, one thousand seven hundred and eighty nine.

THE Conventions of a number of the States, having at the time of their adopting the Constitution, expressed a desire, in order to prevent misconstruction or abuse of its powers, that further declaratory and restrictive clauses should be added: And as extending the ground of public confidence in the Government, will best ensure the beneficent ends of its institution.

RESOLVED by the Senate and House of Representatives of the United States of America, in Congress assembled, two thirds of both Houses concurring, that the following Articles be proposed to the Legislatures of the several States, as amendments to the Constitution of the United States, all, or any of which Articles, when ratified by three fourths of the said Legislatures, to be valid to all intents and purposes, as part of the said Constitution; viz.

ARTICLES in addition to, and Amendment of the Constitution of the United States of America, proposed by Congress, and ratified by the Legislatures of the several States, pursuant to the fifth Article of the original Constitution.

ARTICLE I

Congress shall make no law respecting an establishment of religion, or prohibiting the free exercise thereof; or abridging the freedom of speech, or of the press; or the right of the people peaceably to assemble, and to petition the Government for a redress of grievances.

ARTICLE II

A well regulated Militia, being necessary to the security of a free State, the right of the people to keep and bear Arms, shall not be infringed.

ARTICLE III

No Soldier shall, in time of peace be quartered in any house, without the consent of the Owner, nor in time of war, but in a manner to be prescribed by law.

ARTICLE IV

The right of the people to be secure in their persons, houses, papers, and effects, against unreasonable searches and seizures, shall not be violated, and no Warrants shall issue, but upon probable cause, supported by Oath or affirmation, and particularly describing the place to be searched, and the persons or things to be seized.

ARTICLE V

No person shall be held to answer for a capital, or otherwise infamous crime, unless on a presentment or indictment of a Grand Jury, except in cases arising in the land or naval forces, or in the Militia, when in actual service in time of War or public danger; nor shall any person be subject for the same offence to be twice put in jeopardy of life or limb; nor shall be compelled in any criminal case to be a witness against himself, nor be deprived of life, liberty, or property, without due process of law; nor shall private property be taken for public use, without just compensation.

ARTICLE VI

In all criminal prosecutions, the accused shall enjoy the right to a speedy and public trial, by an impartial jury of the State and district wherein the crime shall have been committed, which district shall have been previously ascertained by law, and to be informed of the nature and cause of the accusation; to be confronted with the witnesses against him; to have compulsory process for obtaining witnesses in his favor, and to have the Assistance of Counsel for his defence.

ARTICLE VII

In Suits at common law, where the value in controversy shall exceed twenty dollars, the right of trial by jury shall be preserved, and no fact tried by a jury, shall be otherwise re-examined in any Court of the United States, than according to the rules of the common law.

ARTICLE VIII

Excessive bail shall not be required, nor excessive fines imposed, nor cruel and unusual punishments inflicted.

ARTICLE IX

The enumeration in the Constitution, of certain rights, shall not be construed to deny or disparage others retained by the people.

ARTICLE X

The powers not delegated to the United States by the Constitution, nor prohibited by it to the States, are reserved to the States respectively, or to the people.

ARTICLE XI

The Judicial power of the United States shall not be construed to extend to any suit in law or equity, commenced or prosecuted against one of the United States by Citizens of another State, or by Citizens or Subjects of any Foreign State.

ARTICLE XII

The Electors shall meet in their respective states, and vote by ballot for President and Vice-President, one of whom, at least, shall not be an inhabitant of the same state with themselves; they shall name in their ballots the person voted for as President, and in distinct ballots the person voted for as Vice-President, and they shall make distinct lists of all persons voted for as President, and of all persons voted for as Vice-President, and of the number of votes for each, which lists they shall sign and certify, and transmit sealed to the seat of the government of the United States, directed to the President of the Senate;—The President of the Senate shall, in the presence of the Senate and House of Representatives, open all the certificates and the votes shall then be counted;—The person having the greatest number of votes for President, shall be the President, if such number be a majority of the whole number of Electors appointed; and if no person have such majority, then from the persons having the highest numbers not exceeding three on the list of those voted for as President, the House of Representatives shall choose immediately, by ballot, the President. But in choosing the President, the votes shall be taken by states, the representation from each state having one vote; a quorum for this purpose shall consist of a member or members from two-thirds of the states, and a majority of all the states shall be necessary to a choice. And if the House of Representatives shall not choose a President whenever the right of choice shall devolve upon them, before the fourth day of March next following, then the Vice-President shall act as President, as in the case of the death or other constitutional disability of the President.14 —The person having the greatest number of votes as Vice-President, shall be the Vice-President, if such number be a majority of the whole number of Electors appointed, and if no person have a majority, then from the two highest numbers on the list, the Senate shall choose the Vice-President; a quorum for the purpose shall consist of two-thirds of the whole number of Senators, and a majority of the whole number shall be necessary to a choice. But no person constitutionally ineligible to the office of President shall be eligible to that of Vice-President of the United States.

ARTICLE XIII

Neither slavery nor involuntary servitude, except as a punishment for crime whereof the party shall have been duly convicted, shall exist within the United States, or any place subject to their jurisdiction.
Congress shall have power to enforce this article by appropriate legislation.

ARTICLE XIV

1: All persons born or naturalized in the United States, and subject to the jurisdiction thereof, are citizens of the United States and of the State wherein they reside. No State shall make or enforce any law which shall abridge the privileges or immunities of citizens of the United States; nor shall any State deprive any person of life, liberty, or property, without due process of law; nor deny to any person within its jurisdiction the equal protection of the laws.

2: Representatives shall be apportioned among the several States according to their respective numbers, counting the whole number of persons in each State, excluding Indians not taxed. But when the right to vote at any election for the choice of electors for President and Vice President of the United States, Representatives in Congress, the Executive and Judicial officers of a State, or the members of the Legislature thereof, is denied to any of the male inhabitants of such State, being twenty-one years of age,15 and citizens of the United States, or in any way abridged, except for participation in rebellion, or other crime, the basis of representation therein shall be reduced in the proportion which the number of such male citizens shall bear to the whole number of male citizens twenty-one years of age in such State.

3: No person shall be a Senator or Representative in Congress, or elector of President and Vice President, or hold any office, civil or military, under the United States, or under any State, who, having previously taken an oath, as a member of Congress, or as an officer of the United States, or as a member of any State legislature, or as an executive or judicial officer of any State, to support the Constitution of the United States, shall have engaged in insurrection or rebellion against the same, or given aid or comfort to the enemies thereof. But Congress may by a vote of two-thirds of each House, remove such disability.

4: The validity of the public debt of the United States, authorized by law, including debts incurred for payment of pensions and bounties for services in suppressing insurrection or rebellion, shall not be questioned. But neither the United States nor any State shall assume or pay any debt or obligation incurred in aid of insurrection or rebellion against the United States, or any claim for the loss or emancipation of any slave; but all such debts, obligations and claims shall be held illegal and void.

5: The Congress shall have power to enforce, by appropriate legislation, the provisions of this article.

Article XV

The right of citizens of the United States to vote shall not be denied or abridged by the United States or by any State on account of race, color, or previous condition of servitude.

The Congress shall have power to enforce this article by appropriate legislation.

Article XVI

The Congress shall have power to lay and collect taxes on incomes, from whatever source derived, without apportionment among the several States, and without regard to any census or enumeration.

Article XVII

1: The Senate of the United States shall be composed of two Senators from each State, elected by the people thereof, for six years; and each Senator shall have one vote. The electors in each State shall have the qualifications requisite for electors of the most numerous branch of the State legislatures.

2: When vacancies happen in the representation of any State in the Senate, the executive authority of such State shall issue writs of election to fill such vacancies: Provided, That the legislature of any State may empower the executive thereof to make temporary appointments until the people fill the vacancies by election as the legislature may direct.

3: This amendment shall not be so construed as to affect the election or term of any Senator chosen before it becomes valid as part of the Constitution.

Article XVIII

1: After one year from the ratification of this article the manufacture, sale, or transportation of intoxicating liquors within, the importation thereof into, or the exportation thereof from the United States and all territory subject to the jurisdiction thereof for beverage purposes is hereby prohibited.

2: The Congress and the several States shall have concurrent power to enforce this article by appropriate legislation.

3: This article shall be inoperative unless it shall have been ratified as an amendment to the Constitution by the legislatures of the several States, as provided in the Constitution, within seven years from the date of the submission hereof to the States by the Congress.

Article XIX

The right of citizens of the United States to vote shall not be denied or abridged by the United States or by any State on account of sex.

Congress shall have power to enforce this article by appropriate legislation.

Article XX

1: The terms of the President and Vice President shall end at noon on the 20th day of January, and the terms of Senators and Representatives at noon on the 3d day of January, of the years in which such terms would have ended if this article had not been ratified; and the terms of their successors shall then begin.

2: The Congress shall assemble at least once in every year, and such meeting shall begin at noon on the 3d day of January, unless they shall by law appoint a different day.

3: If, at the time fixed for the beginning of the term of the President, the President elect shall have died, the Vice President elect shall become President. If a President shall not have been chosen before the time fixed for the beginning of his term, or if the President elect shall have failed to qualify, then the Vice President elect shall act as President until a President shall have qualified; and the Congress may by law provide for the case wherein neither a President elect nor a Vice President elect shall have qualified, declaring who shall then act as President, or the manner in which one who is to act shall be selected, and such person shall act accordingly until a President or Vice President shall have qualified.

4: The Congress may by law provide for the case of the death of any of the persons from whom the House of Representatives may choose a President whenever the right of choice shall have devolved upon them, and for the case of the death of any of the persons from whom the Senate may choose a Vice President whenever the right of choice shall have devolved upon them.

5: Sections 1 and 2 shall take effect on the 15th day of October following the ratification of this article.

6: This article shall be inoperative unless it shall have been ratified as an amendment to the Constitution by the legislatures of three-fourths of the several States within seven years from the date of its submission.

Article XXI

1: The eighteenth article of amendment to the Constitution of the United States is hereby repealed.

2: The transportation or importation into any State, Territory, or possession of the United States for delivery or use therein of intoxicating liquors, in violation of the laws thereof, is hereby prohibited.

3: This article shall be inoperative unless it shall have been ratified as an amendment to the Constitution by conventions in the several States, as provided in the Constitution, within seven years from the date of the submission hereof to the States by the Congress.

Amendment XXII

1: No person shall be elected to the office of the President more than twice, and no person who has held the office of President, or acted as President, for more than two years of a term to which some other person was elected President shall be elected to the office of the President more than once. But this article shall not apply to any person holding the office of President when this article was proposed by the Congress, and shall not prevent any person who may be holding the office of President, or acting as President, during the term within which this article becomes operative from holding the office of President or acting as President during the remainder of such term.

2: This article shall be inoperative unless it shall have been ratified as an amendment to the Constitution by the legislatures of three-fourths of the several states within seven years from the date of its submission to the states by the Congress.

AMENDMENT XXIII

1: The District constituting the seat of government of the United States shall appoint in such manner as the Congress may direct: A number of electors of President and Vice President equal to the whole number of Senators and Representatives in Congress to which the District would be entitled if it were a state, but in no event more than the least populous state; they shall be in addition to those appointed by the states, but they shall be considered, for the purposes of the election of President and Vice President, to be electors appointed by a state; and they shall meet in the District and perform such duties as provided by the twelfth article of amendment.

2: The Congress shall have power to enforce this article by appropriate legislation.

AMENDMENT XXIV

1. The right of citizens of the United States to vote in any primary or other election for President or Vice President, for electors for President or Vice President, or for Senator or Representative in Congress, shall not be denied or abridged by the United States or any state by reason of failure to pay any poll tax or other tax.

2. The Congress shall have power to enforce this article by appropriate legislation.

AMENDMENT XXV

1: In case of the removal of the President from office or of his death or resignation, the Vice President shall become President.

2: Whenever there is a vacancy in the office of the Vice President, the President shall nominate a Vice President who shall take office upon confirmation by a majority vote of both Houses of Congress.

3: Whenever the President transmits to the President pro tempore of the Senate and the Speaker of the House of Representatives his written declaration that he is unable to discharge the powers and duties of his office, and until he transmits to them a written declaration to the contrary, such powers and duties shall be discharged by the Vice President as Acting President.

4: Whenever the Vice President and a majority of either the principal officers of the executive departments or of such other body as Congress may by law provide, transmit to the President pro tempore of the Senate and the Speaker of the House of Representatives their written declaration that the President is unable to discharge the powers and duties of his office, the Vice President shall immediately assume the powers and duties of the office as Acting President.

Thereafter, when the President transmits to the President pro tempore of the Senate and the Speaker of the House of Representatives his written declaration that no inability exists, he shall resume the powers and duties of his office unless the Vice President and a majority of either the principal officers of the executive department or of such other body as Congress may by law provide, transmit within four days to the President pro tempore of the Senate and the Speaker of the House of Representatives their written declaration that the President is unable to discharge the powers and duties of his office. Thereupon Congress shall decide the issue, assembling within forty-eight hours for that purpose if not in session. If the Congress, within twenty-one days after receipt of the latter written declaration, or, if Congress is not in session, within twenty-one days after Congress is required to assemble, determines by two-thirds vote of both Houses that the President is unable to discharge the powers and duties of his office, the Vice President shall continue to discharge the same as Acting President; otherwise, the President shall resume the powers and duties of his office.

Amendment XXVI

1: The right of citizens of the United States, who are 18 years of age or older, to vote, shall not be denied or abridged by the United States or any state on account of age.

2: The Congress shall have the power to enforce this article by appropriate legislation.

Amendment XXVII

No law varying the compensation for the services of the Senators and Representatives shall take effect until an election of Representatives shall have intervened.

Martin Luther King's "I Have A Dream" speech

I am happy to join with you today in what will go down in history as the greatest demonstration for freedom in the history of our nation.

Five score years ago, a great American, in whose symbolic shadow we stand today, signed the Emancipation Proclamation. This momentous decree came as a great beacon light of hope to millions of Negro slaves who had been seared in the flames of withering injustice. It came as a joyous daybreak to end the long night of their captivity.

But one hundred years later, the Negro still is not free. One hundred years later, the life of the Negro is still sadly crippled by the manacles of segregation and the chains of discrimination. One hundred years later, the Negro lives on a lonely island of poverty in the midst of a vast ocean of material prosperity. One hundred years later, the Negro is still languished in the corners of American society and finds himself an exile in his own land. And so we've come here today to dramatize a shameful condition.

In a sense we've come to our nation's capital to cash a check. When the architects of our republic wrote the magnificent words of the Constitution and the Declaration of Independence, they were signing a promissory note to which every American was to fall heir. This note was a promise that all men, yes, black men as well as white men, would be guaranteed the "unalienable Rights" of "Life, Liberty and the pursuit of Happiness." It is obvious today that America has defaulted on this promissory note, insofar as her citizens of color are concerned. Instead of honoring this sacred obligation, America has given the Negro people a bad check, a check which has come back marked "insufficient funds."

But we refuse to believe that the bank of justice is bankrupt. We refuse to believe that there are insufficient funds in the great vaults of opportunity of this nation. And so, we've come to cash this check, a check that will give us upon demand the riches of freedom and the security of justice.

We have also come to this hallowed spot to remind America of the fierce urgency of Now. This is no time to engage in the luxury of cooling off or to take the tranquilizing drug of gradualism. Now is the time to make real the promises of democracy. Now is the time to rise from the dark and desolate valley of segregation to the sunlit path of racial justice. Now is the time to lift our nation from the quicksands of racial injustice to the solid rock of brotherhood. Now is the time to make justice a reality for all of God's children.

It would be fatal for the nation to overlook the urgency of the moment. This sweltering summer of the Negro's legitimate discontent will not pass until there is an invigorating autumn of freedom and equality. Nineteen sixty-three is not an end, but a beginning. And those who hope that the Negro needed to blow off steam and will now be content will have a rude awakening if the nation returns to business as usual. And there will be neither rest nor tranquility in America until the Negro is granted his citizenship rights. The whirlwinds of revolt will continue to shake the foundations of our nation until the bright day of justice emerges.

But there is something that I must say to my people, who stand on the warm threshold which leads into the palace of justice: In the process of gaining our rightful place, we must not be guilty of wrongful deeds. Let us not seek to satisfy our thirst for freedom by drinking from the cup of bitterness and hatred. We must forever conduct our struggle on the high plane of dignity and discipline. We must not allow our creative protest to degenerate into physical violence. Again and again, we must rise to the majestic heights of meeting physical force with soul force.

The marvelous new militancy which has engulfed the Negro community must not lead us to a distrust of all white people, for many of our white brothers, as evidenced by their presence here today, have come to realize that their destiny is tied up with our destiny. And they have come to realize that their freedom is inextricably bound to our freedom.

We cannot walk alone.

And as we walk, we must make the pledge that we shall always march ahead.

We cannot turn back.

There are those who are asking the devotees of civil rights, "When will you be satisfied?" We can never be satisfied as long as the Negro is the victim of the unspeakable horrors of police brutality. We can never be satisfied as long as our bodies, heavy with the fatigue of travel, cannot gain lodging in the motels of the highways and the hotels of the cities. We cannot be satisfied as long as the negro's basic mobility is from a smaller ghetto to a larger one. We can never be satisfied as long as our children are stripped of their self-hood and robbed of their dignity by signs stating: "For Whites Only." We cannot be satisfied as long as a Negro in Mississippi cannot vote and a Negro in New York believes he has nothing for which to vote. No, no, we are not satisfied, and we will not be satisfied until "justice rolls down like waters, and righteousness like a mighty stream."

I am not unmindful that some of you have come here out of great trials and tribulations. Some of you have come fresh from narrow jail cells. And some of you have come from areas where your quest — quest for freedom left you battered by the storms of persecution and staggered by the winds of police brutality. You have been the veterans of creative suffering. Continue to work with the faith that un-earned suffering is redemptive. Go back to Mississippi, go back to Alabama, go back to South Carolina, go back to Georgia, go back to Louisiana, go back to the slums and ghettos of our northern cities, knowing that somehow this situation can and will be changed.

Let us not wallow in the valley of despair, I say to you today, my friends.

And so even though we face the difficulties of today and tomorrow, I still have a dream. It is a dream deeply rooted in the American dream.

I have a dream that one day this nation will rise up and live out the true meaning of its creed: "We hold these truths to be self-evident, that all men are created equal."

I have a dream that one day on the red hills of Georgia, the sons of former slaves and the sons of former slave owners will be able to sit down together at the table of brotherhood.

I have a dream that one day even the state of Mississippi, a state sweltering with the heat of injustice, sweltering with the heat of oppression, will be transformed into an oasis of freedom and justice.

I have a dream that my four little children will one day live in a nation where they will not be judged by the color of their skin but by the content of their character.

I have a dream today!

I have a dream that one day, down in Alabama, with its vicious racists, with its governor having his lips dripping with the words of "interposition" and "nullification" — one day right there in Alabama little black boys and black girls will be able to join hands with little white boys and white girls as sisters and brothers.

336

I have a dream today!

I have a dream that one day every valley shall be exalted, and every hill and mountain shall be made low, the rough places will be made plain, and the crooked places will be made straight; "and the glory of the Lord shall be revealed and all flesh shall see it together."

This is our hope, and this is the faith that I go back to the South with.

With this faith, we will be able to hew out of the mountain of despair a stone of hope. With this faith, we will be able to transform the jangling discords of our nation into a beautiful symphony of brotherhood. With this faith, we will be able to work together, to pray together, to struggle together, to go to jail together, to stand up for freedom together, knowing that we will be free one day.

And this will be the day — this will be the day when all of God's children will be able to sing with new meaning:

My country 'tis of thee, sweet land of liberty, of thee I sing.

Land where my fathers died, land of the Pilgrim's pride,

From every mountainside, let freedom ring!

And if America is to be a great nation, this must become true.

And so let freedom ring from the prodigious hilltops of New Hampshire.

Let freedom ring from the mighty mountains of New York.

Let freedom ring from the heightening Alleghenies of Pennsylvania.

Let freedom ring from the snow-capped Rockies of Colorado.

Let freedom ring from the curvaceous slopes of California.

But not only that:

Let freedom ring from Stone Mountain of Georgia.

Let freedom ring from Lookout Mountain of Tennessee.

Let freedom ring from every hill and molehill of Mississippi.

From every mountainside, let freedom ring.

And when this happens, when we allow freedom ring, when we let it ring from every village and every hamlet, from every state and every city, we will be able to speed up that day when all of God's children, black men and white men, Jews and Gentiles, Protestants and Catholics, will be able to join hands and sing in the words of the old Negro spiritual:

Free at last! Free at last! Thank God Almighty, we are free at last!

Lincoln's Gettysburg Address

Four score and seven years ago our fathers brought forth on this continent, a new nation, conceived in Liberty, and dedicated to the proposition that all men are created equal.

Now we are engaged in a great civil war, testing whether that nation, or any nation so conceived and so dedicated, can long endure. We are met on a great battle-field of that war. We have come to dedicate a portion of that field, as a final resting place for those who here gave their lives that that nation might live. It is altogether fitting and proper that we should do this.

But, in a larger sense, we can not dedicate — we can not consecrate — we can not hallow — this ground. The brave men, living and dead, who struggled here, have consecrated it, far above our poor power to add or detract. The world will little note, nor long remember what we say here, but it can never forget what they did here. It is for us the living, rather, to be dedicated here to the unfinished work which they who fought here have thus far so nobly advanced. It is rather for us to be here dedicated to the great task remaining before us — that from these honored dead we take increased devotion to that cause for which they gave the last full measure of devotion — that we here highly resolve that these dead shall not have died in vain — that this nation, under God, shall have a new birth of freedom — and that government of the people, by the people, for the people, shall not perish from the earth.

INDEX

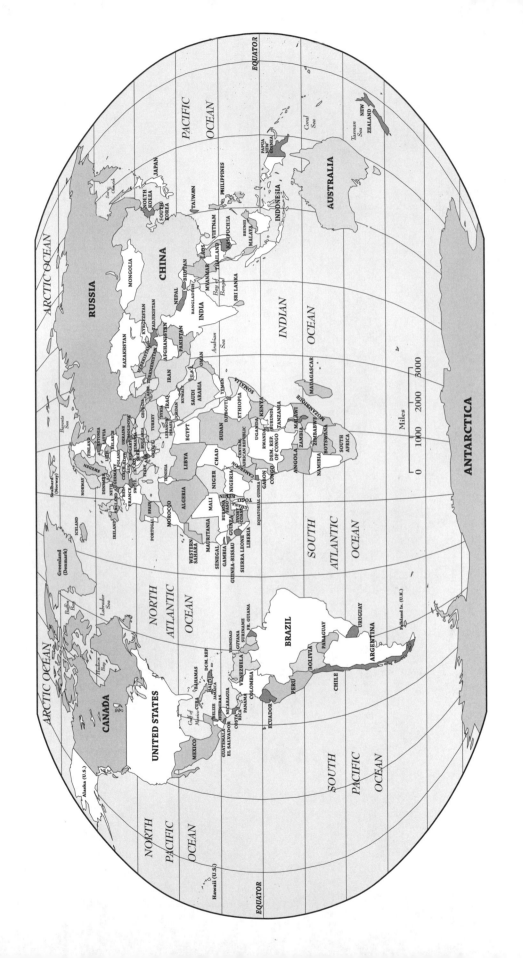